Oxford Studies in Social History

Domestic Dangers

Domestic Dangers

Women, Words, and Sex in Early Modern London

LAURA GOWING

CLARENDON PRESS · OXFORD

Oxford University Press, Walton Street, Oxford OX2 6DP
Oxford New York
Athens Auckland Bangkok Bogotá Buenos Aires Calcutta
Cape Town Chennai Dar es Salaam Delhi Florence Hong Kong Istanbul
Karachi Kuala Lumpur Madrid Melbourne Mexico City Mumbai
Nairobi Paris São Paulo Singapore Taipei Tokyo Toronto Warsaw
and associated companies in
Berlin Ibadan

Oxford is a registered trade mark of Oxford University Press

Published in the United States
by Oxford University Press Inc., New York

First published 1996
Paperback first published 1998

British Library Cataloguing in Publication Data
Data available

Library of Congress Cataloging in Publication Data
Data available
ISBN *0-19-820517-1*
ISBN *0-19-820763-8 (Pbk.)*

Printed in Great Britain
on acid-free paper by
Bookcraft Ltd, Midsomer Norton
Nr. Bath, Somerset

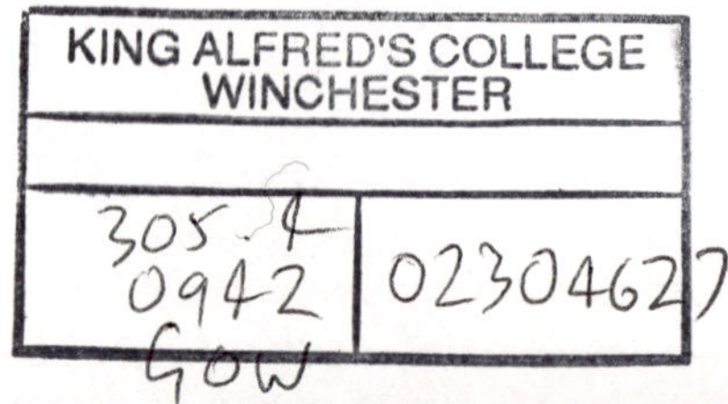

ACKNOWLEDGEMENTS

This academic project is indebted to a feminist politics and scholarship I learnt first outside the academy. Its final shape owes much to Lyndal Roper, who supervised my Ph.D. research from 1989 to 1993: her own work has been an inspiration, and I am deeply grateful to her for the critical acuity and support that brought the thesis together, for talking through endless ideas and problems with me, and for keeping on asking questions until the book was finished. My postgraduate research, and subsequent postdoctoral work, was funded by the British Academy, and Royal Holloway College, University of London, awarded me a tutorial studentship in 1992–3 which enabled me to complete the thesis, and, over the last five years, has provided a stimulating research and teaching environment. For valuable comments as the work progressed, I am indebted to Peter Lake, who acted as joint supervisor early on; Richard Cust and David Dean, examiners of the thesis; the anonymous reader for OUP; the conferences and seminars who listened to versions of the work here; and Keith Thomas, for his painstaking reading of the manuscript. I would also like to thank the staff of the archives and libraries I used, and particularly Harriet Jones of the Greater London Record Office. Many colleagues and friends discussed ideas with me and made suggestions: I want to thank especially Hero Chalmers, Trish Crawford, Faramerz Dabhoiwala, Martin Ingram, Tim Meldrum, Sara Mendelson, Bob Shoemaker, Tim Wales, Garthine Walker, and Helen Weinstein. Trish Crawford, Anthony Fletcher, Cynthia Herrup, and Lorna Hutson all read the work at various stages, and I am most grateful for their advice. My thanks, finally, to Sarah Waters, for talking over gender, sex, and history with me again and again, giving judicious advice on many drafts, and much more.

An earlier version of Chapter 3 was first published in *History Workshop Journal*, 35 (1993), and is reproduced here with permission.

The title comes from St John Chrysostom's commentary on the text of Matthew 19: 8, quoted in several medieval and early modern texts: 'What else is woman but a foe to friendship . . . a domestic danger . . .?'

CONTENTS

LIST OF FIGURES

LIST OF TABLES

CONVENTIONS AND ABBREVIATIONS

Quotations from original sources retain the original spelling and punctuation. I/j and u/v have been distinguished and 'th' substituted for 'y' where appropriate, capitalization has been standardized, and the abbreviations and contractions used by the court clerks have been expanded. Occasional clerical errors (such as repeated words) have been silently corrected, and in a few places commas have been inserted to clarify obscure passages. Matter shown to be omitted consists usually of legal formulas. References to court cases are given as follows: Plaintiff *c.* [*contra*, against] Defendant, with first names added where possible, (date), Greater London Record Office reference. First names are standardized where possible; dates follow Old Style, but the year is taken to begin on 1 January. Unless otherwise noted, references are to records in the Greater London Record Office.

The following abbreviations and Latin terms are used in references to court records and secondary sources:

ad prom.	*ad promotionem*, at the promotion of
als	*alias* (usually used for married women's maiden or previous married names)
et ux.[*or*]	and his wife
GL	Guildhall Library, London
BL	British Library, London
Jl.	Journal
mul. [*ier*]	female
ser.	series
Trans.	Transactions
WSRO	West Sussex Record Office, Chichester
PRO	Public Record Office, Chancery Lane

Archaic monetary values have been retained in quotations, although the abbreviations *d.*, *s.*, and *li.* have been expanded to pence, shillings, and £. In the pre-decimal system of 12 pence (*d.*) to a shilling (*s.*) and 20 shillings to a pound, a noble or an angel was worth 6*s.* 8*d.*; a mark was worth 13*s.* 4*d.*

I

Gender, Household, and City

GENDER AND MORALS

On a doorstep in Whitechapel in the winter of 1610, Alice Rochester insulted Jane Lilham in front of their neighbours, all at work in their doorways. 'Thow art a whore and an arrant whore and a common carted whore and thow art my husbandes whore,' she said, 'my husband hath kept thee a great while at Newcastle and all that he got he spent on thee . . . thow art my husbands whore thow hast lyne oftener with him then he hath done with me.'[1] Six months later, Jane sued Alice at the church court for slandering her, and five women who heard the words came to testify. Hundreds of other women did the same every year. Why did these words carry so much weight, and what happened when women went to court over them to restore their good name?

Alice Rochester's sexual insults tapped into a familiar and potent idiom. The accusation 'whore' featured prominently in disputes between women and men: alone, or elaborated with copious detail, it brought with it a collection of images that explored and condemned women's unchastity. Behind the specifics of Alice's accusation lies a moral framework in which it is acceptable for women to talk about their husbands' infidelity, but where husbands cannot admit to being cuckolded; in which 'whore' is a word of vague yet telling power against women, with no equivalent against men; and where marriage is perceived as a continuous economic and sexual exchange of goods which women's unchastity disrupts.

A closer examination of the language of sexual insult reveals its intimate relation to the organization of gender relations. Insults presumed not just an entirely gendered morality, but a whole order of sexual difference predicated, very largely, on that morality. Bodies and words, sex and marriage were all understood to be shaped by a gender difference which was most distinct on the subject of morality.

[1] Jane Lilham *c.* Alice Rochester (1610), DL/C 219, fos. 196^{v}, 198^{r-v}.

Sexual insult belonged to a culture that perceived women's virtue, honour, and reputation through their sexuality, men's through a much wider range of values.[2] The phrases of insult that women and men exchanged on the streets of London articulated the implications of gendered morality. The understanding of sexual difference that was expounded in verbal insult came into play, too, in the rituals and roles of marriage. It was a model that was, to a certain degree, flexible, drawing on the sources of contemporary culture, familiar formulas, and personal innovation; at the same time, it was based on some constant, rigid perceptions of gender and morality.

At one level, post-Reformation moral theology was keen to stress the culpability of men as well as women for adultery. Puritan writers such as William Gouge noted the unfairness of society's willingness to define women's reputation by their chastity; the Elizabethan sermon on whoredom concentrated entirely on the fornicator as a male figure, who breaks up his household and marriage by his adultery, with only the occasional aside addressed to the female adulterer.[3] In London, the Bridewell authorities led a moral campaign not just against prostitutes, but against their male clients.[4] But at a much deeper level, there was no suggestion that men were morally culpable for illicit sex to the same degree—or even in the same terms—as women. Any contention of an equal culpability for sexual sin was undermined by the constant reiteration of an image of womanhood in which sexual virtue was the essence of feminine integrity. Prescriptive literature, dramatic plots, popular pamphlets and ballads all communicated a vision of morality in which women, not men, bore the load of guilt for illicit sex, and in which women's virtue was premised entirely on sexual chastity. The literature of household advice sought to infuse every element in the domestic hierarchy with a moral value; and at the heart of this project was the distinction between men's morals and women's which, discussing women's virtue in terms of silence, obedience, submissiveness, and restraint, placed the most stress on chastity. Biblical texts and medical theories provided the key to a basic understanding of gender in which women's

[2] Miranda Chaytor, 'Household and Kinship: Ryton in the Late Sixteenth and Early Seventeenth Centuries', *History Workshop Jl.* 10 (1980), 26–7; Susan Dwyer Amussen, *An Ordered Society: Gender and Class in Early Modern England* (Oxford, 1988).

[3] William Gouge, *Of Domesticall Duties: Eight Treatises* (London, 1622), 128. 'Sermon against Adultery', *Sermons and Homilies Appointed to be Read in Churches* (London, 1817), 116.

[4] Ian Archer, *The Pursuit of Stability: Social Relations in Elizabethan London* (Cambridge, 1991), 251.

descent from Eve made them morally weaker than men. Moral frailty was the foundation of feminine weakness.

While women's greater moral weakness was heavily stressed, the ostensible results of that weakness were repeatedly penalized. Morality, in the early modern mind, was very often read as women's sexual conduct; and the governing institutions of early modern England devoted a considerable amount of time to the prosecution of women for sexual offences. The rigour of gendered morality left its mark not just through the courts, but in everyday life. The daily experience of women and men was shaped by sexual standards: not always by a rigorous, consistent morality like that aimed at by literature, law, and the church; but by a spectrum of flexible interpretations of moral rules and their meaning in relations between, and amongst, women and men.

In this vision, men's and women's sexual behaviour were conceived to be incommensurably different. Their sexual acts had different contexts, meanings, and results. In or outside marriage, women were culpable for illicit sex to a quite different degree to men. Because adultery involved the breaking of vows and of sacraments, it was a weightier matter than fornication; but the standards by which both were judged still differentiated in just the same way between women and men. The exact shape of the gendered morality based on marital order which dominated in English culture and law was expounded with precision by Keith Thomas in 1959. At its heart, Thomas argued, was 'the desire of men for absolute property in women', property whose value is 'immeasurably diminished if the woman at any time has sexual relations with anyone other than her husband'.[5] His analysis has remained the touchstone for historians' discussions of sexual morals; but little has been done to elaborate the potential complexities of his model, and 'the double standard' has become a convenient shorthand for the ways in which sex, honour, and gender really worked. Most recently, Lawrence Stone's history of divorce refers to the double standard as the rational model for the unequal rules of marriage, explaining it in terms of its functions for men: the double standard 'made good sense' because of the impossibility of proving paternity, the ease with which men, more than women, can apparently achieve the 'purely physical pleasure of sex' without emotional

[5] Keith Thomas, 'The Double Standard', *Jl. of the History of Ideas,* 20 (1959), 216, 210. See e.g. J. A. Sharpe, *Defamation and Sexual Slander in Early Modern England: The Church Courts at York,* Borthwick Papers, 58 (York, 1980); Martin Ingram, *Church Courts, Sex and Marriage in England, 1570–1640* (Cambridge, 1987), ch. 10.

commitment, and the sexual jealousy that is provoked further in men by the cultural assumption that their wives' adultery imperils their own virility.[6] To some degree, as Keith Thomas's original article suggested, the double standard *does* make sense both because of the physical realities of reproduction and because of what society makes of those facts: because sex may lead to conception in women but not in men, the potential consequences of women's unchastity undermine the very basis of a society structured—practically and conceptually—in familial terms.[7] This version of the double standard effectively naturalizes it; and does so from a man's point of view, as if only men enforced the unequal rules of gendered morals.

In practice the ways women and men spoke of sex, morals, and marriage and the moral understandings that informed social relations and gender relations worked at a different level from the 'good sense' that made the broad structure of gendered morals rational. Like so many elements of patriarchy, the double standard was supported and enforced not just by men but by women: we need to question how it was shared, understood, and deployed by them. Moral principles, and the understandings of honour that were consequent on them, were not a monolithic system, but arose as a series of perceptions, from different sources and with different purposes and effects.

Accepting the broad idea of a 'double standard' of morals, historians have nevertheless neglected its implications for the ideas and practice of early modern morality and its context in families and society. The system of morality in which gender, sex, and marriage had meaning was more complex than a simple scale of sexual culpability, in which logic demanded that women be judged more severely than men. The resonances of gender difference went, I shall argue, deeper and further than that: women's sexual culpability was not just greater than, but incomparable with, men's. However we measure the scale of the difference gender made to morals, it must affect our understanding of the early modern family in far more profound ways than it has so far.

The social historiography of early modern England has come to assume a society in which family life was a miniature patriarchy, a hierarchy ruled by the father, the shape of which mirrored—and was recognized as the analogue of—the hierarchy of the kingdom. Somewhere in this analogy, gender has disappeared. Women's subjection to men figures simply as a relationship like that of subject to

[6] Lawrence Stone, *Road to Divorce: England 1530–1987* (Oxford, 1992), 7–8.
[7] Thomas, 'The Double Standard', 216.

king, servant to master, child to parent. Gender is treated, consequently, as a difference like that of class.

A fundamental problem with this model is that it derives its understanding of gender from normative texts. In prescriptions for household order, gender *was* treated as a social division, with, inevitably, some deep problems that I shall outline later in this chapter. But books and sermons were not the principal source from which women and men worked out the meaning of sex and gender. Moreover, in early modern society, class relations and gender relations were very evidently not the same, and it is not useful, for all sorts of reasons, to read them as analogous. Most basically, the binary, immobile category of gender is visibly rooted in the body, and the multiple, potentially mobile division of class is not.[8] Gender and class were learnt and lived in quite different ways. Finally, the definition of patriarchy in early modern society has rested on a linguistic slippage between two different meanings of the word. Analyses of a society that was patriarchal in the original sense of the word—ruled by the father(s)—have, ironically, subsumed in this sense the feminist analysis of patriarchy, in the sense of a wide-ranging domination of women by men. Discussion of early modern patriarchy has, as a result, been very largely devoid of a considered evaluation of the process, form, and results of women's oppression by men.[9] Correspondingly, gender has become little more than another social variable, like age or class. Yet without taking gender into account, reading it as a both disruptive and conservative element in the structure of society, we miss the point of domestic, sexual, and social relations.

What did gender difference mean to early modern people? In the popular and literate culture of sixteenth- and seventeenth-century England, the definition of femininity was a familiar theme. Culture of all levels stressed the manifestations of gender difference. Sometimes this took the form of extreme misogyny: Joseph Swetnam's *Araignment of Lewd, Idle, Froward and Unconstant Women* (1615) was only one of a series of attacks on women in the gender debate. A few women, or authors signalled to be women, such as Rachel Speght and Jane Anger, responded with proofs of 'how far we women are more excellent than men': women's flesh was purer than men's, because women

[8] Although in a society in which clothes were to some degree a marker of class, and people rarely changed their clothes, the difference between a category marked by the body and one marked by clothes needs to be construed with care.

[9] On the place patriarchy has occupied, and might occupy, in feminist history, see Judith M. Bennett, 'Feminism and History', *Gender and History*, 1 (1989), 251–72.

were made second, and women's bodies, unlike men's, were fruitful. Jane Anger stressed, as well as women's fleshly superiority, their different social role: '[men] are comforted by our means: they nourished by the meats we dress; their bodies freed from diseases by our cleanlines'.[10] More popular literature like ballads underlined the way gender determined social roles by mocking their inversion: 'The woman to the plow, and the man to the henroost', caricatured one.[11] All these types stressed the idea that men and women were fundamentally different, from their flesh to their labour. They assumed, as well, a commonalty of gender identity: 'we women', exhorts Jane Anger. Gender, it seems, is one of the binary divisions that order the world.

Yet to other people, gender seemed less fixed. Jane Anger's conviction that gender difference was rooted in the origin of the flesh seems to sit uncomfortably next to other contemporary models of the body. Thomas Laqueur has shown how pervasive the Galenic 'one–sex' model, where woman's anatomy is an imperfect, reversed version of man's and 'where at least two genders correspond to but one sex, where the boundaries of female and male are of degree and not of kind', remained in early modern physiology. This model was in very many ways a rhetorical one, a tool for physiological investigation and demonstration; and the medical literature does not necessarily, as Laqueur suggests, share 'the same conceptual universe of Renaissance people'.[12] Jane Sharp, a seventeenth-century midwife, invoked Galen's model only to endorse it, 'the difference [between the penis and the womb] is so great that they can never be the same'.[13] The speech of sexual insult, and the words in which adultery was discussed, give us some rare evidence of the ways in which ordinary people spoke about sex. Their main stress is, strikingly, on difference rather than similarity; the sexual organs of men and women are described in quite different terms and are very differently related to desire, pleasure, and

[10] Joseph Swetnam, *The Araignment of Lewd, Idle, Froward and Unconstant Women* (London, 1615); Jane Anger, *Jane Anger her Protection for Women* (London, 1589); Rachel Speght, *A Mouzell for Melastomus* (London, 1617); the quotations are from Anger, sig. C1^{v}. The women's contributions to the debate are published in Simon Shepherd, *The Women's Sharp Revenge: Five Women's Pamphlets from the Renaissance* (London, 1985). For an illuminating discussion of the significance of the pamphlets' disputed authorship, see Diane Purkiss, 'Material Girls: The Seventeenth-Century Woman Debate' in Clare Brant and Diane Purkiss (eds.), *Women, Texts and Histories 1575–1760* (London, 1992).

[11] 'The Woman to the Plow, And the Man to the Hen–Roost', *The Pepys Ballads*, ed. W. G. Day (Cambridge, 1987), iv. 100.

[12] Thomas Laqueur, *Making Sex: Body and Gender from the Greeks to Freud* (Cambridge, Mass., 1990), 68–9.

[13] Jane Sharp, *The Midwives Book* (London, 1671), 82.

disease. The idea that woman's orgasm as well as man's was necessary for conception was very clearly part of the conceptual framework of sex, whatever the experience women had to the contrary. But its theoretical corollary, that female and male were two halves of the same sex, does not seem to have taken root in the popular imagination of gender difference.

If, following Laqueur, sexual difference could sometimes seem a matter of degree, there was also another context to the enticing vision of male–female correspondence. Behind the diagrams of sexual comparability seems to lie a trope meant to make sense of sex between the genders: women's and men's bodies fitted together, not just on paper but in practice. Sexual difference in early modern society—as today—made sense in what Judith Butler has usefully named 'the heterosexual matrix'.[14] Gender was figured, and gender difference played out, in the light of the definition of the category of women through the practice of heterosexuality.[15] The primal scene of gender relations and gender difference was heterosexual relations. It follows that the drama of sex itself, with all the moral weight the sex act carried to the early modern mind, is central to the practice of gender, as it was conceived and played out in society and culture. The language of sexual insult, devoted as it was to describing both the practices of illicit heterosexual sex and their results, was based on a concrete and telling understanding of sex and gender that went to the heart of moral practices and gender difference in society.

In a sense, marriage is as central to the understanding of gender difference in early modern society as sex is. I take issue, throughout this book, with the historical assumption that gender was worked out from the prescriptive texts that made the ideal conjugal household the foundation of society and social order; but nevertheless we cannot understand this society without understanding marriage. Marriage defined women's status, their economic lives, and their social contacts; as Natalie Zemon Davis has suggested, for women, the moment of marital choice could be the moment of deciding an identity.[16] As

[14] See Judith Butler, *Gender Trouble: Feminism and the Subversion of Identity* (London, 1990), 151.

[15] See Monique Wittig, 'On the Social Contract', *Feminist Issues,* 9/1 (1989), 2–12, and Adrienne Rich, 'Compulsory Heterosexuality and Lesbian Existence', *Signs,* 5 (1980) 631–60.

[16] Natalie Zemon Davis, 'Boundaries and the Sense of Self in Sixteenth Century France', in Thomas C. Heller, Morton Sosna, and David E. Wellbery (eds.), *Reconstructing Individualism: Autonomy, Individuality and the Self in Western Thought* (Stanford, Calif., 1986), 61.

I shall go on to show, the records of marriage disputes reveal a marital system in which conduct, roles, and economic positions were defined by gender. Even more than the affectional history of marriage, we need to attend to its function in women's lives as a hard economic exchange, a guarantor of gender difference, and a constituent of identity.

This book takes the language of sexual insult as a starting point for an examination of the workings of sex, gender, and honour in language, law, and popular practice. From litigation over slander, in which the ideas of reputation, credit, and honour that gave sexual insult its import were rehearsed at length, the focus shifts on to the practice of gender relations in the preliminaries to, and at the breakdown of, marriage. In a sense this focus on sex and marriage is fortuitous, for when I started this research I was looking, simply, for the most detailed records of women in early modern England, for a source in which enough of a coherent text survived to make it possible to home in on the meanings, resonances, and contradictions of the words that registered early modern women's contacts with the record-keeping institutions of their society. At the church courts, ordinary women and men fought over sexual words and marital conduct and left behind them testimonies of great length and detail about everyday events and critical life stages. And it is not, I think, entirely coincidental that these most detailed and fruitful records have turned out to be about sex—that subject on which women were expected to be the most silent, and which simultaneously defined the category of 'women'.

As women's history of the early modern period has drawn the sharp and important line between precept and practice, the difficulty of sorting out women's experience from the perceptions of the men who, almost invariably, record it, remains.[17] The analysis of the operation of gender threatens, sometimes, to leave women behind. And yet it is hard to tell what difference gender makes, without looking first for the hidden experiences of women. I try, in this book, to do both. Looking for women in the courts involves, very often, retrieving women from the records of institutions and processes which specifically excluded them. The church court depositions which are the basis of this book, while they record in unusually large numbers testimonies of and about women, are still transmitted through the disrupting and often homogenizing process of legal record-keeping.

[17] Amy Louise Erickson, *Women and Property in Early Modern England* (London, 1993), argues with particular force for the distinction between precept and practice.

Inevitably, records of this sort cannot give us an unproblematic, unmediated access to a recognizable 'women's voice'. My aim, rather, has been to read both women's and men's testimonies with an eye to the deep-rooted ideologies of gender and the daily shape of gender relations.

The moral dimension of sex, words about sex, and marriage brought disputes over these matters to the church courts, the disciplinary arm of the spiritual state. The importance of these courts has begun to emerge as historians have turned to legal records as a productive source for social history.[18] The extraordinarily detailed records of the church courts have always been a fruitful source of social and sexual anecdote, from Archdeacon Hale's compilation of 'Precedents and proceedings' in 1847 to G. R. Quaife's *Wanton Wenches and Wayward Wives* in 1979.[19] More critical studies have presented the church courts in their social and legal context, debating their significance and power as moral arbiters and discipliners and measuring their success or failure in terms of popularity and efficiency. Christopher Hill's picture of a jurisdiction that was anachronistic, inefficient, and ready to collapse by the 1640s, was modified by the work of Ronald Marchant and Ralph Houlbrooke, which established a clearer picture of the courts' daily operations, stressing the relative efficiency and flexibility of ecclesiastical court procedures and practice.[20] Most recently, Martin Ingram has examined the courts' business in far greater detail to argue

[18] See e.g. Keith Wrightson's use of legal records in *English Society 1580–1680* (London, 1982), and for more specific use of the church court records, Amussen, *Ordered Society*, and Marjorie Keniston McIntosh, *A Community Transformed: The Manor and Liberty of Havering, 1500–1620* (Cambridge, 1991).

[19] Victorian selections from the records include W. H. Hale, *A Series of Precedents and Proceedings in Criminal Causes from 1475 to 1640* (London, 1847) (using the London records), and *Depositions and Other Ecclesiastical Proceedings from the Courts of Durham, extending from 1311 to the Reign of Elizabeth*, ed. J. Raine, Surtees Society, 21 (London, 1845); a more recent compilation is Paul Hair, *Before the Bawdy Court: Selections from Church Court and Other Records Relating to the Correction of Moral Offences in England, Scotland, and New England, 1300–1800* (London, 1972). Following similar lines to G. R. Quaife, *Wanton Wenches and Wayward Wives: Peasants and Illicit Sex in Early Seventeenth-Century England* (London, 1979) is John Addy, *Sin and Society in Seventeenth-Century England* (London, 1989); most recently some London records are the source for Jane Cox, *Hatred Pursued Beyond the Grave: Tales of Our Ancestors from the London Church Courts* (HMSO, London, 1993).

[20] Christopher Hill, *Society and Puritanism in Pre-Revolutionary England* (London, 1964), chs. 8–10; Ralph Houlbrooke, *Church Courts and the People During the English Reformation, 1520–1570* (Oxford, 1979); Ronald A. Marchant, *The Church Under the Law: Justice, Administration and Discipline in the Diocese of York, 1560–1640* (Cambridge, 1969).

that the courts were, for the most part, 'in reasonable accord with the values of the wider society'.[21]

The symbiosis which this interpretation assumes between the practice of ecclesiastical justice and popular morals is one that has consistently underlain work on the records of the church courts. The central stress has been on the extent to which the courts' work both moulded and reflected popular opinion: the prosecution of particular 'moral' crimes has been taken as an index of the acceptance of the moral vision they purveyed, and hence of their popularity. I want to question at the start this alliance between law and morality. It is worth pointing out, first, the rather anomalous situation of canon law in post-Reformation England: in contrast to the godly cities of Europe, the canon law which ecclesiastical jurisdiction enforced had never been fully reformed. The reformed code drawn up under Edward VI, *Reformatio Legum Ecclesiasticarum*, never got through Elizabeth's parliaments, and instead only piecemeal alterations were introduced. In the regulation of sex and, most importantly, marriage, therefore, the post-Reformation church was working from a pre-Reformation law, modified by the judiciary's discretion. The law, the courts, and their judges were not necessarily pursuing precisely the same moral aims. My main interest in this book, though, is in the attitudes, experiences, and language of the people who went to court. However cases were sued at the church courts—as disciplinary presentments by church officials informed by parishioners, or as inter-party suits fought between plaintiff and defendant—there was great potential for all sorts of other issues to become entangled with the crimes ostensibly at dispute; the contexts of litigation, as I shall show, make some of those issues clear.[22]

Most importantly, our idea of the moral standards on which canon law operated in practice needs to be adjusted. Litigation over sex and marriage did not depend on a consistent, homogeneous morality: rather, the rules, principles, and beliefs that women and men spoke of and appealed to suggest a range of moral structures and a degree of flexibility. Nor did these moral principles necessarily accord with either the church's ideal moral standards or any uniform popular morality. Rather, in the various contexts of sex and marriage a mass of ideas, adapted or invented, provided the means by which behaviour might be judged. Men might be prosecuted for illicit sex and bastardy; yet some at least were quite ready (as women were not) to boast

[21] Ingram, *Church Courts*, 11.

[22] See also Ingram, *Church Courts*, 313–16.

in public of the women they had 'occupied'. Women and men might judge the acceptability of marital violence in different terms, and act accordingly. The radically different versions of sexual morality that applied to women and to men, among the most rigid of popular moral understandings, were rooted not in the church's teaching but in popular practice. My point here is that we cannot assume an unproblematic community whose moral interests and ideas were more or less in accord with those of lawgivers in the spiritual and secular sphere and more or less the same across the differences of age, class, family, and gender. Even in disciplinary business, and certainly in interpersonal litigation, the church courts both reflected and shaped popular morals precisely because the women and men who presented each other or sued cases acted from individual and shared interests and beliefs. Early modern morality differentiated specifically between men's and women's morals; any study of morals in practice must take into account the different meanings of morals for women and for men.

While the use of law was increasingly part of the fabric of social relations and popular culture, the burgeoning opportunities of interpersonal litigation were very largely closed to women both by law and by social custom. The church courts were an important exception. As the anonymous legal treatise, *The Lawes Resolution of Womens Rights*, declared in 1632, 'Women have no voyse in Parliament, they make no laws, they consent to none, they abrogate none. All of them are understood either married or to be married and their desires ar subject to their husband, I know no remedy, though some women can shift it well enough.'[23] Amongst the women who could 'shift it well enough' we must surely count the church courts' litigants. While in common law, married women's legal agency was vested always in their husbands, ecclesiastical law allowed married women the right to litigate in their own names.[24] The church courts, responsible for the presentment and punishment of sexual offences, also held considerable potential for interpersonal litigation between women and men and the realm of their jurisdiction—the regulation of sex and marriage, including sexual slander—was one in which women were invariably and deeply involved. At ecclesiastical jurisdictions across the country, women fought cases about language, sex, and marriage, and it was in London that they took the most advantage of this opportunity. In the early seventeenth century as many as 250 women a year came to the

[23] T. E., *The Lawes Resolution of Womens Rights: Or the Lawes Provision for Woemen* (London, 1632), 4.

[24] J. H. Baker, *An Introduction to English Legal History* (London, 1990), 551.

London court in slander cases like that sued between Alice Rochester and Jane Lilham.

Already, in pre-Reformation London, women represented a high proportion of church court litigants, suing more often than men in some kinds of cases.[25] In the 1570s, when this study starts, women were suing about half of all sex and marriage cases; over the next fifty years, as patterns of litigation changed, their part in it rose as high as 80 per cent. Between 1570 and 1640 the London church courts witnessed a transformation that put women, uniquely for any court, at the centre of their business.[26] Two dynamics led to the increase of women's participation. Defamation cases, always more likely to be brought by women, rose enormously; and women litigants in all cases about sex and marriage increased. By the 1630s, three-quarters of the consistory court's sex and marriage litigation was brought by women. The church court also saw large numbers of women testifying as witnesses, partly because the women who litigated were more likely than men to bring female witnesses, and partly because of the particular context of church court cases. Consequently, the records of London's church courts between 1570 and 1640 contain around 1,800 suits over sexual slander or marriage, of which 85 per cent had at least one female litigant, and nearly 6,000 witness testimonies in such cases, of which 43 per cent came from women.

The three types of case on which this study focuses, sexual slander, contracts of marriage, and marital separation, each has a language and a conventional story-line of its own. Examined in context, individual cases yield a wealth of detail about custom, expectation, and mentality; together, the cases in which women and men fought about sex, reputation, and marriage can be exceptionally revealing of the experience of gender, sex, morals, and language.

THE METROPOLITAN EXPERIENCE

London's experience, though it reflected and presaged some national trends, was in many ways unique. Topographically and demographically, London was a constantly changing city, regularly fraught with anxieties about plague, inflation, and poverty. Between 1580 and 1640

[25] Richard Wunderli, *London Church Courts and Society Before the Reformation* (Cambridge, Mass., 1981), 76.

[26] The relative levels of women's participation in litigation are summarized in Tim Stretton, 'Women and Litigation in the Elizabethan Court of Requests', Ph.D. thesis (Univ. of Cambridge, 1993), 45–52.

the capital's population tripled, increasing from somewhere between 107,000 and 125,000, to 326,000–380,000.[27] In the 1590s, plague at the beginning of the decade followed by harvest failures made prices rocket; an increasing proportion of taxes were levied on poorer taxpayers, and poverty became an acute urban problem.[28] London's broad base of trades meant that the national depression and the fall in living standards hit it less severely, and recent work has effectively undermined the idea of 'crisis' in the 1590s, but evidence remains of social stresses, conflicts, and anxieties, pointed up by the mobilization of local and central government in pursuit of economic and social order.[29] Demographic change made itself felt in the influx of immigrants that sustained the city's population, in the changing age balance of a community with an unusually high proportion of adolescents and, in particular, apprentices, and in the topography of the city that housed an expanding population. London government from the mid-sixteenth century focused on regulative offences, controlling the growth of overcrowded alleys and tenements, minor delinquencies, and the alehouses and dancing schools associated with popular disorder. Ian Archer has traced the Reformation's early effects on the pursuit of a wholesale reform of manners. The mid-Tudor period saw, simultaneous with this tightening of social regulation, an increasing concern with moral offences, and the prosecution of a rising number of non-professional sexual offenders at wardmotes and Bridewell.[30] The disputes of social and gender relations were staged against these changing circumstances, where demographic and topographic change, poverty, and the threat of disorder were shaping the focus of local government and communal concern.

Much of what distinguishes the patterns of litigation in London was characteristic of the use of law in an urban setting: elsewhere in England, urban areas always drew more women to their courts both as litigants and as witnesses, and in the later part of the seventeenth century it was in the urban areas of London and Middlesex that

[27] Roger Finlay, *Population and Metropolis: The Demography of London 1580–1650* (Cambridge, 1981), 60.

[28] Archer, *Pursuit of Stability*, 9–13.

[29] A. L. Beier, 'Engine of Manufacture: The Trades of London', in A. L. Beier and Roger Finlay (eds.), *London 1500–1700: The Making of the Metropolis* (London, 1986). On the 'crisis', see Valerie Pearl, 'Change and Stability in Seventeenth-Century London', *London Jl.* 5 (1979), 3–34; M. J. Power, 'A "Crisis" Reconsidered: Social and Demographic Dislocation in London in the 1590s', *London Jl.* 12 (1986), 134–46; and Steve Rappaport, *Worlds within Worlds: Structures of Life in Sixteenth-Century London* (Cambridge, 1989); on conflict and order, Archer, *Pursuit of Stability.*

[30] Archer, *Pursuit of Stability*, 242–51.

women's participation in the prosecution of petty offences was maximized.[31] Clearly, urban life made it somehow easier for women to participate. Some of the reasons for this might lie in the character of urban women's work. The opportunities for domestic service drew many young women to the capital; as well, London's trades, crafts, and markets involved women in a range of roles.[32] Many worked with their husbands, in their shops or in victualling houses; others worked on their own or with other women and men, often in informal, semi-legal practices that, as in other early modern towns, made women's work a frequent target for official regulation.[33] Women who witnessed to the court were not immediately identified by their occupation as men were, but they might be asked to explain how they kept themselves. Their responses indicate some of the kinds of work city women did. Magdalena Holmes, aged 34, whose husband was a 'scourer in the Kings privie kitchen', described how 'she helpes to get her owne lyving': she 'useth her nedle and knitting and sometymes washing and starching'. Joan Blackborne of Whitechapel, aged 21, told the court 'she is a wife and lyves partly of her husband labour and partly of her owne by winding of silke and making of buttons for handkerchers'. Ann Barton of St Dunstans in the West, a widow of 60, 'belonged' to Sarjeant's Inn, where she was 'employed ther by the cooke of the howse in the terme tyme to turne the spitt and washe dishes and suchelike druchery'.[34] Other women worked in more public spaces, selling, for example, butter, cheese, oatmeal, and fruit in London's markets or, more controversially, working at the playhouses: 'There are no women that keepe playhouse dores but are whores,' asserted one man in 1607.[35] London women worked in a range of public, semi-public and private workspaces outside their own houses; both work and social life involved public contacts like those

[31] David Souden, 'Pre-Industrial English Local Migration Fields', Ph.D. thesis (Univ. of Cambridge, 1981), 54; Robert B. Shoemaker, *Prosecution and Punishment: Petty Crime and the Law in London and Rural Middlesex, c.1660–1725* (Cambridge, 1991), 207–9.

[32] On the nature of women's work in this period, see Alice Clark, *Working Life of Women in the Seventeenth Century* (1919), ed. Amy Erickson (London, 1992); Lindsey Charles and Lorna Duffin (eds.), *Women and Work in Pre-Industrial England* (Beckenham, 1985); Mary Prior, 'Women and the Urban Economy: Oxford 1500–1800', in Mary Prior (ed.), *Women in English Society 1500–1800* (London, 1985).

[33] See Michael Roberts, 'Women and Work in Sixteenth-Century English Towns', in Penelope J. Corfield and Derek Keene (eds.), *Work in Towns 850–1850* (Leicester, 1990), 86–102; Jeremy Boulton, *Neighbourhood and Society: A London Suburb in the Seventeenth Century* (Cambridge, 1987), 75, 82.

[34] DL/C 226/V, fo. 13^{r-v} (1619); GL MS 9189/1, fo. 76^{v} (1623); GL MS 9189/1, fo. 130^{v} (1624).

[35] DL/C 217, fo. 216 (1607).

of Katherine Pollard, a Stepney widow who witnessed a defamation dispute while she was in an alehouse 'on business'.[36] London women's daily lives were more public and more distant from the home than those of rural women. As a result they were more likely to become involved in the kind of neighbourhood disputes that might lead to litigation. Since men's work, too, often took them out of the house, leaving those women who did stay at home to represent the household in negotiations with authority, women were also likely to fight cases themselves rather than leave litigation to their husbands.[37] In one particular occupational area, circumstances combined to produce the highest level of women's participation in London. East London parishes, like the fast-growing, crowded industrial area of Wapping, were mostly riverside neighbourhoods where as much as three-quarters of the male population might be sailors, absent for long periods.[38] Their wives were both open to accusations of illicit sex and bastardy in their husbands' absence, and well prepared to fight cases alone.

As well as these usually well-established, secure wives, London's households were full of young women in the less protected conditions of domestic service.[39] Many had come to the city after the death of a parent; even if their parents were alive, they were generally at some distance. In the place of close family, servants lived under the authority of their employers. They were probably both freer than their rural counterparts, and more vulnerable. They also had a very different experience from that of the men who migrated at around the same age. The institution of apprenticeship gave young men a fixed status—if a problematic one—in a household, a certain relationship to their master, and a position regulated through their company. Women migrated at a greater variety of ages and to less predictable positions. Helen Spicer came to the household of Sir John Branch from Hereford when she was 15; she was still there fifteen years later. Sicilia Clerke arrived in Elizabeth Smith's household from Northampton when she was 7 or 8, and stayed there until she was 19, when she moved on to service at a brickmaker's, but her fellow servant, Agnes Sherington, who came from Lancashire when she was 21, moved on after six months.[40] Susan More, a 25-year-old servant who had an illegitimate child by a business friend of her master's in 1607 or 1608,

[36] DL/C 231, fo. 543v (1630). [37] Boulton, *Neighbourhood and Society*, 81.

[38] Michael J. Power, 'The Urban Development of East London, 1550–1700', Ph.D. thesis (University of London, 1971), 177.

[39] On women's experiences of service and apprenticeship, see Ilana Krausman Ben-Amos, *Adolescence and Youth in Early Modern England* (New Haven, 1994), ch. 6.

[40] DL/C 213, fo. 395 (1588); DL/C 211/1 fos. 44, 45v (1572).

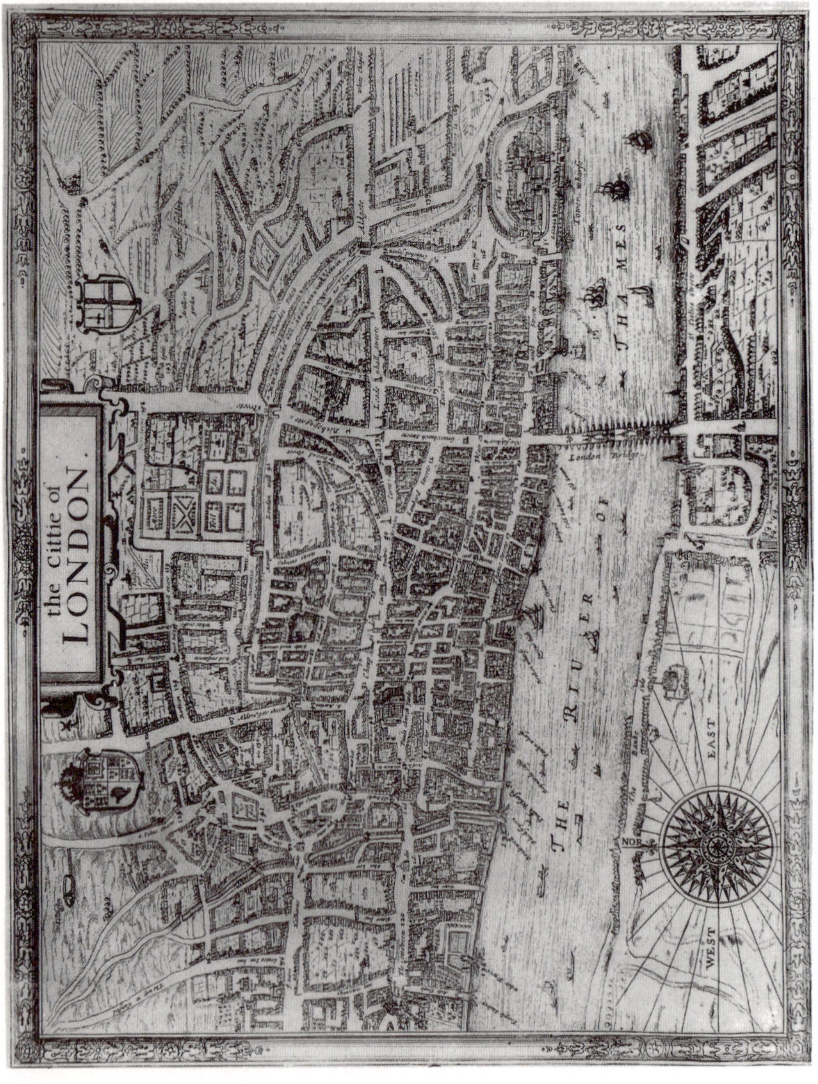

FIG. 1. The City of London, by Cornelius Dankerts, 1645

gave the court an unusually detailed record of her history since coming to London five years before. At the time she testified she had been living with Hugh Jackson, a stationer, in Fleet Street, for six or seven weeks. Before that, she told the court, she had lived with Edward Handby for ten weeks; outside Cripplegate with Randall Birke, a bookseller, working with his wife making points, for a year; in Holy Trinity Minories with Mistress Longe for three months; in St Lawrence Pountney with Arthur Goodgame for a year; with Mistress Lambert in St Margaret New Fish Street for a year; and with a widow, Mistress Lynsey, in St Peter Cornhill for around two years. Susan More had lived and worked in six different houses in five years, even before she became pregnant and had to move from Randall Birke's employment.[41] Dependent very much on goodwill and good luck, women's employment as servants could mean high mobility and an unpredictable future.

London's character was shaped, too, by its changing demography. The population increase of the sixteenth and seventeenth centuries was sustained by immigration: London was a city of migrants, and especially of young migrants, serving their periods of apprenticeship and service in the metropolis. London was also a magnet of employment for women; but the high level of young male immigration gave London, in contrast to most pre-industrial European cities, a sex ratio of around 113 men to 100 women.[42] The city drew young immigrants from all over the country as well as some from abroad. They settled and found lodging, employment, and marriage partners with the help of earlier migrants, often staying in close touch with people from their birthplace. Joan and Richard Aspinwall came to London from Liverpool in about 1579; sixteen years later their London acquaintance still included several other Liverpool emigrants.[43] While young men tended to come to London to fixed contracts of apprenticeship, where they made contacts within their company, women came more informally, often under the protection of kin or friends who had migrated earlier. Of the migrant women who requested marriage licences in the early seventeenth century, over a third had close kin in London (although only a fifth lived with them).[44] The same system

[41] DL/C 218, p. 138 (1608). For more of Susan More's story, see ch. 7.

[42] Finlay, *Population and Metropolis*, 140.

[43] DL/C 214, pp. 579 ff., 592 ff. (1594).

[44] Vivien Brodsky, 'Mobility and Marriage in Pre-Industrial England: A Demographic and Social Structural Analysis of Geographic and Social Mobility and Aspects of Marriage, 1570–1690, with Particular Reference to London and General Reference to Middlesex, Kent, Essex and Hertfordshire', Ph.D. thesis (University of Cambridge, 1978), 220–33.

might work from outside as well as inside Britain. Anne Clemens came from Rouen as a young wife in 1585, followed later by Katherine Auger, who came to London as a servant when she was 14. There were enough immigrants in London for such women and men to live and work largely in a community of their own: when Anne Clemens came to court seven years after her arrival in the city, most of her witnesses were French and she gave her deposition in her own language. As a major port, London might also receive more exceptional immigrants like Isabella Montera de Gamboye from the Azores, taken captive by a ship of Turks, bought as a slave, and brought to London by an English sailor whom she later married.[45]

Together, the different kinds of men's and women's migration had a considerable effect on the character of London neighbourhoods. Witnesses in church court litigation supplied the court with biographical details that give some sense of the effects of migration to the city and the different characters of the urban and rural parishes where they lived. While the pressure to choose creditable witnesses both discriminated against some people with histories of high mobility (like old women and the poor) and in favour of others (servants, a group of extraordinarily high mobility who are over-represented in the group of witnesses), witnesses' autobiographies give a vivid impression of the difference between life in the city and life outside it. The diocese of London encompassed not only the densely populated urban parishes within the city walls, and the separate city of Westminster, but also the emptier, developing suburbs beyond the walls and the rural settlements of Middlesex (illustrated in the map at Figure 2). The city's population was significantly more mobile, even without the regular influx of young servants, than that of rural areas. Of the women and men who came to witness from urban parishes between 1600 and 1640, excluding servants, 41 per cent had lived in their parish for ten years or more, compared to 50 per cent in rural parishes.[46] Urban parishes saw higher levels of annual newcomers, with 15 per cent of London witnesses and 10.5 per cent of rural ones as newcomers of a year or less. Only 9.5 per cent of London witnesses, not counting the large number of migrant servant witnesses,

[45] Examples from DL/C 214, pp. 279, 443 (1592); DL/C 228, fos. 328–9^{v} and DL/C 193, fos. 58–60 (1627).

[46] These figures match almost exactly those calculated from different sources for urban and rural areas by Jeremy Boulton in *Neighbourhood and Society*, 217, and Peter Laslett, 'Clayworth and Cogenhoe', in Laslett (ed.), *Family Life and Illicit Love in Earlier Generations* (Cambridge, 1977), 50–101; see also the figures for persistence of householders in various parishes in Finlay, *Population and Metropolis*, 46–7.

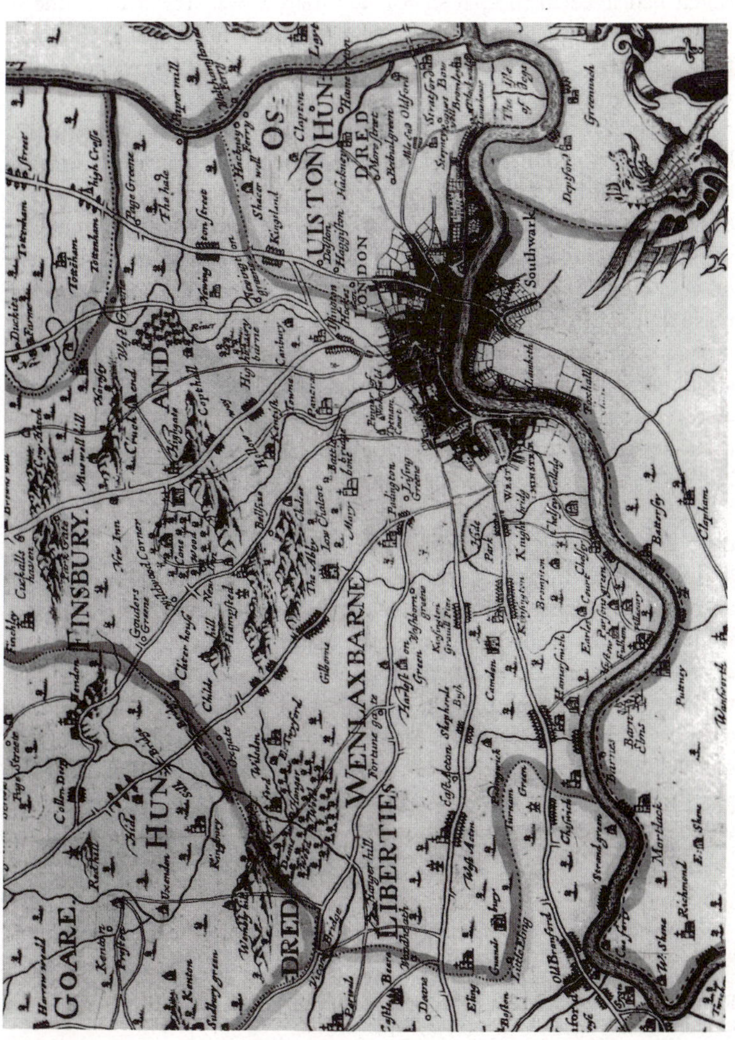

FIG. 2. London and Middlesex, by John Ogilby, *c.*1677

were living in the parish of their birth, although a larger number, 14 per cent, had been born elsewhere in the city; outside London, 45 per cent were still living in the parish where they had been born and brought up. While women and men moved for different reasons and to different situations, and perhaps with different frequencies, overall male and female witnesses were just as likely to be immigrants, some from provincial towns, most from small villages across Britain, and a few from France and Holland.[47] In this sample of Londoners, one in seven had lived in the parish for less than a year; fewer than one in ten lived in the neighbourhood where they had been brought up; and three-quarters had been born and brought up in communities of a very different character.

The social conflicts that sometimes ended as litigation were shaped by these circumstances. The urban experience of daily life, with its crowded conditions and fragile boundaries of privacy, must have exerted considerable strain on those people new to it. Patterns of social behaviour such as courtship may well have been quite different in rural areas, and clashes over expectations in this area might be one reason behind suits for breach of marriage contract. More generally, most people were living in communities where they had a relatively short personal history, and no family past; to their neighbours they were, to some extent, an unknown quantity, and public discussions of their sexual honour provided one forum for anxieties about geographic, and perhaps also social, mobility.

The uniquely large social spheres of the city, while they produced different experiences of neighbourhood and locality to those of towns and villages, did not make London society anonymous. The multiple administrative districts of wards and parishes provided institutional frames for local knowledge and investigation.[48] At court, people were very clear about the positions of their close neighbours, describing women and men carefully as 'next neighbours', living 'two houses away', or 'directly opposite'. From their choice of marital partners, social lives seem to have been very often concentrated within one parish, or a community within it: in later seventeenth-century Southwark, and in East London, around 83 per cent of marriages took place

[47] A breakdown of the areas of origin of another sample of London witnesses is given in Brodsky, 'Mobility and Marriage', 166.

[48] See Boulton, *Neighbourhood and Society*, ch. 10; Archer, *Pursuit of Stability*, ch. 3; Rappaport, *Worlds within Worlds*, ch. 6; Peter Burke, 'Popular Culture in Seventeenth-Century London', *London Jl.* 3 (1977), 159.

between fellow-parishioners.[49] At the courts, most witnesses displayed an intimate knowledge of their close neighbourhood, and relatively little concern with areas further afield. Some had kin or ex-neighbours in other parts of London, but for most, journeys across the city, and over the river, were occasional rather than everyday. For many people support and friendship came not from their closest blood relations, but from the kin acquired through migration, who provided links with both London and their birthplace. One of these relationships was described in 1579 by Anne Hewse, talking about a girl who had asked her advice on her marriage: Margaret Howe was born near her in Leicestershire, and their families were 'speciall frends' there; after Anne had moved to London, she—'bearing some affection to' Margaret, 'then a pretye girle'—sent for her and 'placed her here in London, where she have continued ever since, resorting still to this examinates [Anne's] house and making greate accompte of her following her advice and direction in all her doinges and being out of service placed, at this examinates appoyntmente'.[50] Servants and apprentices, in particular, found a new group of kin when they came to London, and in the formation of marriage they depended on the influence and advice of employers, distant relatives, or their fellow servants. Nevertheless, London did offer some opportunities for anonymity. Bigamous husbands and wives were apparently capable of living for several years in the same city as their estranged or abandoned spouses until they met one day by chance; rediscovery of a previous partner who had been presumed dead depended entirely on the accidents of communication.

The peculiarities of London's topography were a combination of anonymity and closeness. Most people living in the capital had been born and brought up outside it. Accustomed to smaller and more stable communities, they found themselves sharing the public spaces of the street with people whose families and histories were unknown. At the same time they lived at unusually close quarters with these strangers. Outside the city the border parishes were populated by about 15 houses per acre: within the walls the density might be as high as 95 houses to an acre.[51] As London's population grew, its open spaces were built over and its buildings subdivided into tenements. The streets, alleys, and courts which formed one kind of community consisted of a mass of shops backed by kitchens and yards,

[49] Boulton, *Neighbourhood and Society*, 229, and Power, 'Urban Development of East London', 78.

[50] DL/C 213, p. 148 (1587).

[51] Finlay, *Population and Metropolis*, 168–72.

thin-walled and opening out on to one small space. The kind of conflicts that ended up in court as defamation litigation arose initially over issues particular to crowded urban life: boundaries between closely bordering properties, shared walls or fences, the use of communal resources like gutters and water supplies. Social disputes were characterized, often, by an insistence on community morality which might be read as the desire to stabilize shifting people and values. In the parish of St Thomas the Apostle in 1613 Henry Coxson insulted Margaret George: 'Go go thou art a base beggerly queane and not fitt to dwell in such a place as this is amongst honest neighboures but in some out place or backe lane amongst such as thy self art.' We do not know how long Henry had lived in the parish, but his first witness had only lived there around a year.[52] The tensions engendered by London's combination of high mobility and crowded living produced, too, some formulaic themes for sexual insult: suggestions of hidden sins of the past and slurs on the neighbourhood, struggles over territory and the boundaries of privacy.

HONEST NEIGHBOURS

The layers of institutional and social structures of life within London provided a variety of communities and authorities through which discipline and unity were enforced, and whose powers of including and excluding—territorially, politically, and socially—naturally came into play in neighbourhood and marital dispute. The basic unit of society was the household. Its structure was laden with ideological and political implications. In the well-rehearsed rhetoric of domestic advice, household order was the microcosm of order in the state. Households, encompassing husbands and wives, children and servants, were the convenient unit of moral, spiritual, and economic affairs. But in the highly mobile society of the metropolis, the model of a community divided into households did not always fit circumstances. Economically, household workshops—while they constituted the primary or sole means of production for many families—were part of a labour market of mobile craftsmen, multiple occupations, and women's work outside the domestic sphere. Many women and men worked in one household and lived in another; others lived in temporary and semi-permanent accommodation, moving between lodgings. Mary Peters, for example, who came to court in a complex

[52] Margaret George *c.* Henry Coxson (1613), DL/C 221, fo. 1521.

defamation suit in 1627, lived with her husband as lodgers with Elizabeth Welsh in St Clement Danes, as did Helenora True and her husband: Mary's husband was 'towards the lawe' and, according to neighbours, they did not 'keape a house or famyly but do usually lodge . . . and they doe often remove from one place to another'.[53] It was, as far as can be seen, very largely women who assumed charge of managing lodgings like these, whose reputation was a regular point of dispute at the court. In a city with a high proportion of mobile labourers, widows, and widowers, households headed by a husband and father were only one—if the most conventionally recognized—kind of social unit.

In the broader sphere of the civic community, a primary social division for Londoners was citizenship. Steve Rappaport estimates citizens to be two-thirds of London's men in 1600; the companies to which freemen belonged provided both social bonds and some means of discipline.[54] Members of one company often witnessed together in court. But non-citizens organized themselves through trade too, and labourers like watermen, porters, or lightermen came to court together in the same way. What implications did these bonds of occupation and citizenship have for women? Although the customary law of London allowed married women the right to trade separately from their husbands as 'femes soles', a number of companies specifically ruled against the incorporation of women in the mid-sixteenth century and very few women became citizens.[55] In the same way as their husbands, the women who married into particular trades witnessed disputes together, partly because of the occupational character of particular neighbourhoods, like the sailors' wives of Stepney who fought or supported each other in defamation cases. Other women worked together: selling goods at markets, washing, in inns, victualling houses, or playhouses. The social ties of daily life were likely to be based more on geographic location than common occupations, although the two often overlapped. Local government constructed another series of identities and exclusions. Parishes, wards, and precincts constituted a set of overlapping administrative structures that made London's government particularly 'diverse and pluralistic'.[56] Each of these jurisdictions depended for their operation on enlisting the involvement of

[53] Mary Peters *c.* Elizabeth Welsh (1627), GL MS 9189/2, fo. 12^{v}, 12.

[54] Rappaport, *Worlds within Worlds*, ch. 2.

[55] On women and citizenship, see Rappaport, *Worlds within Worlds*, 36–42. Caroline Barron discusses the situation in medieval London in 'The "Golden Age" of Women in Medieval London', *Reading Medieval Studies*, 15 (1992), 44–8.

[56] Pearl, 'Change and Stability', 15.

their members, and through them the middling sort of men were invested with the responsibilities of local administration. Wardmote inquests made regular presentments of offences to the city's aldermen, and many of these offences were presented as violations of neighbourhood standards. Vestries, the governing bodies of the parishes, provided one of the main starting-points for local participation in the administration of communal resources and responsibilities like poor relief, water pumps, or schools, and they enlisted, too, the help of some women, for tasks like plague searching and the watching of the dead. Parishes were manageable as communities: London parishes were relatively small, with an average size of 4 acres, 137 households.[57] When witnesses and litigants came to court the first description of themselves they gave was in terms of their parish. It was there that they attended church, and sometimes joined in vestry meetings over local matters, and it was through the parish that the church court's disciplinary arm dealt with sexual, marital, or religious offences. More loosely defined, and without a particular institutional structure, was the idea of neighbourhood, an area that might be partly coincident with a ward or parish, but which held firmly its own sense of identity; within the neighbourhood, streets, alleys and yards seem to have had their own bonds.

It was customary communities like these, rather than institutionalized ones, that formed the basis of many social bonds. Such communities were cohesive, as Ian Archer points out, because of their power to exclude;[58] their boundaries proved a staple of verbal abuse between neighbours. In the verbal disputes of London streets, men and women often linked sexual misconduct to a particular area, most often Clerkenwell, and threatened to drive dishonest women out of honest neighbourhoods: the idea of neighbourhood exclusivity had an emotive power.[59]

PRESCRIPTION AND PRACTICE

All the regulatory powers of structures of parish or neighbourhood depended to some extent on another level of order: that of the household. Contemporary writers constructed a household that was a microcosm of the whole kingdom, hierarchically ordered by bonds of obedience. The household advice that was expounded in brief

[57] Rappaport, *Worlds Within Worlds*, 215. [58] Archer, *Pursuit of Stability*, 68.

[59] Ian Archer's map of bawdy houses in London shows a large concentration around Clerkenwell and Turnmill Street: Archer, *Pursuit of Stability*, 212.

sermons like William Whately's *Bride-Bush* or exhaustive manuals like William Gouge's *Of Domesticall Duties*, was hardly original to Puritan teaching and doctrine. Its tenets, and much of its phrasing, derived from central humanist texts, most often Heinrich Bullinger's *Christian State of Matrimony*, translated by Miles Coverdale in 1541, and Bullinger's ideas of the household economy came originally from Xenophon's *Oeconomicus*.[60] Every litany of household advice ran along the lines of Ephesians 5: 22–6: 9, detailing the respective duties of every member of an ordered household: husbands and wives, parents and children, masters or mistresses, and servants. Ostensibly, then, every member of early modern society had a place in the household as in the realm, defined by duties to their superiors and responsibilities to their inferiors. But equating the marital relationship with that of parents to children or employers to servants was potentially awkward, and writers like William Gouge proclaimed their position to be a controversial one. Gouge referred specifically to the women of his London congregation who had resisted his theory:

> I remember that when these Domesticall Duties were first uttered out of the Pulpit, much exception was taken against the application of a Wives subjection to the restraining of her from disposing the common goods of the Family without, or against her Husbands consent . . . Other exceptions were made against some other particular duties of Wives. For many that can patiently enough hear their duties declared in generall terms, cannot endure to heare those generals exemplified in their particular branches. This cometh too neere to the quicke, and pierceth too deepe.[61]

To counter such opposition many advice writers dealt specifically with the question of the extent of obedience due from women to their husbands, focusing often on the crux of religion: was the duty of a heretic's wife to her God, or her earthly master? They debated, too, the question of disobedience and its remedies, settling almost unanimously against violence, except, perhaps, in the most extreme cases. An amalgam of animal images attempted to prove women's status: marriage was a yoke of oxen; a wife must be a well-trained horse; a

[60] William Whately, *A Bride-Bush: Or, A Direction for Married Persons* (London, 1619); Gouge, *Of Domesticall Duties*; Heinrich Bullinger, *The Christen state of Matrimonye*, trans. Miles Coverdale (Antwerp, 1541). The unoriginality of household prescriptions is discussed in Kathleen Davies, 'The Sacred Condition of Equality—How Original Were Puritan Doctrines of Marriage?', *Social History*, 5 (1977), 563–80; more recently, Lorna Hutson has pointed out the innovative work of prescriptive literature based on Xenophon's text in *The Usurer's Daughter: Male Friendship and Fictions of Women in Sixteenth-Century England* (London, 1994), 22–30.

[61] Gouge, *Of Domesticall Duties*: epistle dedicatory.

woman must be like a snail, carrying her house always with her. Instead they leave a clear impression of the difficulties of legislating for the marital relationship. Couples needed to be equal 'yokefellows', yet the husband had to be in command. A woman's duty was inside the house, but she needed to work outside it to sustain the household economy.

Susan Amussen has shown how these ideals might shape popular experience of marriage and family, exploring the permeation of the hierarchical model into every sphere of early modern human relations.[62] Clearly, the idea of natural hierarchy illustrated by patriarchy was extremely powerful both culturally and socially. But the application of that idea to ordinary household relations was also deeply problematic. Even without the self-consciously controversial debates of the advice writers, the ideal that literature propagated remained fundamentally inapplicable to the real household. 'Public' and 'private', 'outside' and 'inside' the house were, in fact, no more easily separable than 'domestic' and 'political'. Women had duties, work, and social lives both outside and inside the house.[63] The family itself was infinitely more complex than its literary model, and its relationships more awkward. By no means all households were headed by men: 16 per cent of Southwark households in 1631 were headed by women, and in many of these women were living alone.[64] Households based on a conjugal relationship had their own complications. An estimated 42 per cent of women marrying in the early seventeenth century had been married before, and many of them had children from a previous union to fit into a new household.[65] Widows remarrying were not the young inexperienced girls envisaged in advice literature, but

[62] Amussen, *Ordered Society*, ch. 2.

[63] See e.g. Patricia Crawford, 'Public Duty, Conscience and Women in Early Modern England', in John Morrill, Paul Slack, and Daniel Woolf (eds.), *Public Duty and Private Conscience in Seventeenth-Century England* (Oxford, 1993); Merry E. Wiesner, 'Women's Defence of their Public Role', in Mary Beth Rose (ed.), *Women in the Middle Ages and the Renaissance: Literary and Historical Perspectives* (Syracuse, NY, 1986); Diane Willen, 'Women in the Public Sphere in Early Modern England: The Case of the Urban Working Poor', *Sixteenth-Century Jl.* 19 (1988), 559–75; Ralph A. Houlbrooke, 'Women's Social Life and Common Action in England from the Fifteenth Century to the Eve of the Civil War', *Continuity and Change,* 12 (1986), 171–89.

[64] Boulton, *Neighbourhood and Society*, 126.

[65] Vivien Brodsky, 'Widows in Late Elizabethan London: Remarriage, Economic Opportunity, and Family Orientations', in Lloyd Bonfield, Richard M. Smith, and Keith Wrightson (eds.), *The World We Have Gained: Histories of Population and Social Structure* (Oxford, 1986), 135; rates of remarriage across England are estimated as 30 per cent in the mid-16th c., in E. A. Wrigley and R. S. Schofield, *The Population History of England, 1541–1871: A Reconstruction* (London, 1981), 258–9.

women accustomed to some social and financial independence, with inherited property or businesses. For both women and men, high rates of mortality and frequent remarriage shaped their understanding of the married state, and the records of betrothal and separation reveal experiences that advice literature rarely considered. The mechanics of service, too, became more complicated when many households took in close relatives as servants, and the clear lines drawn between masters and servants were in constant danger of infringement by the possibility, aired so often in other kinds of literature, of sexual relationships between masters and maids or mistresses and menservants.[66] None of the relationships of the household could be as simple as writers assumed.

What use, then, can this weighty body of advice, ostensibly both prescriptive and descriptive, have been to the early modern household? Sermons and books made use of a common stock of ideas and images about marriage and the household to produce an ideal of social and familial order whose details were, for many households, largely irrelevant. One starting-point might be to enquire how members of real households interpreted such ideology, and to what particular uses they put it: not how far household practice and gender order reflected ideology, but in what ways individuals sought to use such prescriptions. The records of marriage disputes suggest violent husbands used the rhetoric of household order to discipline their wives; the language of insult played on the specific rules of feminine behaviour to describe and defame women as whores.

The words of sexual insult, the transactions of marriage, and the literature of precept are all visibly and profoundly organized around sexual difference; at the same time they work continuously to define that difference. Gender is constructed through representation (as, to a degree, its supposedly natural basis, sex, also is).[67] Judith Butler has shown femininity to be not a constant, coherent category, but a definition in progress, mobilized continuously through certain performances and constitutive acts.[68] We might trace in the popular and

[66] On servants in the household, see Marjorie K. McIntosh, 'Servants and the Household Unit in an Elizabethan English Community', *Jl. of Family History*, 9 (1984), 3–24.

[67] Judith Butler points out that the sex-gender distinction ignores the extent to which sex itself is a constructed category: Butler, *Gender Trouble*, 36–8. On the representation of gender as its construction, see Teresa de Lauretis, *Technologies of Gender: Essays on Theory, Film, and Fiction* (Bloomington, Ind., 1988), ch. 1.

[68] Butler, *Gender Trouble*, esp. 139–41.

élite culture of early modern England a particular stress on the terms and means of that definition; certain kinds of culture constituted performances and definitions of sexual difference. The correlation of male and female reproductive systems presented gender as a line of degrees of difference. The authors of prescriptive texts took as their starting-point an impractical understanding of men's and women's gender roles as incomparably different. In the language of insult, descriptions of whores defined the precise characteristics that differentiated dishonest women from honest ones, and assumed a moral world in which women's and men's characters were evaluated in quite different terms. Each such definition belonged to a wider project with linguistic, social, and political implications: the attempt to pin down the elusive subject of gender, and, particularly, of femininity. Of necessity, gender was always being defined.

For this reason, I think the model of 'crisis' that historians have sometimes applied to gender relations in the period *c.*1560–1640 is an unhelpful one.[69] David Underdown's original argument for an early modern 'crisis in gender relations' marshalled the evidence (questioned, since, by Martin Ingram), for an increase of scolding and other 'female offences' around a thesis that particular peaks of anxiety, and hence prosecutions for scolding, occurred in towns and rural 'wood/pasture' areas (rather than in more stable, field-based agricultural economies).[70] The precise dynamics, chronology, and extent of change in gender relations are, of course, matters to which feminist projects of history need to attend urgently, and the exact terms in which we can measure change in women's history are still being worked out.[71] But crisis, I think, is not the best way of measuring those changes. Gender is *always* in contest: gender relations seem to be continually renegotiated around certain familiar points. In a sense, the cases discussed in the following chapters testify to continual crises around gender and gender relations: crises of words, clashes of expectations in the rituals of courtship, conjugal partnerships that are

[69] Here, see also Lyndal Roper, 'Was There a Crisis in Gender Relations in Sixteenth-Century Germany?', in *Oedipus and the Devil: Witchcraft, Sexuality and Religion in Early Modern Europe* (London, 1994).

[70] David Underdown, 'The Taming of the Scold: The Enforcement of Patriarchal Authority in Early Modern England', in Anthony Fletcher and John Stevenson (eds.), *Order and Disorder in Early Modern England* (Cambridge, 1985). Martin Ingram argues against Underdown's thesis in '"Scolding Women Cucked or Washed": A Crisis in Gender Relations in Early Modern England?', in Jenny Kermode and Garthine Walker (eds.), *Women, Crime and the Courts in Early Modern England* (London, 1994).

[71] Bennett, 'Feminism and History'; Joan Scott, 'Gender: A Useful Category of Historical Analysis', *American Historical Review,* 91 (1986), 1053–75.

stretched past breaking-point. At the same time, they record the persistence of an ideology. The words of sexual insult repeated at court expose a series of understandings of gender and its ramifications; the stories of the contested events of sex and marriage testify to what those understandings meant on a daily basis. The mental, social, and material worlds of early modern women and men were shaped by an ideology of gender relations structured around sex and morals that was, in many ways, constant and persistent.

2

Women in Court

THE CITY AND THE COURTS

The phrase 'going to Pauls' was part of London vernacular. The church courts held in St Paul's Cathedral and known across England as 'the bawdy courts' were one familiar jurisdiction amongst many others. The province of spiritual justice was wide: it ranged from church attendance and Sabbath-keeping, through tithes and the administration of wills, to the regulation of sex and marriage. The latter, which extended also to complaints of sexual slander, took up the most time in the sixteenth- and seventeenth-century courts.

Ecclesiastical justice functioned at several levels. In London, the highest jurisdictions were the courts of arches and of audience, which saw appeals from the whole province of Canterbury. The local jurisdiction of the diocese of London operated through the bishop's court, the consistory; the lower commissary; and the archdeacon's court.[1] Before the Reformation, the commissary court in particular was flourishing, with over 1,000 cases a year at its peak in the 1490s.[2] By the 1510s business was falling and the consistory and commissary courts may have been amalgamated for a time; by the late sixteenth century the commissary seems to have been dealing principally with disciplinary and testamentary business, rather than litigation over sex

[1] Susan Brigden, *London and the Reformation* (Oxford, 1989), ch. 3, gives the fullest picture of London's ecclesiastical jurisdiction. Richard Wunderli, *London Church Courts and Society Before the Reformation* (Cambridge, Mass., 1981), covers the business of the pre-Reformation commissary court. Contemporary discussions of the court's jurisdiction include John Bridges, *A Defence of the Government Established in the Church of England for Ecclesiasticall Matters* (London, 1587), and Richard Cosin, *An Apologie: of, and for Sundrie proceedings by Iurisdiction Ecclesiasticall* (London, 1591). For outlines of the court's procedure, see John Godolphin, *Reportorium Canonicum; or, An Abridgement of the Ecclesiastical Laws of this Realm* (London, 1678) and H[enry] C[onsett], *The Practice of the Spiritual or Ecclesiastical Courts* (London, 1685), essentially a translation of Francis Clerke's *Praxis in Curiis Ecclesiasticis* (London, 1596).

[2] Wunderli, *London Church Courts*, 158.

and marriage.[3] The archdeaconry court, which met just outside the city walls at Christchurch, Newgate, was still functioning in much the same way as the consistory, dealing with the same kinds of marital and defamation cases, in lesser quantities; records survive for only a few years of its business. But it was the consistory court, meeting in the Long Chapel of St Paul's,[4] which dealt with most cases. There, numbers of cases increased steadily until 1641, when the act abolishing the court of high commission demolished the church courts' coercive powers and in London, as elsewhere, the machinery of ecclesiastical justice ground to a halt, to be resumed in the 1660s.

Suits at the church courts fell into one of two types of business. In 'office' or disciplinary cases women and men were presented to the court and prosecuted, either by the judge or sometimes at another person's 'promotion', for offences concerning both church matters and moral standards. For the most part such presentments arose from the visitations of bishops and archdeacons and most were dealt with summarily through reprimands and penances. In the early seventeenth century the court for the City and Middlesex dealt with over 1,000 presentments a year, the vast majority concerned with failure to receive holy communion or working on the sabbath, and just over a tenth relating to sexual and marital offences: fornication, premarital sex, adultery, bearing or fathering a bastard, harbouring an illegitimately pregnant woman, or running a bawdy house.[5] Reformers complained of the court's failure to discipline spiritual offences effectively; the 1572 *Admonition to the Parliament* called the archbishop's court 'the filthy quauemire and poysoned plashe of all the abhominations that doe infect the whole realme'.[6]

The records of disciplinary jurisdiction, particularly in London, are vast but brief; they give no more than cursory outlines of the incidents of illicit sex and disrupted marriages.[7] The other kinds of case

[3] See the series GL MS 9065A and GL MS 9065H. The suggestion that the courts were amalgamated is Wunderli's: *London Church Courts*, 158.

[4] The courtroom of the consistory at Chester still survives: a photograph is reproduced in Jane Cox's *Hatred Pursued Beyond the Grave: Tales of Our Ancestors from the London Church Courts* (HMSO, London, 1993), 13.

[5] Calculated from the office business of the year 1610, recorded in DL/C 308 and DL/C 309. On office jurisdiction, see Martin Ingram, *Church Courts, Sex and Marriage in England, 1570–1640* (Cambridge, 1987), 43–6.

[6] 'An Admonition to the Parliament' (1572), *Puritan Manifestoes*, ed. W. H. Frere and C. E. Douglas (London, 1907), 35.

[7] Selections of the office records for London are printed in W. H. Hale, *A Series of Precedents and Proceedings in Criminal Causes from 1475 to 1640* (London, 1847), and for other dioceses, *The Act Book of the Archdeacon of Taunton*, ed. C. Jenkins, Somerset Record Soc. 43 (London, 1928); *Child-marriages, Divorces, and Ratifications, etc. in the diocese of Chester,*

that came to the courts were more complex, longer, and generated very different kinds of records. 'Instance' causes were brought by plaintiffs against defendants on complaints about tithes, disputed wills, contracts of marriage, marital breakdown, and, most of all, sexual slander. Between a fifth and a third of these suits, along with a few office cases, called witnesses to testify, and it is their statements which provide the longest, most detailed records of sex, marriage, and language: the testimonies of near to 6,000 women and men in cases of sex and marriage survive for the years on which this study concentrates, between 1572 when the records begin to form a more complete series, and 1640, when they end just before the collapse of ecclesiastical justice. By the early seventeenth century the deposition books are very largely given over to the meticulous recording of disputes about sexual insult fought largely between and about women.

In late sixteenth-century England, slander litigation was increasing in both ecclesiastical and secular courts. In Wiltshire in the 1560s and Chester in the 1580s defamation cases accounted for around a quarter of all church court business.[8] In London, defamation had already risen to high levels in the early sixteenth century: in 1512–14 about 40 per cent of cases at the commissary, the lower of the church courts, were suits for slander.[9] In the later sixteenth century, when this study starts, the consistory court was seeing a roughly similar balance of litigation to Wiltshire, Chester, and other church courts; by the seventeenth century, defamation was taking over the London court's business. From a third of litigation in the 1590s, defamation suits rose to represent three-quarters of it in the 1630s: the change is traced in Table 1. While numbers of marriage suits barely kept pace with the rise in population, the increase of defamation suits, and with them the participation of women, substantially outflanked demographic change. Between 1590 and 1624, a period when London's population increased by nearly two-thirds, the numbers of both female plaintiffs and defamation cases nearly tripled. Figure 3 illustrates the transformation by which defamation litigation came to dominate the courts.

At the same time another dynamic was shaping the nature of court

A.D. 1561–6, ed. Frederick J. Furnivall, Early English Text Soc., OS 108 (London, 1897); *The Archdeacon's Court: Liber Actorum, 1584*, ed. E. R. C. Brinkworth, Oxfordshire Record Soc., 23–4 (Oxford, 1942–6).

[8] Christopher Haigh, 'Slander and the Church Courts in the Sixteenth Century', *Trans. of the Lancashire and Cheshire Antiquarian Society*, 78 (1975), 1–13; Ingram, *Church Courts*, 68, table 2.

[9] Wunderli, *London Church Courts*, 142–3.

TABLE 1. *Changes in consistory court litigation, 1572–1633*

Year	Total cases	Cases brought by women		Defamation cases		Defamation sued between women	
		No.	%	No.	%	No.	%
1572	119	30	25.2	21	17.6	9	7.5
1590	182	57	31.5	67	37.0	21	11.5
1618	378	164	43.5	(no record)		78	20.5
1624	368	160	43.5	187	51.0	81	22.0
1633	272	147	54.0	198	73.0	116	42.5

Source: London consistory court act books.

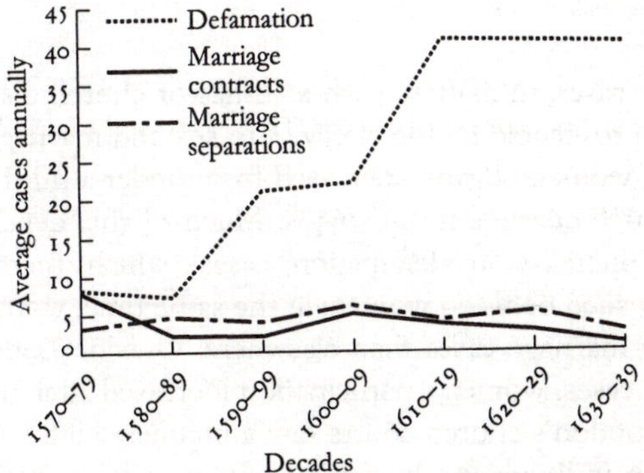

FIG. 3. The increase of defamation suits, 1570–1639

business: the growth of women litigants, shown in Figure 4. Already in the early sixteenth century the commissary court was receiving, rarely for any early modern jurisdiction, as many female as male plaintiffs and sometimes three times as many female defendants: Richard Wunderli suggested that it was 'becoming a women's court'.[10] In the later sixteenth century the consistory court was still well below such levels, but between 1572 and 1640, as defamation cases increased, numbers of women plaintiffs increased fivefold and in 1633 54 per cent of plaintiffs in all inter-party cases were women, even

[10] Ibid., 76.

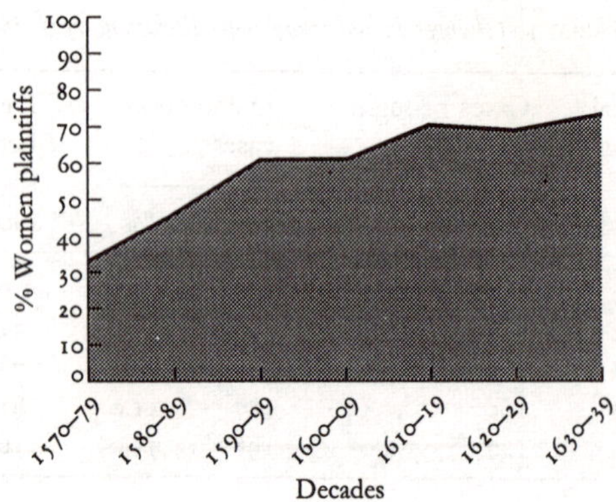

FIG. 4. The increase of women plaintiffs, 1570–1639

when many cases, in matters such as tithes or church discipline, were necessarily prosecuted by the clergy.[11] In sex and marriage cases, proportions of women litigants increased from under a third in the 1570s to nearly three-quarters in the 1630s. Much of this development followed the increase in defamation cases, which themselves were increasingly sued between women; at the same time, women were also suing more marriage cases than elsewhere. Outside London, even in defamation cases, women's participation increased later and to a lesser degree.[12] London's church courts saw a uniquely high level of female participation in litigation; the city's position in relation to the rest of the country's spiritual and secular litigation is shown in Table 2.

The metropolitan diocese was an amorphous one. Its centre lay in the urban parishes within the city walls, whose parishioners brought half the cases that came to the court. But its jurisdiction extended also into the peripheral, suburban parishes around the city: 30 per cent of London's business came from neighbourhoods like Stepney and Whitechapel in the east, Islington and Clerkenwell in the north,

[11] Calculated from the instance act book DL/C 27. Cases brought by the clergy were generally fought as disciplinary, 'office' causes and recorded elsewhere, but a proportion appeared as interparty suits.

[12] In York and Norfolk, numbers of women plaintiffs in defamation cases increased sharply in the later 17th c. (although not, apparently, to this level): see J. A. Sharpe, *Defamation and Sexual Slander in Early Modern England: The Church Courts at York*, Borthwick Papers, 58 (York, 1980), 27, and Susan Dwyer Amussen, *An Ordered Society: Gender and Class in Early Modern England* (Oxford, 1988), 101.

TABLE 2. *Women and the courts in early modern England: proportions of participation*

	Cases brought by women %	Total cases No.
All litigation		
London commissary 1512–13	57	229
London consistory 1590	31	182
London consistory 1633	54	272
Sex and marriage litigation		
Chichester archdeaconry 1574–92*	38.5	44
Chichester archdeaconry 1608–38*	51	51
London consistory 1572–94†	54	210
London consistory 1606–40†	70	1,236
Defamation litigation		
Chichester archdeaconry 1574–1638*	76	26
Wiltshire 1580s	70	67
London consistory 1572–96†	70	124
London consistory 1606–40†	75	1,152
London consistory 1572–1640: urban†	84.5	948
Secular courts		
Sussex Quarter Sessions indictments in criminal causes 1625–40	13	518
London recognizances for petty crime 1663–1722	35	2,039
London indictments for petty crime 1663–1722	18	467

* Sample of selected years only
† Cases from deposition books only, not a full record of suits.

Sources: Ingram, *Church Courts*, 301; Wunderli, *London Church Courts and Society*, 76; Cynthia B. Herrup, *The Common Peace: Participation and the Criminal Law in Seventeenth-Century England* (Cambridge, 1987), 117; Robert B. Shoemaker, *Prosecution and Punishment: Petty Crime and the Law in London and Rural Middlesex* (Cambridge, 1991), 208; Chichester archdeaconry court depositions 1578, 1587, 1596–1608, 1622–38; London consistory court act books 1590, 1633, and deposition books 1572–1640.

Southwark on the other side of the river and, in the west, the whole separate city of Westminster and its environs, Holborn, Marylebone, and Chelsea. The remaining 20 per cent of litigation came from the parishes which made up the rest of the county of Middlesex—rural settlements close to London like Fulham and Acton or further afield like Edmonton and Enfield, and from the peculiars of the Bishop of London in Essex, Hertfordshire, Kent, and Surrey. Each of these different kinds of parish developed a recognizable pattern of litigation, shown in Table 3. The rural parishes exhibit a profile of legal concerns much the same as those studied in other parts of the country: an increasing but not predominant proportion of defamation cases, a low but rising proportion of female participation as plaintiffs and as witnesses. Thirty-seven per cent of plaintiffs were women in 1572–96, 62 per cent in 1606–40. In the City, the pattern was different. With slightly more defamation cases and considerably more female litigants, by the early seventeenth century up to 80 per cent of sex and marriage cases from there were brought by women. In between these two patterns, the parishes that lay between the City and the country, like Shoreditch, Clerkenwell, and Holborn, sent relatively more defamation cases and female plaintiffs to the court than rural parishes but fewer than the City parishes. Exceptionally, though, in the dockside parishes of East London, where many men were away at sea, women went to law even more often than in the City: 86 per cent of plaintiffs in East London sex and marriage cases were female, a level of participation that was surely unique for any contemporary jurisdiction. London's court had its individual character, which manifested itself particularly in the large numbers of cases both fought and defended by women. In Chichester at the same period large numbers of women also brought cases, but relatively few fought them against other women. Jurisdictions everywhere in England were developing their own patterns of business. The London court's receptivity to women's litigation meant that women were prominent not just in slander cases, but in every kind of litigation.

Most studies of the church courts have focused on measuring their effectiveness and efficiency. Martin Ingram's work on Wiltshire has shown how far the church courts were from imminent collapse in the years leading up to 1640, and London was certainly no exception to this. Its levels of business continued to increase steadily, faster than the population rise. But the contours of London litigation suggest, I think, a legal and social history that can be more profitably examined outside the notion of success or failure, however we measure them. The aims of the courts' judges and officers, the principles of canon law on which they operated, and the desires of their litigants were not always united. Ecclesiastical jurisdiction aimed, as much as disciplining its parishioners, to mediate: the role of the judge in court was to help disputing parties come, in 'charity', to an accord, to settle cases

TABLE 3. *Female and male litigants in and around London, 1572–1640*

	Urban		Suburban*		East London		Rural	
	No.	%	No.	%	No.	%	No.	%
Female plaintiffs	595	72	269	73.5	126	78	189	57
Male plaintiffs	231	28	97	26.5	36	22	143	43
Total	826	100	366	100	162	100	332	100
Female defendants	507	59	213	55.5	109	65.5	189	53.5
Male defendants	353	41	171	44.5	58	34.5	165	47
Total	860	100	384	100	167	100	354	100
Cases between women	324	40.5	134	38	78	50	84	26.5
Cases between men	76	9.5	32	9	11	7	51	16
Total litigation	801		354		156		318	

* Excluding East London parishes

Note: The total numbers of plaintiffs and defendants do not tally because there are multiple litigants in some cases.

Source: London consistory deposition books, 1572–1640.

without protracted litigation.[13] But the women and men who came to the court in the seventeenth century looked to litigation as a weapon in the neighbourhood disputes that were expressed through sexual insult: some were looking for mediation and eventual concord, others were seeking revenge. The material they brought as testimony made the court a forum for one particular endeavour: the discussion of women's sexual honour. In 1572 the consistory court was dealing with roughly equal numbers of its traditional kinds of business, tithe cases, testamentary disputes, church discipline, marriage contracts and separations, sexual defamation. By the 1630s its deposition books were filled with suits of sexual defamation between women.

The transformation of the court's business and clients in the early seventeenth century was, most obviously, due to an increase in defamation suits, which were almost entirely about sex and generally sued by women. We might look in a number of directions for the explanation for that: changing social stresses might have made themselves felt through verbal disputes between women; it may be

[13] J. A. Sharpe, '"Such Disagreement Betwyx Neighbours": Litigation and Human Relations in Early Modern England', in John Bossy (ed.), *Disputes and Settlements: Law and Human Relations in the West* (Cambridge, 1983).

that some other jurisdictions lost out as the church courts gained business; it may be, too, that the church courts were simply prepared to accept more defamation cases and able to cope with them. (It seems to have taken no longer, on average, for cases to pass through the system in the 1630s than it did in the 1580s). But the fact that these cases were increasingly sued by women is also important. Defamation was by no means as female-dominated as this elsewhere; J. A. Sharpe's study of the York courts over the same period, for example, found a high proportion of slanders were non-sexual (and mostly sued by men), and elsewhere, even sexual slanders were not always sued by this many women.[14] At a time when the church courts' prestige was under attack, the numbers of women litigants in London's principal ecclesiastical court may have acted both as proof and cause of their decline. In theory, too, canon law was more open to women's legal agency than common law—inevitably so, since its main jurisdiction was in matters that involved women as much as men. This does not, of course, mean that the church courts were more likely to treat women as reliable witnesses or litigants: as we shall see, very often they did not. But women seem to have absorbed, and probably passed on, the message that the church courts were increasingly receptive to women's cases. As much as the increase of defamation and women's suits at the consistory court reflected social changes and pressures, it was related to the court's identity and status, and how it was perceived by contemporaries; it was an identity that remained in many ways similar when the court resumed business after 1660.

THE LEGAL PROCESS

Litigation involved a series of stages, of which the depositions on which this study focuses represented only one. The process of litigation was generally handled by ecclesiastical lawyers, proctors, and advocates, on their clients' behalf. It started with the serving of a citation to summon a defendant to appear. The plaintiff then presented a libel that stated the case in a list of points, and the defendant answered each one, usually with denial. The plaintiff then produced witnesses, who were examined in private on the points of the libel, and their answers were written down as depositions. They might also be cross-questioned at this stage with 'interrogatories' posed by the

[14] See Table 2, p. 35 for these comparative details.

defence. In addition the defence might respond with a counter-allegation of its own, and witnesses to support it, or an 'exception' that questioned the character of witnesses. When this stage was over, the judge assigned a date for the sentence to be given. After judgment was passed the loser might appeal, but in most cases an order was made for the payment of costs and the performance of penance where appropriate.[15] A defamation case that called witnesses and went to final sentence might take a year or eighteen months, a difficult marriage separation could take two, three, or more years to settle. Most cases were dropped or settled before witnesses were called: depositions were only taken for between one in five and one in three of the sex and marriage cases heard at the London court. Even after witnesses had told their stories, out-of-court settlement was still a possibility. The church courts were intentionally flexible. From the Middle Ages they had taken care to encourage settlement rather than confrontation, peace and reconciliation rather than the imposition of penalties. In London, most of the cases that came to the court disappear from the records before sentence was passed. The cursory nature of the surviving sources means that it is only possible to detect which party's request for a sentence was granted: rarely are the details of sentences given, and even after sentence was given, the case might continue with an appeal until it was eventually resolved or dropped.[16] Under a quarter of the cases discussed here are recorded as receiving a sentence. Those that did were settled in 80 per cent of cases in the plaintiff's favour, although proportions varied between different kinds of cases. On the whole, men were more likely to pursue a case to its formal close than women: 27 per cent of men, but only 19 per cent of women, received a formal sentence at the end of their case. As the court's litigation business became increasingly female-dominated, it seems that the men using the court were likely to be more determined suitors; women and men were, perhaps, using the court in different ways, with men coming with a greater expectation of achieving a sentence instead of a series of statements and counter-attacks that were eventually abandoned or possibly reconciled.

[15] For a full account of the litigation process, see Dorothy Owen, *The Records of the Established Church in England Excluding Parochial Records* (London, 1970); and for a guide to the records it produced, J. S. Purvis, *An Introduction to Ecclesiastical Records* (London, 1953).

[16] No records of sentences survive. Act books for the period, which noted the stages in a case's process, record when the proctor of plaintiff or defendant requested the judge for sentence; while marriage cases often reappear after this point as alimony was settled, most cases disappear from the records after this stage.

The sentences that were given involved various judicial orders. In marriage cases, defendants were generally ordered to solemnize a disrupted marriage, to live in harmony with their partners, or to live separately from them with the church's permission. Men separated from their wives for cruelty were assigned sums of alimony to pay, and unsuccessful litigants were charged the expenses of the case, which, for an average case, was around £4; the costs of longer suits could mount as high as £14. Defamation, like illicit sex, called forth specific penances: often, a public confession after Sunday service, sometimes dressed in a white sheet and carrying a wand, or a paper declaring their sin. Defamers might be sentenced to a public apology, a retraction of their libellous words, and a payment of compensation and expenses.[17] Katherine Fayermanners, accused of calling Aveline Grace 'baggage' and 'thief' on the street in Cheapside in the summer of 1591, and telling her 'Newgate was never fitter for her and that she hoped a carte would come and fetch [her] awaye', was sentenced in April 1592 to do penance at evening prayer in St Swithins church: 'before the minister churchwardens and fower other honest men . . . in the chancell of the same church shee shall openlie on hir knees ask allmightie God and Aveline Grace forgivenes for slaundering of hir'. She was also to pay seventeen shillings and forty-six shillings in expenses.[18] In 1590 Juliana Clunye was ordered to pay ten shillings 'or otherwise to give satisfaction' for calling Marcella Lynne's husband a cuckold.[19] Like illicit sex, defamation was construed as a neighbourhood sin that demanded public apology, and some sentences prescribed with care the exact words of repentance. These are the ones given to Ursula Shepherd, accused of adultery by her husband in 1589, to say during the Sunday service in St Mary Woolchurch:

> Good people I doe here before God and yow all confesse that whereas I have been a marryed wife unto Henry Shepherd for the space of twentie yeres I (forgitting god and my dutye unto my husbande) have comitted adultery and playde the harlott with one Richard Mathewe my servant nowe of late tyme And for the same I am by order of lawe devorced from my husband and enjoyned to doe this my pennance And therfore I desire yow all to take example by me and I doe promise herafter to lead a chaste life.[20]

[17] See Hubert Hall, 'Some Elizabethan Penances in the Diocese of Ely', *Trans. of the Royal Historical Society,* 3rd. ser. (1907), 263–77.

[18] Aveline Grace *c.* Katherine Fayermanners (1591), DL/C 214, p. 102; DL/C 13, fo. 242.

[19] Marcella Lynne *c.* Juliana Clunye (1590), DL/C 213, p. 639; DL/C 13, fo. 119.

[20] Henry Shepherd *c.* Ursula Shepherd (1589), DL/C 13, fo. 6[v].

Penance and forgiveness was meant to be a neighbourhood affair. The church's ultimate penalty was excommunication, either in its lesser form of suspension, which excluded the offender from the church, or the greater form, threatening total ostracism from Christian society. Excommunication was a statutory penalty for non-appearance at the courts, and was regularly threatened and used in the London jurisdiction; but both forms could be lifted with relative ease.[21]

Sensing the fragile boundary between welcoming offenders back into the moral community, and publicly humiliating them, the courts were prepared to be fairly flexible in the performance of penance. Oliver Wallett, detected for fornication with Agnes Hayward in 1574, and sentenced to stand in the church porch from the beginning of morning prayer until the start of the sermon with a paper proclaiming his offence over his head, to stand repentantly in front of the congregation through the sermon, and finally to confess and 'desyer all the people to forgyve hym', had his penance mitigated on the grounds that it might hinder his 'towardnes . . . to mary with Agnes Haywarde'. The penances that judges and ministers planned with such care around the Sunday liturgy were rituals whose symbols—the white sheet, the paper on the head—were invoked outside as well as inside the church, and they might be received, correspondingly, not entirely as the clergy hoped. After Oliver and Agnes had performed their penance, two other parishioners were summoned to the court for 'skoffyng and abusinge of them at their goinge awaye'.[22] Like the moment of execution, the drama of penance could be understood by its audience in terms very different from the severity its architects intended.[23]

LEGAL NARRATIVES

The story of adultery that Ursula Shepherd was enjoined to tell her neighbours at her penance testifies to the significance of narrative in the legal process. Justice in the church courts depended on storytelling. When reconciliation was impossible, the court made its decisions based on depositions about sex and honour, slander and reputation, or marriage and its collapse. Such testimonies explain the

[21] The effectiveness of excommunication is discussed in detail in Ingram, *Church Courts*, 340–63.

[22] DL/C 615, p. 25 (1574); ibid. 46 (1574).

[23] See Thomas Laqueur, 'Crowds, Carnival and the State in English Executions, 1604–1868' in A. L. Beier, David Cannadine, and James M. Rosenheim (eds.), *The First Modern Society: Essays in Honour of Lawrence Stone* (Cambridge, 1989).

occasions of misconduct in extended narratives about the world of marriage, family, and neighbourhood and their disruption by dispute. Longer and fuller than most early modern legal records, they provide a unique source for social information. But deposing in the church courts was a complicated process, involving the combination of a series of different voices and a range of purposes. Making sense of depositions, and using them as sources, requires a full attention to the circumstances of their production. Church court depositions are the composite product of a series of reworkings. As witnesses saw a dispute, committed it to memory, told other people about it, and finally reported it to the court, their stories were shaped through a selection of influences: personal concerns, familiar story models, conventional moral judgements. The result is a series of texts that seem to both expand and compress narrative possibilities, that are both surprisingly detailed and full of gaps, coherent and disrupted. These texts played parts in several different kinds of story. Ostensibly, they were part of the grand story of a case: their details were intended to back up the pleas of plaintiffs or defendants. At the same time, testimonies are, in varying degrees, individual. They express, as well as the aims of the litigants and their lawyers, the story of their narrator's participation in the contested events. It was a participation shaped by gender: men and women took different parts in the contested events of sex and marriage, and they made different kinds of witnesses.

In the early modern courts as today the presentation of a case depended upon stories constructed by, in turn, the prosecution, the witnesses, and the defence: the final outcome confirmed which story had won. Story-telling translated contested events into a legally comprehensible medium. As people use narrative techniques to convey selective interpretations of behaviour to others, so story-telling performs a similar function for witnesses testifying in a court, aiming to provide the judge with the evidence for a decision.[24] In a still largely oral society, and in the particular context of the church courts, the narratives of litigation carried a special weight. The relationship between narratives and the legal process took a particular form in the church courts. Unlike other courts, there was no jury to interpret the material of witnesses and litigants: stories went straight to the

[24] W. Lance Bennett and Martha S. Feldman, *Reconstructing Reality in the Courtroom* (London, 1981), 7–10; Bernard Jackson, *Law, Fact and Narrative Coherence* (Merseyside, 1988), ch. 3. For story-telling around another legal context, see Lincoln B. Faller, *Turned to Account: The Forms and Functions of Criminal Biography in Late Seventeenth- and Early Eighteenth-Century England* (Cambridge, 1987).

judge.[25] But the narratives of litigation did not work simply as material for judicial decision-making. Few cases reached the point of final sentence, and the expectations of litigants must have been geared to this: it seems to have been the formal articulation of complaint and conflict, rather than a judicial decision, that was the point. In many cases, it was the narratives of litigation themselves, rather than a final sentence decided from them, that carried the weight of dispute and that brought suits to the point at which they could be resolved or abandoned.

At the church courts, the depositions and defences which made up the legal narratives also had a rather different function to that of the examinations of witnesses at the quarter sessions or the assizes. Disputes over sex and marriage hinged not so much on proofs of crime as on questions of interpretation. In suits for defamation, disputed marriage contracts, and separation, litigants and witnesses argued about the meaning of events, over whether words were spoken in malice or anger, what constituted proofs of marriage, or whether a certain extent of violence was unreasonable enough to constitute marital breakdown. Witnesses were asked by the court who they thought 'had the right'; the question was often not what had happened, but whose interpretation of it deserved to be accepted. When women and men retold the occasions of dispute to the court, the confrontation between two people translated into a contest for the meaning of their actions, as each produced a story for the court and struggled to make its meaning stick there. In a society where the circulation of oral stories and rumours was an important part of the fabric of gender and social relations, the conflicting narratives told at the church courts had wide resonances outside the law.

If the social and legal context gave the content of narratives a wide bearing in the community as well as in court, their precise shape was strictly determined by legal protocol. The first task in tracking down the functions and construction of depositions is to identify the various legal and lay voices that together represent the central events of a case through narrative interventions, omissions, additions, and reorderings. The stories of witnesses and defendants were given in private to a clerk and in answer to questions posed by the plaintiff's libel. Witnesses were asked to say what they knew about the central

[25] On the role of juries, see Kathryn Holmes Snedaker, 'Story-Telling in Opening Statements: Framing the Argumentation of the Trial', in David Ray Papke (ed.), *Narrative and the Legal Discourse: A Reader in Story-Telling and the Law* (Liverpool, 1991); Bennett and Feldman, *Reconstructing Reality*, ch. 1.

allegations of the case, and they did so through recounting their involvement in the disputed events.

First, then, the words of witnesses and defendants were shaped by the original libel to which they were responding. They generally followed its allegations, but elaborated them to make a story. At the archdeaconry court of Chichester in 1631 Thomas Hudson alleged that Hugh French, his parish priest, had defamed him by saying 'Thou or he or Thomas Hudson art or is a whoremaster or whoremonger or Thou or he or Thomas Hudson or Hudson the miller did ly with or hath lyen with Joane Chapman in the mill or in Selsey mill uppon a Saturdaye or uppon Maye daye last past'. From these alternatives his first witness selected a phrase and put it in the context that explained it: 'he was going homewards after they had made an ende of walking theire parish bounds for that day . . . Thomas Woodland said they were like to have a poore parishe . . . Frenche replied it was like to be poorer for Hudson lay with Joane Chapman in the mill, on Saterday.'[26] While plaintiffs, aided by their lawyers, set out the basic points of a case with care, witnesses provided the imaginative elaboration that gives both a context and a personal meaning to the events in dispute. Nominally structured around a question and answer form, litigation in fact involved the creation of stories: while many of the plaintiff's questions requested and got brief answers, some led to much longer explanatory stories which, dealing with two or three questions at once, constituted the heart of the narrative to which the judge would respond.

Both the litigants' statements and those of their witnesses were shaped to some extent by the proctors who acted as ecclesiastical lawyers. The London court depended on a sizeable pool of them: in 1590–1 twenty-nine were practising in the consistory court, one of whom was Francis Clerke, author of a well-used manual on church court practice.[27] Some of the church court's personnel also practised in the Court of Arches and were members of Doctor's Commons.

[26] Thomas Hudson *c.* Hugh French (1631), WSRO EpI/15/3/29, m. 57; EpI/11/14, fo. 243.

[27] From DL/C 13. On Clerke's *Praxis*, see R. H. Helmholz, *Roman Canon Law in Reformation England* (Cambridge, 1990), 128–32. While in most local church courts in this period proctors (roughly, the ecclesiastical equivalent of solicitors) assumed a number of higher duties they were not strictly entitled to practise, in London advocates (the higher branch of ecclesiastical law, equivalent to barristers) played a much greater part. Colin R. Chapman, *Ecclesiastical Courts, their Officials, and their Records* (Dursley, 1992), 33–4. However, litigants and witnesses in these cases refer to 'proctors' and not to 'advocates' so the London consistory court was perhaps more similar here to other local church courts than has been assumed.

Connected as they were with the élite of ecclesiastical lawyers, the personnel of London's church courts must have been a well-informed, well-trained group, probably for the most part far from the incompetent, ignorant lawyers of which contemporary reformers complained.[28] Their contributions to plaintiffs' and witnesses' stories must have had a considerable effect on their shape. It was the proctors' responsibility to make comprehensive legal narratives out of people's words, selecting relevant evidence, ordering it, and ensuring it made sense to the court. Probably it was proctors who had the most hand in deciding what details were the basis of a case: the exact words of abuse in defamation suits, the gradations of violence in complaints of cruelty, or the signs of affection and familiarity that could prove promises of marriage. At the same time, the people who came to the court were often well versed in the rules of litigation. Clearly, 'whore' and other explicitly sexual insults were well known to be actionable words, as love tokens were established as proofs of marital commitment and as life-threatening violence was understood to constitute a reasonable plea for marital separation.

The words of litigants and witnesses were also mediated by the men who wrote them down. The registrars and their deputies who were the scribes to the consistory court added to the everyday speech of litigants the conventional legal usages of Latin and English that made up the court's language. Their names are rarely recorded, but most of them had probably trained in the courts as servants to registrars, possibly taking a specific qualifying examination.[29] Along the way they acquired a style that was virtually uniform across the country, and across several centuries: characterized by long, rarely punctuated sentences, frequent reiterations, and careful explanations of every character's place in the court process, it transposes the spoken language into statements which can be virtually incoherent outside the court. A series of formulas are used to surround the words of the witness. Statements presumably given in the first person ('I saw . . .') are transposed to a third person defined in relation to the case and distanced

[28] Ronald A. Marchant, *The Church Under the Law: Justice, Administration and Discipline in the Diocese of York, 1560–1640* (Cambridge, 1969), 54–7; Martin Ingram, 'Ecclesiastical Justice in Wiltshire, 1600–1640, With Special Reference to Cases Concerning Sex and Marriage', D.Phil. thesis (University of Oxford, 1976), 48–51; Carson I. A. Ritchie, *The Ecclesiastical Courts of York* (Arbroath, 1956), 138.

[29] C. W. Brooks, R. H. Helmholz, and P. G. Stein, *Notaries Public in England since the Reformation* (London, 1991), ch. 1; Ritchie, *Ecclesiastical Courts of York*, ch. 4. Walter Horsell, servant to the court's notary William Blackwell in 1579, and occasionally filling in for him then, was a notary public himself by 1588: DL/C 629, fo. 46 (1579); DL/C 213, p. 415 (1588).

again by the form of reported speech ('she this deponent saieth that she saw . . .'). Every person introduced in the narrative is explained in the light of legal process: 'the said Mr Smith party defendant in this cause against whom this deponent is produced', clerks wrote, making a lengthy, clumsy, but technically unimpeachable statement. The kind of clerical insertions that altered a story are marked here in italic:

[He says and answers] that at the latter end of summer last past *and within the time articulate* he *this deponent* being at work in his shopp situate in East Smithfeild *in the parish of St Buttolph Algate London* sawe *the partie defendant in this cause* come into his shopp and take his wife *and precontest* by the arme into the street before his shopp *in the parishe aforesaid* And *then and there* in a scoffing and jeerieng manner she *the said Philippa Munford the partie defendant articulate* speaking of *the partie plaintiff* Lewse Homes said Yonder is or yonder goes the man that was in the haycocke with Mrs Holmes when she lost hir shoe, she *the said Munford* then pointeing at or sheweing his said wife a man that drove turkeis which went on the other side of the way beyond a cart in the street at that time.[30]

Other formulas are less obvious. Statements to the court must have been produced in conformity to a whole range of hidden textual rules that are now hardly visible. When, for example, testimonies concerned illicit sex, scribes, lawyers, or witnesses themselves shifted into a different register from everyday speech; instead of 'occupying' or 'lying with', witnesses' depositions use the terms 'carnall knowledge', 'carnall copulation', and the stock phrase 'fornication adultery or incontinence'. The legal presentation of sex involved an idiom common to all courts: examinations of women suspected of bastardy and infanticide in the Westminster sessions record their words in very much the same official language. In this transposition from oral testimony to written record, at least some of the original words must have been lost: what the clerks recorded looks, in most cases, as much like a summary of what they heard, as a word for word transcription of an answer. But at the same time, faithful reporting of words was both possible and important. In these courts especially, where so many cases hinged on the exact formulas of marriage promises or verbal insults, clerks were well aware of the vital importance of establishing precisely which words were spoken and which were not.

Even before answers were written down, another kind of mediation took place as witnesses were asked questions and prompted to answer them. The legal form of question and answer was a familiar

[30] Lewse Holmes *c.* Richard & Philippa Munford (1637), DL/C 235, fo. 2.

one. Reproductions of such questionings regularly formed the epigraph in the popular literature of crime; one of the works of Henry Goodcole, the ordinary of Newgate, details the ways in which he conducted his examination of an accused witch, Elizabeth Sawyer, in 1621. Goodcole's account lays considerable stress on his authority as a questioner, creating a relationship between himself and the accused in which he interprets, enjoins, and judges. His questions are explained with comments like 'In this manner was I inforced to speak to her, because she might understand, or give unto me answere, according to my demands, for she was a very ignorant woman'. He attends to the way she answers—'this I asked of her very earnestly and shee thus answered me, without any studying for an answer'. As the tale unfolds, he interposes moral judgements—'a wonderfull warning to many whose tongues are too frequent in these abhominable sinnes . . .'—and as they reach the crux of the allegations against her, he admonishes her 'tell the truth, I charge you, as your [*sic*] will answere unto the Almighty God'.[31] For Henry Goodcole, practised in creating moral pamphlets out of criminal prosecutions and their texts, the process of interrogation was of a particularly public and self-conscious nature. But the convention of questioning practised in the church courts necessarily involved some of the interpreting and explaining reported in his account, and perhaps some of the careful explanatory strategies we see in witness depositions are responses to this kind of prompting. As the church court clerks wrote down the answers of witnesses, they sometimes inserted a similar kind of moralizing. 'Not withstanding her first promyse made unto John Sturton to the grete damage of her soule as she belevethe and grudge of her conscience . . . she . . . solemnised matrimony with the said John Lynney', was the record one clerk at the London archdeaconry court made of a woman's response to the charge of contracting marriage twice.[32]

The clerks' records of witnesses' answers represent, then, a mediated, rearranged, and possibly rewritten version of the real words they heard. While they cannot be taken as a reliable transcription of oral narrative, many testimonies are notably individual and appear to be at least partly verbatim reports; in them, the formulaic phrases of the

[31] Henry Goodcole, *The wonderfull discoverie of Elizabeth Sawyer a Witch, late of Edmonton, her conviction and condemnation and Death. Together with the relation of the Divels accesse to her, and their conference together* (London, 1621), sig. C1, C3.

[32] John Lynney *c.* Agnes Gregory (1567), GL MS 9056, fo. 100.

clerical style mingle with words and phrases that look as if they were remembered, and recorded, in their original detail.

TESTIFYING AT COURT

While the records of the church courts include little information about the litigants who initiated lawsuits, they provide a comprehensive profile of the witnesses whose stories are the foundation of the study. The personal details witnesses gave the court record their age, marital status, occupation, place of birth, and length of residence in the parish.[33] The form of these brief autobiographies hides as much as it reveals: women are described by marital status and never by occupation, except in the case of servants; men are described only by occupation, never by marital status. But from these details we can build up at least a partial picture of the women and men whose texts we are examining and of the kind of concerns that motivated the selection of reliable, plausible witnesses.

Both litigants and witnesses represented a select sample of the community. The poorest members of society, paupers and day labourers, were rarely called to witness, and the costs of litigation, probably generally between £1 and £10, precluded them from fighting cases: skilled workers in London in the first decade of the seventeenth century were earning around 18½*d.* a day, semi-skilled workers 12½*d.* a day.[34] Servants and apprentices made up 16 per cent of witnesses, but were unlikely to bring cases, unless sponsored by their employers. Nor did the gentry constitute a high proportion of participants in the court's business: only 6 per cent of witnesses were gentlemen or women, and as litigants, gentlewomen and men usually came to court only, and occasionally, to decide marriage separations. Marriage contracts and defamation disputes, more amenable in any case to settlement outside the court, were also usually staged in a different kind of social world. Most cases involved women and men who worked, or whose husbands worked, in London's large variety of trades and crafts. Of witnesses, 19 per cent were or had married higher status suppliers such as merchant tailors, drapers, and vintners, 44 per cent

[33] All these details are recorded with varying degrees of accuracy. In particular, age reporting (as is usual in records of this period) is unreliable because of the practice of rounding ages up or down. (Whereas 40% of ages given should end in 1, 3, 7, or 9, only 21% of those given in these records do.)

[34] Details of the London court's fees are recorded in GL MS 25,188 (1598); calculations of wages are from Steve Rappaport, *Worlds within Worlds: Structures of Life in Sixteenth-Century London* (Cambridge, 1989), 85.

lower status tradesmen such as blacksmiths, weavers, and shoemakers, and 6 per cent outdoor workers such as porters and watermen.[35] The trade names can be an unreliable guide to the actual work men, and even more so women, did; several men described themselves by different occupations from those the court named, and women, while they often practised their husbands' trades, also mention their involvement in a range of other, often characteristically female occupations, selling food, nursing, sewing, cleaning and laundering. Often, the members of one trade lived and socialized together, and so they might come to the court together as witnesses to a local incident. In such cases, litigants were likely to share the same occupation as some of their witnesses, but not necessarily the same status: apprentices or employees testified for their masters and sometimes vice versa.

Witnesses were also more likely to be men than women. Although in London women were far more likely to be called to witness than elsewhere, only 43 per cent of London witnesses were women, and only 25 per cent in rural areas.[36] This difference can be directly correlated with the number of women using the courts: only women were likely to produce women as often as, and sometimes more often than, men to testify for them. Table 4 outlines the precise differences. Correspondingly, as the numbers of women suing sex and marriage

TABLE 4. *Sex of witnesses, 1572–1640*

	Male witnesses		Female witnesses	
	No.	%	No.	%
All marriage cases	743	64	420	36
Marriage sued by women	295	58.5	211	41.5
All defamation cases	2,261	53.5	1,947	46.5
Defamation sued by women	1,476	48	1,599	52
Defamation sued between women	748	40	1,123	60

Source: London consistory deposition books, 1572–1640.

35 My division of the trades here is based partly on Vivien Brodsky's analysis in 'Mobility and Marriage in Pre-Industrial England: A Demographic and Social Structural Analysis of Geographic and Social Mobility and Aspects of Marriage, 1570–1690, with Particular Reference to London and General Reference to Middlesex, Kent, Essex and Hertfordshire', Ph.D. thesis (University of Cambridge, 1978), 114, and on that of David Cressy, *Literacy and the Social Order: Reading and Writing in Tudor and Stuart England* (Cambridge, 1980), 138.

36 Cressy, *Literacy and the Social Order*, 114.

cases increased, so did the proportion of female witnesses: from 31 per cent in 1570–80 to 48 per cent in 1630–40. Age also affected women's credibility as witnesses. Only in the group of witnesses aged under 25 were more than half the witnesses female; around 40 per cent were women in the age groups 25–60, and thereafter the proportion of women dropped still further. Older women had a distinctly different standing in the community from old men: if men, with age, acquired a certain power and status that enabled some to mediate in social disputes, older women were just as likely to be defined as a source of trouble, and for female witnesses, the phrase 'old poor woman' was a marker of discredit.

Throughout the witnessing process, credit was in question. Defendants undermined the prosecution case by attacking the veracity of witnesses. Their questions and counter-allegations focused on the conditions which most imperil credit: poverty, youth, previous involvement in court cases, or a reputation for neighbourly disharmony. Both men and women witnesses were subject to attempts to discredit their words; but women were interrogated particularly closely on the truth of their words (as opposed to, for example, questions about compromising financial debts to the plaintiff, or disrespectable poverty). Interrogations of women reflected the lower and more precarious credit of their words. Young women were asked if they understood oaths, wives were asked if their husbands had sufficient money to maintain them, 'old poor women' were asked how they lived (implying financial dependence on the plaintiff). Although the exact words of these questions do not survive, the answers women gave when their credit was under attack reveal the points of doubt the court targeted, and the strategies with which women asserted their credibility and reliability. Over-friendliness with the plaintiff was one common charge, to which one woman answered:

> when this respondent kept a shopp in Newgate markett, where she sould poultrie ware, she did goe as often to other of the neighbours there as she did to the partie producent, and the said partie producent never at anie tyme lent this respondent money as is malitiously dedeuced in this interrogatory . . . neither doth she stand in feare or awe of her.

Ignorance of the meaning of oaths was another allegation, to which women responded with strong assertions of their understanding of what law, oaths, and truth meant. In a 1620 defamation case Susan Freeman, a 14-year-old servant, told the court: 'whoe soever forsweareth them selves are in danger of godes wrath and indignation here in this life and after death of hell fier with out gods especiall grace preventing them'. Dorothy Freeman, her aunt, answered: 'This respondent for her parte hath not ben soe ill brought upp but that she right well knoweth the danger of an oathe, and what state a perjured man and woman standeth in, yf they offend therein.'

It was not just the court who thought women less truthful, but litigants; a number of witnesses, rather more women than men, told the court how plaintiffs had tried, sometimes successfully, to bribe them into telling certain stories with money, presents, or threats. Young female servants were particularly vulnerable in this respect. Elizabeth Plover, a servant, told the court in 1627 that a quarter of a year earlier she had been ignorant of what an oath meant, and so a justice had refused to hear her evidence in a dispute, but now, she said, 'she . . . is almost sixteene yeares of age, and saith that she is not ignorant of an oath, nor what is required of anie who taketh an oath as an wittnes between partie and partie, for she saith that an oath is to testefie and speak a truth and noe more but a truth being taken before a magistrate or judge'. In the same suit another servant, aged 21, admitted being forced by her mistress to accuse a man wrongfully of having had sex with her.[37] When women came to the court, they were made aware from the start that their testimony was understood differently from that of men.

The choice of witnesses was, of course, circumstantial as well as tactical. Men were more likely to be present at marriage contracts, when a formal, authoritative witness might be necessary; women were more likely to witness defamation disputes, which often took place in domestic or labour contexts that were predominantly female. But the different treatment of male and female witnesses indicates exactly where the lines were drawn to measure women's credit. It is clear both from the proportions of male and female witnesses, and the specific questions they were asked, that women's credit could be a very different affair from men's.

The term 'credit', while it had all sorts of wider meanings related to reputation, trust, and name, was fundamentally an economic one. For men its financial meanings, and their relationship to the weight of their words, were fairly simple: the court asked them how much financial credit they had to establish both their general worth and their independence from material bribes by the litigants. For women those financial meanings were much less stably fixed in terms of occupation

[37] GL MS 9189/2, fo. 33 (1627); DL/C 226/V, fo. 18 (1620) and DL/C 226/VI fo. 33 (1620); GL MS 9189/2, fo. 12^{v} and fo. 101^{v} (1627).

and income. Women rarely gave straight answers to the question how much they were worth, which, designed for men, made little sense in the light of women's technically dependent economic status; in strictly financial terms, married women's credit was not easily measured. Outside the court women's credit had a sexual meaning too—women's worth depended on sexual probity—and interrogations of female witnesses cast doubt on their sexual chastity, the legitimacy of their children, and sometimes also the sexual reputations of their mothers or sisters. The especial vulnerability of women's credit to any suggestion of sexual misdealing also had a broader effect. Honesty, for women, was interpreted as sexual honesty; correspondingly, less honesty—in terms of straight dealing and truthful words—was expected of them than it was of men, and they were questioned specifically about their understanding of honest words. Women were less often chosen as witnesses because women's stories were expected to be less plausible, less effective in court, than men's. In defamation cases, many women rejected this reasoning and brought women to witness. Their choice reflected the extent to which slander, both on the street and in court, was becoming established as a women's affair; but it also suggests an understanding of gender, credit, and the court that was rather different from that of men.

The composite exercise of lawyers, litigants, witnesses, and clerks is reflected in the texts of depositions. Natalie Zemon Davis's pioneering work on sixteenth-century French pardon tales has illuminated the narrative crafting and shaping which went into pleas for royal mercy, and the structures on which those tales depended to build a plausible story.[38] Similar narrative processes were at work here; but these tales present a much less coherent narrative project. The different aims and endeavours of plaintiffs, witnesses, and legal personnel meant that these stories were always told by more than one person. What the court required were answers satisfactory to the case, not necessarily coherent outside it. But what witnesses provided was a narrative mould for these facts, the story-telling frame in which they found themselves most eloquent: one where they shifted the focus on to their own behaviour, transforming themselves from audience to actors. The narratives that this meeting produced betray the conflict of their origins. They dwell on some details, ignore others; formulas important to the court are stressed, clauses that make the story's plot more coherent are left out or slipped in later; witnesses are led swiftly

[38] Natalie Zemon Davis, *Fiction in the Archives: Pardon Tales and their Tellers in Sixteenth-Century France* (Cambridge, 1987).

on from introductions, to the main crux of words or deeds; and, while witnesses often provide a conclusive ending to their stories, their testimony in fact opens the way for a new closure to be decided by the court or by the litigants themselves. The story of the production of these texts is, at one level, the history of the struggle between 'answer', in a legal sense that relies on a notion of question and response quite different from that of ordinary speech, and 'story', the model through which witnesses presented their testimony.[39]

Like litigation itself, witnessing had a meaning not just for the court but for the people who engaged in it. In a culture where contact with written texts was so limited, and so distinctly gendered, the transcription of these words by the clerk gave them a value different from most of the other daily words spoken by witnesses. Some of the men who came to the court, churchwardens, constables, or sidesmen, had contact with other official ways of recording their voices; but for most witnesses this was one of the few times their words were likely to be written down. London witnesses were unusually literate, with the proportion of men who could sign their names rising from 57 per cent in the 1580s to 73 per cent by the 1630s. But even in London women's literacy remained low until later in the seventeenth century, and only 13 per cent signed their names to their depositions in the 1630s, most of them gentlewomen. Signing is, of course, by no means a sure guide to literacy: some people who signed their names might have been unable to read while others, particularly women, might have learnt to read but not to write.[40] Nevertheless, the picture that remains is of a society in which most men could write and most women could not.

For the illiterate, the transcription of their oral stories to the signs of script was likely to be a particularly significant experience. Even for literate witnesses, deposing in court was a different kind of expression from anything they might write themselves. In many ways the narratives the court preserved, with all their unexplained absences and gaps, still present a more coherent, fluent story than the other textual

[39] On the peculiar verbal qualities of court speech, see J. Maxwell Atkinson and Paul Drew, *Order in Court: The Organisation of Verbal Interaction in Judicial Settings* (Basingstoke, 1979), ch. 2.

[40] On this problem see Cressy, *Literacy and the Social Order*, ch. 3; Keith Thomas, 'The Meaning of Literacy in Early Modern England', in Gerd Baumann (ed.), *The Written Word: Literacy in Transition* (Oxford, 1986); Wyn Ford, 'The Problem of Literacy in Early Modern England', *History*, 78/252 (1993), 22–37; Sara Heller Mendelson, 'Stuart Women's Diaries and Occasional Memoirs', in Mary Prior (ed.), *Women in English Society 1500–1800* (London, 1985), 182–3.

records that might be left by the same kind of people. In a culture still predominantly oral the act of writing, especially by unpractised writers, effected a detachment of the story from its author, producing a more stilted tale than the transcriptions of the clerks.[41] We might compare the account Henry Machyn, a London merchant tailor, wrote in his diary in 1561 of his punishment for slander with the circumstantial stories of similar events produced for the courts:

> yt was sant Clement day, dyd sy[te] alle the sermon tyme monser Henry de Machyn, for ii [words?] the wyche was told hym, that Veron the French [man] the precher was taken with a wenche, by the rep[orting] by on Wylliam Laurans clarke of sant Mare Maudle[ns] in Mylke strett, the wyche the sam Hare knellyd down [be]for master Veron and the byshope, and yett [they] would nott for[give] hym.[42]

The gaps in this text are not just those left by the book's decay and the abbreviations of Henry Machyn. The story is told almost backwards; it digresses only briefly into explanation and poses as many questions as it answers. Machyn's diary records many of these disciplinary incidents, but this one that concerns himself is as impersonal as those about strangers. Witnessing to a court demands an entirely different kind of story, circumstantial and explanatory, with the skills of oral story-telling as opposed to those of cursory daily chronicling like Machyn's: testifying offered an unusual verbal and narrative opportunity. It was particularly unusual for women, with so much less access to literacy than men. The surviving autobiographical words of women are most often those shaped through the form of a spiritual diary, to be, like Elizabeth Bury's, 'a Witness betwixt God and her own Soul'.[43] In the church courts the clerks recorded a different kind of witnessing, the presentation of stories that incorporated and prioritized the details of daily lives and that focused on sexual acts and sexual language that were meant to be very far from the domain of women's speech.

TELLING STORIES

The narratives of witnesses and litigants were shaped not just by clerks and proctors, but by their narrator's own strategic and uncon-

[41] Walter J. Ong, *Orality and Literacy: The Technologizing of the Word* (London, 1982), ch. 4.

[42] Henry Machyn, *The Diary of Henry Machyn*, ed. John Gough Nichols, Camden Society (London, 1847), 14/11/1561, pp. 272–3.

[43] Samuel Bury, *An Account of the Life and Death of Mrs Elizabeth Bury* (Bristol, 1720), 11; quoted in Mendelson, 'Stuart Women's Diaries', 185.

scious reshapings. Even as witnesses committed events to memory, they interpreted what they saw and heard through the expectations and knowledge of their culture.[44] Remembered stories are already changed. The events which witnesses recount may never have happened exactly as they describe them, whether or not they intended to tell them accurately. For the most part, they told tales that fitted with the plaintiff's story, but tales that were also compatible with contemporary expectations and shaped by set models and literary tropes.

In court, depositions worked as part of the much larger story of the whole case, providing a structure of understanding both for the witness who saw the events and for the judge to whom they were retold. At their heart were explanations and narratives of sometimes extensive detail, the products both of adept reshaping and reliable memory. If the central events of a case were outlined in plaintiffs' statements, witnesses also very often came to the court with their own detailed recall, not just of deeds but of words. The precise details of words were vital in many of these cases; they determined the exact degree of marital commitment, or the offence offered by insults. Plausibly forceful and striking phrases, many of them apparently part of proverbial idiom, distinguish individual stories. Rebecca Askewe remembered the powerful words Anny Cumberland had said of Frances Day: 'she stood like a blazing starre and I am the woorse every time I see her'.[45] The form of church court depositions gave a minute attention to telling detail of which witnesses took full advantage. Many such reports were much longer than these. William Sandes of Great Totham in Essex deposed an account of his minister's sermon in 1613, alleging that he had compared his 'cheifest parishioners' to the sinners of Sodom and Gomorrah:

> Mr Searle did . . . say as followeth or to the like effect wee have some sodamites here amongest us or we have some sodamites in the parishe which do abound in pride fullnes of bread idlenes not strengtheninge the hand of the needye And they thinke to rule the minister and the whole parishe or they go aboute to rule the minister and the whole parishe But I hope that my heart shall be as the heart of righteous Lott and have no conversacon with them for their sinnes are greater then the sinnes of Sodome and Gomorrhe they contemne or refuse the sacraments and service of God but do they thincke to escape the vengeance of God no I doubt not but fire and

[44] On this process, see Anna-Leena Siikala, *Interpreting Oral Narrative* (Helsinki, 1990), 18–22, and Michel de Certeau, *The Practice of Everyday Life*, trans. Steven Rendall (Berkeley, Calif., 1984), 86.

[45] Frances Day *c.* Anny Cumberland (1611), DL/C 219, fo. 377.

brimstone will come from heaven and consume them wee have them here today but wee shall not have them here againe foure or fyve sondaies followeing.[46]

Every cadence of the sermon—to which, after all, its congregation was meant to be paying a memorizing attention—is recorded precisely; the early, hedging phrases that allow for imperfect memory disappear by the end. Yet William's version was not exactly the same as that of his co-witnesses, nor, it seems, as that of the plaintiff.

The stories of witnesses and litigants depended for their power, as much on vivid, apparently authentic detail, as on the chords struck by what they said in contemporary minds. Narratives made sense, both in court and out of it, through their similarity to familiar plots in the stock of common social knowledge: defamatory exchanges, contracts of marriage, or incidents of illicit sex were conveyed through well-known devices.[47] Neighbours intervened in slanderous disputes because they 'heard a great noise', husbands or servants witnessed adultery by looking through holes in walls. In part these were legal formulas that made stories plausible to the court; but they were also part of a popular culture that made sense of real experience. Witnesses to disputes retold them in court as they must also have done outside it, using linguistic practices, familiar story-lines, and shared perceptions through which their audience, lay or legal, could engage in the story. Research on story-telling in the modern courtroom suggests that intelligibility depends, too, on narrative structure: well-told stories are more likely to be believed.[48] So the witness's story needs to present the listener and the judge with the central actions of the case, to surround those actions with connections and descriptions that make sense in the world the listener knows, and to suggest inferences from which an interpretation can be built.

The influences that shaped witnesses' stories must have reflected the variety of strands in popular culture, a spectrum encompassing both oral and written sources. Many of the men who used the church court were accustomed to reading printed texts aloud or using them for specific purposes. Richard Raniscroste, deposing in 1578, spoke of using 'a book of astrologie' bequeathed to him by a friend to confer with a man who 'had cunning that way' about his past and future

[46] Sir Edward Bullock *c.* Thomas Searle (1613), DL/C 221, fo. 1429^{r-v}.

[47] On the place of familiar plots in legal story-telling, see Bernard S. Jackson, 'Narrative Theories and Legal Discourse', in Cristopher Nash (ed.), *Narrative in Culture: The Uses of Storytelling in the Sciences, Philosophy, and Literature* (London, 1990), 28–31.

[48] Bennett and Feldman, *Reconstructing Reality*, ch. 4.

fortunes.[49] Fathers used the Book of Common Prayer to contract their children in marriage. Most familiar and accessible were the words of the Bible. The didactic advice of Solomon was circulated in ballad form and recycled explicitly by at least one defamer, and implicitly in the images of whoredom around which insult revolves.[50] When Edward Locke was trying to contract himself to Sara Johnson in 1623, Sara's stepfather turned to the Bible to prevent it: 'he did turne to or finde out a place in the bible that a daughter ought not to contract herself without the consent of her father'.[51]

Many more people, especially women, lived in a cultural world where print had no place; but they, too, used cultural models to make sense of the world. The different mediums, oral and literate, of early modern culture, shared much of the same content: printed literature was reproduced on a smaller, abbreviated scale to appeal to those who could afford pamphlets or chapbooks; and ballads and broadsheets both passed into, and drew from, oral culture; reading aloud and retelling shared the effects of literacy among the broader non-literate community.[52] The stories of pamphlets and the words of ballads passed easily into oral culture, and lent themselves to a variety of uses. The most elaborate slanders of the time were those composed and repeated verbally in the form of rhymes and songs, sometimes based on contemporary ballads, sometimes ending up in print themselves.[53] Popular printed culture included a fund of stories that existed orally as well. Collections of stories about women, such as *Ar't asleepe Husband?* and *The deceyte of women*, gathered together tales that had their corollaries in oral culture; telling stories about a woman's adultery or deceit was one well-established method of defamation.[54] Roger Die told his mistress and lover Lady Joan Ashbey the story of a young wife whose lover 'contrived her husbands deathe' after which 'the younge man and she lyved contently and pleasantly togither': it was a plot rehearsed at length in popular murder pamphlets and in domes-

[49] Matthew Goodman *c.* Elizabeth Rogers (1574), DL/C 212, p. 61.

[50] E.g. *Solomons Sentences* (c.1615), reprinted in *Ballads and Broadsides chiefly of the Elizabethan period*, ed. H. L. Collman (London, 1912), no. 84.

[51] Edward Locke *c.* Sara Johnson (1623), GL MS 9189/1, fo. 36ᵛ.

[52] On the continuities between oral and print culture, see Adam Fox, 'Aspects of Oral Culture and its Development in Early Modern England', Ph.D. thesis (University of Cambridge, 1992), ch. 1.

[53] Fox, 'Aspects of Oral Culture', 232–4; for a slander based on a ballad see John Taylor *v.* James Cowane (1608), PRO STAC 8 285/27, m. 8.

[54] Philogenes Panedonius [Richard Brathwait], *Ar't asleepe Husband? A Boulster Lecture* (London, 1640); Abraham Vele, *The deceyte of women. to the instruction and ensample of all men, yonge and olde* (London, 1563).

tic tragedy.[55] Other cultural strains are more difficult to trace. Descriptive phrases about sex and honour can sometimes be related to the great corpus of early modern proverbs whose familiar formulas were part of the fabric of everyday speech.[56] Jokes exchanged in conversation might find their way into insults. As well, women and men remembered and told a whole range of stories, from local and family histories to cautionary tales and ballads.

The narratives people told at court reflected the stories they already knew. Popular literature featured a series of familiar plots about sex and marriage: women killing their husbands to marry their apprentices, men catching their wives out in adultery, handsome young men deceiving old husbands to seduce their wives, and women stealing their husbands' breeches were the stock figures of stories that were collected in printed editions, sung in ballads, and shared orally between men and women. These themes were influential. Tales of men gaining mastery over their insubordinate wives, for example, proved a resource for some violent husbands; the stories of domestic murder could serve as both threat and romantic fantasy. Contemporary culture held a stock of stories in both oral and printed form whose contexts, events, and results could be rifled for the tales told in everyday life, in the moments of dispute, and at court.

The depositions that survive in the church court records, the product of several competing and overlapping voices, are both individual and typical, innovative and repetitive. When women and men enlisted the powers of litigation in the pursuit of sexual and marital disputes, they used the court, too, to tell personal stories that uncover the complex operation of gender in the daily life of early modern society.

[55] Sir Francis Ashbey *c.* Lady Joan Ashbey (1619), DL/C 226/III, fo. 8. (This case is discussed in Ch. 6.) See e.g. *The Tragedy of Master Arden of Faversham* (London, 1592) and *A Yorkshire Tragedy* (London, 1608), whose story was also recounted in *Two most unnaturall and bloodie Murthers* (London, 1605). Both plays are reprinted in *Three Elizabethan Domestic Tragedies*, ed. Keith Sturgess (Harmondsworth, 1969).

[56] For contemporary proverbs see James Howell, *Παροιμιογραφια. Proverbs, or Unsayed Sawes and Adages* (London, 1659); M. P. Tilley, *A Dictionary of the Proverbs in England in the Sixteenth and Seventeenth Centuries* (Ann Arbor, 1950). On the use and interpretation of proverbs, see Fox, 'Aspects of Oral Culture', 128–32.

3

The Language of Insult

'I have knowne her a whore these 22 yeares', said Thomas Cockson, warning his wife away from Katherine Fowler in 1610, 'and nowe she waxeth olde she will turne bawde'.[1] The definition of whores and bawds was integral to the rich language in which early modern women and men insulted each other on the streets, in shops, and in the houses of the city and its environs. In the seventeenth century, complaints about such insults came to dominate the church courts: in the early years of the century around 130 women and men came to the court every year to testify to the details, context, and meaning of sexual slander. Their stories of verbal disputes in London's streets, shops, and yards record the precise details of an effective idiom of abuse that targeted women's sexuality. In the language of insult, women and men described sexual misconduct, characterizing it through a central picture of the whore, delineating the emotional, material, and sexual dislocations that whoredom was supposed to effect, and calling for whores to be named and punished. They referred, sometimes, to actual sexual misconduct or rumours about it; but the word 'whore' rarely meant a real prostitute, and the words of insult were understood to be related only opaquely to actual sex. Elizabeth Stokes, a 20-year-old servant who heard Phoebe Cartwright call Margery Hipwell 'impudent quean' in Fleet Street at seven o'clock one April morning in 1613, told the court she did not think 'that Phebe Cartwright by calleing Margerie Hipwell queane did meane that shee had committed fornicacon or adultery or plaied the whore with any man but only spake the same wordes in her anger', after a wrangle between the two women and Margery's husband.[2] Cursory or excessively detailed, the descriptions of whores, queans, bawds, and cuckolds that characterized legally actionable insults added up to a whole language of gendered abuse. It was a language that differentiated persistently and profoundly between the sexual morals and sexual honour of women

[1] Katherine Fowler *c.* Thomas Cockson (1610), DL/C 219, fo. 199^{v}.
[2] Margery Hipwell *c.* Phoebe Cartwright (1613), DL/C 221, fo. 1409^{v}.

and men, and one in which gendered insults marked off the outlines of gender roles in sexual, marital, and social relations. Slander was the linguistic exposition of a model of gender, sex, and morals whose principles governed a much wider sphere; the testimonies of defamation expose the workings of that model both in language and in life.

SLANDERING WOMEN

Sexual insult was a matter for the church courts because it alleged spiritual sins: fornication, adultery, bawdry, and bastardy. While ecclesiastical jurisdiction over defamatory words had, from the late fourteenth century, been increasingly limited by the claims of the common law to judge slanders of non-spiritual matters like theft or murder, by the late sixteenth century secular courts were trying to limit the flood of defamation suits, and in the period of this study the church courts were solidly established as the principal forum for disputes over words and reputation.[3] It was a forum particularly used between women. Figure 5 gives a gender breakdown of the plaintiffs and

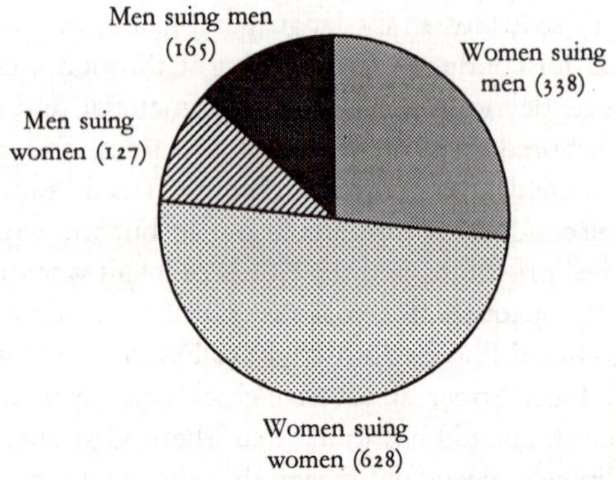

FIG. 5. Women's and men's defamation suits

[3] See *Select Cases on Defamation to 1600*, ed. R. H. Helmholz, Selden Society, 102 (London, 1985), introduction; R. H. Helmholz, *Roman Canon Law in Reformation England* (Cambridge, 1990), 56–68; Martin Ingram, *Church Courts, Sex and Marriage in England, 1570–1640* (Cambridge, 1987), 296–7. The boundary between spiritual and non-spiritual offences was subject to debate in certain areas; bastardy could also be prosecuted at the common law, but, while some commentators argued slanders of bastardy should be tried in the secular courts, it was generally accepted as a spiritual offence and hence within the remit of the church courts.

defendants at the consistory court. Three-quarters of all defamation cases were brought by women, and nearly half were both fought and defended by women. Sexual slander was also predominantly a women's crime: nearly two-thirds of these cases were brought against women. As both plaintiffs and defendants, most of these women were married. In the city, defamation was brought by the wives and daughters of middling status tradesmen and craftsmen, many working with their husbands and sometimes practising skilled and makeshift work of their own; in dockside neighbourhoods most litigants were sailors' wives; in the country, they tended to be married to farmers, husbandmen, and yeomen. Defamation, and especially litigation over it, characterized a particular social milieu; while the status and wealth of litigants varied, none were noble or gentry, and at the other end of the social scale the costs of going to court excluded most servants and the poor.

Early modern constructions of speech and gender gave slanders by women a special dimension. The production of language was a site of particular contest in the definition and prescription of womanhood with which so many writers and preachers were concerned. Women's verbal restraint was one of the cornerstones of virtue: 'She that is talkative is not likely to prove either a quiet wife, or a wise . . . for tis the guise of the harlot to be forever babbling.'[4] Sexual words like those of insult contravened every prescription for women's speech. They also constituted an individual and predominantly feminine model of complaint. The culture and institutions of early modern society provided a multitude of opportunities for men to condemn women, but very few for women to condemn either men or each other. The high number of women's insults, and the contexts in which they were used, suggests that women used public verbal abuse for some of the same purposes for which men had formal or institutional avenues of complaint.

Women's defamation litigation tended to follow a different course to men's. While very few defamation cases got as far as asking for a definitive sentence, men's were more likely to do so than women's. Of cases sued by men, 23 per cent, compared to 18 per cent of those sued by women, received a sentence. Women, it appears, were placing more stress on getting their complaints to the court than on achieving a formal judgment on them; men's disputes, increasingly in a minority, were perhaps more likely to be perceived as more weighty

[4] Matthew Griffith, *Bethel: or, a Forme for Families* (London, 1633), 261.

by the proctors who organized legal proceedings; and women were apparently better at settling their disputes out of court than men. The results of sentences differed, too. Always the majority were given for the plaintiff, and it made little difference whether men or women were suing a case: but as defendants, women were much less likely to win than men. In cases where sentence was given, 23 per cent of male defendants won their cases, but only 14 per cent of female defendants.[5] Women, it seems, were more readily classed as defamers by the judges.

In the exchanges of slander, both the insulter and the insulted were most likely to be women. But even between men, sexual insult was almost invariably about the sexuality of women, not men. Most slander cases were brought by women who had been called whores, or accused of adultery or bastardy; insults of men, in contrast, revolving around words like cuckold or bawd, were directed not at their sexuality but that of their wives. All this suggests that the expanding litigation from and between women had its own character. Women's disputes, by far the largest proportion of defamation litigation, were less likely than men's to be settled in court. Yet the roles and categories of slander fitted women more easily than men. Women were most readily characterized and punished as defamers; and women could be defamed with the briefest of insults, 'whore', a succinct but legally actionable accusation that had no male equivalent.

TERMS OF INSULT

The broad outline and the detail of sexual insult both reflected and constructed a set of specific understandings of the different consequences, implications, and significance of sex and honour for women and for men. Figure 6 illustrates the most basic differences between insults of women and of men. Insults of women were overwhelmingly personal and sexual, using the word whore and its synonyms: jade, quean, or strumpet. The word bawd might also introduce the sexual behaviour of others, and occasionally insults were non-sexual, alleging witchcraft or drunkenness. Insults of men, in contrast, were much less likely to attack their own sexuality.[6] Instead, men were called

[5] Overall, surviving act books for the period 1572–1639 record the passing of sentences for 256 of the 1,339 defamation cases in the deposition books.

[6] The same prevalence of the insult 'whore' can be observed in other communities, e.g. New France, where many insults were interchangeable between men and women, but 'whore' (*putain*) was still the most constant insult for women. Peter N. Moogk, ' "Thieving Buggers" and "Stupid Sluts": Insults and Popular Culture in New France',

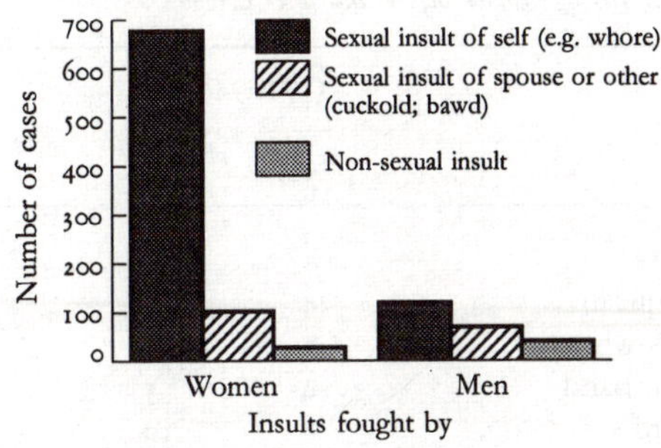

FIG. 6. Gender and the types of insult, 1572–1640

cuckolds or bawds, with the implication that their wives were whores, or they were insulted with non-sexual words like knave and rogue. Some of these, notably whoremaster and whoremonger, did have a sexual connotation, but not a specific one: whoremaster was not used, as whore was, as a preliminary to detailed sexual accusations. On the whole, sexual insults of men revolved around their control of women's sexuality: cuckoldry represented a husband's failure to control his wife, bawdry an investment in another woman's promiscuity. The language of slander divided sexual honour starkly by gender. There was no way of calling a man a whore, or condemning his sexual promiscuity; nor of calling a woman a cuckold, or calling her to account for her spouse's misconduct. Women remained the focus of sexual guilt and responsibility.

The language of slander, organized very clearly by gender, comprised a range of familiar and formulaic insults. The exact words that were used for these insults, and the changes over the period of this study, are analysed in Table 5, a brief typology of gender and insult.[7] The word 'whore' was the most common form of abuse; its centrality to insult, and the elaborations that defamers wove around it, reveal some of the assumptions about gender, sex, and honour that were central to the language of verbal abuse. Regularly, women ended up

William and Mary Quarterly, 3rd ser., 36/4 (1979), 524–47. See also Mary Beth Norton, 'Gender and Defamation in Seventeenth-Century Maryland', *William and Mary Quarterly*, 3rd ser., 44/1 (1987), 3–39; Robert St George, '"Heated" Speech and Literacy', in David D. Hall and David Grayson Allen (eds.) *Seventeenth-Century New England* (Boston, 1985).

[7] For similar analyses for other areas see Ingram, *Church Courts*, 300, and J. A. Sharpe, *Defamation and Sexual Slander in Early Modern England: The Church Courts at York*, Borthwick Papers, 58 (York, 1980), 16.

TABLE 5. *The words of slander before and after c.1600*

	1572–94		1606–40	
	No.	%	No.	%
Slanders of women:				
Whore/jade/quean	24	29	340	39
'My husband's whore'	3	4	27	3
Cuckolding husband	4	5	37	4
Bearing bastard	8	10	59	7
'I have lain with thee'	2	3	12	1
Pox	0	0	30	3
Other specific sex acts	31	37	212	24
Bawd	8	10	131	15
Drunk	0	0	22	3
Witch	3	4	2	0
TOTAL	83	102	872	99
Slanders of men:				
Bastardy	2	5	30	11
'You lay with me' [or tried to]	5	14	12	5
Pox	0	0	12	5
Other specific sex acts	12	32	72	27
Bawd	5	14	38	14
Cuckold/whoredom of wife	7	19	46	17
Knave, whoremaster, etc.	5	14	39	15
Drunk	1	3	17	6
TOTAL	37	101	266	100

Note: Here, since accusations of whoredom were so common, the other details that defamers used to embellish their insults have been used to categorize them: so 'pocky whore' is classed under 'Pox'.

Source: London consistory deposition books, 1572–1640.

in court for saying to each other 'Thou art my husband's whore', and going on, usually, to list absorbing financial and sexual details of adultery. It was a phrase with no possible male equivalent: a man talking about his wife's adultery would in effect be calling himself a cuckold. Over the years, the courts heard a changing range of insults. While the basic terms of abuse, 'whore', 'knave', 'cuckold', remained constant through time, others went in and out of fashion. The variable frequency of 'witch', always a very rare accusation in London, and the appearance after 1600 of allegations of having the pox must reflect changing contemporary concerns.[8] An increase in bastardy accusations as a proportion of men's insults might reflect a changing social policy; it remained nevertheless predominantly a slander against women. As the numbers of cases increased, specific sexual insults, especially those of women, tended to be replaced by vague terms: 'whore', 'jade', 'bawd'. But the distribution of sexual responsibility between men and women remained the same: sexual blame continued to be laid almost entirely on women, by women as much as men. There is no evidence here of the erosion of the double standard that the moral campaigns of London's disciplinary authorities might suggest.[9] If anything, sexual slanders were focusing even more clearly on women's sexual sins. Before 1600, about four times as many women as men came to the court over personal sexual slanders; between 1600 and 1640, it was nearer six times as many.

Unusually for the period, none of these cases feature any allegations of homosexual behaviour.[10] One explanation may be that sexual relations between men had been from the time of Henry VIII a temporal rather than a spiritual crime, and those between women were no crime at all, and so neither were technically actionable allegations at the church courts. Equally important may be the status such relations occupied in popular culture. While contemporary culture, as far as we know, contained few images or words with which to label sex between women, there was much established mythology and satire around sodomy. None of this found an echo in the language of insult reported to the church court. Alan Bray argues that Renaissance thought pictured sodomy through distant metaphors, not the realm of daily life; and it was daily life with which these defamers were most concerned.[11] Their insults focused around the street, the market, and the household.

Clearly, slanders fought at the court do not necessarily represent

[8] In other areas witchcraft was a much more powerful slander, although technically it was a secular and not a spiritual matter: see Peter Rushton, 'Women, Witchcraft and Slander in Early Modern England: Cases from the Durham Church Courts, 1560–1615', *Northern History* 18 (1982), 116–32, and Sharpe, *Defamation and Sexual Slander*, 12–14.

[9] For a suggestion that the double standard was becoming less powerful over these years, see Ian Archer, *The Pursuit of Stability: Social Relations in Elizabethan London* (Cambridge, 1991), 251.

[10] See for comparison Peter Burke, 'The Art of Insult in Early Modern Italy', *Culture and History*, 2 (1987), 68–79, and Preben Meulengracht Sørensen, *The Unmanly Man: Concepts of Defamation in Early Northern Society*, trans. Joan Turville-Petre (Odense, 1983).

[11] Alan Bray, *Homosexuality in Renaissance England* (London, 1982), chs. 1–2.

the range of insults that might be exchanged at street level: for one thing, the rising numbers of insults women complained of at the court probably need to be seen as part of women's increasing use of the courts, rather than a change in types of insult. But from the words of slander, it seems clear that sexual insult consistently permeated verbal attacks on women as it did not those on men. If men were being insulted for their own sexual behaviour on the street, they were unlikely to regard such attacks as damaging enough to take them to court. To a certain extent, the idiom of sexual slander worked as a marker for the severity of a dispute. Most people knew that 'whore' was an actionable word, and defamers regularly dodged around it with phrases like 'I will not call you whore'. The use of the word whore ensured that insults of women were invariably concerned with their sexual behaviour. Even the occasional accusation of 'witch' is phrased as 'witch whore'. 'Whore' does not necessarily have the financial implications of prostitution, although defamers sometimes specify them. Benedict Putnam 'fell a rayling' against Theodosia Merill in 1627 that 'shee . . . gave . . . Norton £3 12*s.* to be his whore': even when it is the man who receives the money, it is still the woman who is the whore. A generic term of abuse, 'whore' also worked as an accusation on its own, as part of a string of similar sexual insults, or as a preamble to a story. Words like 'quean', 'jade', or 'strumpet', understood to have a less specific meaning, were used both to amplify 'whore' and to modify it: in 1614 Isabel Moody said of Grace Aldred that 'she is a droncken whore . . . if I may not call her so then I will call her droncken queane'.[12] And the usage of 'thou' rather than 'you', recorded for most defamations, might indicate a pragmatic verbal insult in itself.[13]

The currency of verbal abuse also sheds light on the values and judgements through which illicit sex, and especially female promiscuity, might be condemned. Many insults connected concerns about poverty, disorderliness, and dirt with the realm of the sexual, combining familiar themes with inventive elaboration along these lines: 'maggottie whore', 'mangy carrion', 'shitten whore', 'pockey lousey hedge whore', 'tinckers truell', 'twopenny whore'; 'scurvie fatt arst

[12] Theodosia Merill *c.* Benedict Putnam (1627), GL MS 9189/2, fo. 67; Grace Aldred *c.* Isabel Moody (1614), DL/C 222, fo. 63.

[13] See Jonathan Hope, 'The Use of *Thou* and *You* in Early Modern Spoken English', in Dieter Kastovsky (ed.), *Studies in Early Modern English* (Berlin, 1994), 142–51.

quean', 'gouty legged whore', 'daggletaile queane'.[14] Women's sexuality was given an animal side: 'worse than anie salte bitche which the dogge followethe up and downe the streete'.[15] Whores were 'common', with a sexuality loosed from male control: in one woman's words, 'as common as a barbers chaire'.[16] With a relatively small vocabulary, defamers could be conspicuously creative, like one man who called a woman 'a common whore and a milke whore', explaining 'thou . . . hast byn occupied under every hedge over thy milke payle'.[17] Nationalities and neighbourhoods constituted another axis of abuse: insults included 'welshe jade', 'high dutche whore', 'Westminster whore', 'Hackney whore', 'St Katharines whore'. Welsh, Dutch, or Londoners, whores were conceived to have come from outside the main thoroughfares of the city where insults were exchanged. Each of these place-names carried its own complex of resonances, from the dockside precinct of St Katharine's, well known for its bawdy houses, to Westminster, the seat of royal government, but each was also well outside the mainstream life of the streets where the insults were exchanged. Central to the language of insult was a project of naming whores and symbolically exiling them from the city, an enterprise whose corollary in actual practice—keeping prostitutes outside the city walls—was an established part of urban moral regulation.

THE COMPOSITION OF SLANDER

Insults were composed along practised lines of style. While many defamers confined themselves to strings of insult, others told detailed slanderous stories against their victims. Michael Richards defamed Luce Birch by telling some people in an alehouse that she had

[14] Insults from DL/C 228, fo. 71 (1621); DL/C 224, fo. 62 (1615); DL/C 221, fo. 1518v (1613); DL/C 228, fo. 110 (1621); GL MS 9189/2, fo. 105 (1627); DL/C 232, fo. 300 (1631); DL/C 224, fo. 208v (1616); DL/C 221, fo. 1561 (1613); DL/C 235, fo. 127v (1638).

[15] Judith Deacon *c.* Reginald Scoles (1620), DL/C 226/VII, fo. 37. 'Salte' means on heat. 'Bitch' is the only animal name used in these verbal insults; on the implications of animal abuse, see Edmund Leach, 'Anthropological Aspects of Language: Animal Categories and Verbal Abuse', in Eric H. Lenneberg (ed.), *New Directions in the Study of Language* (Cambridge, Mass., 1964), 23–63.

[16] Alice Cuttin *c.* Elizabeth Bancks (1631), DL/C 233, fo. 219v. The phrase 'as common as a barber's chair' was a proverb, recorded in M. P. Tilley, *A Dictionary of the Proverbs in England in the Sixteenth and Seventeenth Centuries* (Ann Arbor, 1950). Used of whores, it must have resonances of syphilis and the barber-surgeon: for such implications, see Margaret Pelling, 'Appearance and Reality: Barber-Surgeons, the Body and Disease', in A. L. Beier and Roger Finlay (eds.), *London 1500–1700: The Making of the Metropolis* (London, 1986).

[17] Elizabeth Gooche *c.* Nicholas & Joan Thoruberry (1613), DL/C 221, fos. 1394r–v.

approached a sailor 'and asked if he would have a wench, and then tooke up her clothes and shewed him all her nakednes, but the said sayler did not like her but desired a younger and thereuppon shee . . . sent upp her maide who did the like'. Judith White was prosecuted for defaming her ex-mistress, Alice Arbete, by telling people that 'upon a time when [Alice's husband] was at Bristowe fayr I coming from market and going into an upper roome in his house did see my mistres . . . lieing backward upon a settle with her cote turned upp to her belly and that I didd see her bellye naked and one Mr Hall lening betweene her legges'.[18] Humiliating tales like these replicated themes familiar to popular culture: women's deceit, men's cuckoldry, and sometimes, men's ultimate triumph over their unruly wives. In 1629 Elizabeth Trimmell, a London grocer's widow, claimed to have been defamed by a story that used an archetypal tale of women's dishonesty to play on contemporary anxieties about widows. The court heard that while she was a widow, a Herefordshire gentleman had been advised to pay his suit to her, but that he had been put off by the story Andrew Reade told a group of men in his brother's house on Newgate Market:

I did heare that Mrs Smith the widowe of Wolfraed Smith did make shewe of going to a sermon unto St Antholins Church in London and that her husband mistrusting that she was a dishonest woman of her body, and that she goinge without a man went to play the whore, followed after her, and observed her to goe into a bawdy house in St Swithins Lane in London and her husband went into a barbers shopp neere unto his wife and caused his beard to be shaved and altered his clothes and then went into the bawdy house after his wife and desired to have a wench brought him, and there was answere made unto him by the bawde that there was none in the house, but such as was very deare, and the husband of the said Elizabeth Trimmell als Smith asked how deare and the bawde answered that he might have one for five peeces and he told her the bawde that he would give five peeces if he liked the partie and gave her a peac in earnest whereuppon the said Elizabeth Smith was brought to her husband Wolfraed Smith by the bawde not knowing he was her husband But soe soone as the saide Elizabeth Trimmell als Smith heard her husbandes tongue and perceived that he was her husband she . . . ran away from him and went home and said that she was undone and her husband followed her home and suddainely fell sicke and died with griefe.

All the elements of this cautionary tale—the deception, the disguise, the discovery, and the moral of the dangerous characters of widows—

[18] Luce Birch *c.* Michael Richards (1630), DL/C 231, fo. 543v; Alice Arbete *c.* Judith White (1575), DL/C 212, p. 520.

suggest a well-used story that might have been picked up from ballads, books, or shared story-telling. In these circumstances, it had a special power: Elizabeth's suitor told the court that after hearing the story, he 'did not hould her to be a fitt wife for an honest man and did thereuppon leeve of his intended suite of marriage with her'.[19] Elizabeth had married again, though, by the time the case came to court.

The moment of discovery so central to Andrew Reade's tale is always a crux of defamatory stories. Their climax is the moment when secret immorality is exposed to public view. Husbands follow their wives; servants unmask their mistresses; suspicious neighbours find themselves obliged to find keys or break down doors to get at couples who have locked themselves in. Elizabeth Barwicke told her neighbours that Mary Wharton 'was lockt into a roome with Mr Peirson and that shee was inforced to breake open the doore uppon them, and there found Mr Peirson . . . in a great sweate, and thincke you . . . what they were doing'.[20] When there were no other witnesses, defamers resorted to endowing inanimate objects with the anthropomorphic powers of memory. In 1615 Joan Ashen called Elizabeth Denham 'pissabed whore, and sayd allsoe that yf the Sarasons head staires coulde speake they would tell a tale would hold water'. In a London courtyard in 1614 Thomas Hoskins told a single woman, Ellen Godderd (whom he called 'Bouncinge Nell'), 'If thou art not with child yet thou . . . hast deserved for it as many tymes as there are stones in this courte And if the water gate could speak it would tell many strange tales . . . And if these stones could speake they would justifie my wordes to be true.' And in Wiston in West Sussex Jane Lucye evoked a more rural vision to substantiate her allegations to John Willett: 'Thou . . . wouldest have lyen with mee . . . and committed adultery with mee, or diddest divers and sundry times or once att the least sollicite mee . . . to committ adultery with thee or diddest offer to lye with mee, and that the trees and woode if they could speake would testifye and wytnesse the same.'[21]

Defamers, of course, were themselves exposing hidden sex to the neighbourhood eye: the structure of their stories reflected the drama of words through which insults were staged. They insisted that illicit sex was a public, neighbourhood concern. 'We know what you are',

[19] Elizabeth Trimmell *als* Smith *c.* Andrew Read (1629), DL/C 231, fos. 393^{r-v}.

[20] Mary Wharton *c.* Elizabeth Barret [Barwicke] (1627), DL/C 230, fo. 425^{r-v}.

[21] Elizabeth Denham *c.* Joan Ashen (1615), DL/C 223, fo. 326; Ellen Godderd *c.* Thomas Hoskins (1614), DL/C 222, fos. 80^{v}–81^{v}, 88; John Willett *c.* Jane Lucye (1600), WSRO, EpI/15/3/14, fo. 66.

Thomas Farmer told Joan Farre in her kitchen, invoking the spectre of communal disapproval: 'you laie with a sailor 2 monthes before you wer married'. If defamers presented themselves as the legitimate judges of morals, women were the prime targets of their investigations. In the shadow of the formal mechanisms of detecting, judging, and penalizing women for illicit sex, defamers staged their own trials. At Agnes Fenner's Shoreditch alehouse in the summer of 1610, three men and women discussed a rumour about Barbara Meakins. William Stevenson deposed that he

> called for a pot of drinke . . . and sayd to the sayd Agnes Fenner in the presence of . . . Barbara Meakins, I heare saye you have reported that this woman was delyvered of a child in a coblers howse in Norton Folgate and she the sayd Agnes Fenner sayd Aye she had sayd so then this Jurate sayd there are divers coblers howses in Norton Folgate tell me in whose howse it was then the sayd Agnes Fenner sayd to this Jurate do you thinke I do not knowe you yes, in your howse it was . . . she further sayd there was a childe fownd in the feildes I pray god that were not the child she was brought abed withall and moreover she sayd she would not stop theyr mouthes with 40 shillings worth of bread that would speake as muche as she the sayd Agnes spake.

The repetitive exchange of question, answer, accusation, and speculation builds up a full story; both listeners and tellers contributed their judgement. The circulation of this tale by Agnes Fenner brought Barbara Meakins before the JP to be examined about the child in the field and about allegations that a man was seen in her chamber 'with his breches tyed about his wast', but she was found not guilty. Agnes's vision of the irrepressible force of rumour was a common one. In 1614 Elizabeth Clay said to Frances Dan 'I have heard saye that thou . . . hadst had a bastard and that thou were delivered therof in Moore Feildes'; later, in the evening, she repeated the words, adding 'and a bushell of wheat would not stopp the mouthes of those that had spoken them'.[22]

Defamers' insistence that illicit sex could not be concealed reflected, on one level, the difficulty with which privacy was attained in the early modern household. The architecture of crowded city housing left as little privacy between houses as between rooms; keys, locks, and bolts could furnish in themselves the causes of suspicion. In the summer of 1632 Jane Rostell leant out of her window, overlooking Foxehold Court near St Sepulchre's, to call to Anne Sills, at her own window, 'I was

[22] Joan Farre *c.* Thomas Farmer (1631), DL/C 233, fo. 182v; Barbara Meakins *c.* Agnes Fenner (1610), DL/C 219, fo. 278v; Frances Dan *c.* Elizabeth Clay (1615), DL/C 224, fo. 76v.

never locked into a chamber with a coachman in a bedd'; below, Mary Johnson and John Edwards, at their doors, heard the words. Locks and keys provided, too, a metaphor for sex, as here: 'John Taverner . . . hath a key fitt for Besse Matthewes locke, and she hath a locke fitt for John Taverners key'.[23] Often the tales of insult resemble the evidence the court heard in prosecutions of fornication or adultery, using the conventional motifs of thin walls or holes in doors. Henry Wiltshere's accusations of Elizabeth Stott in 1629 stressed the failure of her attempts at privacy: 'Thou art a privat queane and a base queane and . . . thou keepest privat knaves in thy house or els thy bed would not goe jigge and jogge so often as it doth.' In St Sepulchre in 1627, Joan Whitehead told Dorothy Buck, her next-door neighbour, 'that she had a hole in her garrett . . . and that she sawe a man and her . . . naught together on her bed when her husband was out of towne'.[24] Such details are testimony as much to a particular kind of legal fiction, necessary to prove adultery, as to the real structures of city houses; they were, nevertheless, at least plausible.[25] Clearly, the structures of housing made privacy both scarce and suspicious. At the same time the insistence of defamers on exposing sex was an attempt to problematize privacy, to move sex from a private incident to a subject of public debate. The persistence with which defamers stress the discovery and exposure of illicit sex hints at the tensions between privacy and publicity in urban life.

While defamers' inquisitions and testimonies of sex echoed in many ways the practices of formal justice, their enterprise was an entirely different one. They were not concerned so much with punishing sex (although, as we shall see, the threat of punishment loomed large in the language of insult), as with talking about it: much of the power of slander lay in the social drama of speaking about sex on the street. With the heavy role both spiritual and secular courts had in regulating what we would now think of as private life, and the degree of publicity with which, for most people, everyday life was conducted, the concept of privacy was still one that was significant and sometimes fraught. Seeing, hearing, and witnessing were all powerful storytelling poses for defamers; in conjunction with the conventions of spying and the derogatory use of 'private', the language of defamation testifies to a world in which the boundaries of privacy and publicity

[23] Anne Sills *c.* Jane Rostell (1633), DL/C 630, fo. 41.

[24] Elizabeth Stott *c.* Henry Wiltshere (1629), DL/C 231, fo. 380; Dorothy Bucke *c.* Joan Whitehead (1627), GL MS 9189/2, fo. 84.

[25] Archer, *Pursuit of Stability*, 67, and Ingram, *Church Courts*, 245; for a Bridewell defendant's reference to an invented story hinging on such a device, see GL Bridewell Court Book III, fo. 369^{v}, *re* Susan Makenas (1578).

were very much in contest, where insults played productively on the tensions of those boundaries. And as much as the rules of morality and 'honesty', defamers who tried to make the private public were concerned with the social implications of illicit sex: betrayed hospitality, bawdry, or the pollution of neighbourhood morality.

This insistence on exposing sex was complicated by gender. Slander might represent for women a way of telling the stories about dishonest behaviour, claiming as they went moral superiority and a right to sanction dishonesty, that men had more opportunity for telling in court. Female and male, defamers told stories that implicitly claimed the right to comment publicly on the sexual behaviour of any woman. But women rarely claimed this authority over men's sexuality. Rather, they complained of men's misconduct only when they could testify to it personally. Some claimed that men had propositioned them, and used this as a frame for further accusations. Isabel South accused Richard Todd in front of his wife in Turnbull Street 'Thow art a whoremaster and thow diddest offer to give me an angell of gold to occupie me and thow diddest offer an other mans wife the making of an oven to occupie her.' Mary Walker complained that Henry Colman had accosted her verbally: 'Yonder roague Colman hath so misused me that it is most shamefull to be heard for he did hem at me in the strand and made all the boyes in the streat to wonder at me.' She went on to accuse him of adultery and to plan her exposure of his behaviour: 'but when he comes home lyke a roague and a rascall as he is I will tell him what a whoremasterly roague he is and that he might have hemd at his whore Haywardes wife'. Her apprentice reported that when she got home she told him to hang a pair of horns on Colman's door.[26] When women accused men of sexual misconduct, they put their own reputations on the line first, as if only this could make their words stick.

In incidents like these, men and women confronted each other in a battle for public credit. Every legal and social understanding of women's speech and status meant that men's words were more likely to be taken seriously than women's. In response, some women developed personal strategies of complaint and attack. In 1586 one woman confronted a minister with his sexual misdemeanours, using his church as her stage and his congregation as her audience. Just before Christmas the parishioners of St Margaret Pattens were gathered in the church for a vestry meeting, when one of them brought his sister-in-law, Ann Symes, into the church. There,

[26] Richard & Katherine Todd *c.* Isabel South (1610), DL/C 219, fo. 242^{v}; Henry Colman *c.* Mary Walker (1610), DL/C 219, fo. 102.

> being come in presence of Mr Lisbye the parson . . . she very bouldlye and shamefastlye before the whole assemblye begann to accuse the said Mr Lysbye in theise wordes . . . viz Thowe . . . hast most shamfully committed carnall copulacon with me and hast occupied me dyvers and sundrye tymes as namelye twise in one Treales house a cook by Pye Corner and there thow gavest money to the mayd to kepe the dore while thow didst occupye me/ and another tyme at the signe of the black lyon withowtt bishoppsgate and dyvers other tymes since thow haste had thy pleaseure and use of me and in occupieinge me thow didst use me more ruffanlike than honestlye. All which words was spoken by the said Ann Symes very bouldlye and withowtt blushinge or any shame att all or womanlike modesteye . . . to the great slaunder and ignomynye of Mr . . . Lisbye, whoe seeinge the untrue . . . reporte false unmannerly and unwomanlike behavior and order of the sayd Ann Syme before the whole assembly earnestlye denyed itt and wishe the grownde mighte open under hym if the accusacon of Ann Symes were true.

Edward Reo, who gave this account to the court, made his own perception of the incident unusually clear; his experience as a churchwarden of long standing and a witness in other cases might account for his ability to present so long and detailed a deposition. The focus of both his testimony and Ann Symes's story is shame. He centralizes the scandal of her bold speech; she brings her complaint to a climax with the 'ruffanlike' behaviour of the parson. In interrupting an ecclesiastical and community event in such a way Symes was taking some calculated risks to turn her account into a dramatic event. Her story of the sexual relations between them reverses the expected forms of women's speech. The church was one place where women did talk about sex: confessions of adultery and fornication were ordered by the courts and made in the church door with the offender dressed in a white sheet, exhorting the congregation for their forgiveness. Symes uses this whole convention to provide a venue for her humiliation of the minister from whom, in other circumstances, she might be asking absolution. She steals his place as the focus of the meeting, produces a confession and, at the end, adroitly passes judgement upon his behaviour, while Edward Reo, in the audience, is judging hers. Her words had some effect: a number of the parishioners then refused to receive communion until the charge against their minister was examined, and Lysby was defamed again by another parishioner the following year.[27]

[27] John Lysbye *c.* Ann Symes *als* Hills (1587), DL/C 213, p. 142; St Margaret Pattens Churchwardens' Accounts, GL MS 4570/2, p. 434 (1587). The words of the later defamation, by a man, were reported only as 'tendyng towards the paryll of the said Lysbies lyff yf they had been trew': they may have related to sodomy, punishable by death, or 'lyff' might simply refer to livelihood.

Ann Symes's confessional idiom was a familiar one for women talking about sex. Women bearing illegitimate children were pressed to confess the name of the father, in the presence of the midwife and other women who could be brought to testify to her words when proof of fatherhood was needed: these confessions were themselves sometimes cited as defamations. Confessions of sexual sins in public was one of the punishments imposed by the church courts, and women were more likely than men to be detected for fornication and so to confess it in this way. The very words women use about sex are often those of sin: Ann Symes started 'Thow hast most shamefully committed carnall copulation with me', before she went on to use more popular words like 'occupy'. Speech about sex was presented through the confessional language of the church.

Men conceptualized their experience of sex differently. They, too, were prosecuted for talking about their own sexual behaviour; but their speech shows no signs of the sense of guilty self-implication that characterizes women's defamations of men. Philip Clarke used his own experience to substantiate his accusation of Elizabeth Moore: 'that shee was a whore and a base whore and that there was not a baser whore in the stewes and that he knew it by experience in that he himself . . . had had the use of her body'. His proof is meant to be enough to condemn her. William Pullman insulted a single woman, Ann Bird, in 1615, 'in greate malice and detestacon on the open street': 'thou . . . mayest hold thy peace for I . . . have occupied thee, and thou knowest it', 'thou . . . art a whore and my whore, and I . . . can occupie thee behinde the dore or where I list'. James Granger made a specific threat to Alice Marsh, saying that 'Ales Marsh was an arraunde whore and that he had lyen with her, and that he wold send letters to her husband to declare the same'. Such words had behind them the potential of prosecution for adultery or fornication: they reflected the security of men's position in the sexual system. Women did not threaten men with exposure to their wives. Instead the wives of adulterous men united with them to condemn their female partners. In Boar Head Alley in Fleet Street in 1579, Susan Symonds looked out of her window, which was just beneath the stairs to Alice Amos's chamber, and called to Alice 'Thow art a whore: And I sawe my husband stand between thie legges and thow didst put thy hande into his codpiece very rudely'. From inside the house her husband called 'remembre the quart of creame remembre the quart of creame', and looked out to say 'Yea thow art a whore indeed: for I . . . did occupy the[e] myselfe sixe tymes for one messe of creame.'[28] Both Richard and Susanna were quite clear about where to lay the blame in this case. In contrast, women's defamations of men have about them a certain desperation, an awareness of the inequalities of penalties for sex and the unlikelihood of bringing a man to account for his sexual transgressions except through the financial responsibilities of bastardy.

Most revealing of these difficulties are the experiences of women who spoke about sexual assault and rape. A number of men prosecuted women for claiming in public, at court, or in private that they had attacked or raped them. In 1624 in the parish of St Benet Fink a servant, Susan Turton, complained to a local JP of her master's behaviour towards her and her fellow servant. 'She could not be in quiett for . . . William Holmes for he would fynde her out in anie roome of the house'; 'he would be tousing and mousing of them and urging them to follie and did take upp their clothes and would have had the carnall knowledg of their bodies'. Three months later William Holmes sued his servant for 'much abusing' him. Another servant faced this charge in 1582, with her mother who had supported her complaints. William Gould, a London merchant, took his servant Isabel Burroughs and a friend of her mother's, Katherine Socklyn, to court after Katherine, Isabel's mother, and other women had talked about reports that Isabel was being abused, and had brought a midwife and other friends to William's house to investigate. One witness reported that when Isabel's mother came to her daughter's lodgings in St John Street, she refused to speak with her, 'as Gulde hath made her a whore . . . soe lett hym take her and hang her upp att his dore for the signe of a whore'. The woman with whom Isabel later boarded deposed that

> perceiving her to be sadd this deponent asked her the cause of her sadness; to whome with muche adoe privatlye togither the said Izabell with wepinge eyes toulde this deponent . . . that Mr Gould . . . came thither to her, and sent her up to one of Mrs Burnettes chambers of an arrant: and so sone as she was gone upp, he followed her, and there stryving withe her and had to deale with her, and therefore she was so sadd.

One of the women who had accompanied Isabel's mother to see her testified that she and the other women had examined her and 'did well perceive that . . . Izabell had bynn very ill delt with all and strayned

[28] Elizabeth Moore *c.* Philip Clarke (1631), DL/C 233, fo. 190ᵛ; Anne Bird *c.* William Pullman (1615), DL/C 223, fos. 48ᵛ, 49; Alice Marsh *c.* James Granger *et ux.* (1574), DL/C 211/2, fo. 263; Alice Amos *c.* Richard & Susan Symonds (1579), DL/C 629, fo. 176ᵛ, 177ᵛ.

(in partibus secretis) and then askinge . . . Izabell who did soe hurte her: she saide Mr Goulde had make her soe, and none but he had had the use of her bodye, and that he did it againste a beds syde.'[29]

As well as being sued for defamation in the consistory court, Isabel was also brought before the masters of Bridewell, where she repeated the confession she had made to her landlady; and this confession provided another item for William Gould's allegation against her. The difficulties of penalizing a man for behaviour like this were amplified by the way that the confessional speech encouraged of women who had committed sexual sins could become dangerous in itself. Public and semi-private complaints were one way for women to draw attention to crimes that were rarely prosecuted in the courts.[30] But the language that women had for male sexual misbehaviour remained limited. In the reports of witnesses Isabel's mother calls her daughter a whore, but has no word for her master: the only articulation she has for her daughter's experience is through the language of sexual insult.

When women talked about sex, the question of their own honesty was rarely far from the surface. Even for those women who were not talking about their own sexual experiences, discussion of another woman's morals also had implications for their own. Women used the words of slander to proclaim their own virtue by defining its opposite. Many women's defamations made this comparison explicit. Joan Searles told Thomasine Hayward 'I . . . did never play the whore with John Knight for a wastcoate and holland smocke.' Winifred Bland, in a dispute with Elizabeth Hollinshed and her husband that led to three cases in 1608, said to her: 'I never rode 12 myles on a bare horseback nor ever carried a payer of sheetes out of dores to Ned Bird . . . Bes Bes when I have any children I will have but one father to them.' A useful tool for introducing sexual details, comparisons like this also asserted an idea of honesty based on competition between women. In it, the established female virtues—chastity and fertility—could be played off against suggestions of dishonesty. Thus, when Frances Powell called her neighbour 'base jade base whore base queane base bitch' in Little Drury Lane in 1638, she responded 'Noe gossipp noe, noe bitch I have beene the mother of sixteene children.' And when

[29] William Holmes *c.* Susan Turton (1624), DL/C 229, fo. 89^{r-v}. 'Touse' and 'mouse' mean to 'pull about' and to 'handle roughly but goodnaturedly' (OED). William Gould *c.* Katherine Socklyn (1582), DL/C 213, pp. 123, 124; William Gould *c.* Isabel Burroughes (1582), ibid., pp. 125–7.

[30] On the low levels of prosecutions for rape, see Nazife Bashar, 'Rape in England between 1550 and 1700', in London Feminist History Group (ed.), *The Sexual Dynamics of History* (London, 1983).

Frances called her whore again, she countered 'when anie bodie will make either of us whores we must put our heads in a bagge'.[31] This was a proverbial vision of testing honesty: 'Putt a Miller, a Tailor, and a Weaver in a bagg and shake them, the first who cometh out will be a thief.'[32] But it worked only between women. Men's honesty, as it is discussed in defamations, seems to lack the potential of competition that is so fruitful a ground for women's insults.

Comparisons of honesty also proved impossible between men and women: there appears to be no common ground on which women can be compared with men. Samuel Adams, insulting Anne Ayscough in 1630, turned to his wife for an example, telling her 'he scorned to compare his wife to soe base a woman . . . for my wife never crept to bed to her master and had a bastard'.[33] William Pinge and Roda Greenrise, arguing over a piece of ground in Colchester in 1610, became enmeshed in a battle over 'honesty' frustrated by the impossibility of comparing men's with women's. When Roda advised William to 'go to law' for the ground that was in dispute, William countered with an attack on her use of the law, which Roda interpreted as a slur on her honesty:

> Holde your peace woman for that you had lawe late enoughe your belly full and Roda Greenrise sayd what lawe had I, had I any more lawe then an honest woman should have? I never went to lawe in my lyfe, and she urging him mutche about her honestie the sayd William Pinge sayd as for honestie let that alone if thy honesty and myne were put both in a sacke it would cracke out.

But while the sack test might work for two women, it failed for a man and a woman. Urged by Roda to specify her dishonesty, William could offer nothing but 'it was knowne what she was and what house she came of . . . touch a galled horse and he will kicke'[34] and 'he knewe no dishonestie by her but that she would play with a thinge which she had nothing to do withall'. Finally he returned to the metaphor of the

[31] Thomasine Hayward *c.* Joan Searles (1628), DL/C 231, fo. 277v; Winifred Bland *c.* Elizabeth Hollinshed (1608), DL/C 218, p. 267; Ireland *c.* Frances Powell (1638), DL/C 235, fos. 136–8.

[32] James Howell, *Παροιμιοτραφια. Proverbs, or Unsayed Sawes and Adages* (London, 1659), 3. The phrase may also be related to the punishment of 'sacking' derived from Roman law and in use in Germany, where criminals were drowned in a bag with two animals.

[33] Anne Ayscough *c.* Samuel Adams (1630), DL/C 231, fo. 524v.

[34] This phrase was popularly applied to women as well as horses, in, e.g., the introduction to a ballad of 1634: 'if anyone take in ill part what's here said | Sheel shew by her kicking that shee's a gauld jade', 'Have among you! good Women' (London, 1634), BL Roxburghe Ballads, i, 146.

heads in a bag, turning it, significantly, not towards Roda's honesty, but her husband's, telling him 'yf thy head and mine were put into a sacke, but that thy head is bigger then mine it would be the first that would come foorthe'.[35] The familiar idiom worked particularly well if one man was, as Roda Greenrise's husband was meant to be, a cuckold whose horns pushed him out of the bag first. At the heart of this prolonged exchange of words was the problem of the definition of women's honesty: while originally only a piece of land was in dispute, it proved impossible for William Pinge to complain about Roda Greenrise's honesty other than through references to her sexuality. While men's and women's dishonesty might cover some of the same areas, any comparison was complicated by the implications the word 'honest' had for women's chastity. As William Pinge discovered, it was impossible to put a man and a woman in the same bag: sexual honesty was so distinctly gendered as to allow no space for effective comparison of male and female honesty.

Central to all these stories was the suggestion of illicit sex; but only some defamers described the actual act. Those who did made quite clear their different perceptions of men's and women's sexual roles. Men 'solicit', 'commit adultery', and 'occupy'; women 'suffer' or 'entice' men to do these things. While men were consistently described as looking for sexual satisfaction, women's agency seems to lie entirely in consent. Margaret Burbage was called to the court for defaming Ann Gibbons: 'Thowe jumpinge Jade . . . where is the rogue that laide thee downe upon the bedd and occupied thee nyne tymes and bid thee Nan lie still for he had not enough yett.' Men might also be accused of impotence, or simply sexual exhaustion, as William Large was: he was 'seene (by two men) in a field with a woman his breeches being downe, and when he had done enough those 2 men which saw him said unto him Large pull upp pull upp your breeches for you have done as much as you can'.[36] In contrast the play between satisfaction and pleasure was a fruitful ground for insults of women: and considerably more attention was given to what exactly women did and why whoredom was so pleasurable for them. Stephen Melbury told Mary Addison in 1635: 'Anthony hath tickled thy cory whilest a dishe of collops and egges were makeing readie at thy house in the docke.' In particular whores were credited—by both men and women—with a rapacious interest in men's codpieces. Elizabeth

[35] Roda Greenrise *c.* William Pinge (1610), DL/C 219, fo. 174v.

[36] Ann Gibbons *c.* Margaret Burbage (1623), GL MS 9189/1, fos. 69v–70; William Large *c.* Robert Sewell (1630), DL/C 231, fo. 637v.

Harris insulted Anne Barnes: 'It is no honest womans parte to put her hande into a mans codpece and pull out his members and kisse it and saye she liked it better then her husbandes.' Frances Hurlstone told the headborough of St Giles in the Fields that 'Sibill Tracie did use to put her hand into mens codpeeces, and . . . a man to whome shee had soe donne did saie that shee . . . coulde not bee honest in puttinge her hand in anie mans codpeece.'[37] Explicitly sexual insults attempted to give a moral tone to the erotic, to define the honest limits of women's sexual pleasure. It was a project with which advice literature, with its careful delineation of the difference between healthy sexual pleasure and the dangers of brutish lust, was allied.

DEFINING THE WHORE

The focal theme of defamatory speeches was female sexual behaviour; the central character, the whore. Defamers constructed an image of whoredom, associating it with particular kinds of behaviour and appearance, and creating a recognizable vision as a reference point for female honesty. In part the language of insult was an endeavour of definition, one with which contemporary culture was also concerned: as one London minister explained in 1616, in relation to 'the character of a Painted woman': 'she is a creature, that had need to be *twice defined*, for shee is not what she seemes'.[38] At one level, dishonesty was understood as the direct opposite of honesty: the definitions of honest women as chaste, silent, obedient, and confined to the home which were stated in household manuals and sermons also provided a source for the definition, against these measures, of dishonesty.[39] As well, early modern culture defined the whore specifically. Her qualities, like those of the honest woman, could be found in some key biblical passages. One defamer attributed his words directly to those of Solomon in Proverbs. Henry Blyth, asked by Lucretia Treat to move out of her shop doorway, abused her : 'Thou brasenfaced queane thou hast a whore face of thyne owne, and as Salomen saith one may

[37] Mary Addison *c.* Stephen Melbury (1635), DL/C 234, fo. 187v (Mary's response was to say 'that Melburys wifes gowne was an old gowne that hung at the Brokers'); Anne Barnes *c.* Thomas & Elizabeth Harris (1620), DL/C 226/V, fo. 12; Frances Hurlstone *c.* Sibyl Tracie (1617), DL/C 224, fo. 306.

[38] Thomas Tuke, *A Treatise against Painting and Tincturing of Men and Women: against Murther and Poysoning: Pride and Ambition: Adulterie and Witchcraft* (London, 1616), 57.

[39] On the advice literature, see Susan Amussen, *An Ordered Society: Gender and Class in Early Modern England* (Oxford, 1988), ch. 2, and Kathleen M. Davies, 'The Sacred Condition of Equality—How Original Were Puritan Doctrines of Marriage?', *Social History*, 5 (1977), 563–80.

knowe a whore by the trampling of her foote and the twinckling of her eie, and further sayd Oh thou audatious whore.' Like so many defamers, Henry was not primarily concerned with Lucretia's appearance or her sexual chastity: the enmity between the two was due to Henry's 'encouraging and animating' his brother, her husband's apprentice, in his 'lewd deboysht and disobedient course of life'.[40] More relevant to these defamers than the detailed rules of contemporary advice to women was the elaborate picture of the whore that provided their obverse. It was on this that they focused their vision of whoredom.

The 'whore face' that Henry Blyth described was a distinctive one. In the language of insult, the visibility of dishonesty was a key motif. As some defamers dwelt on their part in discovering secret sexual misconduct, others insisted that unchastity could always be detected in women's appearance. Especially, whores used falsifying cosmetics. Sara Wood, thinking a group of women in her Stepney street were talking about her, leaned over the pales and called Martha Rawe 'a painted whore and a gowtye legged whore and a bastard bearing whore', and said 'Thou . . . dost carry a boxe of complexion about thee and thou art a painted gille.' Visions of whoredom were characterized by a recurrent tension between the allurements of sexual availability and the marks of physical ugliness: 'painted faced curled locke curr'; 'thou art an ugly whore . . . thou lookest like the backe syde of my barrell of small beere'.[41] Most noticeable are whores' noses: women were called 'flatt nose whore', 'saddlenosed whore', or told 'your nose turns up like a drabbs tayle'. In part, noses stood for the tails they were compared to. The face is meant to make whoredom visible, to enable a perceptible distinction between honest and dishonest women.

The invisible physicality of whores—the tails that noses stood in for—was imagined just as powerfully. In talk about sex, men's and women's sexual organs were characterized quite differently. Medical treatises, until the late seventeenth century, lacked an anatomical language for female genitals, relating them instead, as Thomas Laqueur has shown, to the male body: women's anatomy was the reverse of men's.[42] But there is little evidence that this particular vision shaped

[40] Lucretia Treat *c.* Henry Blyth (1628), DL/C 231, fo. 237; DL/C 193, fo. 309v.

[41] Martha Rawe *c.* Sara Wood (1613), DL/C 221, fo. 1561v, DL/C 222, fo. 383v; Burges *c.* Wells (1639), DL/C 235, fo. 233; Richard & Katherine Todd *c.* Isabel South (1610), DL/C 219, fo. 242v.

[42] Thomas Laqueur, *Making Sex: Body and Gender from the Greeks to Freud* (Cambridge, Mass., 1990), 96–8.

popular perceptions. Men's members feature regularly in defamations, described with exactitude. Infection destroyed men's members graphically: one woman said to another in 1620 'my husband doth not looke lyke thy husband for my husbandes pricke was never burnt with the pocks nor halfe of it cut of in Newgate Market as thy husbandes was'. Men's members were an object of fascination both to men, and—in the popular culture of sex—to women. In front of the Bishop of London at Fulham Palace, Edward Jones complained that Edmund Harman 'wold have had to doe with his . . . wife and that he did offer her 10 shillings with one hand and held his pricke in the other hand and said he wold give her that 10 shillings to make it stand'. John Ashenden told the court of a conversation in a tavern: 'on the wall there was the similitude of a mans privie members made with a cole or some such like thinge . . . some of the company . . . demanded of . . . John Burrell whether his the said John Burrells pricke were of that length'. John answered 'No yet . . . my wief is with childe.'[43] Women's genital apparatus is described in very different terms: no one reported pictures of it on tavern walls. The broad word 'tail' is the only one used with any regularity. Tails are, however, a key focus of sexual insult of women. They were imagined as the locus of sexual pleasure, and the acts women were supposed to have engaged in to satisfy that pleasure were visualized with bawdy exaggeration. One woman insulted another: 'William Dixson the miller was once plucked out of thy tayle and hee will be plucked out of thy tayle agayne one of these days.' In the same manner Joan Gregorie accused Isabel Smallridge 'that she the said Isabell did suffer one Henrie Hackell to dippe in her tayle up to the elbow in whitefriers lane whilst she did consent thereunto and did laughe or cry aloud hah hah hah'.[44]

While men's members were imagined as appealing and attractive to women, women's tails were figured differently. Images of the corruption of syphilis were particularly powerful, and combined with more general suggestions of decay and degeneration, made women's tails grotesque in a way men's members never were. Leaky women, those mainstays of early modern physiology, were a powerful image in sexual talk. In the language of insult, men are solid beings with members that appeal to women, who take hold of them or kiss them;

[43] Acton Corveth *c.* Petronell Hinshawe (1620), DL/C 226/V, fo. 33; Edmund Harman *c.* Edward Jones (1611), DL/C 219, fo. 413; Roger Herrenden *c.* John Burrell (1615), DL/C 223, fo. 99ᵛ.

[44] Katherine Tale *c.* Mary Popkyn (1613), DL/C 221, fo. 1484; Isabel Smallridge *c.* Joan Gregorie (1628), DL/C 231, fo. 297ᵛ.

women are unstable vessels with dangerous, leaking orifices. 'My mistres . . . is not like thie mistres,' one woman servant told another in a shop in 1620, 'to suffer, or permitt a man to clapp her arse whilest the matter runs about his hand or his fingers.' 'Burntarse whore' and 'blackarsed queane', were typical images of the pox's effects on women; 'cuttailed whore', 'goodwife cuttarse', may have carried the same meanings. Other defamers, women even more often than men, expanded on the possible forms of infection with a fascination with the grotesque: 'Yf I were [a whore] . . . I should have clients enough for I have no scabbe upon my arse'; 'she hadd as many maggottes in her tayle as ever had a sheepe'; 'I felt thee or took thee by the privie parte and there was no heire on it'.[45] Men's members were never described with such absorbed repulsion: they might be lost, but, as far as defamers were concerned, they were not grossly infected. In the language of abuse, men's genitals were objects of desire, women's were objects of repulsion. The difference articulated with clarity here ensured that the interplay of desire, blame, and shame when sex was talked about was shaped, fundamentally, by gender.

The clothes that hid whores' grotesque bodies were important too. In the light of contemporary prescriptions for the relations of clothing to class and gender, defamers saw whores' clothes as violating sumptuary convention. One indicator of whoredom was meant to be the clothes bought with the sale of sex. 'Thow hast never a cote to thy back but thou hast gotten it by plaieng the whore,' Katherine Higgins insulted Joan Robinson in 1574. In an alehouse in Holborn in 1572, Margery Wright defamed John Thomas's wife, and he responded 'well . . . she was an honester woman then thow art, for she never occupyed for a taffatay hatt, as thow diddest'.[46] Any suggestion of luxurious materials implied violation of the degrees of apparel appropriate to social class that were enshrined in law until 1604, echoed by the advice writers' insistence that women should dress to reflect the status of their husbands. Taffeta in gowns, at least,

[45] Mary Harrison *c.* Grace Mace (1620), DL/C 227, fo. 176^{v}. (The words meant, according to the other servant, that her mistress had 'gott the poxe or some other loathsome disease'. The alternative words here ('suffer or permit') were probably added for the court rather than at the time.) Harrison *c.* Mace, DL/C 227, fo. 181^{v}; Elizabeth Dymcross *c.* John More (1591), DL/C 214, p. 22; Elizabeth Willey *c.* John & Anne Hooper (1627), GL MS 9189/2, fo. 106.

[46] Joan Robinson *c.* Katherine Higgins (1575), DL/C 212, p. 396; Margery Wright *c.* John Thomas (1572), DL/C 211/1, fo. 107^{v}. Margery had previously told John 'That he kylled his old wyff with kyndenes, and therefore she wold go with hym, that he might have her skynne full of farthinges' (fo. 108^{v}). 'Kyndenes' here might refer to sex, or just to love.

was confined to 'Gentlemen's wives, bearing arms, and all above that rank, etc.', by the Elizabethan royal proclamation of 1597.[47] The over-luxuriousness of whores' dress contrasts with their base natures. Elizabeth Leigh, going to visit Grace Drury in a green damask petticoat in 1627, was accosted by Thomas Bridle who told her 'If Mrs Drury respected her credit she would not have or suffer such huswife as thou arte come unto her house . . . a sackcloth petticoatte was more fitt for the[e] . . . then that thou wearest'.[48]

As well as social order, women's dress was also supposed to be liable to confuse the order of gender. James I's complaints about women wearing broad-brimmed hats, short hair, and doublets were followed by the pamphlet debate started by *Hic Mulier* in 1620, which interpreted androgyny as sexual availability. These debates were mostly about upper garments: there was little chance of any of the women about which James or the pamphleteers inveighed really being taken for men.[49] The concern was, rather, that their doublets were 'all

FIG. 7. The fight for the breeches: from the 'The Jolly Widdower', *The Pepys Ballads*

[47] F. E. Baldwin, *Sumptuary Legislation and Personal Regulation in England* (Baltimore, 1926), 229.

[48] Elizabeth Leigh *als* Henley *c.* Thomas Bridle (1627), GL MS 9189/2, fo. 145^{r-v}.

[49] For the political and cultural contexts of actual female transvestism, see Natalie Zemon Davis, 'Women on Top: Symbolic Sexual Inversion and Political Disorder in Early Modern Europe', in *Society and Culture in Early Modern Europe* (Stanford, Calif., 1975); and Rudolf M. Dekker and Lotte C. van de Pol, *The Tradition of Female Transvestism in Early Modern Europe* (Basingstoke, 1989).

unbutton'd to entice'.[50] Popular literature and ballads were more concerned with the lower parts, notably with breeches, the traditional and proverbial signifier of male dominance.[51] Defamations linked the licentiousness of cross-dressing with its implications for gender order. Some defamers invoked the breeches as metaphor. Near Paul's Wharf in 1613, Alice Baker called Elizabeth Edwardes 'saddlenose queane and saied that her nose turned up like a drabs tayle'; Elizabeth replied 'I would be ashamed to have a husband and weare the breeches', and Alice retorted 'Thou . . . art an arrant whore to say that I weare the breeches'. After the falling out Baker's husband apparently pulled a paper off a post near their door 'wherein . . . was written that Alice Baker . . . did weare her husbandes breeches'. The accusation of wearing the breeches was enough to compose an effective slanderous paper without the proliferating accusations of whoredom that are repeated in spoken defamations. Other women went into more detail about the specific items of clothing that were at issue. In 1593 Anne Webb was accused of abusing Margery Dunne with the words:

> thow hackney queane thow hackney jade comon ridden jade . . . codpeece quean thow monster thow, putt of thy long pettycote put on a pair of britches putt of the white kerchiff and putt on a flatt capp for thow hast a snaffle for thy husband to make him ly upon the boords all night and by the selfe upon two or thre feather bedes.

Keeping husbands in a horse's bridle, forcing them to sleep on the floorboards, were established images in popular ballads and woodcuts; the careful list of garments ties marital misconduct directly to cross-dressing.[52] Like the defamers who accused women of playing with men's members, Anne Webb starts with the codpiece; but she treats it as the locus not so much of male sexuality, as of the economic order that is manifested in clothes. Her elaboration of the difference between male and female garments concentrates crucially upon the work clothes, breeches and the flat cap, that symbolize male economic dominance over women. The assumption of men's clothing is seen

[50] *Hic Mulier; Or, the Man-Woman* (London, 1620), sig. A4^{v}, followed by *Haec-Vir: Or, the Womanish Man* (London, 1620). The context of these debates is explored in Jonathan Dollimore, *Sexual Dissidence: Augustine to Wilde, Freud to Foucault* (Oxford, 1991), ch. 19, and Marjorie Garber, *Vested Interests: Cross-Dressing and Cultural Anxiety* (London, 1992), ch. 1.

[51] On breeches, see e.g. 'The Woman Wears the Breeches', in Thomas D'Urfey, *Wit and Mirth* (London, 1707), ii. 63.

[52] Elizabeth Edwardes *c.* Alice Baker (1613), DL/C 221, fos. 1542^{v}–1543, 1523; Margery Dunne *c.* Anne Webb (1593), DL/C 214, p. 406. (A snaffle is a horse's bit.) For matrimonial ballads featuring images like these, see Ch. 6.

entirely in the context of the disruption of gendered division of labour, and its results for marital order: the climax of the speech has the husband subdued in a horse's bridle, kicked out of the marital bed. Matrimonial ballads worked in a very similar vein.[53]

As much as the sexual behaviour of 'whores', defamers were concerned with their social conduct. The outward signs of disorderly life were carefully marked. Mary Crompton allegedly said Sara Powell

> had an ill report and yf it were true shee was sorry for it and would be loath to keep her the said Sara company because shee . . . did frequent the company of married men, and kept a noise of fidlers all night in her shop, and that her . . . night walking and day walking got her noe good name and that shee was accompted noe better than shee should be.

Others suggested ways of regulating disorderly women. In 1609 Alice Costedine attempted to stop Margaret Read, a prisoner at Bridewell, getting bail, by calling her 'a notorious whore and her mother is a bawd . . . and her husband . . . was a cuckold . . . if I weare a man and had a wief I would sett her in a garden to weed or pull upp thistles rather than she should ride into the cuntrie with prentices or kepe boyes company'. This vision of disorderly femininity and its control might owe something to the prescriptions of household order so prevalent in early modern culture, but it twists them towards a different focus. Confinement to the household provides, here, not the insurance of chastity against temptation, but the humiliation of uncomfortable labour. The ideology of the household might also be inverted and used against men, as it was by Abigail Hellam to Richard Painter. Richard was trying to arrest one of Abigail's servants for defaming his wife, when Abigail intervened with her own insults: 'Thowe art a troublesome fellowe and it were more fitter for thee to be at home with thie wife, and meddle with thie bastardes.'[54] Her words both supported her servant's allegations, and effectively attacked Richard Painter's fitness for his public duty.

The literature of women's advice warned that the rules of honest femininity were easily infringed. William Vaughan, who wrote a treatise on detraction in response to defamatory rumours about his wife,

[53] E.g. 'My Wife will be my Master' (*c.* 1640), Roxburghe Ballads, ii. 576. On humour and gender regulation in ballads, see Elizabeth Foyster, 'A Laughing Matter? Marital Discord and Gender Control in Seventeenth-Century England', *Rural History*, 4/1 (Apr. 1993), 5–23.

[54] Sara Powell *c.* Mary Crompton (1629), DL/C 231, fo. 479; Margaret Read *c.* Alice Costedine (1609), DL/C 218, p. 597; Richard Painter *c.* Abigail Hellam (1618), DL/C 225, fo. 319.

explained that certain circumstances might reasonably bring women's chastity into question:

Some againe doe but gather by presumptions and circumstances, that chast women prostitute their bodyes, because they go gallantly attyred in the fashion, with strange Periwigs, with false bodyes, truncke sleeves, verdingales, and with costly Jewells belike beyond their Husbands meanes . . . because they gadde to stage playes, to publike daunces, and showes upon Sundays and Holy-dayes.

These assumptions which lead people to 'blurt out scandalous impeachments of honest womens fame' are seen as being only reasonable: 'And in truth their reasons fall out many times currant; for that such things being devised by devilish people, as allurements to spiritual fornication after the pompous gods of the earth, be likewise the fore-runners of fleshly fornication.'[55] Vaughan's condemnation of such unfounded defamation simultaneously condones its premise: that promiscuity can reasonably be inferred from disrespectable behaviour. Dorothy Leigh encoded the same message in her advice to her son: 'Some of the fathers have written, that it is not inough for a woman to bee chaste, but even so to behave her selfe, that no man may thinke or deeme her to be unchast.'[56] But defamers were noticeably less rigid in their attention to women's behaviour. Realistically, no one suggested that working and socializing outside the house imperilled women's honesty, nor did they defame women for breaking the rules of feminine behaviour laid down in advice literature and sermons. More interesting, and useful, to them was the picture of the dishonest woman that lay behind these prescriptions.

In the ideal vision of the ordered household, the honest wife was tied to the house and its concerns. Her concern for her family, in Daniel Rogers's 1642 marriage sermon, 'rivets her into the house'. Unchastity broke those bonds: 'the unchast,' Rogers preached, 'having lost his or her heart, is loosened from the whole body, thinks nothing pertaining to her: is ready to part the children, leaving the lawfully, and chusing the misbegotten for her portion, that so she may goe to her Paramour'.[57] It is this vision of the unchaste woman, 'loosened' from the ties of the household body, that is mirrored in the

[55] William Vaughan, *The Spirit of Detraction, Coniured and Convicted in Seven Circles* (London, 1611), 345–6.

[56] Dorothy Leigh, *The Mothers Blessing: Or, The godly Counsaile of a Gentle-woman* (London, 1627), 39.

[57] Daniel Rogers, *Matrimoniall Honour, Or, The mutuall Crowne and comfort of godly, loyall, and chaste Marriage* (London, 1642), 169.

words of defamers. It taps into the pervasive image of whoredom from Proverbs. Barnabe Rich's more aristocratic audience were presented with a very similar version of that image: 'The harlot is mooveable . . . *now shee is in the house, now in the streetes, now she lieth in waite in every corner*, shee is still gadding from place to place, from company to company.'[58] Robert Cleaver's commentary on Proverbs glosses a quite different passage to mean exactly the same. 'She sitteth at the doore of her house, on a seate in the high places of the City' (Prov. 9: 14) is interpreted 'her whole property is to bee abroad in the streets to meet with companions, and to entice men to follie by her lookes and behaviour'. Commentators like Cleaver found in Proverbs a vision of whoredom that could be used to condemn women's 'gadding'; earlier, Cleaver's much-reprinted household advice had outlined an exact division of the spheres of domestic labour, the indoors to the woman, the outdoors to the man.[59] That concern had resonances for defamers, and more than the prescriptions of the ordered household, it was this familiar and fascinating vision of the harlot that preoccupied them.

The harlot of Proverbs, adapted by commentators as far apart as Robert Cleaver and Barnabe Rich to fit contemporary discourse about honesty, was most importantly a 'strange' woman, representing both a danger to men and a competitive opposite to the honest wife. 'Her qualities are, first, that she is a strange woman, one with whom thou oughteth to have nothing to doe: for strange standeth in opposition to a mans lawfull wife.'[60] This competitive confrontation between strange whores and lawful wives was very often the foundation on which women defamed each other: as they defined other women as whores, they proclaimed themselves models of honesty.

THE CONSEQUENCES OF WHOREDOM

Defamers turned these visions of whoredom into insults by expanding on the consequences of sexual misconduct. They described at length the results of illicit sex, bastardy, and disease; they asserted that

[58] Barnabe Rich, *My Ladies Looking Glasse. Wherein May be Discerned a Wise Man from a Foole, a Good Woman from a Bad* (London, 1616), 43, quoting (his italics) Prov. 7: 11.

[59] Robert Cleaver, *A Briefe Explanation of the Whole Booke of the Proverbs of Salomon* (London, 1615), 150; id., *A Godly Form of Householde Governement: for the ordering of private Families, according to the direction of Gods word* (London, 1598), 168.

[60] Cleaver, *Briefe Explanation*, 27, on Prov. 2: 16. On the development of the idea of the 'strange woman', see Léonie Archer, 'Virgin and Harlot in the Writings of Formative Judaism', *History Workshop Jl.* 24 (1987), 1–16.

illicit sex had emotional and material effects on individuals, households, and neighbourhoods; and they called for punishments to match the offences.

The most personal effects of whoredom were those it visited upon the body: bastardy and disease. Defamers used both to insist that whoredom left permanent marks on the bodies of men and women. In the language of insult, pregnancy and bastardy served more as proofs of whoredom than offences in themselves. Their meaning differed for women and for men. When men were accused of begetting illegitimate children, the principal consequence was perceived as the financial results of abandonment.[61] As with accusations of fornication, a number of such insults were claims by the pregnant women themselves. Accusations of women took place in a different context. They were made most often by other women and they concerned the physical and permanent results of pregnancies that were visualized as the bodily retribution of whoredom. In Pudding Lane in the summer of 1608, Timothy Hollinshed insulted Winifred Bland, imagining for her a liaison that would produce nothing but grotesque offspring: 'thou art a nastie suttle queane, for halfe a crowne I will hier an Italien that shall gett nothing but jack an apesses and munckes uppon the[e]'. Other detailed allegations listed the stages of illegitimate pregnancy and the way whores evaded them: 'thow arte a whore and I will prove thee an arrant whore, and a child thow hadste, and a childe thow hast made away, And a childe I will make the[e] to fynde'. Margaret Batchelor told Catherine Walker one day in 1629 that she was a 'base queane and a whoare, and that shee . . . had taken phisicke to destroy her child'. Often accused of aborting their own pregnancies, whores were also apparently powerful enough to induce miscarriage in other, legitimately pregnant women. Elizabeth Stawton accused Mary Day that 'shee . . . and . . . Mr Wood did walk soe often together that Mr Woodes wife had thereuppon got a mischance'. George Barnard was less specific, accusing Adrian Bishopp simply 'goe goe thou queane thou wilt miscarrie someon'.[62]

The most detailed of these accusations were made by women. Like the ceremony of childbirth, pregnancy involved specific and exclu-

[61] See Walter J. King, 'Punishment for Bastardy in Early Seventeenth-Century England', *Albion* 10 (1978), 130–51.

[62] Winifred Bland *c.* Timothy Hollinshed (1609), DL/C 218, fo. 264^{v} ('munckes' here means, I think, monkeys, a not infrequent figure in defamatory language, rather than monks); Isabel Anslowe *c.* George Lowe (1590), DL/C 213, p. 745; Catherine Walker *c.* Margaret Batchelor (1630), DL/C 231, fo. 522; Mary Day *c.* Elizabeth Stawton (1630), DL/C 233, fo. 176; Adrian Bishop *c.* George Barnard (1618), DL/C 225, fo. 242.

sively female rituals.[63] Married women might be the subjects of careful calculations of the time between marriage and delivery; other women detected pregnancy in their relatives, neighbours, or servants by the signs of the pregnant body, summed up by one woman as 'her great belly milking of her brests her lookes and shortnes of her coates'. In 1634 Mary Heale suspected her neighbour's servant was with child, and squeezed her breast to check it for milk. In Wapping in 1613 Susan Chaddocke used her female expertise to accuse Elizabeth Barwicke of being pregnant while her husband was away at sea, by examining her urine, as midwives did. She later told a neighbour:

> That she had found in the house of Elizabeth Barwicke an urinall And that she the said Susan Chaddocke did looke upon the water which was in the same urinall and saied that whose water soever that was they were with child wherupon the said Elizabeth Barwicke . . . did take the same urinall and did throw the water which was in it into her parlour chimney saieing unto her the foresaid Susan Chaddocke that she had asmuch skill as the dog.

Four years later Elizabeth was to assert her own skills in the matter of pregnancy and paternity, using the occasion of a christening to accuse John Dearsly of fathering a bastard. Once children were born their looks were expected to provide proof of their paternity, and women had the first chance to examine their features. When Ellen Fanch went to visit Mary Harman as she lay in childbed, Mary asked after Ellen's sister-in-law and her young daughter. Ellen replied that 'she cared not how they did and further . . . said that Richard Wood didst beget her husbands brothers wife . . . and I will take mine oath that he . . . didst begett . . . the child . . . and it is like his children . . . and I . . . cannot love it'.[64] The enclosed female world of childbed could provide the ideal forum for the discussion of paternity and illegitimacy.

In somewhat the same way as pregnancy, venereal disease was imagined as the visible evidence of illicit sex; but unlike pregnancy, it

[63] See Patricia Crawford, 'The Construction and Experience of Maternity in Seventeenth Century England', in Valerie Fildes (ed.), *Women as Mothers in Pre-Industrial England* (London, 1990), and on the occasion of childbirth, Adrian Wright, 'The Ceremony of Childbirth and its Interpretation', in the same collection.

[64] Office *ad prom.* Layton *c.* Elizabeth Francis *als* Elkes (1634), DL/C 630, fo. 291^{v}; Elizabeth Bowles *c.* Mary Heale *als* Hale (1634), DL/C 630, fo. 330^{v}; Elizabeth Barwicke *c.* Susan Chaddock (1613), DL/C 221, fo. 1291; John Dearsly *c.* Elizabeth Barwicke (1627), DL/C 230, fo. 292; Richard Wood *c.* Ellen Fanch (1631), DL/C 233, fo. 229. On the evidence of pregnancy to be found in urine, see Jane Sharp, *The Midwives Book* (London, 1671), 104; Sharp also discusses the resemblances between parents and children, 120–4.

affected both sexes, although in different ways. The potential grotesqueness of whores' bodies allowed defamers to explore the corrupting effects of pox on them in more imaginative detail than they did for men. Men were called 'pocky knave', with occasional graphic details such as 'he . . . had lost halfe of his yard'. But it was the bodies of women that provided the best opportunities for insult. Anne Reynolds abused Laurence Hickenson 'he did keepe whores wherof there was one of them had her commodite or cunt eaten half off with the pox'. In the same vein Hester Collins 'scolded' Patience Proctor 'hath not the poxe eaten the[e] upp yett . . . I had thought . . . that thowe hadst ben rotten before this time' and Hester Forest said that Anne Carrington 'didst swett and froth for the pox'.[65] The pox was also visualized as eating away women's noses, as it did men's members, and damaging their eyes, teeth, and legs. In the language of insult, the effects of whoredom upon women's and men's bodies were distributed as exactly as was sexual blame.

For many defamers the central effect of whoredom was not physical but economic. Sexual misbehaviour might be linked with a general evasion of financial responsibilities. William Dawson accused Joan Granger that 'she lived like a quean for he payed scott and lott in the parish and she payed none'. More regularly, the word 'whore' conveyed not so much the exact meaning of prostitution as a range of connections between money and sex. Some defamers made specific accusations about the amount of money women were supposed to have charged for sex. In Stepney in 1627 Elizabeth Willey and Elizabeth Eaton both insulted Anne Hooper, reputed to keep a bawdy house, for lying with a Flemish man, Willey alleging in particular that she had charged him less than an English client: 'away you whore you lay with a fleminge for 2 shillings and with an English man for halfe a crowne I would have used an English man better than a fleminge you whore'. In rural Enfield in 1625 another woman translated her accusations of whoredom and bawdry into suitable material terms: 'thou didst give thy mayd a paire of white sleeves to keepe thy counsell . . . And . . . thou didst play the whore . . . for a bushell of wheat and slave for it till harvest'.[66] Other defamers thought in the

[65] Israel Willett *c.* Petronell Hinshawe (1620), DL/C 226/IV, fo. 35; Laurence Hickenson *c.* Ann Reynolds (1624), GL MS 9189/1, fo. 179^{v}; Patience Proctor *c.* Hester Collins (1619), DL/C 226/VIII, fo. 10; Anne Carrington *c.* Hester Forest (1628), DL/C 231, fo. 73.

[66] Joan Granger *c.* Michael Dawson (1609), DL/C 219, fo. 2; Anne Hooper *c.* Elizabeth Willey (1627), GL MS 9189/2, fo. 100^{v}; Alice Cooper *c.* Susanna Croxon, DL/C 230, fo. 329.

broader financial terms of consumption and expenditure. They presented whores as expensive, extravagant consumers, whose demands for maintenance constituted the material costs of dishonesty. The implications of illicit sex for the household focused on the crux of consumption. The expensive dress which was meant to signify dishonest women was one of these: Frances Rolf, jostled by John Sutton in the street in Saffron Walden, retaliated with the words 'Out you rascally roague and you whoremasterly jacke, you maintaine and keepe a whore in her silke stockings pumps and pantophles.' Another crux was food. The everyday meals of the household rarely figure in defamations; instead, luxury food prompts and sustains illicit liaisons outside it. 'Thowe didst ride behind Henry Goodwyn from Storeford faire, and he tooke thee by the geere fortie tymes, and thowe still . . . wilte entice him . . . for pies or cakes to be naught with him,' alleged Sisley Wayte in 1619. Food played a similarly central role in one woman's seduction tale:

> Peter Marsh had bin twice at her house and would have had her abroad with him to eate artichoks and drink wyne with him; And further that he the said Peter Marsh would have plucked her down into his lapp and would have putt his handes under her coate but that she would not suffer him; and strived to kisse her and would have putt his tonge into her mouth.[67]

Eating and drinking were intimately associated with the circumstances of illicit sex.

Imagining whores as consumers gave the misdealings of whoredom wide financial implications. In this picture, whores consume domestic resources for their maintenance; they also bring into the household profits from illicit sources, making their relatives and servants bawds. Whoredom creates a financial exchange that disrupts both the income and expenditure of the household, and it has particular implications for the place of gender in domestic labour and economics. In Warwick Lane, off Newgate Market, in 1590, Juliana Cluny abused Marcella Lynne's husband, who had reproved her for her 'sluttishe penthouse': 'goe to yow cuckolde yow arrante cuckolde gett yow in a dores lyke yow cuckolde yow maynteyne yowre wife to gett your lyvinge'.[68] In an urban society where, although many women worked alongside their husbands or outside the house, men's labour was

[67] John Sutton *c.* Frances Rolf & Frances Rolf (1611), DL/C 220, fo. 799^{r-v}. (The two were mother and daughter; these words are those of the daughter.) Priscilla Brett *c.* Sisley Wayte (1619), DL/C 226/III, fo. 29; Peter Marsh *c.* Swanton *mul.* (1630), DL/C 231, fo. 662.

[68] Marcella Lynne *c.* Juliana Cluny (1590), DL/C 213, p. 638.

understood to provide the principal income of the household, the financial relations imagined for whoredom could be profoundly disturbing.

This understanding of the economy of whoredom played a central part in women's insults. Women defamers evaluated with care the exact disruptions that whoredom wrought, and unlike men, they discussed their own households as well as those of their neighbours. The phrase 'thou art my husband's whore', a stock of the language of women's insults, was often expanded with details about the alienation of sexual relations, affection, and material resources. A dispute between Dorothy Hove and her husband in Essex in 1609 involved an audience of women in the bakery where they were working. Dorothy, 'being falne out with her sayd husband as oftentymes she was', said to him 'Gett thee to thy whore on the hill,' meaning Jane Hertford, and said to the other women: 'Com, lett us all be whores for they are better beloved than honest women yonder is my husbandes whore on the hill better beloved then I am I fare the worse for her fyne tayle, she is a whore and a bitche.' Later a neighbour, John Feltham, tried to persuade her to make peace with Jane Hertford, and she answered 'I will never be frendes with such a brasen faced whore as she is, she is a glewe whore she hath stolen away the love of my husband from me.' John protested 'I do not think she is any suche manner of woman, her carriage is so good,' to which Dorothy responded 'Yes, the more whore, the better carriage.' Her language conflated financial and economic betrayal. In a tavern in St John Street in 1611 Elizabeth Fryer confronted Margaret Yard with an even more exact appraisal of her emotional and financial displacement: 'thou art Stephen Yards wife and my husbands whore moreover thou art a whore an arrant whore and a filthy whore . . . he can be contented to spend 10 shillings on thee but he will not spend 2 pence in my company'.[69] Insults like these displaced the blame for men's adultery on to women, reinforcing a system in which, inside or outside marriage, women carried the weight of sexual culpability. Yet at the same time, words like Elizabeth Fryer's shifted the results of men's adultery back into the domestic sphere. The inventory of material, economic, and sexual alienation with which wives charged their husbands' alleged mistresses kept the discussion of men's adultery within the marital sphere: at stake in these accusations was not moral

[69] Jane Hertford *c.* Dorothy Hove (1609), DL/C 218, pp. 345, 615 ('glewe' probably means 'squinting'); Margaret Yard *c.* Elizabeth Fryer (1611), DL/C 219, fos. 436–7.

guilt, or complaints about 'honesty', but the material goods of marriage.

The whoredom with which women were charged was also, though, dangerously close to another marriage. At the root of allegations like these was the idea of 'maintaining' whores, and while whoredom was frequently perceived in terms of luxurious and excessive consumption, in these accusations women also indicated how near this kind of 'maintenance' could come to the legitimate financial balance of marriage. In Whitechapel in 1579 Agnes Seare, a carman's wife, made several long and specific allegations against Alice Leland, first to her husband in public and later, when Alice had already commenced a suit for defamation against her, to the official who delivered her a citation to appear in court. According to witnesses, when her husband and she were at a neighbour's house about a cart that was being mended, she complained to her husband of Alice Leland: 'Thow hast occupied her . . . rownd abowt the howse: And thow hast occupied her as often as thow has occupied me,' and 'It was long of Alice Leiland . . . that thow didst beate me so as I lay bedred therupon three yeeres after.' As well as these complaints, she also envisaged the illicit relationship becoming a legal one, claiming that 'her brother . . . offred the[e] . . . £10 or a horse and a cart worth £10 with her . . . if I weare dead and the[e] to marrie with her'. When the court official came to serve a citation on her as she was at market in Leadenhall, Agnes told him

> Shee . . . is an harlott and my husband hath spent £40 on her, her brother . . . came home to my husbands howse when my husband and I were at variance and then he saied to my husband: lett thy wife alone and come home to me and I will give the £10 and a horse and a carr with my sister . . . my husband hath sold all that he hath to mainteyne thee: And . . . I have called her . . . whore any time theise 5 yeeres and yett I will stand to it.

Here, two rather different kinds of financial transaction are threatening Agnes Seare's position at once: her husband is both maintaining a 'harlott' with the household money, and being tempted away with the offer of a marriage settlement on her. That the currency of marriage settlement was not just money but carts was only suitable. The boundaries between the economy of adultery and that of marriage or its preliminaries were not as rigid as they appear, and whoredom threatened not just because of its distance from the legitimate sexual economy, but because of its potential overlap with it. Early modern marriage involved a series of negotiations, commitments, and ceremonies. The potential confusions and blurs between these meant it was possible for one woman to accuse another: 'she is a whore and shee . . . lieth with my husband every night and plaieth the whore with him and is married to him'.[70]

While the exact estimates of the marital disruptions caused by men's adultery were of interest mostly to the women directly involved, women's sexual behaviour was the focus of a more widespread concern. In the family, street, and neighbourhood women and men were ready to expose adultery by talking of its effects and implications. In the definition of sexuality which ruled sexual insult, women's adultery, unlike men's, signified the loss of the whole character; it led to a permanent state of whoredom; and it had profound implications, as men's did not, for the honour of their spouses and their households. Men were held responsible for the chastity of their sisters and mothers: Katherine Betts said that Richard Elston was unfit to marry her daughter 'for that as she sayd he was a base fellowe and his eldest sister had byn a captaines whore many yeares and that he had afterward married her to a welche gentleman'. But most importantly, they were responsible for their wives: women's adultery dishonoured their husbands. Insults played on this vision of dishonour, elaborating it with the rhetoric of possession and authority that underlay early modern discourse about conjugal relations. On one of the few occasions when a man spoke about his own wife's adultery, he conceived its damage in terms of violation of his property: 'thow didst occupy my wife uppon my owne stayres'.[71] That stress on property was maintained in accusations of cuckoldry. Defamers presented cuckoldry as a loss of men's marital authority, a failure to maintain household order. Cuckolded men have lost control over their households: they are actively, culpably ignorant of their wives' whoredom. Winifred Bland, 'chiding with her neighbours' in 1609, told Timothy Hollinshed 'Howld thy peace Peter while thou art abrode a bobbing for fishe, ther is some body bobbs at home with thy wief.'[72] Equally culpable is men's failure to exact satisfaction for their wrongs. During a brawl in his shop in the city in September of 1619, Richard Smith said to William Cherry: 'William Cherry . . . by Gods bloud thou art a cuckold and . . . Jacke Bullock . . . did lye with thie wife, and after-

[70] Alice Leland *c.* Agnes Seare (1579), DL/C 629, fos. 135^{v}–137^{v}, 139^{v}; Edith Bestoe *c.* Katherine Jones (1614), DL/C 222, fo. 67^{v}.

[71] Anne Harris *c.* Katherine Betts (1611), DL/C 220, fo. 627^{v}; John Gamble *c.* Matthew Smithe (1615), DL/C 223, fo. 14.

[72] Elizabeth Hollinshed *c.* Winifred Bland (1609), DL/C 218, p. 310^{v}; Winifred may have been calling Timothy 'Peter' in allusion to the apostle, since he had been fishing. The words were part of a larger dispute, quoted above.

wards did beate thee, and then was contented to give thee 5 shillings or a noble and a breakfast to be friends.' Defeated sexually by his wife's adultery, William Cherry compounds his own humiliation by allowing himself to be beaten physically by his rival, and further, to be cheated out of his rightful compensation.[73]

As cuckoldry damages honour, so it threatens the physical structure of the house. The horns imagined upon cuckolded men, illustrated in one contemporary woodcut (Fig. 8), are a constant danger. Cuckolds

FIG. 8. A horned cuckold: from 'Mirth for Citizens', Roxburghe Ballads

[73] William & Mildred Cherry *c.* Richard Smith (1619), DL/C 226/IV, fo. 8 (a noble was 6*s.* 8*d.*)

put their heads out of windows and get stuck, they break doors and exclude themselves from their own houses: 'Alas poore cuckold,' said Edith Andrewes to a neighbour in the kitchen of a victualling house in 1640, 'thy hornes are soe great thou canst not come into that doore.' On the street in Holborn in 1637 Mary Okeham taunted Mr Bushwell 'cuckold and cuckoldy foole and bid him make his door bigger or wider for his hornes to come in at and asked him how he could turne him selfe in his bed for his hornes'. This exclusion is highly symbolic: women's adultery takes away men's place in their houses. It can also undermine the stability of the neighbourhood. One day in the summer of 1609 Anne Phesey stood outside her back door and said to William Dynes, standing at his own door across the street 'Go thow cuckoldy slave thou wittall thy hornes are so great that thow canst scarce get in at thyne own doores, take heede thow doest not breake a hole with thy hornes thorough thy neighbours wall.'[74] The cuckold's contented tolerance of his wife's adultery has not only caused his imaginary horns to grow so large that he is excluded from his own household; it is so dangerous that it threatens the very structure of his neighbour's walls.

In the same way, defamers envisaged household order being disrupted by bawdry. Parents were accused of being bawds to their daughters, and servants to their mistresses; all these suggestions involved dishonourable and disordered household economies. Michael Kendall came to court in 1573 to counter the accusation that he was a 'gagge mouthed drunken chorle and a drunkard and that he hadd a whoore to his daughter and maintayned her therin'.[75] Another set of disruptions comes into play with allegations that servants are bawds to their mistresses. Household advice was specific about the duties of women to their servants: 'She must have a diligent eye to the behaviour of her servants, what meetings and greetings, what tickings and toylings, and what words and countenances there be betweene men and maides; least such matters being neglected, there follow wantonnesse, yea follie within their houses, which is a great blemmish to the Governours.'[76] The social and sexual behaviour of household servants was an important preoccupation for the women of London's trade and craft communities. The idea of bawdry by ser-

[74] [Mrs] Child *c.* Edith Andrewes (1640), DL/C 235, fo. 329^r–v^; Bushwell *et ux.* *c.* Mary Okeham (1639), DL/C 235, fo. 186; William & Elizabeth Dynes *c.* Anne Phesey (1610), DL/C 219, fo. 71. 'Wittall' means a contented cuckold.

[75] Michael Kendall *c.* Joan Belves (1573), DL/C 211/1, fo. 196.

[76] Cleaver, *Godly Form*, 86.

vants reversed these concerns absolutely: in the language of insult, servants oversaw their mistresses' sexual conduct. Underneath the straightforward model of women's responsibilities in the household presented by the advice writers were considerable anxieties about the powers this gave women. The dangers of older women's conversation for the virtue of young girls are constantly rehearsed in women's conduct books; the vision of women as bawds to their daughters and their mistresses expresses these anxieties. As with cuckoldry, the symbolic injury bawdry did to the household was represented in physical damage. Broken windows were meant to signify a bawdy house: Emma Bacchus was accused 'thow art a bawd . . . and thow diddest breake thy glasse windowes because thow wouldest have thy house knowne to be a whore house'; other women had their windows broken for them.[77]

Like whoredom, bawdry constituted an occupational identity only for women. Men might be called bawd, but such accusations were founded on specific circumstances like these, outlined by John Dawkes to Henry Dixon in 1610: 'Thow art a bawd thow haddest 30 shillings of me for being my bawd when thow foundest me in the feilds.' Henry's wife Clement Dixon, talking to Dawkes's wife about the same incident, spoke with more outraged detail about the financial consequences: 'thy husband is a bawd he did take 30 shillings of my husband for bawdry and I will have my money againe . . . thow mayest well were copper rings when thy husband can get 30 shillings in a morning for playing the bawde'.[78] 'Bawd' alone is not enough to condemn men; nor, for them, does it have the extra power it gains by its association with whoredom. It was very difficult to use against men the kind of sexual labelling that was regularly applied to women.

The disruptions that whoredom caused extended, too, beyond the family. Sexual dishonesty was visualized as polluting the honesty of women, households, and neighbourhoods. Within the household, women's reputation was built on a foundation of fragility, on the understanding of honesty presented by one contemporary conduct-book writer: 'a woman that regardeth her owne credit, ought to refuse the company of a woman that hath an ill name, or deserveth any cause of suspition'.[79] Robert Cleaver's commentary on Proverbs explains some of the reason for this, glossing the text 'come not neere the

[77] Emma Bacchus *c.* Anne Barber (1610), DL/C 219, fos. 46^{v}–47.

[78] John Dawkes *c.* Henry & Clement Dixon (1610), DL/C 219, fo. 115^{r-v}.

[79] *The Court of Good Counsell. Wherin is set down the true rules, how a man should choose a good Wife from a bad, and a woman a good Husband from a bad* (London, 1607), sig. D1.

doore of her house': 'hee would not have us to come to her house or the place where she is, yea to the very doores of her house, because the disease is so dangerous, that the place itselfe is full of evill'.[80] This stress on the doors of the house found a corollary in the incidents of defamation. The vast majority took place outside, in the street; and as many witnesses note, the doorstep was a crucial vantage point for the exchange of insult. Many arguments were conducted across streets with both women standing in their own doors and others standing on their doorsteps to listen. From there, women reinforced their position in the households from which stemmed their standing in the community. Sara Johnson, describing a dispute between Sicely Thornton and Edith Parsons in Clerkenwell, noted carefully the staging of an insult that was particularly concerned with a woman's misbehaviour outside the house:

> It happened this deponente heeringe a noise in the corte . . . where she dwelleth to goe forth unto her dore where she saw Sicelye Thornton standinge in the dore of her owne house and Edithe Parsons in her owne seller windowe . . . skolding at the same Sicelye Thornton and calling her . . . Thow . . . arte an whore an arrant whore and worse then a bitche thow goest sawghtinge up and downe the towne after knaves and art such a whott tailed whore that one nor tenn nor twentye knaves will scarce serve the[e].[81]

Sara's stress on work and speech within, and on the borders of the house, makes an effective contrast with Edith's insistence on Sicely's misconduct outside it. Such careful attention to the details of staging disputes acquires a special significance in the light of household advice about where women should spend their time. If the street is so dangerous a place for women's virtue, and the walls of the home such a safeguard of chastity, the doorstep of the house makes a particularly good position from which to call another woman whore.

The closeness of city dwellings made the house and the household less self-contained than those imagined by most contemporary writers. Several couples often shared one house, a situation liable to provoke dispute. In one case, the three litigants and two of the three witnesses lived in one house, and the defamation took place on the stairs. Even between houses, privacy was not guaranteed: one woman prosecuted a case based on having heard her next door neighbour call

[80] Cleaver, *Briefe Explanation*, 85 (on Prov. 5: 8).

[81] Sicely Thornton *c.* Edith Parsons (1590), DL/C 213, p. 649; another witness noted that the exchange took place in service time, and described how she was 'busy about some necessary work in her house', ibid. p. 648.

her whore through her kitchen wall.[82] Defamations rarely happened inside private houses, at meals, or within private conversation, but were staged, often in the open, with an audience provided by the witnesses who, 'hearing a great noise' in the street, left their work or their houses to investigate or intervene. One witness reports a crowd of 'above half a hundred people' looking on an incident in a shop in London; on another occasion William Hopwood and his wife were roused from their bed at eleven o'clock at night by their maid to hear two of their neighbours chiding.[83] The occasion of defamation was clearly as important as its content; and the stress that defamers laid on the way whoredom polluted the community was reflected in their use of the neighbourhood as a stage and audience for insult.

Defamers tried to exclude the women they named 'whores' from the local community. Dishonest women were represented as a danger to all women. Whoredom could be inherited, from mothers to daughters, between sisters, or more distantly: in Cheshire the word 'tilling' was used to mean 'not only a whore but the grandmother of a whore'.[84] Contemporary advice to women understood their honour as a compound of inherited name and individual behaviour: it was mothers, rather than fathers, from whom women's most important virtue, chastity, descended.[85] Whoredom was also contagious between unrelated women. Robert Dainty, courting a woman in 1628, told her 'if he married hir she must not kepe companie with Mrs Ireland . . . for that she spoiled his former wife'. Elizabeth Wootten, a 59-year old widow from West Ham selling oatmeal near St Peter's Church in Cornhill on a market day, heard Thomas Bradocke threaten Ann Marshall with the pollution of her house and her appearance after Olive Maddock had called her a pander:

thowe art a queane . . . and did not the woman . . . reporte and saie of thee that thowe wast a pander and that thowe kepst a whore in thie howse, And I would . . . thowe didst but see howe like an ould jade thowe doest

[82] Sara Flower *c.* Anne & Thomas Tayler (1629), DL/C 231, fos. 453–4v; Amy Cumberland *c.* Frances Day (1611), DL/C 220, fos. 445v–446v.

[83] Elizabeth Raymen *c.* Katherine Socklyn (1590), DL/C 213, p. 756; Anne Holstead *c.* Katherine Wharton (1591), DL/C 213, p. 82.

[84] John Addy, *Sin and Society in the Seventeenth Century* (London, 1989), 114; the definition is that of the deputy registrar in a case from 1635.

[85] E.g. C[harles] G[ibbon], *The Praise of a Good Name* (London, 1594), sig. A1; Richard Brathwait, *The English Gentlewoman* (London, 1631), epistle dedicatory. On these two notions as the constituents of honour, see Julian Pitt-Rivers, *The Fate of Shechem or The Politics of Sex* (Cambridge, 1977), ch. 1.

looke like ever since thowe tookest or didest take Mris Browne into thie howse.[86]

His words elided the dual dangers attached to whoredom; a moral infection, it was also legally compromising, making women who witnessed it into bawds or panders.

Defamers used the language of actual dirt to describe the corruptions of whoredom. In 1626 a passer-by heard Elizabeth Walsh and Mary Peters chiding in the street:

Elizabeth Walsh said . . . Thou art a base queane and a strumpett . . . gett thee out of my house into Turnball Street for I will keepe noe bawdy house for thee . . . And this deponent then and there also heard the said Elizabeth Walsh bid or comand some servant of hers to pull or dragge out the said Mary Peeters by the haire of her head unto the pumpe and to washe her and further saying that if she . . . would not doe it she would pull or dragge her out of her house unto the pumpe herselfe.

It was important for the honesty of the community that whores could be confined to a particular area like Turnbull Street (now Turnmill Street, in Clerkenwell), notorious for its bawdy houses. When Susan Lark moved to Shoe Lane, her ex-neighbour Margaret Wild came and stood by her door, and 'speaking in a loud manner' insulted her daughter, calling her a whore and saying 'Turnebull Streete is more fitt for hir to live in then amongst honest people.' A few months later she went to see Nicholas Heild, and told him 'that there was a neighbour of hers come to live neere him' and said 'hang her whore'.[87] Real prostitutes were circumscribed in the same way, through the branding introduced under Henry VIII, their control through marked brothels, and the confinement to particular areas that was enforced in other European cities.[88]

Behind many accusations of whoredom lay a disturbing anxiety about women's sexual histories. Women who had just moved into an area were particularly open to speculation that might turn into insult. Their new neighbours expressed doubts and rumours about their

[86] Powell *c.* Ireland (1639), DL/C 235, fo. 192ᵛ; Ann Marshall *c.* Thomas Bradocke (1620), DL/C 226/VII, fo. 1.

[87] Mary Peters *c.* Elizabeth Walsh (1627), DL/C 231, fo. 151; Susan Lark *c.* Margaret Wild (1631), DL/C 233, fos. 214, 216ᵛ.

[88] Ruth Mazo Karras, 'The Regulation of Brothels in Later Medieval England', in Judith M. Bennett, Elizabeth A. Clark, Jean F. O'Barr, B. Anne Viles, and Sarah Westphal-Wihl (eds.), *Sisters and Workers in the Middle Ages* (Chicago, 1989); Gāmini Salgādo, *The Elizabethan Underworld* (London, 1977), 52; Jacques Rossiaud, *Medieval Prostitution*, transl. Lydia Cochrane (Oxford, 1988), 56–8; Mary Elizabeth Perry, *Gender and Disorder in Early Modern Seville* (Princeton, NJ, 1990), ch. 7.

pasts: 'I never came away and left a childe behinde mee in the countrye'; 'shee neede not be so bragg for shee kept a bawdy house before she came to dwell in that parish as I heard say'; 'she was a whore and was hunted from the place from whence she came'.[89] The high mobility of London's population provided ready grounds for anxiety and insult.

RESPONSES TO WHOREDOM

It was women, most of all, who hunted out whores and called for their punishment. Their words suggest a new way of looking at the ideology of household morality. Early modern conceptions of order, morality, and honour placed all the responsibility for household honour on women: unchaste women made themselves whores, their husbands cuckolds, their houses dishonest. In the language of insult, some women turned this responsibility around so that their duty was not just towards their own honesty, but towards that of other women. 'I have a priviledge to call the[e] whore as long as I live,' Joan Hardie asserted to one woman, and 'Thou art a strumpet and I will declare thy name in the streete whersoever I meet thee,' Blanch Lincks said to another. Women insisted, too, on their special responsibility for following, as well as detecting, illicit pregnancies: Alice Hammer told Susan Wilkinson 'Thoue art . . . a puritane whore and thoue art with child and that child is not thie husbands but yt is a merchants child and I will keepe reckoning for thee, and thoue shalte be delivered of that child a month before Christmas next.'[90]

In line with this kind of 'reckoning', women also called for whoredom to be punished. They demanded a response that was broader than the legal sanctions of church and secular courts: it extended to the rituals of community censure, reflecting the combination of popular and institutional sanction that was characteristic of contemporary punishments for illicit sex, and referring to the symbols of punishment. In the gamut of punishments available for whoredom, women had a particular role. The formal legal routes of complaint were more open to men than women: they could, and many of the men who

[89] Alice Nem *c.* Elizabeth Hopkins (1628), DL/C 231, fo. 289; Emma Burston *c.* William Ayres (1630), DL/C 231, fo. 533; Hanna Hamblett *c.* John Linx (1616), DL/C 224, fo. 175^{v}.

[90] Rowe *c.* Joan Hardie (1635), DL/C 234, fo. 21; Frances Day *c.* Blanch Lincks (1611), DL/C 219, fo. 375^{v}; Susan Wilkinson *c.* Alice Hammer (1621), DL/C 227, fo. 228^{v}–229.

came to this court did, hold office as churchwardens or constables, and even without such positions they were considerably more likely than women to present people for sexual or other offences. If men's wives committed adultery, they had a route of complaint through the church courts, leading to a judicial separation; women rarely if ever attempted to use this option against their husbands. In the language of insult, women might assert a claim to moral responsibility and a right to punish.

Insults drew heavily on the imagery of the ritualized, communal punishments of early modern society. Defamers threatened punishment through talking of, and sometimes actually producing, the symbols traditionally associated with community censure of behaviour. The most pervasive are the cuckold's horns, conjured up for example by Margaret Wigge in a dispute with Joan Drake, who with her husband lived at the sign of the Golden Calf: 'hold it upp to thy master his signe, I will have . . . a paier of hornes clapte up to make the calfe a bull'. Others hung up actual horns, waved two fingers to represent them, or called 'cuckoo'. Scolds were offered their own traditional symbols: wisps, figures of straw at which they were meant to rail. Accusations of unchastity led directly to the idea of unruly speech, as the words witnesses reported hearing Richard Langley say to Elizabeth Awsten in Alveley in Essex in 1609 suggest: he apparently 'set up a wispe' against her and said 'Thow art an owtlawed jade and an owtlawed javell . . . there is a wispe for thee for thow hast deserved it.'[91] Like the rituals of rough music recorded in other areas, the banging of basins and pans at women was used to accuse them of whoredom or scolding, and this too found its way into the vernacular of defamation.[92] Alice Fullham and Ellen Allsop called each other 'quean' and 'bitch' in the street in 1611, and Alice said to Ellen 'a cart and a basen tyng tyng, a cart and a basen tyng tyng, a cart and a basen if thou wilt not be quiet'.[93] Here, as so often, verbal and sexual incontinence were conflated.

Between women, the words 'thou art my husband's whore' were also part of a ritual of punishment, peculiar to women and representing a rare opportunity for complaining about men's adultery. The

[91] Joan Drake *c.* Margaret Wigge (1590), DL/C 213, p. 656; Elizabeth Awsten *c.* Richard Langley (1609), DL/C 219, fo. 9^{v}.

[92] See Martin Ingram, 'Ridings, Rough Music, and the "Reform of Popular Culture" in Early Modern England', *Past and Present,* 105 (1984), 79–113, and 'Ridings, Rough Music and Mocking Rhymes in Early Modern England', in Barry Reay (ed.), *Popular Culture in Seventeenth Century England* (London, 1985).

[93] Ellen Allsop *c.* Alice Fullham (1611), DL/C 220, fos. 540^{v}, 547.

culture and legal practice of early modern society contained few avenues for condemning male sexual misconduct, and instead some women turned to public confrontations and threats, directing the blame conveniently outside their marriages on to other women. In 1632 three men and women testified how, in midsummer of that year, Mary Sadd had come to Horne Alley to find the woman she called her husband's whore. Sara Saunderson, hearing 'a greate noise' in the alley, went down 'and finding a woeman standing at her husbands house door railing with a great company of people about her she . . . demanded of the woeman what she meant to kepe such a railing at her doore'. Mary pointed at the house where Margaret Eddis lodged and replied 'I would have the whore out of that howse . . . for she is a base whore and an hospitall whore' and said that 'her [Mary's] husband pawned her goodes and not soe much but her childrens clothes to maintaine her [Margaret], and that she had rousted her out of one place allready and yf she staied but till tomorrowe she would roust her out of this'.[94] Men's adultery and its consequences, here, are translated into a battle between women, one with its own language and expedients.

A more personal punishment involved an actual mutilation of the whore, to make her as visible as she was meant to be. In Stepney in 1618 Alice Squire scratched Katherine Berry's face and said she had given her a 'whores marke'. Other women made explicit exactly what a 'whores mark' was: a slit nose. In Watford in 1619 Joan Hickman accused her neighbour Joan Bird of 'keeping her husband' and threatened to 'slitt her nose and marke her for a whore'.[95] In the culture of medieval and early modern Europe damaging noses signalled sin, specifically sexual sin, and dishonour; it had currency both as a threat, sometimes from municipal authorities, and an actual species of physical assault.[96] In the popular culture of early modern England slitting the nose was conceived as the injured wife's revenge on her husband's mistress. Witnesses to Joan Hickman's threats said she had 'used her pleasure of Joane Bird in speeches': the familiar phraseology of sexual pleasure was echoed in the shape of the pleasurable verbal revenge for it. Noses also suggested phalluses, and as the syphilitic infection of women's noses mirrored, for defamers, the destruction of men's

[94] Margaret Eddis *c.* Mary Sadd (1632), GL MS 9057/1, fo. 13^{r-v}.

[95] See e.g. the ballad, 'Have among you! good Women', Roxburghe Ballads, i. 146. Katherine Berry *c.* Alice Squire *et al.* (1618), DL/C 225, fo. 351^{r-v}; Joan Bird *c.* Joan Hickman (1619), DL/C 226/III, fo. 42.

[96] Valentin Groebner, 'Losing Face, Saving Face: Noses, Honour and Spite in the Late Medieval Town', *History Workshop Jl.* 40 (1995), 1–15.

members, slitting or cutting women's noses carried echoes of castration. The language and gesture of insult focused on noses as a place on women's bodies on which, as on the phallus, discredit could be visibly marked out.

Women and men also resorted to and threatened other kinds of physical violence. More severe assaults, and particularly those by men, probably ended up in the secular courts, but lesser attacks and threats were presented to the church courts as part of the circumstances of defamation. Many women used as weapons or threats the household objects with which they were eating or cooking. In 1575 an 'old controversye' between Jane Davies and Katherine Brisley was revived at dinner in Lombard Street with some of their neighbours, leading to Jane 'behaving herself very rudely in disquieting the company and throwing loves of bred and a trencher' at Katherine and saying to her 'Thow art a drabbe and an harlott and the evell favoured knave thy landlord keepeth thee.' At another meal in 1618 Elizabeth Morris threw a plate of butter and cheese at William Elkin when he said she was Richard Price's whore. Sibyl Brosse attacked Catherine Ripon with a gridiron and called her 'witch saying that shee would cut her as small as hearbes to the pot'.[97] Other disputes happened in the street and ended in blows. In a confrontation 'in the open street' Jane Young was alleged to have beaten or kicked Frances Harrison, causing her to miscarry; Sara Pridden and Dorothy Foster were seen fighting in the fields, Dorothy pulling the headcloth from Sara's head and calling her 'ugly whore a base whore and a damned whore'; Elizabeth Moorefoote struck Sibyl Doe on the head with a stick, making her bleed, and was carried by William Crowther to the stocks, scratching him and tearing his ruffs on the way; and Catherine Ripon was accused of calling Sibyl Brosse whore and breaking, not only her head, but her glass windows, in an action that combined the symbolizing of whoredom with physical violence against the whore.[98]

As well, women claimed a part in the more formal punishment of whoredom. While it was men who decided and enforced the penalties of temporal and spiritual law, women made explicit claims to a stake in that power. In many ways legal punishments invoked as powerful a symbolism as communal ones. Women found guilty of whore-

[97] Katherine Brisley *c.* Jane Davies (1575), DL/C 212, p. 330; Richard Price *c.* William Elkin (1618), DL/C 225, fos. 289–290^{v}; Catherine Ripon *c.* Sibyl Brosse (1628), DL/C 231, fo. 27.

[98] Frances Harrison *c.* Jane Young (1628), DL/C 231, fos. 192^{v}–193; Sara Pridden *c.* Dorothy Foster (1628), DL/C 231, fo. 154; Sibyl Brosse *c.* Catherine Ripon (1628), DL/C 231, fo. 28^{v}.

dom or bawdry were regularly sentenced to be carried in a cart through the city, as Elizabeth Holland, found guilty of keeping a brothel, was in 1597: 'she shalbe put into a carte at Newgate and be carted with a paper on her hed shewinge her offence, from thence to Smythfeilde, from thence to her house, from thence to Cornehill, from thence to the Standerd in Cheepe, from thence to Bridewell, and all the waye basons to be runge before her.'[99] Defamers claimed their own share in the ritual humiliation and emphasis on place that the courts dictated. Margery Hipwell threatened Phoebe Cartwright 'Thou art a queane and a wrymouth queane and I will make thee . . . do pennannce with a white sheet And I will have thee . . . carted out of the street': her attack combined ecclesiastical and lay sanctions to threaten both shame and symbolic exclusion.[100]

The white sheet that was sometimes used for penance in the parish church conveyed a powerful symbolism. In 1592 Roger Bady sued three women for their attack on him: 'all three of them with one voice each of them repeating the words said that . . . Roger Bady was a bawdy knave', and Joan Miller 'said she would stand to it for if the said Bady had not bought it out he should have stood in a white sheet in Stepney church'. Anne Johnson was sitting in her shop selling fruit, holding Marie Buckle's child, when Elizabeth Lee came past and 'tooke the said child in her arms and kissed yt sayeing thowe art a prettie child and Marie Buckle did not stande in a white sheet for nothinge, and sayeing further that Alice Clerke . . . was a bawde and she would cause her to be carted for a bawde, which words she . . . spake verie lowde and in malitious manner'.[101] In these insults, women claimed a power to punish whoredom that belonged in law to men. While institutional and legal restrictions excluded them from most of the powers of community control in which their husbands might have a stake, many women insisted on their own part in that authority.

HONESTY AND HONOUR

From the range of sources available to them men and women produced a detailed and apparently rigid understanding of sexual honour, the system in which honesty had meaning. Unchaste women were

[99] *Middlesex County Records*, ed. John Cordy Jeaffreson (London, 1886), i. 234.

[100] Phoebe Cartwright *c.* Margery Hipwell (1613), DL/C 221, fo. 1190.

[101] Roger Bady *c.* Joan Miller, Joan Sellwood, & Mary Coly (1592), DL/C 214, p. 174; Alice Clerke *c.* Elizabeth Lee (1620), DL/C 226/IV, fo. 28.

depicted as the dishonest opposites of the ideals of wifehood; honesty was a state for which women were meant to compete through the comparison of modesty. Both honesty and dishonesty were defined through the household. In sermons and marriage advice, the walls of the house provide the context of wifely obedience; insults present women's dishonesty through its direct and material effects on their whole household. Its first implications are for husbands, in danger of the dishonouring humiliations of cuckoldry and the material threats it might pose through the potential of bastard children. The husbands of unchaste women are most damaged, because of their own investment in the continence of their wives. The sexual link leads to an economic one: a cuckolded man is in danger of being fooled into accepting another man's son as his own, into supporting a bastard and passing his inheritance on to a usurper. The honour of the household is invested in a monogamous sexual bond, a joint marital honour which gives words like 'cuckold' and 'whore' implications for both partners.[102] But the responsibility for that honour rests in practice upon women: only women's sexual misconduct damages the household honour.

Brothers, fathers, and sons are implicated less closely by the understanding that women's honesty and dishonesty was the responsibility of her male relatives. It has ramifications too for the fragile honour of other women in the family, as the numbers of defamations of mothers and daughters as bawds and whores show. Women's honour extends to affect the whole household, with implications for the house itself as well as specific family members. In 1613 Anne Gibbons complained of a series of sexual insults directed at her husband but focusing on her: 'cuckold' , 'wittoll', and 'every one that passeth by thy house and seeth thy wife saieth there is a whore and there is a bawdye house'.[103] In the marital division of sexual honesty, the honour of the whole house reposed with the wife.

Meanwhile, men's honesty was also the subject of debate, both in sexual slanders and outside the church courts. Indeed, it was men's honour, rather than women's, that was the main subject of discussion for contemporary writers: the sexual slander of which women were

[102] See the analysis of the exchange of honour through sex in Sandra Cavallo and Simona Cerutti, 'Female Honor and the Social Control of Reproduction in Piedmont between 1600 and 1800', trans. Mary M. Gallucci, in Edward Muir and Guido Ruggiero (eds.), *Sex and Gender in Historical Perspective* (Baltimore, 1990), 74–81.

[103] Anne Gibbons *c.* John Stronge (1613), DL/C 221, fos. 1539^{v}–40.

the brokers received little attention from men.[104] The barrister John March's definition of defamatory speech outlines the issues of honour which slander could affect:

all scandalous words which touch or concerne a man in his life, Liberty or Member, or any corporall punishment; or which scandall a man in his Office or place of Trust, or in his Calling or function by which he gains his living; or which tend to the slandering of his Title or his disinheritance; or to the loss of his advancement or preferment, or any other particular damage; or lastly which charge a man to have any dangerous infectious disease.[105]

Here, a man's life, public identity, financial standing, and penis are all vulnerable. Imputations of venereal disease or impotency affect a man's life in the same way as material allegations. Accusations like 'Traitor, Felon, Theefe, or Murderer' 'call a man's life in question'. None of them are perceived as damaging women, and their only sexual implication is through venereal disease. March's few references to slanders of women at the common law concern sexual insults like those that came to the church courts: 'shee hath a Bastard', 'shee is a Bawde, and keepes a Bawdy House'.[106] Apparently, then, whether fought at church or secular courts, women's reputation was always at heart about sexual honour, and in contrast, male honour covered a whole range of different fields.

Those fields are explored in litigation at other courts. John March suggests some occasions on which defamations harm men: 'of a merchant, *that he will be Bankrupt within two dayes*', of an officer '*that hee is a corrupt Officer or Judge*', of a free man, that he is someone else's villein.[107] Such accusations had temporal implications and were sued at common law. The Middlesex and Westminster sessions saw a small number of cases over such insults; most often it was office-holders who complained. William Cratchman was accused in 1609 of abusing the Justice of the Peace, Sir William Warde, 'saying the divell shatt justices when he was made one'.[108] For most cases, only the brief

[104] John March, *Actions for Slaunder, Or, a Methodicall Collection under certain Grounds and Heads, of what words are Actionable in the Law, and what not?* (London, 1647), deals primarily with slander at the common law, and its effects upon the material livelihoods of men; Vaughan, *Spirit of Detraction*, 345–7, goes into more detail about slanders of women; John Godolphin, *Repertorium Canonicum; or, An Abridgement of the Ecclesiastical Laws of this Realm* (London, 1678), 514 ff., explains the effects of defamations of women through their marital prospects.

[105] March, *Actions for Slaunder*, 10–11. The same point is made in Godolphin's *Reportorium Canonicum* and Vaughan's *Spirit of Detraction.*

[106] March, *Actions for Slaunder*, 57.

[107] Ibid. 43, 53.

[108] GLRO MJ/SR 472/84 (1609).

recognizances survive, and they give no details of insults, using instead terms like 'abusing', 'provoking', and 'threatening' to describe the confrontations between constables, justices, and ordinary people. At Star Chamber, where some litigants took their cases to appeal, witnesses and plaintiffs went into much greater detail about the language of men's insults. Most Star Chamber cases involved litigants of higher social status than those at the church courts; it was there, it seems, if anywhere, that the gentry were likely to pursue slurs on their reputations. Of the middling status litigants there, some men complained of material allegations of theft or corruption. Again, most were office-holders, their position both making them a target of abuse and enabling them to fight effectively at law. Others were concerned about religious insults. John Cunditt of Dorchester complained of the circulation of a series of rhymes that began 'Tall sturdy Puritan knave' and 'You Puritans all wheresoever you dwell / imitating your master devill of hell'. Another point of attack was descent: in London in 1618 Susan Mouns said William Taylor, a merchant tailor, and his wife, were 'basely and beggerly descended'.[109]

But even at Star Chamber, very many defamations of men turned out to concern their wives, and the insults of which they complained focused, like those that went to the church courts, on men's betrayal by their wives' adultery after marriage or their promiscuity before it. In longer, more complicated insults, frequently in lengthy doggerel verse, the drama of cuckoldry was enacted in detail. Walter Robbins, his wife Avice, and her mother Alice, came to Star Chamber from Cornwall in 1610 to complain of a libel being circulated around their town, purporting to be a letter warning Walter of his wife's duplicity, aided by her mother. The author tells Walter how Avice's lover comes to the house when he is at work, and brags openly of his position: 'so soone as you are out hee wilbee in, and hee wilbee in the chamber when you are in the hall . . . you did mistrust him a great while but now hee doth use his witts so fynely that you have left it, and now hee may doe what hee please, so that hee sayeth that hee will hold in comons with you'.[110] In insults as in ballads, drama, and literature, the story of cuckoldry focuses on the deceit of women and the betrayal of hospitality. And it regularly proved the most effective way of

[109] John & Elizabeth Cunditt *v.* Matthew & Margaret Chubb (1609), PRO STAC 8 94/17, m. 12; William & Mary Taylor *v.* Susan Mouns (1618), PRO STAC 8 284/23, m. 2.

[110] Walter, Avice, & Alice Robbyns *v.* John & Honor Cornishe and others (1610), PRO STAC 8 254/29, m. 2.

defaming men. But despite its popularity as a means of insult, the lawyers who wrote of defamation and honour mentioned nothing about the power of such accusations. No legal treatise was prepared to deal explicitly with the exact damage to masculinity effected by a husband's loss of sexual control over his wife.

Both at the church courts and elsewhere, women were the focal point of a whole repertory of verbal insults. Insults of women played on a culpability for illicit sex that was unique to them. The personal, verbal, social, and institutional sanctions against 'whores' and 'bawds' had no counterpart for men. Men were less likely than women to be presented for illicit sex; men's adultery was never an accepted ground for marital separation as women's was; and the word 'whore' had no male equivalent. Sexual honour was imagined entirely through women, and in the language of abuse women's dishonesty was interpreted through its direct and material effects on the whole household. The reputation of the house itself rested on women. Women were at the pivotal centre of the circulation of blame and dishonour for sex: responsibility was channelled entirely through them.

That responsibility made women the natural targets of sexual insult. But it also gave some women an investment in the regulation of sexuality inside and outside their households. Sexual honour was overwhelmingly a female concern, and while women were the targets of the regulation of honesty, they also made themselves the agents of its definition. Women used the broad and powerful possibilities of the word 'whore' in every sort of local and personal conflict. They called other women whores as one weapon in disputes about money, goods, or territory, or they told circumstantial stories of actual, rumoured, or imagined sexual transgressions. The knowledge of female bodies with which women were credited and their authority in the area of childbirth established one source of power which was immensely productive in the shaping of abuse. Symbolic actions like slitting noses and threats of community punishment sustained a tradition of women's sanctions, encompassing sexual sin in contexts as broad as the neighbourhood and as narrow as the household. For women, the rituals of slander could perform a wide range of functions for which men were more likely to look to official, institutional, and legal spheres.

In many ways, then, the language of slander offered particular linguistic powers to women, through which they asserted their verbal, physical, and legal agency to judge and condemn other women. But such sexually explicit speech had its risks for women. Using sexual insult to prove other women dishonest left slanderers themselves open to charges of impropriety; and the dangers of women's speech about sex were particularly apparent when women alleged seduction, assault, or rape. Ready to insult women with the phrase 'my whore', men regularly sued women for their attempts to fix sexual responsibility on them; both their use of the courts, and the words of their insults, proclaim their control over the institutional and cultural machinery of sexual judgement.

The language of sexual insult that both men and women employed embodied the perceived model of gender that made men's and women's experience of defamation so different. Its idiom depended on a binary gender division that treated men's and women's honour as incommensurable. The imagery of whoredom provides the linguistic elaboration of a system of honour that determined women's and men's experiences in conflicts over sex and marriage. Women's relationship to standards of sexual behaviour was radically different from that of men, not just in the scale of culpability, but in the very terms in which it was constructed.

4

Words, Honour, and Reputation

Early modern England was a society in which spoken words still wielded enormous power. Few people, and especially few women, used the written word with any frequency, and when accurate memory was so important, oral speech could have far-reaching echoes. What people said was accepted, too, as a measure of character. The concept of 'common fame', which carried legal weight, for example, in proving contested marriages, and in the use of compurgation by a group of neighbours to decide a defendant's innocence or guilt, was primarily an oral one. Words, then, were crucially linked with reputation; and the concept of reputation held considerable sway both legally and socially.

This link between words and reputation was the basis on which litigation for defamation worked. The victims of insult who, increasingly, responded by going to court did so on the grounds that their reputations had been severely damaged in the eyes of people who mattered.[1] To historians, the increase in slander litigation through the late sixteenth and early seventeenth centuries has suggested the possibility of tracing a growing popular intolerance of illicit sexuality through the currency of insult. The records of defamation have been interpreted as testimony of a widespread concern both with a sexual morality more or less corresponding to that of church teaching, and with a sexual honour that read slander as profoundly discrediting. Yet, as historians have recognized, both insults and the litigation that followed them arose from broader local and personal conflicts; and to contemporaries, the growth of litigation looked like a pollution of neighbourliness by malicious dispute.[2] Slander was a creative project.

[1] 'Cum infamatus non sit apud bonos et graves' (*Auctoritate dei Patris*, 1222), discussed in *Select Cases on Defamation to 1600*, ed. R. H. Helmholz, Selden Society, 102 (London, 1985), pp. xxxiv–xxxvi.

[2] J. A. Sharpe, *Defamation and Sexual Slander in Early Modern England: The Church Courts at York*, Borthwick Papers, 58 (York, 1980), 24–6, 22; Martin Ingram, *Church Courts, Sex and Marriage in England, 1570–1640* (Cambridge, 1987), 165–6, 304–6, 313–16; John March, *Actions for Slaunder, Or, a Methodicall Collection under certain Grounds and Heads, of what words are Actionable in the Law, and what not?* (London, 1647), esp. 4.

While defamers relied, for the most part, on conventional visions of female whoredom and its associations, they could also be imaginative, and of necessity, they were sometimes (particularly as women insulting men) forced to replace convention with invention. Recognizably different from church and literary moral teaching, the ideologies of insult were also not identical to the practical workings of morality in daily life. We cannot read off from sexual insult a popular intolerance of illicit sex. And while ostensibly defamers spoke to attack dishonesty, and plaintiffs came to the court to attack false words, the contexts of words and litigation testify to a more complex use of both language and law. In the seventeenth century the church courts were filled by women and men complaining of sexual insult. Brief insults and longer stories about illicit sex were the basis for long and fairly expensive cases based on the principle that slander damaged a person's reputation. What was so damaging about sexual insult? Why did so many women and men turn to the courts? And how was the gendered morality so integral to insult followed up in the concepts of name, fame, and credit that litigants invoked at court? The meaning of slander—on the streets and in the courts—depended on an intersection of words, law, morals, and honour. The precise connections between insults and dishonour, between slander and morals, and between litigation and reputation, were complicated and variable; and they were shaped at every level by gender.

HONOUR AND MORALS

For the most part the words of insult assumed and stressed a morality which differentiated sharply between women and men. In it, women's responsibility for sexual morality made them 'whores', but men 'cuckolds': women's honesty was defined by their sexuality, men's by that of the women connected with them. This made for a system of culpability with particularly acute gender differences in the implications of extramarital sex. The relationship between sex and marriage was cast differently for men and women. Women's sexual misconduct had implications for the whole honour of a marriage; blame for men's misconduct, though, was diverted on to the women involved, both by the men who called their sexual partners whores, and by the wives who called other women 'my husband's whore'. The conventions of slander assumed that adulterous men and adulterous women stood at very different ends of the battlefield of sexual words. Adultery made women vulnerable to insult, but gave men, instead, the power to abuse: while adulterous women and their husbands were at the receiving end of sexual slander, the men they had allegedly had sex with joined with their wives to call them whores and their husbands cuckolds. The language of insult revolved around a rigid and precise vision of the difference gender made to sex.

The shaping of the words of slander, and the pursuit of them at court, presupposed an intimate relationship between such words and dishonour. The spectre of dishonour made slander effective: while the word 'whore', it could be argued, represented a real offence which might lead to material penalties, its corollary for men—'cuckold'—had no such implications. Only the idea that words could be discrediting in themselves gave insult the power that made it slander. The discussion of honour by anthropologists in the context of Mediterranean 'honour and shame' societies, as a rigid moral code in which the suggestion of a woman's illicit sex shames both her and her family members, is not particularly useful here;[3] but the term 'honour' can still be a helpful one. It was not a word contemporaries made much use of: for the people embroiled in slander disputes, terms like 'credit', 'name', and 'reputation' more accurately summed up the issues over which they were fighting. The moral ideals they expressed, though, were part of an overall system of beliefs and ideals in which a definition of morality was used to judge reputation. That definition was not necessarily constant, although at certain times it might draw strength from apparent rigidity: one of the arguments of this book is that women and men were able to interpret and deploy ideas of honour, as well as absorbing and being ruled by them. Honour, in other words, was a variable, not a constant. In association with ideas of morals, of reputation, and of credit, it was a powerful tool in the daily negotiations of gender relations.

Studies of sexual honour, whether from the perspective of historians or that of anthropologists, have tended to be one-sided. A system of honour that valorizes female chastity protects the property of husbands: it attempts to ensure their wives are faithful to them, and that their material wealth passes on only to their own children. But the use of slanderous language in early modern London testifies to a concept of honour that was also useful to women. It was women, more than men, who ended up in court for calling other women whores, jades,

[3] This is pointed out by Sharpe, *Defamation and Sexual Slander*, 19–20, and Susan Dwyer Amussen, in 'Gender, Family and the Social Order 1560–1725', in Anthony Fletcher and John Stevenson (eds.), *Order and Disorder in Early Modern England* (Cambridge, 1985), 207.

and queans. The ideas of honour that held sway in early modern society need to be examined now in the light of their functions not for men, but for women.

The elaborate condemnations that slanderers constructed suggest a clear moral code, where the unacceptable could be readily marked out. Slanderers proclaimed themselves concerned with moral standards; and historians have tended to take their proclamations at face value, reading slander as one means of enforcing communal norms of behaviour.[4] Insults stemmed from more complex roots than this. The morals slanderers expressed were closely related to those of various kinds of contemporary culture, but they were not identical to them, and often, they represented creative adaptations of familiar ideas. More than the absorption of contemporary moral teaching, sexual slander testifies to a use of the ideas and targets that popular, élite, and ecclesiastical culture set up. The emphasis of clerics on equal culpability for illicit sex made little difference to the dichotomy between women's and men's sexual morality that was integral to the practice and experience of slander; nor did the more detailed behavioural rules of household prescription. Rather, the images of whoredom that were promulgated in popular and prescriptive literature proved a useful source for some powerful insults.

Insults played on the ideas of honour presented in contemporary oral and printed culture, but did not entirely reproduce them. They also represented some personal definitions of honour and dishonour. Sexual insults of men could rely on none of the conventions of the dishonour of whoredom from which insults of women drew strength. The word whore and its multiplicity of dishonouring associations had no male equivalent; contemporary discussions of slander made no reference to the possibility of men being sexually defamed, outside imputations of having syphilis. While popular oral and printed culture bears little traces of concepts of male sexual culpability, in practice it *was* possible for men's sexual transgressions to be discrediting. The lists of complaints women directed at their husbands' alleged 'whores' also registered with force men's violation of the economic and sexual relations of marriage. Words like 'knave' or 'whoremaster', not by definition about men's own sexual behaviour, could be deployed to insult men for their part in sexual misconduct. There were also rumours about women falsely accusing men of seducing them, stories which whether true or not, suggest that at the level of practical morality men

[4] Sharpe, *Defamation and Sexual Slander*, 25; Ingram, *Church Courts*, 165–6.

could be, and were, quite severely blamed for the faults of illicit sex, rape, and especially bastardy.[5] The women who accused men of these transgressions, implicating themselves as they did so, were still engaged in a particularly original, and sometimes risky, project. Arguably, such accusations were more closely related to actual events than many sexual insults of women; rather than random verbal attacks, many of them represented attempts by women to fix the blame on men after illicit sex or sexual assault. Whether they were true or not, women who made such accusations were redefining the conventional grounds of dishonour to insist upon a male culpability that, in practice, would rarely be realized.[6]

To the extent that slander represented a project of moral regulation, it was one that was not always consonant with legal and cultural convention. It was a project, too, that was by no means always directed at actual immorality.[7] The 'whores' of the language of insult are not, generally, real whores. Yet on some occasions and to some extent the words of slander reflected some very real concerns. Most obviously, the women accusing men of assault and rape were often making genuine complaints, rather than shaping effective insults. The language of insult might, however, also provide such women, as in the case of Ann Symes who insulted the minister in front of his parish, with a means of humiliating the men concerned. Accusations between women are just as hard to disentangle. The insult 'my husband's whore' sounds as if it was based on some firm evidence, and often this is supported by the details of sexual and economic betrayal; yet it was also accepted as a meaningless, common insult. Two women appeared in front of the wardmote court of Aldersgate in 1586, after each had accused the other 'to be nought with . . . her husband'; while the wardmote concluded 'yt apperethe no sufficyent proofe, that wherby we may indyte eyther of them', they also decided that one of the women was probably guilty, since she had also been indicted 'for a common barratter and a very discencious woman' and she had come, with her husband, from another ward with no certificate of good behaviour. The couple were told to leave their house and she was ordered to 'refrayne the company' of the other woman's

[5] See e.g. Thomas Derrifield *c.* Mary Thompson (1630), DL/C 232, fo. 282.

[6] See also Mary Beth Norton, 'Gender and Defamation in Seventeenth-Century Maryland', *William and Mary Quarterly*, 3rd ser., 44/1 (1987), 3–39.

[7] Truth was not, technically, an accepted defence in slander cases: even true words could be defamatory, although plaintiffs generally claimed insults to be false: *Select Cases on Defamation*, intro. pp. xxx–xxxi.

husband.[8] Thus one woman's accusation was taken as evidence; the other's was treated as barratry. Even—perhaps especially—where formulaic, familiar insults were concerned, it was not always easy to distinguish between truth and fiction. While some defamers may have been complaining about actual sexual misdemeanours, for many others sexual insult was not primarily a response to sexual transgression. It was, rather, a language to which women and men resorted on a whole range of occasions in the relations of the household, the street, and the community. The circumstances of dispute, as they are related by witnesses, bear out the difference between public slander and communal morality.

In the testimonies of witnesses in defamation suits, a set of detailed descriptions of the background to slander clarifies the meaning of insult and its relationship to the sexual standards it espoused. While the words of insult might not necessarily be related to any actual incidents, their stress on disordered households, economies, and neighbourhoods does provide a distorted reflection of the concerns over which urban and rural communities fell into dispute. The strategic place that doorsteps occupy in the staging of defamations suggests their symbolic power and the boundary they represented. Household order was a prime focus for complaint, conflict, and insult. The principal subjects of household control, children and servants, were frequently at the centre of conflict: in different ways young children, adolescents, and apprentices were all liable to disturb or infringe domestic boundaries. Disputes over children led readily to accusations of bastardy. In 1611 Alice Fullham's young son swept dust into Ellen Allsop's child's face; Ellen called the boy a 'base roague', Alice said, 'what doest thou call my boy bastard if he be a bastard then must I be a whore', and called Ellen 'wrimouthd queane and a wrimouthd jade' and 'filthy ridden bitch'. Another two women came to court after a dispute provoked by the behaviour of older children. In the parish of St Sepulchre in 1574, Margery Swinton brought a constable to inspect the house of her new neighbour, Anne Lenthropp, on the grounds that it was 'a nowghtye and a bawdye house, and that . . . Anne Lenthropp had a dowghter there . . . unto whome her sonne did moch resorte unto and spente all that he could gett uppon her'. When they arrived there, Margery said 'Here is the arraund bawde . . . and haith bene this twentie yeares, and there is the whore her

[8] Aldersgate Wardmote Minutes (1586), GL MS 2050/1, fo. 1.

dowghter.' Instead of managing to get her neighbours arrested, she found herself sued for defamation.[9]

Conflict over the behaviour of servants and apprentices, in a society where masters and mistresses were expected to oversee their moral conduct, led in the same way to suggestions of immorality. In a yard at Coldharbour in the summer of 1614 Ellen Godderd sued Thomas Hoskins and his wife for calling her whore and for complaining that she was 'enticeing our servants to lewdnes any tyme these foure yeares'. Grace Hutchinson and Elizabeth Ivott fell out in 1614 because Elizabeth's servants kept coming to Mr Hutchinson's shop, offering brass tokens instead of money for his goods. Jane Holliday defamed Thomas Wells by saying 'thou dost kepe a base house and doth harbour other mens servants to spend their masters goodes in thy house'.[10]

Other disputes arose about the household's physical boundaries. In the crowded streets of the City much conflict revolved around the contested territories that marked out houses, walls, yards, and gutters. In Shoreditch in 1611 Richard Ingles called Audrey Levis a whore because her apprentices had broken his wall. Near Chancery Lane in the same year Elizabeth Jacob complained to Elizabeth Chare that her husband's new building was obstructing her light, and the exchange between them moved swiftly into one about honesty, bastardy, and cuckoldry: starting with one telling the other 'that shee was as good a woman as shee was', it went on 'I have ten children and thou hast never a one'; 'Aye . . . but who gotte them? Your husband . . . gotte none of them but alas poore nynny horner he . . . is faine to father them'. Anxieties about the limits of the house extended too to shared resources, such as water, the focus of a dispute between three wharf-side neighbours in 1630. Frances Humfreys complained that Peter Marsh had placed a scaffold by the wharf which prevented her drawing her water, John Swanton took her part, and Marsh called him 'a sawcy jacke a base fellowe a druncken knave a druncken rascall and a copper nose drunkard' and 'thou . . . art the basest fellowe in the parish and thou didst abuse thy owne father'.[11]

[9] Ellen Allsop *c.* Alice Fullham (1611), DL/C 220, fos. 540^{v}–541, 542; Anne Lenthropp *c.* Margery Swinton (1574), DL/C 212, pp. 3, 5.

[10] Ellen Godderd *c.* Thomas Hoskins *et ux* (1615), DL/C 223, fo. 6^{v}; Grace Hutchinson *c.* Elizabeth Ivott (1614), DL/C 222, fo. 120^{r-v}; Thomas Wells *c.* Jane Holliday (1628), DL/C 231, fo. 203.

[11] Audrey Levis *c.* Richard Ingles *als* Daniell (1611), DL/C 220, fo. 780^{r-v}; Elizabeth Chare *c.* Elizabeth Jacob (1611), DL/C 220, fo. 815^{r-v}; John Swanton *c.* Peter Marsh (1630), DL/C 233, fo. 142^{v}.

Outside the boundaries of household and neighbourhood a whole range of other concerns had their own echoes in defamatory language. Most prominent were disagreements over property and money. Both men and women became involved in defamation as a result of financial conflicts; but, particularly where women were concerned, the issues at stake were rewritten to focus on sex.[12] In 1629 Peter Eldredge called Elizabeth Champneis a whore, because a dispute about 'a bargaine of a parcell of allmonds' between his brother and her had been referred to the Lord Mayor and judged in her favour. Elizabeth White and Rachel Townsend fell out while attempts were being made to settle a difference between their husbands about some debts. When Elizabeth heard Rachel persuading her husband not to pay Henry White and to tell Elizabeth to 'take her course by law', she told Rachel 'she was a scurvy woman in soe doing', and Rachel responded 'openly in malitious and angrie manner . . . I . . . am not so scurvy a woman as you . . . for I never sould my daughters maydenhead for money', and accused Elizabeth of taking £5 for her daughter's virginity. Intervening in a financial dispute, Rachel transposed it into a different economic arena, focusing it on the sexual. Other disputes were concerned with women's own financial enterprises. In the twopenny gallery of the Red Bull playhouse in Clerkenwell, Joan Hewes, taking the money and selling fruit with other women, became embroiled in an argument with Luke Bryan, a 60-year-old member of the King's guard on his way in: he 'asked how they did, Well quoth Joane Hewes . . . if you will paie me for your admittance, paie quoth the said Bryan you are a scould, a scould quoth the said Hewes it would sett your kitchen on fier to keep manie such scoulds, the said Luce Bryan replyeinge said unto . . . Joane Hewes thou art an arrant whore and a theefe'.[13] Bryan's refusal to pay is geared specifically towards the (female) context; because it is a woman demanding money, he shifts the emphasis of the exchange first on to her words, characterizing her demand as scolding, and then on to her body, calling her first whore, then thief.

The words of slander, ostensibly about sex, turn out to be about almost everything else. The sexual insult of women absorbed and refracted every kind of female transgression. When Isabel Morley said in 1614 that Grace Aldred was 'a scurvie queane for enticing away her

[12] Norton, 'Gender and Defamation', 9.

[13] Elizabeth Champneis *c.* Peter Eldredge (1629), DL/C 231, fos. 376 ff.; Elizabeth White *c.* Rachel Townsend (1629), DL/C 231, fo. 321^{v}; Joan Hewes *c.* Luke Bryan (1618), DL/C 225, fo. 341^{r-v}.

servant', she used a typical and familiar way of turning a specific complaint into a discrediting form of abuse, hinging on stereotypes and associations that could be obliquely related to her accusation.[14] The insults whore, quean, and bawd were particularly useful in grievances about households and economics, because the vision of whoredom that was the touchstone of sexual insult had such strong resonances in those areas: whores disrupted households, economies, and neighbourhoods. So while the convergence of every complaint about women on to their sexuality, which was hardly new to this period, makes it hard to see slander as evidence of increasing moral concern, some connections between slander and morality remain. The people who created and circulated rumours about the sexual behaviour of their neighbours spoke with self-conscious and individual purposes. The themes of insult drew on and were shaped by the concerns of contemporary moral projects, but defamers discussing sexual behaviour were not enforcing one standard of behaviour: rather, their words defined images of acceptability and transgression which gave insult its power. The norms of insult were used to judge only some members of the community. As a weapon in neighbourhood relations, slander was a most convenient response to alliances and disruptions between men and women over the regular incidents of everyday life. Reinforced by a long history of images of whoredom, the language of insult gave women and men powerful words with far-reaching implications.

THE POWER OF INSULT

In a taxonomy of early modern forms of speech, slander occupied a well-established place. The definitions litigants, witnesses, and contemporary commentators gave to show the discrediting power of slander give some idea of the kind of speech it was conceived to be. Plaintiffs and defendants contested the nature of slander: joking or angry, kindly or malicious. Contemporary writers were keen to draw the line—a line that slanderers themselves tried to blur in their own defence—between helpful moral regulation and malicious slander. In 1656 Edward Reyner, a Lincoln minister, prescribed some rules for moral advice, a 'work of charity and a general office of Neighbour to Neighbour'. Made in a spirit of love and meekness, reproof was to be seconded with arguments, 'to set it off with evidence'; it should be

[14] Grace Aldred *c.* Isabel Morley (1615), DL/C 223, fo. 13.

'founded on some text of Scripture, so as the party admonished may see himself reproved rather by God than by us'; and it required certain verbal forms, like illustration by stories, comparison with the speaker, or insinuation through phrases like 'I wish your good'.[15] At the opposite end of the admonitory spectrum to the well-intentioned moral adviser were those who damaged good names: 'talebearers, backbyters and slaunderers', whose tactics were characterized in *The Praise of a Good Name* in 1594, 'when one speaketh evil of another with fine prefaces and preambles, saing that he is very sorry that his neighbour hath done such or such a thing: that he speaketh it not of malice, but of a good minde; that he is constrained to speake; that he speaketh not all that he could speake'.[16] Reyner's distinction between malice and neighbourliness was a hopeful one: defamers used not only the types of speech he identified as backbiting, but just as often, his models for charitable advice: they told stories, drew comparisons, and even invoked the scriptures in their support.[17]

The crucial difference between reproof and slander, though, was its context. Public reprimands, Edward Reyner noted, had quite a different effect from private reproof; and the public performance of slander was essential to its power. Many insults were staged in front of a large audience, but even private slanders were frequently informed by the idea of exposure, of making private sins public property. The slanderous stories with which defamers insulted their neighbours played on, and fed into, tales and rumours that could be passed round the neighbourhood and elaborated. Historians have characterized slander as 'gossip', using the anthropological interpretation of gossip as a means of regulating social norms and expressing group values.[18] Certainly, slander suits emphasized the importance of the circulation

[15] Edward Reyner, *Rules for the Government of the Tongue* (London, 1656), 199, 174–6, 181–3; similar advice was given by William Perkins, *A Direction for the Government of the Tongue according to Gods word* (London, 1615). The possible relationship between such literature and the context of defamation sued at the common law is developed in Annabel Gregory, 'Slander Accusations and Social Control in Late Sixteenth and Early Seventeenth Century England, with Particular Reference to Rye (Sussex), 1590–1615', D.Phil thesis (Sussex, 1984).

[16] C[harles] G[ibbon], *The Praise of a Good Name* (London, 1594), 31, 80.

[17] John Heywood, *A ballad against slander and detraction* (London, 1562), stanza 10, puts slander in this same context of reproof.

[18] Roger Thompson, '"Holy Watchfulness" and Communal Conformism: The Functions of Defamation in Early New England Communities', *New England Quarterly*, 56/4 (1983), 520–2; Sharpe, *Defamation and Sexual Slander*, 20–1; Norton, 'Gender and Defamation', 35–9. The classic anthropological approach on which these depend is that of Max Gluckman's article, 'Gossip and Scandal', *Current Anthropology*, 4/3 (1963), 307–15.

of stories, of 'rumour' and 'common fame'. In Stondon, Hertfordshire, in 1618, rumours about George Butcher and Mrs Osbaston were passed around in words, rhymes, and writing, ending up in court, where George Curlewes deposed that he had heard William Serle say, 'George Butcher hath had carnall copulacon with the widowe Osboston, and if all thinges hit right he hath given her that, that will sticke by her forty wekes' and that 'there is a libell made of the widowe . . . yf you will go downe to the chequer, there you may see it.' He had also heard that 'the report was that William Searle . . . taught one Watson' a rhyme about Mrs Osbaston. Grace Curlewes, George's wife, heard that Robert Hills had found the rhyme on a bridge and carried it back to his alehouse. Hills was also prosecuted for passing the story on to William Barfoote.[19] Ostensibly, such story-telling was concerned with the health of the community, with the affirmation of its social identity through sexual regulation. But behind those concerns can be traced a deeper and more personal mass of meanings: the motives from which defamers spoke, the manner of their speech, and their intentions. Gossip can have considerable social power, but its force is shaped by the way individuals use it.[20] As important here as the implication of sex and pregnancy in the libel is the fact that a story is circulating, orally, in verse, and in writing: the very existence of gossip, even more than its content, can be discrediting. As well, moral regulation is not the most obvious aim of the words of insult. Frequently, slanders were very obviously driven by the impulse to develop a good tale: malice and humour were more important than reprimand. When John Lowther alleged Winifred Royse had committed fornication, he said 'that a man had her upp against a barell butt in a sellar and that one of her sonnes came out and cried oh gaffer gaffer doe not kill my mother'.[21] His embroideries, playing on Winifred's difficult position as a widowed mother, were designed not to regulate morals, but to humiliate.

More useful for our understanding of slander is a concept of gossip that stresses the gendered meaning of the word. In early modern society, women's talk about sex had different implications to that of men. In these testimonies, women's references to their own sexual experience frequently invoke ideas of shame and the model of

[19] Sara Osbaston *c.* William Serle (1618), DL/C 225, fos. 189, 191, and Sara Osbaston *c.* Robert Hills (1618), ibid. fos. 294v–5.

[20] Robert Paine, 'What is Gossip about? An Alternative Hypothesis', *Man*, NS 2/2 (1967), 278–85.

[21] Winifred Royse *c.* John Lowther (1627), DL/C 230, fo. 399.

confession; men talk, or boast, with none of this sense of moral responsibility. As well, for women, any kind of public speech, and most of all that about sex, could be interpreted as discrediting. Richard Brathwait's image of the ideal gentlewoman, presenting, despite its different target audience, many of the same ideas as the advice to women in household manuals, took as its antithesis a picture of a woman 'with a virago's heart':

> Nothing desir'd she more then to give affronts in publike places, which she did with that contempt, as the disgrace she aspers'd on others, was her sole content. Places of frequent were her Rendevou, where her imperious tongue runne descant on every subject ministred . . . Now could these courses anyway choose but cause that to be irreparably lost, which by any modest woman should be incomparably lov'd?[22]

The power of his virago's tongue discredits others; and at the same time, disgraces her own honour. In law the same connection was made. Defaming, marked out as a particularly female offence, was linked with scolding, the more explicit focus for public concern over women's disorderly speech; in New England law, defaming, like scolding, was punished by ducking.[23] While the actual scale of punishments for scolding is still in dispute, it is evident from the testimonies in slander cases that the nature of the crime and the symbols of its punishment loomed large in the popular imagination.[24] In the London courts, complaints against scolds raised some of the same issues as slander litigation. Catherine Barnaby was prosecuted in 1637 for 'scouldinge' words that used the familiar defamers' idiom of 'my husband's whore': 'that druncken queane that sitte there . . . hath made my husband spend £500 and hath nowe spent him beyond sea, and that she keepes company with none but pedlars and roagues and theeves'. And, aware of her neighbours' attempts to condemn her as a scold, Catherine Barnaby manipulated the very symbols of scolding back at them: 'if that any of them do give her an answer she presently runneth and fetcheth a bottle of hay and setteth it up and sayeth she

[22] Richard Brathwait, *The English Gentlewoman* (London, 1631), 124.

[23] Clara Ann Bowler, 'Carted Whores and White Shrouded Apologies: Slander in the County Courts of Seventeenth-Century Virginia', *The Virginia Magazine of History and Biography*, 85/4 (1977), 413.

[24] For this debate, see David Underdown, 'The Taming of the Scold: The Enforcement of Patriarchal Authority in Early Modern England', in Fletcher and Stevenson (eds.), *Order and Disorder*, and Martin Ingram, '"Scolding Women Cucked or Washed": A Crisis in Gender Relations in Early Modern England?', in Jenny Kermode and Garthine Walker (eds.), *Women, Crime and the Courts in Early Modern England* (London, 1994).

cannot be quiet for these roagues and Rascalls and therefore she setts it up for them to scould at'.[25] The 'bottle of hay' was what scolds were meant to scold at: it was a symbol that might very well have been used against Catherine herself. The idiom of defamation, and the familiar penalties for women's disorderly speech, ensured that women and men spoke with an awareness of the fundamentally different implications of their sexual talk. The gossipy talk of which slander might be a part, identified and condemned as typically female, gave women a particular standing in neighbourhood social relations. Telling stories and judging morals made women the brokers of oral reputation.[26]

Allied to other familiar forms of early modern speech, like reproof, gossip, or scolding, defamation also had an established identity of its own. Defamers and their victims in this period show themselves well aware of the legal rules of slander and the boundaries between actionable and nonactionable insults. They use the phrase 'whore of thy tongue' to avoid the penalties consequent on the word whore, or formulate careful, but still insulting, insults like this: 'I will not saie Thou art a whore nor that thou didst lie with thy master.'[27] The drama of defamation and its potential repercussions was a familiar one. It was represented too in contemporary culture. Defamation was depicted as the crisis point of tragedy in *Othello*, or of comedy in Nathan Field's *A Woman is a Weathercock* (1607).[28] In *Two Angry Women of Abington* Henry Porter constructed instead 'a womans jarre' between neighbours, with Mistris Barnes chastising her neighbour through her husband: 'She is a strumpet, and thou art no honest man | To stand in her defence against thy wife.'[29] The shift of blame, from a husband to his alleged mistress, was a manœuvre around which defamations persistently revolved.

Legally, the essential element of slander was malice. The determining factor in slander was whether it was 'uttered out of a malicious

[25] Office *c.* Catherine Barnaby (1637), GL MS 9057/1, fo. 174^{r-v}. See also Martin Ingram's reading of this case in '"Scolding Women Cucked or Washed"', 69–70.

[26] See, for perceptive comment on this aspect of gossip, Susan Harding, 'Women and Words in a Spanish Village', in Rayna R. Reiter (ed.), *Toward an Anthropology of Women* (New York, 1975), 301–5.

[27] Margaret Barrett *c.* Thomas Middleton (1635), DL/C 630, fo. 357^{v}.

[28] See Lisa Jardine, '"Why should he call her whore?" Defamation and Desdemona's Case', in Margaret Tudeau-Clayton and Martin Warner (eds.), *Addressing Frank Kermode: Essays in Criticism and Interpretation* (Basingstoke, 1991); Nathan Field, *A Woman is a Weathercock* (1607), ed. J. P. Collier (London, 1829), ii. p. i.

[29] Henry Porter, *The Pleasant history of the Two Angry Women of Abington* (London, 1599), I. ii. 522–7.

and angry mind'.[30] Slanderers defended themselves by claiming to have spoken jokingly or friendlily; witnesses against them describe their speech as 'angry', 'in choller' and 'uncharitable'. Defamation was legally about malicious imputations of crimes for 'hatred, profit or favour', and sixteenth-century literary conceptions of slander relied upon the same malicious root and its product, envy.[31] Contemporary works about speech and its dangers were particularly concerned with the difficulties of verbal control, calling for the tongue to be 'reared and hedged in with a double fence, to the end we might speake without offence'.[32] But as much as the result of impulsive 'choller', defamation could be the product of malicious forethought. The careful recital of corroborating circumstances, the choice of shaming adjectives, the drama of their presentation, suggest that many defamers watched their subjects and chose their moments. Either way, slander was constructed not as a project of normative moral regulation, but as one of creative malice.

Witnesses at the court paid an acute attention to the way and the place in which slander was spoken, not just to testify to the publicity of the allegations that were made, but because the circumstances and style of insult were as crucial as its content. The verbal exchanges of insult were, in many ways, like those of physical violence; insults shouted in the open street, with a crowd gathering to listen, were discrediting in themselves, whatever was said. It was being on the receiving end of malice like this, as much as the immoral or unacceptable nature of the deeds that were alleged, that the victims of slander felt discredited them.

To stress the range of non-sexual concerns that the words and style of insult expressed for its users and its victims, and the primacy of the drama of insult rather than its content, is not to deny the relationship between slander and sexual honour. It might, however, be productive to read that relationship slightly differently, by focusing not on the nature of sexual offences defamers described, but on the gendered moral standards that they referred to, but never discussed. Behind the stories of sex, a narrative about gender was being articulated. Sexual insults, as public social dramas, might perhaps be seen

[30] As defined in *Auctoritate Dei Patris* (1222), discussed in *Select Cases on Defamation*, Intro., pp. xxxii–xxxiv; see also H[enry] C[onsett], *The Practice of the Spiritual or Ecclesiastical Courts* (London, 1685), part VI. March, *Actions for Slaunder*, 104.

[31] Robert St George, '"Heated" Speech and Literacy', in David D. Hall and David Grayson Allen (eds.), *Seventeenth-Century New England* (Boston, 1985); Joyce Sexton, *The Slandered Woman in Shakespeare* (Victoria, BC, 1978), 16–35.

[32] C.G., *Praise of a Good Name*, 30.

as one of the repetitious acts or performances that, following Judith Butler, constitute gender.[33] We might usefully interpret the conventions and performances of sexual slander as one kind of definition, differentiating men and women through the implications of their sexual behaviour, describing women as the opposites of men, and whores as the opposite of honest women. Sexual insult defined whores again and again; in this way the meanings of gender are established through the sheer force of verbal repetition. Slander is one of the constitutive acts that establishes gender, repeating and rewriting its definitions of wives and whores, husbands and cuckolds.

THE EFFECTS OF SLANDER

If insult was often related only opaquely to real sexual events, this was reflected in litigation for slander. The legal definition of defamation presumed a direct correlation between insults like 'whore' and their material effects on a defamed person's reputation: defamation litigation was intended to be a response to the attack on reputation and honour that slander represented. But the effects of slander are less tangible than the high levels of litigation might suggest. Contemporary lawyers and commentators devoted little attention to the results slander had for women or the reasons women might go to law, concentrating instead on the various effects of slander on men. 'Actions of *defamation* are of a higher Nature, than they seem *primo intuitu* to be (a mans good Name being Equilibrious with his Life)', wrote John Godolphin in 1678, and it was men he meant.[34] This focus on men's reputations involved a close attention to the financial mechanics of defamation, effects that were less simply quantified for women. Slander affected, according to legal commentators, a man's calling, living, or profession, his inheritance, or his advancement; through these effects, the words of defamation could damage a man's whole life. The same kind of effects were understood to apply to women, but women's livelihood and 'advancement' were conceived in a much narrower sphere than men's. In place of the damage to trade or occupation by which men's dishonour could be measured, the effects of slander on women are related invariably to their marriage prospects. Marriage is women's only opportunity for the kind of advancement

[33] Judith Butler, *Gender Trouble: Feminism and the Subversion of Identity* (London, 1991), 139–41.

[34] John Godolphin, *Reportorium Canonicum; or, An Abridgement of the Ecclesiastical Laws of this Realm* (London, 1678), 516.

that makes up men's careers: 'a Woman not Married, cannot by intendment have so great advancement as by her Marriage, wherby she is sure of maintenance for her life, or during her Marriage, a dower and other benefits . . . and therefore by this *Slander* she is greatly prejudiced in that which be her Temporal advancement'.[35] So for women, sexual insults are both temporal and spiritual in effect because they damage material advancement and because livelihood depends on sexual good name. The same reasoning lay behind William Vaughan's righteous condemnation of those who slandered women: 'cursed be those Sycophants, who with their runnagate rumours and reports doe hinder Gentlewomen from their promotions in honest marriage'.[36] For contemporaries, marital advancement was the only measure of women's reputation.

At the courts, witnesses for single women sometimes used this measure. Ellen Brittanne's allegation that John Taverner and Elizabeth Matthewes were sexual partners was interpreted by a witness: 'yt cannot chuse but be a greate discredite unto her the said Matthewe to be soe evill spoken of by Ellen Brittanne in such manner . . . being a mayden and in the waie of preferment in marriage'. At Star Chamber, Richard and Agnes Nightingale from Staffordshire complained of a scurrilous rhyme circulated before their marriage about Agnes and her supposed suitors, alleging that the three authors had 'confederated amongst themselves . . . howe they might hinder the preferment of Agnes'.[37] Their word, 'preferment', echoes the financial language evoked by writers on honour, of 'advancement' and 'promotions'. And yet it was not until after her marriage that Anne Nightingale took this slur on her 'preferment' to court. It may be that only her husband's resources enabled her to do so; but it looks, too, as if the slur on her husband for marrying her was a more potent motive for litigation than the damage to her prospects.

Writers and preachers against slander focused on the honour of unmarried women, understanding 'chastity' always to mean 'virginity'.[38] But the women who sued for slander were mostly married, and

[35] Godolphin, *Repertorium Canonicum*, 517; Godolphin goes on to argue that women can sue for such insults in the common law, because of their material implications, but there is no evidence of women having used this argument.

[36] William Vaughan, *The Spirit of Detraction, Coniured and Convicted in Seven Circles* (London, 1611), 346.

[37] Elizabeth Mathewe *c.* Ellen Brittanne (1620), DL/C 227, fo. 176; Richard & Agnes Nightingale *v.* John Rotton & others (1610), PRO STAC 8 220/31, m. 14.

[38] See Clarissa W. Atkinson, ' "Precious Balsam in a Fragile Glass": The Ideology of Virginity in the Later Middle Ages', *Jl. Family History*, 8 (1983), 131–43.

their marital 'preferment' already established. William Vaughan's long treatise on detraction was a personal response not to attacks on an unmarried woman, but to slanders of his wife.[39] The most obvious effect of such slanders on married women was severe: female adultery, in the eyes of many, could lead to the sundering of the marriage bond; for more radical Protestant reformers, it could dissolve it entirely. Contemporary commentators made surprisingly little of this. While they were prepared to imagine suitors withdrawing from a woman reputed to be unchaste, they were not, apparently, ready to argue that rumour could be enough to discredit a woman in the eyes of her husband. In the courts, the logical consequences of slander's potential to injure married women was explained more fully. Witnesses and defamers assumed more readily that men might reasonably treat suspicion of their wives' infidelity as a threat to their marriage. When Margaret Smith was accused of saying to Anne Fanne 'thow art a whore thow hast dishonested my howse for I did see Hopkins and thee togither he with his breeches downe and bothe your bare bellies togither', one witness testified that Anne's husband had been so offended he would not let her lie with him and Anne had gone to her mother in the country.[40] Star Chamber plaintiffs, more concerned than those of the church courts to show the exact dimensions of potential damage, sometimes alleged that defamers had a conscious intent to provoke separation between husband and wife.[41]

While commentators focused exclusively on the effects dishonour had on women's marriages, litigants at the courts made some more wide-ranging assessments of dishonour. As sexual behaviour had implications for women's whole characters, so, in theory, sexual insult could affect their whole lives. Like men, women might be concerned with their professional name: Elizabeth Ashley, slandered by Alice Gibbes as 'a whore and a maggottie whore and a maggottie jade', brought a witness to depose that she had been 'discredited in her reputacon and calling to be soe evell spoken of'.[42] Few women, though, made any reference to the kind of occupational identity that 'calling' suggests.[43] Other witnesses talked about their own reactions to the

[39] Sharpe, *Defamation and Sexual Slander*, 3. Neighbours had apparently suggested that her death, through being struck by lightning, was divine retribution for a sinful life.

[40] Anne Fanne *c.* Margaret Smith (1610), DL/C 219, fos. 245ᵛ–6.

[41] See e.g. John Bennett *v.* Thomas Forster (1614), PRO STAC 8 62/23, m. 2.

[42] Elizabeth Ashley *c.* Alice Gibbes (1621), DL/C 228, fos. 70ᵛ–71.

[43] By the 18th c., according to Anna Clark, women's role in the public workplace was a central issue in the use of 'whore' as a sexual insult: Anna Clark, 'Whores and Gossips: Sexual Reputation in London 1770–1825', in Arina Angerman, Geerte

defamation, telling the court when, and how, they had started to think ill of former friends. Witnesses in another case spoke of the effect on their friendships with the plaintiff. When Mary Wharton accused Anne Holstead that someone had 'rubde the skynne of thy knees and thy thighes', Elizabeth Jacob testified that having heard the words, 'she thincketh not so well of the producent Ann Holsteed as she did before the speakinge of the said woords . . . And presentlye upon the speakinge of the said woords imagined veary ill of the producent and she yet doth till she hath cleard her selfe.' William Hopwood deposed in the same case that 'he did verily think . . . the producent had played the whore . . . and notwithstanding that [he] was great friends with the producent he did tell his . . . wife that he was persuaded that the words about the falling out of the producent with Mary Wharton was a bad matter and very suspicious and as yet this deponent cannot think well of the producent until she hath cleared herself'.[44] The key words here, 'imagined', 'persuaded', 'suspicious', suggest the potent ambiguity of reputation: influences, suspicions, and rumours were the evidence of honour and dishonour.

Most witnesses, though, said no more than that the plaintiff was 'much injured' in her 'reputation', 'name', or 'credit'. These terms are more specific than they look: each suggests a different understanding of honour and dishonour, based on personal history, 'common fame', family, or material standing. Most complex, and multivalent, was the word 'credit', a term both witnesses and clerks resorted to again and again. As a measure of honour, its financial implications suggest a reputation that can be spent, wasted or accrued. As well, its Latin form provides the witnesses' initial—and often their sole—response to questions in court: *credit*, s/he believes it, or *non credit*, s/he does not believe it. Its English form still carries the implications of belief, which are echoed again in the use of 'credit' to define witnesses' honesty, often under attack in the more complicated cases.[45] A central word in slander litigation, 'credit' encompassed a series of overlapping meanings that included good neighbourliness, trustworthiness, financial independence, sexual virtue, and social class. Personal credit was a central issue for the court: litigants regularly challenged the credit of witnesses on the other side, and the men and women who came to

Binnema, Annemieke Keunen, Vefie Poels, and Jacqueline Zirkzee (eds.), *Current Issues in Women's History* (London, 1989).

[44] Anne Holstead *c.* Simon Wharton (1591), DL/C 214, pp. 83, 95.

[45] On the intersections of different meanings of credit, see Susan Dwyer Amussen, *An Ordered Society: Gender and Class in Early Modern England* (Oxford, 1988), 52–5.

depose had to give accounts not just of their own standing but that of their fellow witnesses. Good credit was described in assessments like these: 'of good name', 'of honest conversation'. For men, another crucial phrase was 'able to live of himself'. While women were not expected to be financially independent, other pointers to their discredit were available: 'very poore', 'mends old stockings in her stall'. A name for scolding, defaming, and living unquietly—a kind of reputation that attached itself particularly to women—made women's words suspect: 'a very disquiett woman amongest her neighbours for the which ther was first a warrant . . . to duck her', 'a scoulding and a very unquiett woman'; 'a disquieter of her neighbors', 'a whisperer betwene neighbor and neighbor and a harkner at mens dores and one that maketh disaffection betwene neighbors', and 'a comon slaunderer of her neighbours and hath therafter been presented to the official of the Archdeacon of London and before him was convicted'.[46] Women's credit was measured, too, by social standing and sexual morals: 'married but liveth apart from her husband', 'delivered of a child . . . within fourteen weekes or thereabouts after she was married to her now husband'.[47]

For both men and women, then, credit was measured through a combination of factors; but for women, that combination was filtered through the lens of sexual honesty. Sexual morality was not the only gauge of female reputation: for women, neighbourly behaviour, hard work, and quiet living were some of the factors that might give a good name. The nature of the source material leaves us relatively little information about these areas: we know far more about dishonour than about honour. What is clear is that for women, sexuality remained a vulnerable point in the construction and destruction of reputation. Whatever made a good reputation, sexual discredit could threaten it. A slanderous dispute in the parish of St Alphage in 1593 illuminates the interplay between different kinds of reputation and credit for women. At its centre was Margaret Durrant, a married cook, whose maid, dismissed from her service for theft, had gone to Roger Pepper who, according to witnesses, 'kept her . . . to get from her what he could' about Margaret's behaviour. Roger soon began saying, first to neighbours and then to the parish officials, that Margaret had lived incontinently with a beer brewer. One of those to whom Roger told the story, the parish constable, explained that he was unwilling to convict Margaret because of the differences between her credit and that

[46] DL/C 218, pp. 247, 231 (1608); DL/C 213, pp. 297–9 (1587).
[47] DL/C 230, fo. 458 (1627); DL/C 218, p. 233 (1608).

of her servant. Margaret's credit was higher because of her reputation for hard work: the constable deposed that he 'because he saw that the said producent Durrant allwayes took great paines and laboured hard for hir living was loth to draw that woman into discreditt withowt desert'. Her maid's credit was lower because her claim to have locked Margaret and the brewer in a room together put her own sexual morality in question, and because of the reputation of Roger Pepper who was backing her accusation: the constable deposed that

> considering with him selfe the quality of the accused and that she [the maid] had in effect confessed that she was bawd unto the said producente he told hir that if it wear so she was being the bawd was as bad as they and hee doubted whither hir credit wear such as that creditt might be geven to hir woordes but if she could bring forth any person of creditt that wold give testimony of hir good beehavior he wold then give creditt unto hir.[48]

Here, each party's credit is weighed carefully and comparatively. For women as well as men, money and hard work could define credit. But the constable's unwillingness to accept the word of a servant who could be accused of bawdry, and his ready conception of how easily Margaret Durrant could be discredited by his decision, reveal how far women's credit also depended, precariously, on sexual reputation.

More tenuous than men's, women's credit comprised some of the same concerns, but was always liable as men's was not to be devalued by sexual rumours. Credit such as that Margaret Durrant had attained, depending on financial independence and a reputation for honest work, was harder for women to achieve than men; once established, it was still conceived vulnerable to any suggestion of sexual unchastity. Words, and especially men's words, were endowed with an extraordinary power in deciding women's reputation. Elizabeth Wilson was slandered by a man in 1632: 'I will prove her to be a whore by other mens speeches.'[49] Samuel Rowlands's dramatized gossips' conversation imagined the speech of a husband to his 'gossiping' wife, with the familiar ring of men's confidence in their own credit:

> But for my wife I do not care a Pin
> What scurvy minde soever she be in
> To slaunder me with Whores; my credit's knowne,
> She hath a lying tongue (friends) of her owne.[50]

[48] Marmaduke Butler [the man named in the accusation of adultery] & Margaret Durrant *c.* Roger Pepper (1593), DL/C 214, pp. 402, 421, 437, 438.

[49] Elizabeth Wilson *c.* Pritchard (1632), DL/C 233, fo. 323^{v}.

[50] Samuel Rowlands, *A Crew of kind Gossips, all met to be merrie: Complayning of their Husbands, With their Husbands answeres in their own defence* (London, 1613), sig. E1^{v}.

When credit was measured, men's speeches were valued higher than women's.

Yet while oral culture and print reiterated that women's credit was entirely vulnerable to slurs on their sexual reputation, the women who complained of sexual slander rarely brought any evidence of the devaluation of their reputation by the names they had been called. In the records of slander litigation there are very few suggestions of the concrete effects of the injuries that were so great as to impel injured parties to prosecute. Only occasionally did plaintiffs allege their marital prospects or their current married life had been damaged. One witness in 1590 measured a woman's loss of name in exact, economic terms, after she was called 'an arrant whore . . . that laye firste with the master and then with the man in myll lane': 'Susan Mores name', he deposed,

> is by reason of the saide scandalous wordes . . . spreade about in all the cuntry thereaboutes and she the producent become to be talked of comonly amongste the neighbours, to the greate discreadit of the producent, And . . . he verily thinketh the producent to have rather given £20 then to have had suche a speach goe upon her, as throughe the saide speaches is gonne and doth yett goe, and is talked of, for he saieth the producent hath bynn taken of the neighbours thereaboutes for a very honest woman.[51]

Even from this unusually lengthy and precise account of the damage defamation did as it circulated, the only substantial effect of slanderous talk seems to be more talk. Susan Higgambottom's testimony on the damage Christopher Thompson did to Anne Pridgen by calling her whore strikes the same note: 'forasmuche as people are commonly given to speake the worste of a woman whome they heere to be evell spoken of she thincketh the good name of Anne Pridgen to be impayred and hurte by the said Thompson.'[52] Evil words lead to more evil words, nothing more substantial.

At the same time as witnesses tried to pin down the discrediting of slandered women, they felt impelled to stress the credit of the plaintiff whose case they were supporting. Elizabeth Harwood, witnessing for Alice Collet after she was called a whore by Agnes Simpson, deposed that Alice's good name was 'much impeared among hir honest neighbours . . . and yet she thincketh hir an honest woman'.[53]

51 Susan More *c.* Elizabeth Dymsdalle (1591), DL/C 214, pp. 18–19. The dispute was continued in a subsequent case, Elizabeth Dymcross [Dymsdalle] *c.* John More (ibid. 21), in which Susan's husband was accused of attacking Elizabeth Dymsdalle both physically and verbally and she of throwing a pail of burning coals at him.

52 Anne Pridgen *c.* Christopher Thompson (1588), DL/C 213, pp. 432, 445.

53 Alice Collet *c.* Agnes Simpson (1593), DL/C 214, fo. 399.

Reputation in the neighbourhood was understood to be a reliable measure of credit not just socially, but in the courts, where compurgation by neighbours could prove innocence or guilt. Plaintiffs complaining of damaged reputations trod an uneasy balance between proving that damage and suggesting they had lost all credit.

The relationship between slander and litigation was problematized still further by the ways in which women's use of the law was represented. While litigation cannot have been the only accepted response to insult, the two were very closely linked in the popular imagination. It could be conceived as dishonouring in itself to let an insult go unchallenged. In a dispute with Christopher Mortymer about the mistreatment of her maid, Elizabeth Aldeworth mentioned 'honesty', and Christopher took it up: 'Alas alas, I cannot tell what you call honestye, but you wer called whore, and prevye whore to your tethe, and ye wer gladd to take it quyetlye and putt it upp.' Elizabeth sued these words as a slander; apparently, failing to respond to such slurs could be read as proof of guilt.[54] But concepts of honour might also problematize litigation. Discussing one's sexual reputation in court was, in theory, hardly the action of a perfectly chaste and honourable woman. Self-defence against accusations of whoredom could be seen as contributing to dishonour, in perpetuating the discourse about sex. One woman defended herself against such suggestions in 1610, 'Had I had any more lawe than an honest woman should have?'[55] Clearly the argument about defending modesty by litigation could be used both ways.

Battles over honour and words were evidently more complex and more intangible than the legal process assumed. The power that words had to damage reputation had its roots in the very nature of that reputation: reputations, in a largely oral world, were what people said. The material effects of oral reputation remain hard to trace. Slander might have serious practical consequences; equally, in many cases the insults reported to the court may have had little or no quantifiable effects. What, then, does slander tell us about honour in practice? Most of all, these records suggest that the ideologies of morals, represented as rigid, were in practice fairly flexible. Anna Clark has argued that women in eighteenth century London defined to a certain extent their own codes of sexual morality, dependent on other values than the precepts of sexual honour: the same is surely true for this period.[56] In the language of sexual insult, women and men con-

[54] Elizabeth Aldeworth *c.* Christopher Mortymer (1572), DL/C 211/1, fo. 104^{v}.

[55] Roda Greenrise *c.* William Pinge (1610), DL/C 219, fo. 174^{v}.

[56] Clark, 'Whores and Gossips'.

structed verbal abuse that mostly followed the moral norms of contemporary culture in blaming women for illicit sex, but that sometimes used other words and different ideas to condemn men instead. Evidently, not everyone believed, voiced, and acted on the same moral standards; the records of the moral offences the church courts dealt with testify not to a shared, internalized morality, but to standards that were defined and redefined in public, repeated in church, in the street, and in print, and reinterpreted as insult.

THE CONTEXT OF LITIGATION

If slanderous words did not necessarily lead to quantifiable damage, and litigation was not the obvious response to such damage, the dynamics of defamation are more complex than they seem. The context of defamation cases reveals their part in the broader fabric of social relations: as insult proved a vehicle for diverse neighbourhood disputes, so too did litigation. In many cases the momentum of litigation came to be part of the whole fabric of neighbourhood dispute. Complexes of cases, between a circle of litigants in one street or one neighbourhood, built up as one pair after another took a case to court; 30 per cent of defamation cases were connected to others at the same court, often involving both the same parties. In the seventeenth century an increasing number of cases were part of a larger network of litigation involving spouses, neighbours, and relatives. An incident in the churchyard of Waltham Cross in 1617, where Edward Turner pushed Mary Weatherhead, Mary insulted him, and with three other women, pulled off Mary Turner's apron and called her 'a scurvy queane', led to four separate defamation cases, each alleging a different sequence of events and words.[57] People might also develop a habit of litigation: 10 per cent of litigants appeared at the court more than once, and another 4 per cent had spouses who had also been litigants.[58] Most of these multiple litigants were simply responding to cases against themselves with further lawsuits, but some were involved in webs of neighbourhood dispute and litigation. In the early seventeenth century one woman and her neighbours came regularly

[57] John & Mary Weatherhead *c.* Edward Turner (1617), DL/C 225, fos. 1 ff.; Mary Turner *c.* Mary Weatherhead, ibid. 7 ff.; Edward Turner *c.* Mary Weatherhead (1617), ibid. 101 ff.; Edward Turner *c.* Susan Muckley & Elizabeth May (1617), ibid. 101^{v} ff.

[58] These figures refer to cases that reached the deposition books; the total proportion of interrelated cases is probably higher. Of these cases, 242 out of 2,454 litigants came to the court more than once, and their spouses account for a further 99 reappearances. Of 1373 defamation cases, 409 involved multiple litigants.

to the consistory court with a series of cases that dwelt on some long-running themes. Elizabeth Barwicke, an innkeeper and the wife and later the widow of a sailor in Wapping, was involved in at least twelve cases in fifteen years. In 1612 her father, a churchwarden, presented one of their neighbours, Susan Chaddocke, for being with child when her husband was at sea; a few months later Susan took her revenge by telling her neighbours that Elizabeth, whose husband was also away, was pregnant, and bragging of this to Elizabeth's father, saying 'nowe it was quid for quo or it was come home by his owne dore'. Elizabeth's mother was also at the receiving end of slanders about her daughter, one from a constable saying 'all the bread in wappinge would not stopp the mouthes of them that did say that . . . Elizabeth Barwicke . . . was a whore'. In Wapping, with its high proportion of husbands absent as sailors, accusations of illegitimate pregnancy were always rife; four years later Susan accused Elizabeth of bastardy again, and Elizabeth herself used similar allegations to defame her neighbours, disrupting a christening in 1626 by claiming one of the men present was the father of another child. These particular slanders also made much use of the idea of a family honour vested in a woman. Elizabeth was insulted not only to her face, but through her parents; allegations of her whoredom were meant to reflect on them. Much later in 1628 she herself adopted the same strategies against another woman, Susan May, telling Susan that she was 'Captayne Greens whore and had layd with as many men as there were tiles on side her house' and backing this up by telling Susan's mother that she was 'bawde to her own daughter'. Through fifteen years of neighbourhood and family disputes, the same strategies of abuse provided the foundation of conflict: accusations of bastardy and of family dishonour provided running grievances which brought Elizabeth, her family, her neighbours, and her witnesses into confrontation with each other on a regular basis.[59]

In disputes like these, minor disagreements, often themselves the symptoms of a wider tension, escalated through sexual insult into vio-

[59] Elizabeth Barwicke *c.* Susan Chaddocke (1613), DL/C 221, fo. 1293; Elizabeth Barwicke *c.* William Mott (1613), DL/C 221, fo. 1319; Elizabeth Pett [Barwicke's mother] *c.* Susan Chaddocke (1613), DL/C 221, fo. 1506; Elizabeth Barwicke *c.* Susan Chaddocke (1617), DL/C 225, fo. 75; John Dearsly *c.* Elizabeth Barrett [Barwicke] (1627), DL/C 230, fo. 292, and see also Mary Wharton *c.* Elizabeth Barret [Barwicke] (1627), DL/C 230, fo. 425; Susan May *c.* Elizabeth Barwicke (1629), DL/C 231, fo. 109; Elizabeth Barwicke *c.* Susan May (1629), DL/C 231, fo. 114; Susan Johnson *c.* Elizabeth Barwicke (1629), DL/C 231, fo. 115^{v}; and Elizabeth Barwicke *c.* Susan Johnson, ibid. 115.

lent words, sometimes physical actions, and litigation. Particularly for women, taking insults to court was a powerful way of continuing dispute. The instant transformation of victim into plaintiff meant that the defamer who had insisted on her power to determine sexual reputation ended up on trial as well as the defamed; at court the reputation and credit of both were at stake.[60] The legal costs added to slander cases a financial investment. Christopher Thompson, sued once by Anne Pridgen in the Court of Arches, and accused of continuing to call her whore 'or otherwise entreate her evell if no bodie were bye', responded 'why sholde I not I must have some sport for my money But . . . I will not call the whore no more I have paied for it'. Another man boasted 'I have fower score poundes nowe to spend and when that is spent, I can fetch fower score poundes more to spend to prove thee a whore.'[61] As much as a disincentive to litigation, the penalty of paying costs might come to be perceived as a profitable investment in devaluing another's credit.

In the eyes of contemporaries, litigation, like sexual insult itself, might be born out of malice and connected with earlier disputes. Complaints about the increasing numbers of suits assumed that the suing of defamation was a part of broader social relations, and that unnecessary suits were started by the use of the courts for private contentions: 'that a man should flee to the law out of malice, and make the Courts of Justice maintainers of every small and vaine brabble, this seems to me utterly unlawful and intolerable', wrote John March.[62] Here, it does not seem helpful to distinguish, as historians have tended to do, a particular brand of 'vexatious litigation'; rather, litigation very often took place in a social context fraught with established conflicts and frayed tempers. To these litigants, going to court seemed not a malicious legal manipulation, but a legitimate weapon in neighbourhood dispute, one that answered testimony on the street with testimony in the court and that lifted a dispute about sexual behaviour into a whole new register where everyone's credit and reputation was in question.

The resort to litigation rarely meant pursuing it to its close. Final sentences were potentially both humiliating and expensive. Penances

[60] Here, see also Clare Brant's exploration of the interactions of law and authorship for women seeking to vindicate themselves: Clare Brant, 'Speaking of Women: Scandal and the Law in the Mid-Eighteenth Century', in Clare Brant and Diane Purkiss (eds.), *Women, Texts and Histories, 1575–1760* (London, 1992).

[61] Pridgen *c.* Thompson (1588), DL/C 213, pp. 431–2; Joan Manning *c.* John Jent *als* Joyner (1620), DL/C 227, fo. 108v.

[62] March, *Actions for Slaunder*, 4.

for defamation were as public as the offence, and defendants might be sentenced to make a formal retraction of their words and an apology to their victim in church.[63] For most people the costs of litigation were an even greater concern. Defendants found guilty were liable for the plaintiff's expenses as well as their own, and a complex case could easily cost as much as £10. But such endings were rare: far more often than other cases, defamation cases were dropped after witnesses had given evidence. Fewer than one in five defamation cases requested and were granted a formal sentence. For many people, the articulation of their dispute in court just once enabled them to reach a compromise before the judge's decision. Friends, family, and neighbours took an active part in bringing parties to terms, doing so most often over meals and drink, at the end of which the disputants would make public resolutions of peace sealed by a familiar toast: 'I drincke to you and all the malice or hatred I beare to you I putt into this glasse.'[64] Clergy and local gentry were also enlisted to intervene. Rarely do the specifics of these settlements survive, but one case suggests the particular arrangements that might be made to satisfy injured parties. The minister of St Margaret Pattens, John Lysbye, who was defamed in the church by Ann Symes in 1586, complained to his vestry the next year that another parishioner, Richard Baker, had also insulted him, in words 'tendyng towards the paryll of the said Lysbies lyff yf they had been trew'.[65] The meeting settled the dispute by arranging that Richard Baker would provide Lysbye's wife and servants with paid work sewing hose for him: it is a peculiar example both of the potential for translating words into actual pecuniary damage and compensation, and of the potential for conflating the sexual honour of one member of the household with the income of others. Evidently, achieving a judicial decision was not the main purpose of defamation litigation. More important was the power that prosecution could be used to invoke in the community. The familiar threats of the law, and the penances that, however infrequently they were used, loomed large in many people's imaginations, gave the church courts a considerable significance in neighbourhood discourse.

The church courts actively supported out-of-court settlements, with an eye to conciliation between the parties. It might, then, be argued

[63] Ingram, *Church Courts*, 294. For other examples of penances, see Hubert Hall, 'Some Elizabethan Penances in the Diocese of Ely', *Trans. of the Royal Historical Society* 3rd ser., 1 (1907), 263–77.

[64] This one is from Anne Haynes *c.* Rachel Cheereseley (1622), DL/C 228, fo. 140.

[65] St Margaret Pattens Churchwardens' Accounts, GL MS 4570/2, p. 434 (1587).

that one function of litigation was to promote reconciliation. The courts, however, were not the obvious choice for this purpose. The formal processes of making complaints and calling witnesses aroused hostility and divisiveness. Defamers and defamed men and women who wished to reach an amicable settlement could avail themselves of a wide range of more informal ways of 'making friends', using the mediation of respected neighbours, gentry, or ministers, and the social ceremony of eating and drinking together to bind their reconciliation.[66] While litigation rarely led to judicial penalties, it was essentially used as a confrontational process, in which litigants enlisted friends and neighbours to defend their own story and undermine the words and credit of their opponents. The courts, although they rarely passed sentences, represented nevertheless a forum for continuing and formalizing dispute, as much as a place of reconciliation. Invoking the process of litigation seems more likely to have perpetuated a dispute than to have ended it; the response of some defendants to litigation was to start their own case.

It was in the light of this use of the courts to 'maintain', in the words of John March, local and personal disputes that contemporaries complained of the increase in slander litigation. Slander and its prosecution were seen primarily as occasions, not of regulation or reconciliation, but of disruption and dysfunction. Inside and outside the court, the language of insult disrupted, rather than consolidated, social relations. By contrast, it *did* confirm gender relations, repeating the established vision of whoredom that acted as the admonitory contrast to honest womanhood. Yet insulting words, guarantors as they were of the patriarchal sexual order, gave women a surprising scope for action: in response to them, women grasped the legal responsibility for their reputations and ended up, in ever-increasing numbers, fighting legal battles over their names.

The intersection of slander, morality, and honour was more complicated than the apparent logic of litigation suggests. Insult was more than a project of moral regulation; the material effects of sexual slander were rarely substantial enough to constitute the main motivation for litigation; and honour was sufficiently flexible to make credit and discredit, reputation and disrepute, a nebulous yet powerful affair. It was precisely this flexibility that made honour so potent both as an idea and in practice: it was the power of naming the sin, defining

[66] See J. A. Sharpe, '"Such Disagreement Betwyx Neighbours": Litigation and Human Relations in Early Modern England', in John Bossy (ed.), *Disputes and Settlements: Law and Human Relations in the West* (Cambridge, 1983).

honesty and dishonesty, that gave slander its weight. Similarly, the intangible, unquantifiable effects of slander made it both manageable and uncontrollable. Materially incalculable, the implications of spoken insult could still be huge.

The morality to which insults laid claim bore some relation to the ideals asserted variously by church, state, and culture; it could also be more individual and flexible. But the fairly negotiable ideas of honour articulated by slanderers were always shaped by the implicit rules of gender roles and gender relations. The constant and persistent gender difference in insults, in physiological perceptions of the sexes, and in the implications of sex meant that as sexual insult defined sexual honesty, it also defined gender itself. The profound misogyny that underpins so many of these insults—whether they are used by women or by men—is absolutely central to them: the word 'whore' stood for a whole way of defining women. Sexual honour, negotiable and flexible to a certain degree, was also a potent representation of the understandings and rules of gender that shaped women's experience of sex and, as we shall see in the next chapters, marriage.

5
The Economy of Courtship

The moral culture of sexual honour centred on the marital relationship. Cuckolded husbands, whoring wives, and women who wore the breeches were the prime targets of insults that focused not just on sex, but on the organization of the household economy, on transactions of money, consumption, and power in marriage; and it was, most often, married women who responded to insult with allegations that their reputations had been defamed. How did the marital household work in practice? What were the rules of conjugality by which marriages were shaped, and judged, in daily life? The next two chapters turn from litigation over disturbed relations between neighbours, to that over conflicts between men and women: betrothed, married, and separated couples. Before the solemnization of marriage, couples came to the court in battles over the establishment of a conjugal relationship, pleading or denying proofs of contracts to marry; after it, they came to obtain separation, on the grounds that the marital relationship had been destroyed. Testimonies in both cases describe at length the economic, affectional, and sexual relations that constituted conjugality, and the different parts men and women were expected to play both before and during marriage.

Before marriage, litigation came to the court on the grounds of broken contracts of marriage. Such contracts, promises to marry exchanged in public, supported by both an established popular ritual and a well-defined legal context, marked a key point in the series of stages of commitment that constituted the process of early modern marriage.[1] In medieval custom marriage contracts had themselves constituted legally valid marriage, but by the sixteenth century they functioned more as the foundation for solemnization in church.[2]

[1] On the process of marriage, see Beatrice Gottlieb, 'The Meaning of Clandestine Marriage', in Tamara K. Hareven and Robert Wheaton (eds.), *Family and Sexuality in French History* (Philadelphia, 1980), 49–83.

[2] On this development see Martin Ingram, 'Spousals Litigation in the English Ecclesiastical Courts, c.1350–c.1640', in R. B. Outhwaite (ed.), *Marriage and Society: Studies in the Social History of Marriage* (London, 1981), 35–57. On marriage law and social

Litigation over contested contracts was a stock part of church court business in medieval England and Europe. By the sixteenth century the ambiguities of customary betrothal were suggesting to commentators both inside and outside the church a threat to the dual investments of family interest and church ceremony in the establishment of conjugality.[3] In Europe, Catholic and Protestant reformations achieved a regularization of the rules of private contracts.[4] Similar projects in England never came to fruition, but the church courts did their own work: apparently increasingly uncomfortable with the ambiguities of verbal contracts, judges were less likely to give favourable decisions to plaintiffs and by the early seventeenth century contracts had dwindled to a tiny part of the courts' business. The advantages of betrothal remained clear. Advice writers, many of them clergy, pointed out the useful function such contracts could perform, providing a period of exploration and reflection before the final marriage, a time when couples entered a new status: 'neither simply single, nor actually married'.[5] The ambiguities of betrothal were its strength as well as its weakness.

At the courts, litigants and their witnesses fought over the interpretations of those ambiguities. Their stories present personal, original versions of the preliminaries to marriage. Most importantly and most usefully for the historian, litigants and witnesses were concerned to interpret conjugality. As women and men fought to establish or to deny a binding commitment, they referred both to the words of

practice in the earlier period, see Charles Donahue, Jr., 'The Canon Law on the Formation of Marriage and Social Practice in the Later Middle Ages', *Jl. of Family History*, 8 (1983), 144–58, and Michael M. Sheehan, 'The Formation and Stability of Marriage in Fourteenth-Century England: Evidence of an Ely Register', *Mediaeval Studies*, 33 (1971), 228–63. The political dimensions of the marital contract are examined in Mary Lyndon Shanley, 'Marriage Contract and Social Contract in Seventeenth-Century English Political Thought', *Western Political Quarterly*, 32/1 (1979), 79–91.

[3] Gottlieb, 'The Meaning of Clandestine Marriage'; see also Sarah Hanley, 'Family and State in Early Modern France: The Marriage Pact', in Marilyn J. Boxer and Jean Quataert (eds.), *Connecting Spheres: Women in the Western World, 1500 to the Present* (Oxford, 1987).

[4] On the changes, see James Brundage, *Law, Sex and Christian Society in Medieval Europe* (Chicago, 1987), ch. 11.

[5] William Gouge, *Of Domesticall Duties: Eight Treatises* (London, 1622), 199. On judicial attitudes in the mid-sixteenth century see Ralph Houlbrooke, 'The Making of Marriage in Early Modern England: Evidence from the Records of Matrimonial Contract Litigation', *Jl. of Family History*, 10 (1985), 350, and for a longer period, Ingram, 'Spousals Litigation', 53. Other Puritan advice writers who advocated spousals included Matthew Griffith, *Bethel: or, A Forme for Families* (London, 1633), 272, and Daniel Rogers, *Matrimoniall Honour, Or, The mutuall Crowne and comfort of godly, loyall, and chaste Marriage* (London, 1642), 121.

betrothal and to a set of rituals and customs which provided their context. They focused, in particular, on the transactions of courtship: the exchange, offer, or refusal of words, gestures, emotions, and gifts. In those transactions gender roles were carefully defined. Men offered words and gifts with implications; women refused, accepted, or gave conditional answers to gain time. The shape and meanings of these rituals were both specific to the special time of courtship, and intimately related to what happened after marriage. The words and gestures of courtship, then, are significant as evidence of a particular life stage for women and men, a time with its own rules and rituals, and one of particular import to women, as Natalie Davis has suggested: if women's identity in early modern society was constituted in part by the sense of 'being given away', the time when they answered marriage proposals and 'gave themselves away' could constitute a special moment of self-definition and autonomy.[6] Rituals also carried important implications for the understanding and practice of gender in marriages, households, and communities. The roles women and men played in courtship, and the relationship that was established between them before they became domestic partners, were laden with connections to the conventions of gender roles both in marriage and in wider society: courtship, for early modern couples, both presaged marriage and constituted an entirely different and unique state. The records of litigation also represent some very individual interpretations of marital convention. Within the gendered rituals of courtship, men and women found ways of investing conventional exchanges of words and gifts with personal meanings, making them specific to place, age, and status. In London, litigation about marriage contracts reflected the city's unique conditions, and the court heard stories that were shaped by its individual marriage market. The depositions made to the London church courts between 1570 and 1640 expose the particular functions and the gendered meanings of marriage ritual for women and men in the city. As historians using these records as a source for early modern courtship have argued, while the courtships recorded in them are exceptional in that they did not end, as they were expected to, in marriage, they record a vast amount of detail about both typical behaviour and deviations from it. Not just these details, though, but the stories in which they are embedded are

[6] Natalie Zemon Davis, 'Boundaries and the Sense of Self in Sixteenth Century France', in Thomas C. Heller, Morton Sosna, and David E. Wellbery (eds.), *Reconstructing Individualism: Autonomy, Individuality and the Self in Western Thought* (Stanford, Calif., 1986), 61.

important; designed specifically to prove the existence of a bond of marriage, they focus intentionally on the material, affectional, and physical exchanges that define conjugality.

In London as elsewhere, cases of disputed marriage contracts were becoming rare in the late sixteenth century. They came to the church courts, as part of the spiritual jurisdiction's authority over the conjugal state, only when other formal and informal attempts at conciliation failed. About thirty cases a year came to the London consistory court in the 1570s, constituting a third of all sex and marriage litigation; by the 1620s this was down to nine cases a year, and marriage contracts represented only 6 per cent of sex and marriage suits. The number of cases calling witnesses, whose details are discussed here, fell correspondingly, from five a year in the earlier period to one or two in the later. The London court does not seem to have followed the trend elsewhere, towards a lower rate of sentencing and in particular, sentencing in the plaintiff's favour; but the drop in numbers in the seventeenth century had a similar effect, in that by the 1630s, contracts of marriage were no longer a significant part of the church courts' business.[7] Nevertheless, suits for marriage contract continued to follow an established convention and to hold a place in the culture of courtship. They also played a certain part in the growth of women's litigation that characterized the London court between 1570 and 1640. While in the sixteenth century male plaintiffs predominated in London as they did elsewhere, by the 1620s and 1630s the proportion of women's suits had increased from a third to two-thirds.

Male and female, most of the litigants at the London court were young, marrying for the first time. Some were the children of London tradesmen and craftsmen, working and living with their parents. Some belonged to London's large group of servants and apprentices, living with employers away from their birthplace and family. Others were widows and widowers, with children, businesses, and property to consider as they made a new settlement. A number of them were noticeably better-off than the litigants in defamation suits: the size and

[7] For the cases in this study, 70% (16 of 23) of final sentences in the years 1572–92 were in the plaintiff's favour, as were 60% (9 of 15) in the 1620s and 1630s. This is a much higher proportion than cases in Ely, where Martin Ingram has found that only 20% of sentences were in the plaintiff's favour in the 1580s. However, London cases less often received a final sentence: 32% (23 of 83) of cases in the 1570s and 1580s, compared to over 70% in Ely in the 1580s, were being sentenced: see Martin Ingram, *Church Courts, Sex and Marriage in England, 1570–1640* (Cambridge, 1987), 207–8. The two sets of figures are not entirely comparable since the London sample includes only cases which called witnesses.

payment of marriage portions was a regular stumbling-block before marriage as it was after. Others were dependent entirely on what they earned as servants, and sometimes ran into problems with premature marital promises. At court, their stories of courtship recorded the interplay of established gender conventions and personal circumstance that characterized the transactions leading to marriage.

The making and breaking of marriage contracts were governed by established legal rules. In the formal, witnessed contract that most plaintiffs alleged, the established words of the marriage service were used to bind a couple together in preparation for the solemnization in church. Couples could contract themselves *per verba de futuro*, promising to marry in the future, or *de praesenti*, taking each other as husband and wife in the present tense. Future promises were soluble, unless they had been sealed by sexual intercourse; present contracts, made by mutual consent and without conditions, were legally binding.[8] Careful litigants observed these rules, and provided the regulation two witnesses to testify to the ceremony. Their words consistently echoed the formula of the marriage service, either briefly, with a promise of their 'faith and troth' or at length, with the words 'to have and to hold, from this tyme forwarde, for better for worse, for richer and poorer, in sicknes and in health, til death us departe'.[9] Their vows were made in public, often at a meal, in front of parents or friends and sometimes 'led' by an older friend or a minister. Afterwards, the couple drank to each other and the man offered a ring, or broke a piece of gold to seal the contract.

Outside the specific words of betrothal, men and women came to court with a range of proofs of commitment, emotional relations, and material exchange. Over the years between 1570, when marriage contracts were a central part of the church courts' business, and 1640, when they were rare, the shape of their stories changed. Before 1600, men's suits depended heavily on the words of a contract, the technical proof of conjugality, supported by evidence of the exchange of marriage tokens which showed a couple's commitment to each other, and of courtship, the context for betrothal. Women, suing fewer cases than men, brought suits that were less likely to depend on the correct words of contract, and more likely to claim sexual intercourse as

[8] The church's position on contracts is presented in Henry Swinburne, *A Treatise of Spousals, or Matrimonial Contracts* (London, 1686, written earlier). On the practice of ecclesiastical law in this area, see R. H. Helmholz, *Marriage Litigation in Medieval England* (Cambridge, 1974), ch. 2; Ingram, *Church Courts*, ch. 6.

[9] This example is from John Bulkley *c.* Agnes Modye (1572), DL/C 211/1, fo. 50.

evidence of commitment. After 1600, as litigation became less common, men's suits too relied less often on contracts, and more, in particular, on the social and physical circumstances of courtship, and the existence of what was frequently called a 'common fame' of being, or planning to be, married.[10] For both women and men, the legal definition of a contract was being augmented or replaced by a much broader definition of commitment. But while women and men used quite similar stories of the transactions of courtship to prove marital commitment, those stories assigned different roles and expectations to women and to men.

THE WORDS OF BETROTHAL

In their stories to the court, witnesses and litigants made careful reference to the verbal particulars of tense or phrase that made their contracts legally binding. Vows of marriage had to be spoken in the present tense and unconditionally; promises in the future tense represented no more than an intention, and additions like 'if my friends consent' made a contract conditional. In a set of courtship rituals which depended on men's initiative and women's response, women's mastery of these rules could be crucial. Ann Frier, sued in 1579 by two men who each claimed a contract with her, manipulated the rituals of public betrothal in the face of parental pressure with particular care. Ann had already contracted herself to one man, Richard Robinson, when her father sent him away and tried to persuade her to make a contract with another, Peter Richardson. Ann attended her betrothal dinner but, at the moment of contracting, offered Peter her left hand instead of the customary right: she explained to the court that she had already betrothed herself with her right hand to her first suitor, and so could not do so again. Ann's grandmother, however, proved just as observant of this possible loophole and made sure her granddaughter gave the right hand to her prospective husband, though Ann continued her evasions by saying, as she pointed out, 'I take Peter', not, 'I take him as my husband'.[11] Courtship assigned to

[10] For example, 25 of 38 men's cases in 1606–40 presented details of courtship, while only 17 of 50 cases did so between 1572–96; and in the later period 25 men gave the correct words of a contract, compared to 43 in the earlier one. Women's proofs, by contrast, remained more similar over time, with around a third of cases citing the circumstances of courtship in both periods, and more women than men referring to sex, marriage plans, and the idea of a 'common fame' of their marriage in the neighbourhood.

[11] Richard Robinson *c.* Peter Richardson & Anne Frier (May 1579), DL/C 629, fos. 93–8^{v}; Peter Richardson *c.* Anne Frier (May 1579), ibid. 99, 142^{v}.

women the role of receiving, hearing, and responding to men's propositions, and popular and legal convention established a range of differently inflected answers. Women's idiosyncratic but commanding mastery of those conventions could give them the power to make their marital choices and to evade, deny, or postpone them. As these women gave themselves away, their role in the rituals of courtship provided one focus for strategies of autonomy.

Both women and men used their knowledge of custom and law to evade binding commitment: men as they made proposals, women as they answered them. Elizabeth Frith told the court she had told William Hill 'he shoulde be as welcome to her as any other man shoulde be'. Cuthbert Penny said that, questioned by Elizabeth Stringer's mistress at the Red Lion in Bucklesbury, 'who delte earnestly with this examinate to make promisse of marriage to the said Elizabeth her servante', he

> dyde say to the sayd Elizabethes mistres in the presence of the said Elizabeth that if he wold marie any woman yt shold be with her the said Elizabeth whereuppon the said Elizabethes mistres saieinge that that was not ynough without a token geven by this examinate this examinate to satisfye her like ymportunitie did deliver to the saide Elizabethe a suffran of golde.[12]

Specifics of phrasing could, as Elizabeth's mistress realized, undermine or invalidate apparently binding promises. At the same time, since phrases like these were also part of the repertoire of customary lovers' exchanges, their implications might not always be clear. In 1574 another woman reported exchanging the same words, but for her—although she was in court to defend herself against allegations of marital commitment—they were part of a 'perfecte contracte':

> [he] did promes her by his faith and troth, that if ever he did marye any woman he wolde marye her . . . and at the same tyme she . . . sayd agayne to hym, that if ever she did marye with any man she wolde marye hym, and thereuppon gave unto hym her faith and trothe, and so after that made a perfecte contracte.[13]

As the exact phrasing of contract words could invalidate a promise, so might their occasion. Edward Brooks explained that his youth and position meant he could not marry Susan Powell. Questioned by her master, he asked him 'to make some good ende betwene the producent

[12] William Hill *c.* Elizabeth Frith (1573), DL/C 211/1, fo. 123ᵛ; Elizabeth Stringer *c.* Cuthbert Penny (1580), DL/C 629, fo. 291ᵛ. For the difficulties that faced judges in a medieval York case using the same formula, see Helmholz, *Marriage Litigation*, 41–5.

[13] Rodes *c.* Cole, DL/C 212, p. 78.

. . . and hymselfe, and to consider that he was a yonge man newly entering into the worlde'. On these grounds he passed off the contract as meaningless, confessing 'that their had some kyndnes geven betwene the producent and hym, and that he had geven her some tokens, and that likewise yf every woman should take hould of him as the producente did, he shuld have 100 wyves'. Witnesses to another contract claimed it was invalid because the man involved was physically and mentally disturbed. Margaret Hodges and Moore Fortune were said to have contracted themselves when Moore was 'fallen into a fitt of madnes': Margaret had looked after him during his illness, and in his 'distempature' Moore 'would sometymes say that God badd hym marry . . . Margaret Hodges', finally making a contract with her 'haveing somewhat distempered himself with a full supper the night before and being then full of good cheare'. Moore Fortune's equivocations were ultimately unsuccessful, and he ended up marrying Margaret Hodges a few months later.[14]

COURTSHIP IN PRIVATE AND PUBLIC

The words of betrothal which formed the centrepiece of so many contract suits took place in a particular context: courtship in the presence of family, friends, and neighbours. The private process of courtship acquired its significance through the familiarity it represented, and the signs of that familiarity were studied not just by courting couples, but by their wider household and community. A special kind of social intercourse, described often as 'resorting in the way of marriage', marked the social rituals of courting. Men did the resorting, women received them. Agnes Newman, a servant in an alehouse in Holborn, came to court to deny making a contract with Robert Chapman, but she recognized nevertheless the implications of his visits to her:

> Chapman sitting aloane drinkinge and eatinge would call this respondent to hym and drinke to her, and fall a jestinge with her, after a kynd of love sorte . . . and had this respondent sitt by hym: by reason of which kynde of courtesye he so showed every time att his cominge . . . and familiaratye with such a kynde of fashion as he then used . . . this respondent did well perceive that the saide Chapman did thinke well of her.

[14] Susan Powell *c.* Edward Brooks (1590), DL/C 213, p. 747; Margaret Hodges *c.* Moore Fortune (1613), DL/C 221, fos. 1191^{v}–2; *International Genealogical Index for St Giles Cripplegate Register of Marriages*, 4/1/1614.

Her other responses are revealing of the boundaries that might rule social intercourse between the sexes. She answered to further questions that 'for that she was a servant and not to goe abroad att her pleasure . . . Robert Chapman would oftentymes come and desier her . . . and the other maydes . . . to walke . . . but that ever this respondent walked aloane with Chappman she doth not believe'. Agnes's insistence that she and Robert were never alone together underscores the tension between publicity and privacy in the rituals of courtship. Privacy was compromising to young women. They, and their guardians, worried not just about the vulnerability of their chastity, but about their words: left alone, they might agree to an unsuitable match, and even if they disagreed, their denial would carry little weight without witnesses. Mary Sweeting evinced the same awareness of the dangers of privacy when Robert Smith came to speak of marriage to her:

> she this respondent being in bedd the said Robert Smithe came to her fathers house, and made requeste to come upp to the chamber to this respondent to speke with her, so worde being brought to her that he was there, she wold not graunte that he shuld come upp to her but yet through sute and menes that he did make, he was brought upp to her chamber to her, where he did move talke of maryadge.

A father's fears for another young girl proved well founded. In 1610, Anne Foote went to deliver some washed bands from her mother's shop to one of their customers, Lancelot Grimshawe, a scrivener; she took so long that her stepfather Edmund Hawes had put on his cloak to go and look for her, when Lancelot came back with her. Edmund said to him 'I was coming to you for I mervayled that my daughter tarried so longe,' and he replied 'You might well mervaile at it for there was some matter in it and therefore I thought good to come with her my selfe . . . I have a matter to imparte to you which happely when you heare you will thinke your daughter hath played the foole . . . the truthe is your daughter hath given me her faith and her trothe in the waye of marriage . . . I pray you let me intreate your favour and good will and furtherance of our marriage and that you will no longer accompte of her as yours but as my wife.' Edmund ensured the contract was repeated in front of a minister, but Lancelot's words about foolery proved only too apt, for he did not return to get a licence and shortly afterwards they heard he had 'fled for debte'.[15]

[15] Robert Chapman *c.* Agnes Newman (1588), DL/C 213, pp. 416–17; Robert Smithe *c.* Mary Sweeting (1572), DL/C 211/1, fo. 68v; Anne Foote *c.* Lancelot Grimshawe

The arrangement of roles in more conventional courtships did not guarantee men success in their initiatives: the apparently passive part accorded to women in answering proposals was one that allowed for manœuvres and negotiations for which men did not always plan. In 1593 a typical courtship project ended in conflict between two suitors bent on the same purpose. Richard Houghton asked a friend to go and see Katherine Hawes with him, but when he found out that Katherine was already involved with Thomas Evans he went to confront his rival, who then withdrew his claim, saying 'seeing as she was so fickell of her promisse he would medle no longer or farther with her'. Katherine herself argued that she had made no contract with either man although Richard had persuaded her to accept a ring, and six months later she betrothed herself to and married someone else.[16] When men made all the arrangements, settling their 'claims' to women, women still exercised the power of evasion and refusal.

FRIENDS AND KIN

As couples moved from courting to planning for marriage, the influence of the friends and family who stood on the sidelines in courtships came to bear more directly. The relationships of both young couples and older, remarrying women and men were influenced, mediated, or sanctioned by the people they knew, and if their arrangements ran into conflict, those people provided vital witnesses. Prominent in the social world of courtship were friends. In the context of marriage, 'friends' were a very special group, a particular kind of kin who advised or intervened in marriage plans.

Kinship in early modern England operated flexibly, dependent on social contexts; in the case of marriage, as Diana O'Hara has shown, it extended to non-biological ties through a framework that was about trust and responsibility rather than blood relationships.[17] In London, the special circumstances of a predominantly young and immigrant marrying population demanded an especially flexible definition of the kinds of 'friends' who might help in making marriage. Of daughters in the city, 47 per cent had lost their fathers by the age of 20; the

(1610), DL/C 219, fos. 135–7. On courtship, see John Gillis, *For Better, For Worse: British Marriages, 1600 to the Present* (Oxford, 1985), ch. 1.

16 Richard Houghton *c.* Katherine Hawes *als* Moore (1594), DL/C 214, pp. 550–2, 541–2.

17 Diana O'Hara, '"Ruled by my Friends": Aspects of Marriage in the Diocese of Canterbury, c.1540–c.1570', *Continuity and Change*, 6/1 (1991), 9–41.

death of a parent itself was often what prompted migration.[18] Women, and to a lesser extent men, in this situation referred, when necessary, to a broad group of 'friends': distant relatives, acquaintances, and old family connections from the same part of the country, fellow-servants and co-workers, or employers. The wealth of information these cases furnish about such friends, however, does not provide a direct vision of the patterns of urban kinship. The context of references to friendship is crucial: in these cases, 'friends' feature for one set of very specific functions, advocating or sanctioning marriage matches. A marked gender difference also makes the use of kin in these records very specific.[19] The evidence of courtship suggests that women were at once more constrained and more supported than men by the role of friends and parents.[20] Women were expected to need more guidance and to be less reliable; most of all, their credit, the capital they had to invest in the preferment of marriage, consisted in an imperfectly regulated commodity: chastity. Far more than men, migrant women in London were expected to look to the friendship and advice of older relatives or distant acquaintances. Anne Hewse explained her responsibility for Margaret Howe, for whom she helped arrange a marriage in 1579:

> Margarett Howe is . . . borne in Leycestersheire where this examinate dwelt and was greatly acquainted with the saide Margaretts and one of their speciall frends which they made accompte of By reason of which this examinate about 18 years ago bearing some affection to [Margaret] then a pretye girle sente for her downe to Leycestersheire, and placed her here in London, where she have continued ever since, resorting still to this examinates house and making greate accompte of her following her advice and direction in all her doinges and being out of service placed at this examinates appoyntmente.

Margaret told Anne that Edmund Ellis bore her good will, and Edmund, 'hearing that the whole matter of his suite depended upon [Anne] and Margarett woulde doe nothing (as she herselfe confessed) withoutt [her] advise' came to Anne with his proposal. She told the court that she, 'having care for . . . Margarett Howes preferements and honest matching did willinglye graunte' the couple her approval,

[18] Vivien Brodsky Elliott, 'Single Women in the London Marriage Market: Age, Status and Mobility', in R. B. Outhwaite (ed.), *Marriage and Society: Studies in the Social History of Marriage* (London, 1981), 90.

[19] For an introduction to the anthropological debate about kinship in the light of gender, see Jane Fishburne Collier and Sylvia Junko Yanagisako (eds.), *Gender and Kinship: Essays Toward a Unified Analysis* (Stanford, Calif., 1983), intro.

[20] Keith Wrightson, *English Society 1580–1680* (London, 1982), 76.

and they were contracted on Easter Monday over a large dinner at Anne's house.[21] Judith Wrott, another woman in service, this time in an aristocratic household, had a married friend who advised her to be cautious in courtship. She came to visit Alice Beardon with her suitor, John Wrothe (probably also a relative), several times. On one occasion, Alice came into the room to find John with his head in Judith's lap and expressed concern—which angered John—that he would make Judith content, telling her 'Mres Wrott I would have you be careful that you do not give too much credite, beleve not mens othes for in time of wooing men will sweere anythinge', and saying 'she did not lyke that he should so long deferre and protract the marriage'. John asked her why she said so, and she told them 'I have been abused in the same nature experience teacheth me to say so.' 'Though you have met with an unhonest man, must I needs be dishonest?', John asked, and Alice responded 'no sir . . . I hope not, but the tyme was, when I held him as honest as Mres Wrot can hold you to be'. John vowed then that Judith would have 'no cause to compleyne of' him; but it became increasingly clear, as he delayed the marriage and later, argued that she was of too poor position to be his wife, that she did.[22]

Away from home in service, some women found another kind of 'friend' in their employers. Household advice to women stipulated that part of the duties of running a house was the supervision of the moral relations of servants. The legal ban on young people marrying while still in service, although it did not prevent them doing so, did invest some employers with a sense of authority over their servants' courtships. Both women and men took upon themselves the role of questioning the prospective suitors of their female servants; some threatened dismissal to those who betrothed themselves, but others made attempts to ensure that their servants became properly contracted, enquiring first about their suitors' intentions and financial ability. A witness in one case in 1635 explained how he moved himself in the interests of his servant. Thomas Neale had been 'making suit' to Anne Gardiner for about a year and a half. Eventually her employer

> wisheing well unto the said Anne Gardiner who for divers yeares before had been his nowe wifes servant in the said house and something doubting that the said Thomas Neale would not be constant with his love and affection

[21] Isabel Dye *c.* Edward Ellis (Margaret Howe *pro interesse*) (1587), DL/C 213, pp. 149–50.

[22] Judith Wrott *c.* John Wroth (1619), DL/C 225, fos. 181–2.

> . . . because he so long triffled and would not consummat his said suit by marriage unto hir . . . he this deponent invited the said Thomas Neale to supper . . . and . . . invited thither one Mr Rigge a minister . . . and his wife and another neighbour . . . and his wife . . . and at that time after supper . . . he this deponent moved the said Thomas Neale to be contracted unto the said Anne Gardiner that thereby he might testifie to the world the sinceritie of his love and affection unto hir the said Anne.

As a result of this efficiently organized and witnessed ritual, Anne's contract was confirmed by the court.[23] In contrast, men were not expected to need this quasi-parental supervision, and the records of marriage leave no descriptions of how they found their friends. In practice, as in the ideas of contemporary writers on honour, women's 'preferment' in marriage was seen as precarious, demanding constant supervision and intervention to cement a binding future.

At the moment of marital decision, men and women used their friends differently. The gendered roles of courtship shaped the part friends played. Men used their friends as allies in the initiatives of courtship, asking them to accompany them on visits to 'talk of marriage'; the culmination of the alliance of male suitors and their friends came in projects of forced marriage and abduction. In 1575 Joan Smith, an orphan in the wardship of the Lord Mayor and heir to an inheritance from her father, a freeman, was abducted by Henry Eaton and his friends, who, she said,'looketh to spoyle this respondent of all that her father hath lefte her'. She was rescued by her sister and friends, and gave a long and spirited account to the court of her ordeal. Another young girl, Elizabeth Rogers, was abducted in 1574, by a Mr Dale, to marry Matthew Goodman; Dale had been promised £40 on the solemnization of their marriage.[24] Attempts at abduction were joint endeavours, like the expeditions other men made to propose marriage with their friends: a successful investment in the marriage market would then produce shared profits.

The network of investment that was associated with marriages of women of some wealth was complicated when they had been married before. In an Essex village in 1572 Elizabeth Church found herself under pressure to marry from some of her kin, the sister and brother-in-law of a man to whom she had been betrothed, but who had died, leaving her a sum of £20, before they married. Partly because of this inheritance, Elizabeth's links with the family remained strong, as she

[23] Anne Gardiner *c.* Thomas Neale (1635), DL/C 234, fos. 96ᵛ–97ᵛ, DL/C 28, fo. 181.

[24] Henry Eaton *c.* Joan Smith (1576), DL/C 212, p. 126; Elizabeth Rogers *c.* Matthew Goodman (1574), DL/C 212, pp. 40–68.

explained: 'she called William Crampehorne brother by reason she was betrowghted unto his wiffes brother, and should have been maryed unto hym, if he had lyved'. Traditional kin influences on marriage could thus be modified to take account of the particular circumstances of high mortality rates: the kin acquired in one union acquires here a say in the next. Elizabeth also relied on other kin, particularly her uncle and aunt; while her parents were still alive, according to the parish curate, 'her father is often tymes owte of his wyttes, and when he is in best case, he is but an idyott and so simple that he cannot deserne of any wronge offered unto hym . . . as for her mother, she haith somewhatt more wytt, but not moch'. William Crampehorne and his wife endeavoured to get Elizabeth to marry a clergyman, Matthew Levett, apparently in the hope of a pay-off of 20 marks from the inheritance Elizabeth would bring with her to the marriage; another man involved in the attempt expected to get a horse and 'the beste oke that grew in the ground' she would inherit at her father's death. William Crampehorne came to her after church one Sunday and asked her to come home with him, where he sent her upstairs to meet Matthew Levett 'whome [she] never sawe before . . . takying [her] by the hand [he] byd her welcome, and bye and bye asked of her, if she could fynd in her harte to love hym'. Elizabeth refused to commit herself without first asking the consent of her uncle and aunt, despite Matthew's insistence, and although he forced twopence upon her to buy a pair of gloves, her uncle sent it back. A further meeting was arranged a week later by another man, who interrupted her when she was sowing her uncle's fields; they spoke again, but Elizabeth's defence to the court this time was that she was too confused to remember what they said: 'there was certayn speech moved unto her, but what it was, or what answer she did make unto it, she doth not nowe remember, for she was so sore amased, at the so soddayn meatinge of so manye persons in the high way'.[25] Men's friends, then, were invoked as allies and collaborators in the project of marrying. Women's friends helped them from a different angle: receiving and answering the proposals of men.

Whatever kind of proposals men made, in the customs of marriage and at the court the exact words of women's answers were critical. Some women, like Elizabeth Church, claimed to have forgotten what they said; others gave noncommittal formulas to their suitors; many

[25] Matthew Levett *c.* Elizabeth Church (1572), DL/C 211/1, fos. 98^{v}, 102^{v}–104. A mark was 13*s.* 4*d*: 20 marks, therefore, was a significant proportion—over half—of Elizabeth's inheritance.

also gave answers which invoked, as a protection, the name of their friends. Elizabeth Church refused to give a reply without the consent of her uncle and aunt, transferring the power of influence in marriage from one group of her kin to another: referring to kin or friends in this way enabled women to give careful answers without commitment. Alice Dawson's encounter with John Bothewyd at Christmas, 1587, illustrates perfectly the different roles friends could play for men and for women. John's friends tried to persuade her to marry him, telling her he was 'a fitt mache for her and able to mantayne her yf she would marry with him'. She responded with a call to her friends: 'she not having any entent to contract matrimony at that pointe did without any deliberacon answer Aye yf her frends good will might first be therunto obtained and otherwise not'. Her prudence ensured the court decreed in her favour.[26] The occasion also illustrates nicely the different manifestations friends made in the courtships recorded in these cases. Men's friends make physical appearances and persuasions, women's are reduced virtually to figures of speech: frequently invoked as protectors and counsellors, they rarely appear in person. In a more threatening attempt at persuasion in Harlow, Essex, in 1575, Mary Perry relied on the same kind of defence to protect her from marital commitment. She told the court she had happened to meet Robert Bridges at a victualling house where they had been dancing, and he 'in talke and communicacon of marriadge' asked her 'Marye can you fynde in your harte to love me above all other'; she replied 'ther ys noe haste but that I may tarry well inoughe I am but a stranger to you and you a stranger to me you may here of me and I maye here of you'. At this point the owner of the inn intervened, urging her 'godes bloode speake it is but a woorde', to which Mary responded with an invocation of the authority of one relative: 'I will goe from you and talk with my cosen goodwiefe Stanes.' Robert 'fell into a rage' and threatened her 'godes bloode speake you shall speake before you goe or els you shall not departe this nighte'; and she, 'for feare and onelye to satisfye his mynd bycause she wold be gon', agreed, carefully referring to another relative: 'yf you can gett the goord of my mother I shalbe contente to have you before anye other but I must tell you that whotte love is sone cold.' Mary's narrative, an entirely different tale from the conventional version Robert's witnesses gave of promises exchanged freely after music-making and dancing, describes an occasion where she is surrounded by the persuasions and angry

[26] John Bothewyd *c.* Alice Dawson (1588), DL/C 213, p. 345; DL/C 611, p. 618.

threats of Robert and his friends. With no friends of her own there, verbal references to the authority of her kin are her only resource, but an effective one, enabling her to give in at the time, but to argue herself free from a binding contract later.[27]

When women were unwilling to make a final marriage decision, the invocation of such authority was a particularly useful strategy; suggesting the proposal was being taken seriously, it also provided them with a legal way out of it. Whether women actually used conditional responses like these, or whether they found in them a useful story with which to defend themselves at court, the formulas that invoked the advice and goodwill of friends in marital decision-making were clearly well-established ones. Cloaked in the language of dependency on parents, friends, or kin, they gave women the opportunity to broaden the largely passive part allotted to them in the process of courtship and marriage.

The function of friends in women's marital decision-making was, perhaps, not as significant as the frequent references to them suggest. Compared to the visibility and activity of men's friends, women's friends play a faint, even imaginary part in the stories of broken contracts. Friends—as opposed to parents—do not, in these stories, impede or sanction women's marriages. From the details of these stories, the part friends and wider kin played for women looks to be much less than their answers to men claim. In the urban context, the term 'friends' had a broad and powerful meaning, especially for women, who relied so heavily on the idea of functional friendship: in a community of high levels of migration and mobility, particularly amongst the young people who brought many of these cases, imaginary friends might prove plausible and helpful, as well as real, visible ones. The prominent figures in battles over marital choice are not employers, neighbours, or distant relatives, but parents.

The most manifest influence and power was that of mothers over daughters. Elizabeth Taylor, a haberdasher's wife, testified that she had banned her daughter Susan's suitor John Browne, an apprentice, from the house:

> albeit . . . John Browne oftentymes requested this deponent to geve her consent unto him to be contracted unto her doughter, yet she alwaies tolde him that she never woulde geve her consent that her doughter shoulde be contracted with anie mans apprentice, neyther was she made pryvey to anie contracte . . . And . . . whereas [he] was verie importunat in his suete unto her

[27] John Bridges *c.* Mary Perry (1576), DL/C 212, pp. 466–7, 439–40.

doughter, she willed him to refraine her companie and forbade him her howse for that she nor her husband did like of that match.

While Elizabeth invoked the name of her husband, Susan's stepfather, it was she rather than he who withdrew the family's hospitality. Men's claims that women had reneged on promises of marriage often laid the blame at the feet of their mothers, alleging a maternal influence that could be powerful and intimidating. In 1579 Roger Barrett and his witnesses told the court how his contract with Ellen Shawcock had been dependent on the friends and kin of both of them, but most of all on Ellen's mother. As they discussed the matter in Roger's shop with male friends of his and Ellen's sister (also called Ellen), Ellen was confident that 'my father [her stepfather] will not gainsaye any thinge that is done nor denie to gyve me his consente yf my mother do consente'. Both Ellen and her sister were sure she could persuade her mother to agree: 'I will espie sutch a time to move my mother of it as I wilbe sure to gett her good will', Ellen said, and her sister added 'my mother will not denie my sister any thinge that she askethe of her'. Roger's friends, particularly Walter Horsell, the servant of a consistory court official and thus well up in the problems of private contracts, were still worried, and the subsequent exchange underlines the potential prominence of parents, in different ways, in courtship. Roger said to Ellen,

> If you come to me you shalbe as welcome as my owne mother but if your mother be willing to matche you with another man rather than with me as I know not her minde, she perhappes will send you awaye so that I shall not come at you and terrifie you in sutch sorte that you shalbe forced although against yor will to denie both me and your promise.

Ellen's response was as dramatic as Roger's fears: 'thinke not so Mr Barrett for If I be sent awaye from you (as I knowe I shall not) I wilbe torne in pieces with wilde horses before I will denie either you or my promise'.[28] This menacing vision of maternal power is at once romantic and plausible; it plays both on a rhetoric of forbidden love, and on the drama of real parental authority. Other witnesses report mothers' words to their daughters, giving some indication of the language of familiar but brutal phrases that came into play in conflicts over marital choice. Anne Frier's mother reputedly said 'she had rather see her buried quick than mary with . . . Peter'. John Bulkley's witnesses said Agnes Modye's mother had boxed her ear when she

[28] John Browne *c.* Susan Davers (1574), DL/C 212, p. 157; Roger Barrett *c.* Ellen Shawcock (1579), DL/C 629, fo. 57r–v.

found out they planned to marry, telling her she 'shuld never have pennye nor halfpennye of her purse, neither wolde she take her for her daughter' if she married him; according to them, she also turned her daughter out of the house and eventually persuaded her to marry another man. Margaret Inman's mother, the wife of a freeman and fishmonger in the City, deposed to the court that she had 'declared . . . that she had rather see . . . Margaret sett in ground and stoned to death than to see hir matched and placed with such a generation or stock' as that of her suitor, Thomas Bedle.[29]

The power of these mothers was a physical one, grounded in the daily domestic power of women over daughters who were still living at home, doing housework or errands for their parents' businesses, and dependent on their mothers' hospitality; in several of these cases, too, mothers are the only surviving birth parent. For the frustrated suitors who told these stories of broken contracts, the parental power so regularly invoked by women answering proposals had a firm basis in the physical, familial authority of mothers over their daughters. To that extent, it was a familiar part of the context of courtship. Stories like these, though, were also useful at court. Roger Barrett and John Bulkley ensured their witnesses told the court these narratives in detail, because they both showed how committed the daughters were to the marriage, and suggested a possible reason why the match had run into trouble; both of them seem to have won their cases.[30]

The problem of parental power in marriage was a constant concern for reformers in England as on the Continent. Medieval interpretations of the laws of consent were criticized for giving too little weight to family interest and too much licence to clandestine matrimony.[31] The canons of 1604 compromised by insisting on parental consent for those under 21, without invalidating marriages with no consent. In practice, parental influence on marriages seems to have been low at social levels below the élite: parents approved, rather than enforced, their children's choices, and in these cases, as we have seen, even the authority of parents and friends to which young women so frequently referred could be notional rather than actual. The spectre of parental

[29] Robinson *c.* Frier & Richardson, DL/C 629, fo. 138ᵛ; Bulkley *c.* Modye, DL/C 211/1, fos. 36, 56ᵛ; Office *ad prom.* Thomas Crosbie *c.* Margaret Inman & Margaret Bloise (1635), DL/C 234, fo. 52ᵛ.

[30] DL/C 11, fo. 302; DL/C 8, fo. 256ᵛ. Roger Barrett, though, ended up losing his case after an inhibition was filed from the Court of Arches.

[31] See John T. Noonan, Jr., 'Power to Choose', *Viator*, 4 (1973), 419–34, Sheehan, 'The Formation and Stability of Marriage in Fourteenth-Century England', and Ralph Houlbrooke, *The English Family 1450–1700* (Harlow, 1984), 69–72.

disapproval, the influence of friends, and the domestic power of mothers, buttressed by cultural insistence on women's lack of autonomy, remained strong enough to feature prominently and usefully in the language women used in courtship, and the stories men told about women.

The story of maternal authority was countered by another kind of tale, which stressed young people's freedom from their parents' and friends' influences. The fears that led Continental reformers to insist that clandestine contracts without parental consent did not constitute binding marriages were amply justified for at least some English parents. Edmund Hawes, hearing that his stepdaughter Ann had suddenly contracted herself to a scrivener with few means, found himself 'abashed' and questioned her 'mayd have you done this? have you contracted your selfe without my consent? without my knowledge?' Shortly after, when the match ran into trouble, Edmund wrote down his memory of the conversations he had with Ann and her suitor; Ann's reply to him, as he reported it to the court, asserted the power of secret contracts and the limits of parental control: 'looke what he hath sayd is true I have given him my fayth and my troathe to be his wife and promised to lyve with him and not to parte till God shall parte us by death and sayd I am his wife and he is my husband'.[32] If young women evading commitment turned to the idea of dependence, women who gave themselves freely—or who were argued at court to have done so—expressed in the language of marital choice an assertion of autonomy. Ellen Shawcock was quoted as saying, 'my father and mother may thinke me to be a lewde girle, but . . . I am to make my choice myself'; Sage Povey, as declaring 'I am past twise 7 yeeres old And therefore will take my choise where I shall like'.[33] But when such choices went wrong, the value of parental and friendly support, and the room it left for prudent negotiation, might emerge even more clearly. Witnesses to the troubled betrothal of Joan Mortimer and Richard Campion, which continued for at least four years before Richard took Joan to court in 1591, testified that Joan had refused to follow her parents' advice against 'matching with' him, telling friends 'she would have [him] to her husbande whatsoever became of her all thoughe she begged with hym . . . neither her father nor mother should chuse for her'. But Katherine Hawfield, a 27-year-old servant, told the court that after the contract she had found Joan Mortimer

[32] Foote *c.* Grimshawe, DL/C 219, fo. 135^{v}.

[33] Barrett *c.* Shawcocke, DL/C 629, fo. 64; Ralph Stafford *c.* Sage Povey (1575), DL/C 212, p. 189.

sitting in the kitchen 'very dumpishe and grevouslie weepinge'; when she asked her what was wrong, Joan replied 'that she had cast hir selfe away, contrary to all hir frends goodwill, and had doon that which she could not undoe, but said shee, if he wear a good workman I cared not, but now it cannot be undoon'. Katherine 'willed hir to content hir self . . . and . . . further tould her that she might do very well with him', but Joan answered 'that could never be but thear was no remedie it could not then bee undoon again.'[34]

Not all litigants fitted this context of dependent youth. After widowhood, women found themselves in a very different social situation from that of their first courtship, with both the freedoms of living alone and the precarious reputation that might come with those freedoms. Susan Jason, an Enfield widow sued by Henry Bowles in 1610, defended a case that came to focus on a story of courtship in the particular context of widowhood. Susan deposed that she had turned Henry down because his estate was not as large as he had promised; but his witnesses, both gentlemen, told a longer story of the making of a contract, in which Susan is particularly conscious of her social status as a widow. She invites Henry and another man to dinner, showing him 'many signes and tokens of her love', talking to Henry as they sat down of 'the good that you shall receyve by me', and telling him 'Sir you are the onely man that I make accompt of and I hope you will be an honest man and be loving and kinde to me and you shall be sure that I will be loving and kinde to you . . . for that is all I desyre . . . as for wealthe I do desire it not.' The whole event takes place in the context of her hospitality, apparently at her persuasion; it was only widows, apparently, who could be imagined as offering themselves in marriage, rather than simply receiving men. As the contract was arranged, Susan continued to stress her age and independence, telling him that her son would be angry 'but never the lesse sayd she I am at my owne disposing and will not be ruled by him', refusing at first a gold ring with a diamond in it for 'it was to youthful for her to weare', and insisting that after the marriage, she would go home to her own house, 'for she sayd she would not lye out of her owne house a night'. Urged by Henry to be constant to him, 'for you are going to my Lady Wrothe and I know she will urge you to marrie some other', she asked him in return 'how shall I stand secured for my estate?' He gave her the name of two aldermen as sureties, which she accepted 'if they will be bound that you shall not make

[34] Richard Campion *c.* Joan Mortimer (1591), DL/C 214, pp. 32–4.

away with any of her estate during my life . . . And if you die before me you shall leave me your estate except £100 which you may bestowe where you please.' These are the words reported by one of Henry Bowles's witnesses; they might represent the role he thought suitable to be played by a widow keen to ensure her financial security, and a narrative of courtship that gave her no reason for not marrying him. Ultimately, though, the court rejected this story, awarding sentence to Susan and ordering Henry to pay £10 costs.[35]

THE ECONOMY OF GIFTS

While the verbal exchanges of formal contracts were the accepted proof of betrothal and the culmination of courtship, a set of more material transactions gave premarital commitment an economic context. During courtship, and at the moment of betrothal, lovers exchanged gifts and money as tokens of marriage. The exchange of gifts between lovers, a well-established part of courtship ritual, often came to be a key point of contest at the court; the extensive details about tokens and analyses of their meaning that plaintiffs and defendants gave focused on material exchanges as a proof in themselves of commitment to marry.

At the moment of contracting, couples exchanged rings or broken pieces of gold; before it, they engaged in a much broader range of material and economic transactions involving clothes, purses (empty or full), shoes, hats, and household goods. Diana O'Hara has shown how effectively gifts operated as a form of communication in courtship, so that the occasion as well as the nature of the token furnished its significance.[36] But that significance was potentially ambiguous, and at court, women and men fought carefully over the exact implications of every transaction in which they had taken part. The gifts allegedly exchanged in these cases suggest, too, a broader range of meanings than has generally been assumed. In the context of courtship, material exchange could serve to carry the message of emotional commitments. But it might serve, too, as a symbol not just of premarital relations, but of those of man and wife; in particular, of the financial dependency meant to characterize woman's role in marriage, and the labour she offers in exchange for that support. The gifts exchanged before marriage relate not just to the relations of courtship,

[35] Henry Bowles *c.* Susan Jason *als* Jackson (1610), DL/C 219, fos. 311ᵛ–312, 312ᵛ–314ᵛ; DL/C 15, fo. 280.

[36] O'Hara, ' "Ruled by my Friends" '.

but to those of marriage, and they have ramifications for the whole marital relationship and its context.

Some gifts were specially designed to mean love and courtship: handkerchiefs with posies embroidered on them, or love notes. Susan Hills was claimed to have received gifts of this sort from Robert Lowther, while he was away at sea. A witness to their courtship told the court that Susan had showed her 'a broken peece of gould being the halfe of a halfe crowne' that she said Robert gave her as part of their contract before he went to sea, and that Robert had written to her from abroad enclosing a letter to Susan, 'Thus beginning viz. Susan my love remembred, and ending, I feare you can hardly read this because you do not practise, and in the same letter a ring of gould with a redd stone in it'. Most people mentioned more ordinary gifts, whose context made them significant and whose implications were recalled months afterwards to the court. In 1574 Susanna Cole admitted making a contract with John Rodes on a bench under the window in her father's house in Hounslow, and described to the court the various gifts she received during their courtship:

> before the said contracte so made she this respondent receaved of . . . John Roades two payres of gloves in the way of matrymonye, uppon talke that was betwen them, And after the foresayd contracte so made she receaved of hym one purse one payre of hose and 11 shillings and four pence in monnye, which he gave her to carye in her purse, and to bye such thinges as she needed, and thereuppon she taketh her self to be assured to the said John Roades, and they two to be man and wyff togither.[37]

Women and men both gave and received the gifts of courtship, but it was women who found themselves most obligated by them, and who made efforts to avoid accepting gifts with implications. A man's gifts held, as a woman's did not, the implication of an emotional and, potentially, a marital bond, and a woman's receipt of gifts implied consent to that bond.[38] In Holborn in 1590 Thomas Wye promised his laundress Katherine Freame a reward if she would speak on his behalf to a girl much younger than himself, Agnes Bushey, and asked her 'to get some tokens from Agnes Bushey or take hould of her words if she uttered any whereby he might see, he could gett her to yield to be his wiff', but Agnes would give neither material nor ver-

[37] Susan Hills *c.* Robert Lowther (1626), DL/C 230, fos. 116^{r-v}; John Rodes *c.* Susanna Cole (1574), DL/C 212, p. 78.

[38] On this gender imbalance, see Peter Rushton, 'The Testament of Gifts: Marriage Tokens and Disputed Contracts in North-East England, 1560–1630', *Folk Life*, 24 (1985–6), 26.

bal commitment. Again, women's responses constituted the main point of courtship negotation. Women who accepted tokens and regretted it tried, when they came to court, to explain how they were received unwittingly. Joan Mortimer said that Richard Campion gave her a gold piece in the dark, when she could not see what it was; Joan Frith defended herself that Thomas Sweeting gave her nothing but made her gifts such as a whistle out of oddments, 'which she being of small yeres and lesse discretione receaved at his hande'; Elizabeth Cole explained that the money she received from Martin Mullens was payment for lambs from her mother and for butter at the market, where, as Elizabeth was bargaining with a customer, Martin had paid the penny difference between her price and her customer's offer, to persuade Elizabeth to go and drink with him.[39] Explanations like these, designed to neutralize the meaning of gifts men alleged they had given in the way of marriage, reveal also the potential complications of marriageable women's dealings with money and men in the marketplace.

In their defence, other women repudiated the meanings of gifts by counterbalancing them with payment or gifts in return. Jane Salisbury's meticulous list of exchanges shows her fighting constantly to keep the balance straight:

> while the sayde Lloyde was a sueter unto her she hadd occasyon to sende for a payre of hoose and a payre of sleapers whereof the sayde Lloyde having understandinge payde for them him selffe and att the delivery of them to this respondent caused it to be signifyed unto her that he bestowed them uppon her which this respondent mislyked because she purposed to deserve no suche matter . . . partley for his money layde owte in that behalffe and partlye for wyne which he wolde sende unto her chamber againste her will she sent unto him 10 shillings in golde further she saithe that the sayde Lloyde beinge uppon a tyme in her chamber in greate rage he left there halfe an angell which this respondent dirst not then presse uppon him backe againe for feare he shulde have donne some hurt/ other of his goodes she never receaved but certaine parcells here mentyoned as the scarffe and stomacher the scarff worth 15 shillings and the stomacher worthe a mark and no more . . . beinge delyvered to her servante without her privitye she caused to be sente unto him backe again which he receaved.[40]

Jane's story has her refusing, where she could, the gifts pressed on her; another woman defended herself with an equally careful account

[39] Thomas Wye *c.* Agnes Bushey (1591), DL/C 213, p. 830; Campion *c.* Mortimer (1591), DL/C 214, pp. 10–11; Thomas Sweeting *c.* Joan Frith *als* Ampcotts (1575), DL/C 212, fo. 258; Martin Mullens *c.* Elizabeth Cole (1592), DL/C 214, p. 168.

[40] William Lloyde *c.* Jane Salisbury (1574), DL/C 211/2, fo. 281^{v}.

of how she repaid her suitor for unwanted presents. In 1591 Joan Mortimer listed to the court the financial exchanges between herself and Richard Campion, valuing and counterbalancing each gift of his with one of hers. '[H]e gave her a payre of gloves att the tyme of their first acquaintance which he then sayde did cost him twelve pence And afterwards delyvered her a girdle, which he likewise affirmed did cost him 2 shillings and 5 pence'; he told her the girdle was for a friend of his, but refused to take it from her. He also accompanied her to buy a waistcoat, and insisted on paying for it (2*s.* 4*d.*); when he went into the country she lent him a handkerchief and a pair of cuffs and 'did pay him money namely three shillinges and foure pence againe which he hath laied outt for the gloves and wastcote'; and 'att another time she gave him a shirte bande which cost this respondent two shillinges and sixpence in recompense of the girdle . . . which severale thinges he received thankfully as she beleveth'.[41] Exchanges like this became self-perpetuating: Joan's responses to Richard's gifts could be read both as attempts to neutralize their implications, and as an affirmation and extension of their economic relationship, creating an apparently eternal cycle of gift and receipt. In this context any kind of financial exchange between men and women, like the buying of butter and lambs from Elizabeth Cole, could be rewritten to prove conjugal intent. And conversely, the loaded exchanges of courtship could be represented as balanced transactions in a broader market.

In this discourse certain rules were established that concerned, as much as the promises made by lovers, the relationship between man and wife. Francis Locke, in the words of one of his witnesses, 'gave [Margaret Dyngley] 5 shillings in monye and wylled . . . she shold want for nothing': money like this was intended not just for buying the small gifts of courtship, but for everyday maintenance. Women and men spoke of gifts as evidence that a woman was being 'maintained' by a man, an economic and sexual term which suggests at once the financial relations of prostitution and those of marriage. In 1572 Henry Richardson and Godfrey Stevenson urged Joan Lewes to settle a contract with Godfrey by reminding her of the money he had spent on her. Godfrey proposed to her, 'in respecte of the goodwill that haith bene betwene us . . . and of the cost that I have bestowed uppon you lett us now come to some perfecte ende', and Henry also advised her to 'consider the charges', noting in his deposition 'That . . . Joan Lewes lyved at his hows . . . at the chardges of . . . Godfrey

[41] Campion *c.* Mortimer, DL/C 214, pp. 10–11.

Stevenson who payd [him] 2 shillings 4 pence a weke for her borde'; Henry's wife Margaret also remembered 'Godfrey would divers tymes give her moneye to buye her apparell'. The several assessments of the implications of their relationship held water, and the court apparently pronounced in Godfrey's favour. But establishing women in lodgings or houses was also open to another construction: the situation of service. One London couple, Elizabeth Vyes and Edward Symons, met when they were both servants of Sir Henry Barker. Later Edward hired a house at Parsons Green and placed Elizabeth there 'to undergo and performe all necessary business . . . to the house ground and cattle'; he 'had often accesse unto her', and the neighbours believed they would marry. Witnesses for Elizabeth's suit against Edward concentrated upon the proofs offered by Edward's keeping Elizabeth in his house. From joint servants they had gone to master and servant; the next step was meant to be husband and wife. Instead the couple ended up locked in a dispute in which both sides enlisted the court, Elizabeth (unsuccessfully) to prove a marriage contract, and Edward, a few months later, to sue Elizabeth for calling him 'a knave a rogue and a whoremaster, and that he had had the carnall use and knowledge of her body'.[42] Maintenance could suggest either illicit or licit sexual relations; in this case, Elizabeth's hopes that it meant a promise of marriage were frustrated and she ended by using the language of illicit sex to enforce her claims against Edward.

One group of men and women used material gifts to represent the entry into marriage in a different way: not by prefiguring a future union, but by recalling a previous one. The 'gold ring with a deathes head in it' that one man offered as a token had very real implications in a marriage market where more than half of all unions lasted no longer than ten years. Under half the marriages in London were between men and women who had not been married before. Few of the images available to marrying couples reflected this picture: marriage sermons and advice, and courtship ballads, clung to the idea of one lifetime union, entered by the young, and in popular literature the widow featured as a stock subject for comedy, the widower not at all.[43] But the older litigants at this court were generally entering a

[42] Margaret Dyngley *c.* Francis Locke (1573), DL/C 211/1, fo. 170; Godfrey Stevenson *c.* Joan Lewes (1572), DL/C 211/1, fo. 94, and DL/C 8, fo. 301^{v}; Elizabeth Vyes *c.* Edward Symons (June 1629), DL/C 231, fos. 357^{v}–360, fo. 384, and DL/C 25, fo. 229; Edward Symons *c.* Elizabeth Vyes (Oct. 1629), DL/C 231, fo. 400.

[43] Vivien Brodsky, 'Widows in Late Elizabethan London: Remarriage, Economic Opportunity, and Family Orientations', in Lloyd Bonfield, Richard M. Smith, and Keith Wrightson (eds.), *The World We have Gained: Histories of Population and Social*

second or third marriage after widowhood, and they exchanged gifts that provided a vivid reminder of their status: 'a saff gard of worsted that was his wiffes'; 'a coate garded being one of her majesties liverie and a velvett capp which was . . . her former husbands'; 'his first wifes wedding apparell'; a 'seale ring which was given unto her by her former husband, when he did lye uppon his deathes bed'.[44] This kind of incorporation of the goods of a previous marriage into the foundation of a new union constitutes a startling recognition of the realities of early modern marriage. Remarrying men and women established perhaps the most individual interpretation of marriage custom, inscribing the particular meanings of their unions on to the traditional elements of betrothal.

THE LANGUAGE OF GESTURE

Material gifts provided one language for emotional investment; other stories concentrated on the physical and sentimental expressions of courtship. Physical familiarity was one proof of emotional commitment. William Andros said that 'Susanna Coles came unto . . . John Roades and sett on the bench there with hym usynge herselfe vere famylyarlye and lovinglye unto him', before they made a contract. Thomas Thorpe and Alice Jackson were 'very familiar togither as lovers use to be'. Margaret Richardson observed of Joan Lewes and Godfrey Stevenson, 'And by all tokens that this deponent could see or judge by there outward gestures and famyliaritie together, either of them did beare good will tother, for they wold talk and toye togither, after the accustomed manner of woers'. Betrothed or courting couples drank out of the same cup, shared food, or played games. Jane Clifton deposed that while she and her daughter were at the house of their kinsman, Nicholas Reynolds, in Charterhouse Lane in February 1575, one Mr Roule came to visit and 'happened to finde . . . Robert Prowdfoote and Margery Holte this deponents daughter (who wer of familier acquaintance togither) throwing snow thone at thother

Structure (Oxford, 1986), 135–6. The ring was offered by Meredith Powell, in Meredith Powell *c.* Elizabeth Horton (1624), DL/C 193, fo. 106v. On the stereotype of widows, see Barbara J. Todd, 'The Remarrying Widow: A Stereotype Reconsidered', in Mary Prior (ed.), *Women in English Society 1500–1800* (London, 1985), and Charles Carlton, 'The Widow's Tale: Male Myths and Female Reality in Sixteenth and Seventeenth Century England', *Albion,* 10 (1978), 118–29.

[44] Dyngley *c.* Locke, DL/C 211/1, fo. 170 ('saff gard': an outer skirt); Henry Procter *c.* Alice Deacon (1590), DL/C 213, p. 764; Jane Grigge *c.* Robert Eastfield (1578), DL/C 629, fo. 53; Edward Jones *c.* Anne Thurston (1614), DL/C 222, fo. 309.

wheruppon . . . Mr Roule (knowing Margery Holte) asked . . . Nicholas Reynolds what fellow that was that threw snow at her wherto . . . Reynolds answered that is one that should marry with her.' On hearing that they were not assured before witnesses, he asked Robert his intentions and caused them to join hands and make a contract.[45] Familiarity was interpreted, particularly, in terms of women's readiness to accept men's physical gestures. There are no references in these accounts of courtship to the ritualized night-time fondling and 'bundling' that Lawrence Stone and others have found in different periods and places.[46] The social and domestic world of these London women involved regular social contact with young men, and often, clear public signals of familiarity with lovers and suitors; most courtship seems to have taken place outside, rather than inside women's houses.

Sex before marriage, a far more significant proof of commitment than mere physical familiarity, carried meanings as keenly contested as those of material gifts. Sex before the church ceremony was, by this period, by no means legitimated by betrothal: the phrase 'man and wife' that contracted couples used to decribe their relationship did not necessarily imply the sexual relations of marriage. Allen Browne and Sibilla Green, contracted to each other with an arrangement that ensured she would inherit his property if he died at sea, were described as taking 'communion together as man and wife and dayly conversant togither as man and wife the bed excepted'. Some men tried, sometimes successfully, to follow contracts with sex. After Elizabeth Drake and Edward Goodene contracted themselves in 1623, he said 'nowe we are man and wife together let us go to bed', and they did; but the contract was never solemnized, and Edward betrothed himself to another woman in 1626. Another man said to his partner 'Now wee are man and wife togither I pray the[e] coom to bed to me . . . the marriage is but for satisfieng of the people.'[47] Just over one in five of women's suits claimed sex as evidence of marital contract, relying on the special status sexual intercourse had to seal a marital promise; for many, the case was forced by a pregnancy, and

[45] Rodes *c.* Cole, DL/C 212, p. 82; Thomas Thorpe *c.* Elizabeth Jackson (1609), DL/C 219, fo. 13^{v}; Stevenson *c.* Lewes, DL/C 211/1, fo. 96^{r-v}; Margaret Fisher *c.* Robert Prowdfoote & Margery Holte (1575), DL/C 212, pp. 335–6.

[46] See e.g. Lawrence Stone, *Uncertain Unions: Marriage in England 1660–1753* (Oxford, 1992), 66.

[47] Allen Browne *c.* Sibylla Greene *als* Johnson (1609), DL/C 219, fo. 23^{v}; Elizabeth Drake *c.* Edward Goodene (1626), DL/C 230, fos. 109^{v}–111; Elizabeth Spakeman *c.* Tide Clear (1593), DL/C 214, p. 385.

few had sufficient grounds to win their plea. Men, who only occasionally used claims of premarital sex themselves, tended to admit women's allegations against them, denying that the sex had involved any promise of marriage. Women's allegations linked sex with commitment; in their defence, men denied the connection. Robert Scawe defended himself against Ellen Tinckham in 1609 on the grounds that he had only 'had the carnall use of her body' when she came to his bed after he had been drinking, and that the public fame of a contract had been raised by her 'slanderous report'. Annabel Merriall, whose illegitimate child Thomas Hearn was supporting, alleged that he had promised her marriage when they had sex two years earlier. He responded by explaining to the court how it had happened:

> this respondent fell into more familiar acquaintance with hir by reason they wear servantes togither in one howse and in thend . . . obteined to have, and then had the carnall knowledge of the body of the said Annabell Meriall shee beeing as willing and ready thearto as this respondent and reither inticing this respondent to that wickednes then denieing or resisting him when hee offred him self, onelie shee desired that this respondent wold not thenceforth call her whore, and so she consented unto him, never having had any talk of marriage.

And Thomas Perry, sued by Elizabeth Newgate, admitted to the court that he

> in an unfortunat tyme havinge had carnall knowledge of the bodye of the sayd Elizabeth, And for that facte beinge convented before the judge of this courte in his chamber in the Doctors Commons did in deede in hope of avoydinge punishement and publique pennance for his offence confesse (though untrewelye) then before the judge of this courte that he and the sayd Elizabeth weare contracted together, upon which confession this respondent was . . . moved and drawne by the sayd judge of this courte to contracte himselfe agayne to the said Elizabeth . . . which he did in hope of releasinge his publique pennance And for no other cause . . . never intendinge or meaninge to marry the said Elizabeth Newdigate.

Presumably Thomas finally decided that public penance was a better fate than being forced into marriage.[48] Aware of the special binding power sex had, men and especially women were still not entirely clear about the exact rules that made it the evidence of commitment; most of the time, the desperation of an impending illegitimate birth made women come to court with claims based on sex and little else.

[48] Ellen Tinckham *c.* Robert Scawe (1609) DL/C 218, p. 303; Annabel Merriall *c.* Thomas Hearn (1592), DL/C 214, pp. 164–5; Elizabeth Newgate *c.* Thomas Perry (1591), DL/C 214, p. 68.

MAKING CHOICES

The litigants who sought to prove and disprove conjugality also told the court stories that explained their choice or refusal of partners. Material interest, affection, practical considerations, and the influence of friends combined to shape marital choice. At court, litigants often reduced their accounts of these factors to simple, pragmatic reasons aimed at convincing the court they were, or were not, committed to the marriage. Others brought witnesses with longer stories about the precise balance of material goods or emotions that women and men looked for when they married.

For many people the first question was one of economic viability. While couples did marry when they were still in service, marriage was generally linked with setting up a household: Hugh George told the friends of Mary Vaughan, who were pressing him to marry her: 'a man must first be provided of a house and thinges necessarie before he should marrye'.[49] More broadly, marriage for these couples involved an economic transaction for which parents, friends, distant relatives, and the couple themselves might all pledge money. Before contracting themselves, many men and women made careful enquiries about the 'ability' of men, and the 'provision' for women; financial standing was part of the general background into which both women and men made enquiries before planning marriage. Alice Colstock, a widow who ran a lodging house, told her suitor William Yorke 'That she was not as yet disposed to marrye but she wold lerne further of hym and of his habilitye, and willed hym likewise to lerne further of her and of her habilitye, and when she had so lerned of hym, she wold be ruled by her own frendes, and partly by his also,' although she agreed to ride with him to his house 'to se what he was worth and partely to make merye'. When she did enquire of her friends, she discovered 'that the sayd William Yorke both was a greate dyser [dicer] and also contracted to another woman', and refused him.[50]

Other people made specific financial conditions a prerequisite for marriage. William Meriton defended his failure to carry out his marriage to Joan Leetes on the grounds that 'her mother promised him he should have such lands as were the said Johan her fathers in mariadge with her daughter so as upon consideracon and promise this respondent contracted matrimonie with her daughter but now her mother intendeth not to fulfil that her promise'. Women imposed

49 Hugh George *c.* Mary Vaughan (1576), DL/C 212, p. 483.

50 William Yorke *c.* Alice Colstock (1573), DL/C 211/1, fos. 149v–150.

such conditions too. In 1591 Joan Mortimer claimed to have made her contract with Richard Campion conditional on claims she expected he could not substantiate. He, she said,

finding this respondent unwillinge to consente to marye with him did to thend that he mighte drawe her to yeilde unto his suit . . . affirme that he should be worth 20 poundes in money and 20 nobles in howshold stuffe she believeth that the sayde Richarde Campion being very importunate to procure this examinate to consente to be contracted in matrymonye unto hym she assuring herself that he could not be worthe the severall sums mentioned did promise hym that if betweene that tyme and Candlemas next ensewing . . . itt should appeare unto this respondent of certainty that he the saide Richard Campion weare worth 20 poundes she would then geve him her fathe and trothe.

Ultimately, though, Richard won the case with a story of a firmer contract, supported by the exchange of tokens.[51] Joan Sayers claimed she had consented to marry Christopher Smith in 1574,

if his father would performe his promise which was to gyve him the farme at Aldstock to his marriage and to make her . . . a joynter thereof . . . which promise she saith was not performed for the said Christophers . . . father refused to seale to the bondes being made for the performance thereof.

A fine line separated reasonable practical concerns and excessive preoccupation with financial arrangements. In 1592 Anthony Mitchell, the sexton of St James Garlickhithe, reported an exchange between Tide Clear and Elizabeth Spakeman, whom he was encouraging to get married:

I faith quoth the articulate Clear, if she have so much money as she saith she hath I will marry hir . . . she saith she hath £20 and if she will by and by or within these 5 dayes give me £10 let her bring her clothes and com to me when she will and I will marry hir and make her my wife tush quoth this deponent we wil have a match of it before we goe and wished the said Clear to be contracted with the producent but he wold not but still stuck upon the money and then this deponent being sexton of the parish called his boy and willed him to take a noat of ther names that they might be asked in the church on the sunday following . . . but Clear said well do what you will I will consent to nothinge except that I have the money first.

Elizabeth eventually tired of this, and when Anthony Mitchell asked her two days later if she had the money, 'she said no for . . . if he like the money better than he like me let him goe where he list'. To a cer-

[51] Campion *c.* Mortimer, DL/C 214, p. 9, DL/C 13, p. 399.

tain extent, though, this kind of trouble over money seemed relatively predictable, and a situation where marital preference was quite independent of financial provision was sufficiently remarkable for a few litigants to make a point of mentioning it. It featured impressively in Frances Gates's case against Henry Hancock: her relatives and friends told the court that her suitor, Henry Hancock, had insisted he wanted to marry her despite her lack of portion, saying 'it is noe matter for that I had rather have hir in hir smocke than another with a hundred pounds'. Significantly, though, Henry told the story the other way around, and his witnesses reported him as saying Frances's brother had promised him £100 in marriage with her.[52]

Those couples who were older, where one or both partners were widowed and settled with both a greater degree of financial independence and other responsibilities, found different priorities shaping their practical negotiations. The fairly sizeable estates and trades that widows and widowers, unlike younger women and men, had established made the balancing of financial arrangements a potential minefield; in particular, the expectation that husbands 'maintained' their wives did not always make sense in the light of widows' and widowers' economic situations. In 1626 one widowed London clothworker, James Edwards, effectively inherited his suit to Joan Nevill, a widow who kept a victualling house and a cookshop, from her former suitor, John Frank, a turner, who said he had given up his own 'interest' in Joan because of James's greater 'abilitie'. John reported his speech of renunciation to the court,

> I thought I had had some interest in the said Joane Nevill but if I had three times more interest than I have I now resigne all the same my interest unto you because I know you are a man of abilitie and able to maintain her farre beyond my ability and the said Mr Edwards seemed verie thankfull unto this deponent.

Joan Nevill and James Edwards then made a contract, dependent on his conditions: his daughter and his maidservant were both shortly to be married, and 'he would see them married out of his house, and then he and the said Jone would marry together, and . . . he would give over his trade and they would live together and serve God'. Alice Alden, a witness to the contract, said to them 'I will be your bridesmayd and I hope I shall have a paire of gloves', to which James

[52] Joan Leetes *c.* William Meriton (1579), DL/C 629, fo. 88^{v}; Christopher Smith *c.* Jane Sayers (1574), DL/C 212, p. 137; Spakeman *c.* Clear, DL/C 214, fo. 322^{r-v}; Frances Gates *c.* Henry Hancock (1635), DL/C 234, fo. 143.

replied generously 'You shall all have gloves if it cost me £3'.[53] Presumably James was wealthy enough to contemplate retirement (and buying gloves) at this stage, supporting Joan with his estate; he told her as they contracted he would 'take . . . [her] from her drudgerie'. As James changed his mind about the match, he became much less sanguine about his economic future. They did not marry, and James later said that if Joan had 'come to bed to him' after they made the contract, he would have married her the next morning; instead, worried that she would force him to marry her by law (as she later tried to do), he made his estate over to his children, telling the scrivener who was writing down his business arrangements, that if Joan forced him to marry her, she should have 'noe benefite of or by his estate' and further, 'soe longe as he the said Edwards was whole in the fiste she the said Jone should not be whole or sound in her head'. Each time he went to consult the scrivener about his relations with Joan and their legal ramifications, he gave him wine, telling him that he would rather spend his money than let Joan have it.[54] James's estate, at first an asset to him in his courtship, ended up a considerable source of anxiety; his vows to keep her from working, at first a romantic promise, ended up looking to him like a menacing drain on his estate.

Widows' responsibilities for their dependents, and the frequently precarious nature of their livelihoods, were also liable to unbalance the marital equation. Some women depended on an inheritance that would be cut off on their remarriage; others carried on a husband's business which they would lose if they married a non-citizen. In 1620 Ellen Walker, the keeper of a victualling house in the parish of St Sepulchre, made her own attempts to secure her position when she decided to marry a man who was not entitled to run it with her. Ellen told a neighbour that 'she could have had at that time manie good matches far exceeding him in wealth yett her conscience gave her that she could not fancie noe other nor would she marrie annie other' and solicited him to 'be a meanes to Mr Hugh Middleton that the said Ashmore might be made a freeman of the Cittie of London to the end she might marrie him and not lose the benefitt of keeping a victualling house'. Although this was achieved, somehow the match came apart and Ellen had a bond drawn up in which they agreed to end all

[53] Joan Nevill *c.* James Edwards (1626), DL/C 230, fos. 125v, 127v–128. For comparison, £3 was the sum at which the goods of this witness, a shoemaker, were valued for tax purposes.

[54] Ibid. 312v.

matters between them and 'never to moleste or trouble eche other herafter', saying 'she knewe what she did and that she did yt for the good of her and her children'. A year later Henry broke this by suing her, and she went on to sue him for defaming her by writing notes saying she was a whore and telling others she kept a house 'little better than a bawdy house', by which he must have constituted another kind of threat to the victualling trade by which she lived.[55]

It was mostly money, rather than status, with which litigants in these courts were concerned; most were of middling status and interested rather in the financial means of prospective partners, than their social standing or descent. For one couple with aristocratic connections descent became central. Judith Wrott, in the service of Lady Mary Wroth, took her distant relative and suitor John Wroth to court in 1619. John, after a long and semi-public courtship, had refused to marry her on the grounds that Judith was not worthy of him: 'if it were knowne that he should marry one with no posicon he should neither take up money nor be trusted or go forward with his intended busines'. The case came to focus on Judith's descent, with witnesses for her testifying that she was of 'worshipfull parentage', and that her father was a JP, and witnesses against her deposing that her sister had married a seal cutter 'of no great abilitie'. In the end, although John, already involved in disputes over Mary Wroth's husband's estate, claimed to have promised Judith a total of £700 to avoid further lawsuits, Judith's proofs of marital commitment held sway and the sentence was in her favour.[56]

More influential for some men than these concerns of status was the issue of the moral reputation of their prospective wives. But given the stress laid on sexual honesty in contemporary definitions of femininity, the disputes over disrupted courtships devote a surprisingly little amount of attention to women's sexual chastity. Those men who claimed the collapse of a betrothal was due to a woman's unchastity argued that they had made chastity and virtue, as other people did financial standing, a condition of the match. John Jackson, sued by Amy Sturry in 1611, defended himself: 'thinking that the said Amy Sturry had bin a younge woman of good parentage . . . he hadd a good opinion of her and thought her to have bene a vertuous younge woman . . . he did in his private affection towards her wishe her well

[55] Henry Ashmore *c.* Ellen Walker (Jan. 1621), DL/C 227, fos. 155ᵛ, 157; Ellen Walker *c.* Henry Ashmore (Feb. 1621), ibid. 236–241ᵛ.

[56] Wrott *c.* Wroth, DL/C 225, fos. 378, 179–81, 185–8; DL/C 192, fos. 38, 47; DL/C 19, fo. 11ᵛ.

and made love unto her, and they both had . . . some speeche and conference together as lovers and wellwillers'. They exchanged gifts, which he later insisted were 'as matters in curtesy betwene them but not for or in consideracon of any matter of marriage promise or contract of matrimony'. Later, when 'upon inquiry of her freinds' he 'found that she had abused him with many untruthes he presently withdrewe his former opinion and affection from her'. John Browne explained his refusal to marry his fellow-servant Agnes Knott by her 'lewd' behaviour after betrothal. He said that when they talked of marriage, he told her that

> there is a good space betwyxt that and Michaelmas next, and that if she could during that tyme gett her frends good will to lyke of him, and he for his parte allso at that tyme like well of her the said Agnes, they would then proceede to marriage.

'But', he told the court,

> sithence that promise so made by him, shee the said Agnes hath so lewdley behaved her sellfe during that tyme of pawse that he this respondent could not like well of her, and therefore cannot perswade him sellfe to marrie with her.

It is not clear what Agnes did; perhaps she and her prospective husband had different expectations and understandings of the 'time of pawse' between betrothal and marriage, which could be so ambiguous a period. Another defendant, Anthony Bassett, made the correlation of financial and moral standing explicit, arguing, successfully, that he had made his contract to Martha Kirton conditional on both: in his promise, as he reported it, he 'said unto her that if [he] should be offered of the said somme of foure score pounds and conditionally that the said Martha should remaine chaste and honest he . . . would marry with her'.[57]

The stories told by defendants and plaintiffs about why they did or did not make binding contracts automatically favoured pragmatic, easily explained reasons; it was much harder to make a plausible argument to the court out of the emotional considerations that went side-by-side with practical ones. The references in testimonies to attraction, affection, and love are often confined to the familiar phrases and proverbs that men and women used as advice or warn-

[57] Amy Sturry *c.* John Jackson (1611), DL/C 220, fo. 753^{r-v}; Agnes Browne *c.* John Knott (1575), DL/C 212, p. 165; Martha Kirton *c.* Anthony Bassett (1629), DL/C 193, fo. 333^{r-v} (misnumbered: actually, fo. 323), DL/C 25, fo. 261.

ings: 'whotte love is sone cold'; 'marriage is neither for a day nor a year'; 'what is done cannot be undone'. When stories about broken courtships did focus on emotion, plaintiffs, defendants, and witnesses concentrated on singular, original summaries of the reasons for preference or indifference. They lit especially on the prospects of a practical, successful marriage. Rebecca Bowling wanted a husband who was like her brother-in-law: witnesses for him deposed she had said 'she would rather have him . . . than any man els in regard he was so lyke to one that married her sister'. Alice Oliver, a widow, cited among her reasons for declining Anthony Tristram that her brother 'was not willing that she should go into Yorkshire as that it was tolde hir that it was a barren country' and 'hir friendes thought that he beeing a serving man was a very unfit match for her'. Agnes Bushey drew a fine distinction between accepting love and being in love, telling the court that when her older suitor 'required her leave to love her . . . she answered that he might love her as he loved other folke for that she tooke him then to be married'; but when she 'understood . . . that he was a suter unto her . . . [and] a woman his laundress in Holborne came and tolde her how far he was in love with her', she answered 'she was sorry for it . . . for . . . she culd neither like nor love him'. According to the laundress who mediated between them, she explained this was because 'he was an ould man and going out of the world and she younge, and that his lyving lay at sea, which she could not awaye with'.[58] If stories like these do not explain the whole spectrum of influences on marital choice, they do reveal some of the very specific details that were understood to affect decision-making for marriage. The sexton Anthony Mitchell recommended Tide Clear as a husband to a 'good enocent maid' of his acquaintance, Elizabeth Spakeman, because, as he told her, 'with he . . . you may live well and use him as you list'.[59] Husbands might even be recommended in this way to children. In Sussex in 1609 the 20-year-old Margaret Hudson was sued by Thomas Ayling on the grounds that she had assented to her father's suggestion that she take Thomas to be her husband; depositions by witnesses later revealed that she had done so at the age of 5, and Ann Gauys recalled how she had recommended Thomas to Margaret when Margaret was 6 or 7. Thomas and her husband had

[58] Thomas Savage *c.* Rebecca Bowlinge *als* King (1617), DL/C 225, fo. 9. The words, however, did not convince the court that a contract had been made: sentence was passed against Savage, DL/C 18, fo. 26. Anthony Tristram *c.* Alice Oliver (1592), DL/C 214, fos. 240, 216; Wye *c.* Bushey, DL/C 213, pp. 806, 830.

[59] Spakeman *c.* Clear, DL/C 214, p. 323.

been working together, and she sent Margaret to her husband for a piece of cheese, which he cut to the size of 'the breadth of her three fingers and not above'; Margaret, coming back with the cheese, said 'there is a husband indeed I would give as bigge a peece of cheese as this to a dogge'. Ann said 'Why Megge wilt thowe have him and she said noe not I', Ann went on 'noe you will have Thomas Aylinge', and Margaret replied 'yes that I will why should I not'.[60] Even eight years before marriage came into question, acquaintances and friends might play with the idea of suitable husbands, and so the rhetoric of good husbands started earlier, often, than the language of courtship. The stress on husbands and wives rather than lovers held true in particular for widows and widowers. Thomas White, a widowed sailor, proposed to his servant because he 'had manie children and had good liking unto' her. Anne Wickham allegedly chose William Thomas for a second husband because 'she knew Mr Thomas would take more care of her sonne than a stranger would he being his godfather'; at the betrothal, he 'took William Wickham the sonne of the said Mrs Wickham in his armes and said kisseing of the said Child That now we are concluded if it please god I shall now be both father and godfather to him'.[61]

Stories like these presented preference and pragmatism as united motives for marriage; but other narratives foregrounded a version of courtship more about romantic involvement than marital suitability, a vision of love with considerable potential for dramatic story-telling. Both as a background to betrothal and, sometimes, as a proof that stood on its own, this vision could provide potent evidence of commitment. Courtship involved not just rational choices, but irrational dramas of love. Joan Symonds, sued in 1617 by James Cartwright, told a friend that 'when . . . James Cartwright lay sicke in her fathers house . . . she saw him in great extremitie and that as she thought he was at the point of deathe, which sight strooke her with such greife that if her sister had not come in and cut her lace she thought she should have dyed presentlye'.[62] John Bulkley, suing Agnes Modye in 1572, brought witnesses to produce a narrative about the conflicts of their emotional involvement, focusing around the power of Agnes's mother. Ralph Kybley told how, meeting the couple at Pie Corner

[60] Thomas Aylinge *c.* Margaret Hudson (1609), WSRO EpI/11/11, fos. 135, 128ᵛ.

[61] William Cock *c.* Agnes Chester *als* Tuckerman (1592), DL/C 214, p. 152; William Thomas *c.* Anne Wickham (1636), DL/C 234, fos. 178ʳ⁻ᵛ, 180 (misnumbered: actually, fos. 278, 280).

[62] James Cartwright *c.* Joan Symonds (1617), DL/C 225, fo. 136.

near Newgate, he had found them arguing, with John threatening to go away. Ralph joined the weeping Agnes in grasping John's gown to keep him there, but they let go when he offered to leave the gown behind. John left, and Agnes begged Ralph to go and fetch him, saying

> Now I see it is trewe that is tolde me, for I do heare saye that he is towarde to have another to his wyffe but I have had for hym manye a sore strype besydes manye fowle wordes but yet I will never forsake hym and said farther (with a cryeinge voyce and wringinge of her handes, confirmynge it also with an othe) that she did love hym . . . before he did love her as she thowght, and said farther, that she was sure unto hym . . . and that she wolde have never none to her husbande excepte she had hym . . . neither sayd she shall I love any man so well as I do love hym.

Ralph brought the two together again further down the road, where Agnes begged John

> John what have I offended you, that you be so angrye with me and he answered her agayn and sayd have you geven me no cause to be angrye with you, when you came before your mother the laste day, and denyed that you wer sure unto me when ones you gave me your faith and your trothe to be my wyffe . . . To whome the said Annes Modye answered agayn, Indede I do confesse I did so, but my mother and all the frendes I have shall never make me do so agayne.

Agnes wanted John to come to her cousin's house, but he refused; she wanted to talk more, but she 'was loth to stand in the streate but he said he cared not who saw hym stande in the streate and with that went from her', leaving her crying out so loud that 'one standinge by her in the streate byd her hold her peace'. The next day the three met again in Holborn and this time they did go to Agnes's cousin's house, where they made a formal contract, and Agnes swore 'That I have said I will never denye whils I do lyve no not for all the frends I have.' This narrative of promises and betrayal, told by one witness and repeated in substance by others, laid the ground for allegations that Agnes had broken her oath, and presented her as at once a pursuing lover and a weak daughter. The dominant role is still John's but the emotional expressions that prove marital commitment are attributed entirely to Agnes. A plausible and effective story, accepted by the court, it also suggests some of the conflicts that disturbed women's courtships. Agnes and John do much of their conversing in the street, in the crowded corners of Holborn and Cheapside, but she tries to avoid this; at home, Agnes's mother's power (surely exaggerated for the purposes of testifying) loomed large enough to threaten her daughter's future.[63]

Men's love produced some equally dramatic stories, with a different stress. Love makes women like Agnes Modye and Joan Symonds powerless, weak, and desperate; they faint, cry in the street, or weep and beg. When men suffer the powerlessness that desire and love can bring, they react, instead, with rage, anxiety, or madness. When John Lippett, a feltmaker, became contracted to Martha Pegge, a servant, at a Bankside inn in 1631, he spoke publicly about his fears that love would make a fool of him. A young woman servant, one of John's witnesses, reported their exchange:

> [John said] Martha canst thou love me or noe and wilt thou marrie me whereto the said Martha replied I doe love thee and I could find in my hart to make thee my husband and noe other man but the[e] And . . . John Lippett requested the said Martha to deal plainelie with him and not to leade him into fools paradise nor to make him believe that she loved him when indeed she did not whereuppon the said Martha againe replied that she would marrie with no man but him And then the said John Lippett took hir the said Martha by the hand and said to hir I take thee to my wife and my faith and troth and all that I have I give unto the.

Earlier, another woman had warned Martha 'not to make a foole' of John, but to get her mother's consent and make a contract.[64] In 1570 another man reacted more extremely when he fell in love, taking to his bed 'verie sicke and in some daunger'. Witnesses recalled 'the dysease seamed strange to the physitians', until his mother asked him 'whether he had not conceaved some phansie of love which shold be thoccasion of his sicknes'. Having diagnosed his illness as lovesickness, and discovered him to be in love with her maidservant, she took steps to cure it by arranging a contract with the girl, 'although there were small cause why she should like that match'. The symptoms of lovesickness were familiar, potentially powerful signs: in an attempt to trap Margaret Inman into marriage with him in 1632, Thomas Bedle allegedly 'did faine himselfe madd or distempered for the love of hir . . . he brake one of his neighbours glasse windows and rann a knife at one of the servants of the said house and beate or strock the master of the said house'.[65] Other thwarted men threatened suicide. Joan Frith claimed Thomas Sweeting had told her he would kill himself if she would not

[63] Bulkley *c.* Modye, DL/C 211/1, fos. 35–7, 54–5, 50–1; DL/C 8, fo. 256^{v}.

[64] John Lippett *c.* Martha Pegge (1633), DL/C 630, fos. 37^{r-v}, 35.

[65] Sebastian Briskett *c.* Jane Hugman (1574), DL/C 212, fos. 32 ff.: four years after the contract the couple had not yet married and Jane Hugman, the servant, was involved with someone else. On the medical conception of lovesickness whose

accept his gifts; Sage Povey said her suitor threatened, via a friend, to hang himself if she would not accept some rings.[66] While women's love is commonly called to prove itself through assertions of independent choice, a will to love that defies the influences of friends and parents, men's love is conceived within different parameters: it appears as a frustration, not an assertion, of their will. The subjugation that love threatened, the possibility of being fooled, were not easily reconciled with the assertive role men expected to take in courtship.

Attraction, affection, and love were, of course, foundations of many marriages long before the period to which Lawrence Stone dated the beginnings of affectional marriage, the mid- to late seventeenth century.[67] Detailed stories of the stages of courtship and narratives of romantic love were more frequent in seventeenth-century marriage suits not because feelings had changed, but because litigation over marriage was expanding, in these courts at least, to encompass a wider field of evidence for the bonds that constituted conjugality. The stories of promised marriage had come, by the early seventeenth century, to focus on the grounds by which conjugality was defined in the popular imagination as much as those the law understood: material exchange, financial promises, rituals of courtship, physical familiarity and emotional ties. And while the canon law of marriage contracts placed little weight on most of these grounds, the courts showed a tendency to favour, in particular, stories that supported allegations of a contract with a narrative of conventional courtship ritual.

THE RESULTS OF LITIGATION

Through the sixteenth and seventeenth centuries the church courts listened less and less willingly to the narratives of courtship and contract. By the late sixteenth century success rates for plaintiffs in marital contract cases were already low, and they continued to fall; the same developments, concurrent with a decrease in cases coming to the court, have been noted outside London. The fall in litigation

symptoms Mrs Briskett detected, see Mary Frances Wack, *Lovesickness in the Middle Ages: the Viaticum and its Commentaries* (Philadelphia, 1989). Office *c.* Inman & Bloise, DL/C 234, fo. 25.

[66] Thomas Sweeting *c.* Joan Frith (1575), DL/C 212, p. 210; Stafford *c.* Povey, DL/C 212, p. 201. Suicide for love was supposed to be free from the taint of sinful despair: see Michael MacDonald and Terence R. Murphy, *Sleepless Souls: Suicide in Early Modern England* (Oxford, 1990), 95–103.

[67] Lawrence Stone, *The Family, Sex and Marriage in England 1500–1800* (London, 1977).

suggests several kinds of change. Martin Ingram has concluded that this period saw 'a growing acceptance of the principle that solemnization in church was the only satisfactory mode of entry into marriage, and a corresponding decline in the custom of contracting binding spousals'.[68] Contracts of marriage seem, though, to be still part of marriage convention in the first half of the seventeenth century; what seems to have changed is the readiness to litigate. With the transition of the church courts into a forum dealing largely with defamation disputes, and the evidence of the court's decreasing willingness to confirm unsolemnized contracts, the law—at least in London—must have appeared a less hopeful answer for disputing couples.[69]

What, in any case, would a successful outcome offer a plaintiff? A marriage ordered by the court might seem an unlikely basis for satisfactory conjugal relations, yet in a society where outside intervention—friends, parents, and institutions—played so large a role in making and regularizing marriage, it must have made some sense. Litigants might also look for an enforced marriage for financial gain: men who refused to cohabit with a partner could be ordered at least to maintain them. Yet although the court decreed in around one in five cases to confirm the alleged contract, for most of these couples no evidence survives to prove that they actually married. If the court's decisions were not always enforced, why did litigants pursue cases? As one man asked the woman suing him in 1614, 'Why do you sue me for marriage seeing the more money we spend it is the worse for mee and you too[?]'[70]

To answer that question we need to look not so much at the results of litigation, as at its meanings. Only a minority of alleged marriages proceeded through all the judicial stages to a formal sentence: most were abandoned, and probably settled out of court, at an early stage, and with the court's support. Far more plaintiffs abandoned their claims than enforced them. Many litigants went to court looking for some form of settlement, not necessarily an official one. For some, the ambiguities of betrothal led to confusion and difficulty, and they became anxious that the period between betrothal and solemnization had been too long, unclear of the status of the promises they had made or received, or convinced of the inconstancy of their intended partner. Often, the men and women in these cases speak of 'wishing to make a good end' to their confused situations. Some came to court

[68] Ingram, *Church Courts*, 193.

[69] Ibid. 209.

[70] Elizabeth Willoughby *c.* John Goodyeare (1614), DL/C 222, fo. 14^{v}.

with more ambitious attempts to manipulate the legal process. In Canterbury in 1621 Margaret Smith testified that her fellow servant, William Sanders, and his mother and aunt had tried to persuade her to abandon the marriage contract suit she was suing against him, promising her that William would still marry her because he expected to win £20 towards his expenses in the case he himself was suing against another woman supposed to be betrothed to him. £20, he said, 'would be a good beginning for them'.[71] Bringing a contract case was one way of establishing, through a formal or informal settlement, some control over a public process and its private manifestations.

These detailed stories of courtship and betrothal, at once conventional and individual versions of the foundations of marriage, suggest another dimension to such litigation. Going to court was a familiar threat with substantial symbolic power and, whatever the result, it constituted a public assertion of right. Once at the court, even litigants with the least plausible or correct forms of evidence were given the space to put their claims, retelling the material, verbal, and emotional exchanges of courtship and calling witnesses to support and expand it. As the conclusion to a courtship, it must have had particularly powerful implications for women whose role thus far had centred on listening and answering: when they took a case to court, they initiated an action and through it, told their own story.

The transactions of courtship were at once intimately associated with the marital relations they were meant to precede, and representative of a quite separate sphere of action. For both young men and young women, courtship could represent a time of new independence, an occasion for a degree of personal choice and autonomous decision-making. But throughout courtship, and in the stories that witnesses told of marriage promises, men behaved as if they expected to assert their own will, women as if independence from influences, sanctions, and threats had to be fought for. Men made proposals; women answered them with cagey references to friends whose power ranged from the illusory but useful, to the real and physically threatening. The male and female youth of this class were expected to marry generally in line with their own wishes, but the ideology of dependency which cloaked women's identity gave a different cast to their marital decision-making. In the light of that ideology, women developed their own tenuous strategies of autonomy to decide their futures, and to defend themselves in the face of legal action.

[71] William Sanders *c.* Anne Marten (1621), (Canterbury Cathedral Archives, Consistory Court Depositions x.11.19, fo. 4^{v}.

6

Domestic Disorders: Adultery and Violence

The making of marriage in early modern society laid out the different meanings of conjugality for women and men; but it was as marriages came apart that the precise implications of those meanings emerged most starkly. When marriages broke down, a whole edifice of economic transactions, sexual relations, and social roles came unstuck. The complaints women and men made to the court then reveal the great difference between what conjugality meant for men, and what it meant for women. Structured around two kinds of complaint which in themselves reveal much about the difference made by gender to the rules of marital conduct, testimonies of broken marriages describe the domestic, economic, and sexual organization not just of exceptionally troubled marriages, but of ordinary conjugal life in the city and its environs.

The grounds on which marriages were formally ended were quite different for men and women, and they were founded on the understanding that men and women's sexual behaviour had incomparably different meanings. Men sued their wives for adultery; women sued their husbands for extreme cruelty. Effectively, only women could be penalized for extramarital sex and only men could be guilty of violence. The meanings of these two offences were central to the gender relations of marriage. Sexual conduct, the entire foundation of women's honour, became also the only measure of their marital conduct; adultery was a betrayal of the marital bond whose implications were well rehearsed in popular culture and religious rhetoric. Extreme cruelty was an offence much less easily definable because of its semi-legal status and much less discussed in contemporary culture. At court, both types of complaint were the focus for much wider stories of marital conflict whose details reveal the gendered rules in whose light conjugal relations were conducted and judged.

At the courts, pleas of either cruelty or adultery could achieve only a limited resolution. England emerged from the Reformation with a uniquely unreformed canon law on marriage: while Protestant states in Europe were moving towards separations which allowed at least the innocent party to remarry, England's church courts remained empowered to do no more than grant judicial separations, 'from bed and board'.[1] Such separations allowed couples to live apart, but precluded remarriage by either party, guilty or innocent. Remarriage was only possible if a union could be annulled on the grounds of bigamy, precontract, non-consummation, forced marriage, or the minority of either partner. Annulment on most of these grounds was extremely rare: the majority of marriage cases were suits for separation prosecuted either by the injured party, or sometimes by the couple together, 'negotiating' for separation, and in both types of suit the allegation centred almost invariably on women's adultery or men's cruelty.

A formal decree of separation was, technically, the only way in which a couple could live apart: the courts were empowered to, and sometimes did, proceed against couples living apart unlawfully. Many couples, nevertheless, must have separated without any legal decree, and the testimonies this court heard in suits for bigamy and annulment reveal the extent to which women and men might reinterpret the church's rules of marriage, deciding for themselves how soon to presume an absent spouse dead, what made a marriage irregular, or whether to prosecute a spouse caught out in bigamy.[2] As well, the court procedure established a financial settlement, granting provision for women when litigation started, and alimony if separation was granted, unless adultery had been proved. A relatively high proportion—42 per cent—of complaints sued by men, centring on women's adultery, were sentenced; suits alleging men's violence, sued by women, were much less successful, and only 26 per cent received a final sentence. In both cases, virtually all sentences were given in the plaintiff's favour; cases that the court was unlikely to accept were presumably abandoned earlier, and couples were either reconciled, or lived apart without the court's sanction.[3] Legal separation also led, for some people, to remarriage. Theological debate on divorce reform continued through Elizabeth's reign, and some clergy were prepared

[1] On the legal and practical aspects of separation in this period, see Roderick Phillips, *Putting Asunder: A History of Divorce in Western Society* (Cambridge, 1988), chs. 1, 2; Lawrence Stone, *Road to Divorce: England 1530–1987* (Oxford, 1992), 51–9; Thomas Max Safley, *Let No Man Put Asunder: The Control of Marriage in the German South-West* (Kirksville, Miss., 1984), 28 ff.

[2] For further discussion of this, see my 'Women, Sex and Honour: The London Church Courts, 1572–1640', Ph.D. thesis (University of London, 1993), 165–70.

[3] Out of 120 cases where witnesses were examined, 39 were sentenced in the plaintiff's favour, one in the defendant's.

to marry separated couples—including, in 1605, William Laud.[4] The canons of 1604 reaffirmed the bar to remarriage, and in the same year bigamy was made a felony, but both before and after that date, a number of separated women and men argued that they were entitled to remarry, and some of them ended up in this court accused of bigamy, claiming in their defence that clergymen had advised them they could remarry.[5] Many more must have done so undetected.

Separation at the church courts offered legal and financial settlement of dispute. But going to court to end a marriage also set in train another process: the articulation of marital discontent. The proofs demanded by the court, for the endings as well as the beginnings of marriage, constituted only the focal point for the long histories of affection and conflict which husbands and wives came to the court to conclude. Their testimonies, constructed both within and around the cultural and legal models for marital breakdown, explain the economic, affectional, and material relations that bound or divided couples.

CONFLICT AND THE COURT

Suits for separations and annulments were unusual both in London and throughout the country.[6] Marriages were very rarely annulled, either on grounds of forced marriage or non-consummation. Cases of bigamy were far more frequent: in London between 1572 and 1640 witnesses came to testify in forty-four such suits, a quarter of all marriage separation litigation. The conventional story of the presumed death, and subsequent reappearance, of a spouse, was not the only tale behind bigamy: what litigants and witnesses say also reveals the poverty, or antipathy to a spouse, that could make the presumption of death and the possibility of remarriage convenient. In both cases, discovery of bigamy depended very largely on a tenuous chain of communications and coincidental meetings: many other bigamous couples must have remained undiscovered. The laws that regulated

[4] Stone, *Road to Divorce*, 301–8, explains the legal situation and the debate. For a contemporary argument, see Edmund Bunny, *Of Divorce for Adulterie, and Marrying Againe* (Oxford, 1610).

[5] See e.g. Elizabeth Pinchbeck *als* Thimblethorpe *c.* Nicholas Thimblethorpe (1616), DL/C 223, fo. 371ᵛ; Cicely Grimes *c.* Thomas Grimes (1625), DL/C 193, fo. 147.

[6] See e.g. Martin Ingram, *Church Courts, Sex and Marriage in England, 1570–1640* (Cambridge, 1987), 181–2, on Wiltshire, Chichester, and Ely, and Susan Dwyer Amussen, *An Ordered Society: Gender and Class in Early Modern England* (Oxford, 1988), 127, on Norfolk.

remarrying (only after seven years could an absent spouse be presumed dead) were in many cases reinterpreted or ignored. The largest part of litigation to end marriage, though, was concerned with separation on one of two grounds, adultery or extreme cruelty.[7] Almost invariably, and in roughly equal numbers, men sued for separation on the grounds of their wives' adultery, women on the grounds of their husbands' violence; some were presented instead as suits for restitution, where plaintiffs sought the restoration of cohabitation, often provoking counter-allegations of adultery or cruelty like those of separation suits, and aiming, like them, for a financial and legal settlement of dispute.

Between 1570 and 1640, all these kinds of suits were in decline. In the late sixteenth century, eight or ten separation and bigamy cases came to the court a year, and around three of them called witnesses, a third of cases receiving final sentences, usually in the plaintiff's favour. After the turn of the century, cases fell to four or five a year, and by the 1630s there was often no more than one a year.[8] At the same time, women's suits for separation and annulment did not expand in the way that their litigation over marriage contracts and defamation suits did in this period: overall, while slightly more women sued for separation than men did, there was no noticeable rise in women plaintiffs, and in bigamy suits, the number of cases brought by women actually fell.[9] Evidently, the opportunity the courts provided for fighting the battles of heterosexual relations was quite different from the forum it provided for disputes between women.

Separation suits involved a particular range of litigants. With alimony settlements so central to the legal battle of separation, many litigants were fairly wealthy; as well, it was harder to settle separations out of court than unsolemnized marriage contracts, or defamation disputes. As a result, the gentry and aristocracy made a significant use of the London church courts for separation, as they did not for other disputes. Of witnesses in separation suits, 12 per cent called themselves gentry, compared to only 4 per cent in defamation and marriage contract cases; and

[7] This contrasts with Martin Ingram's finding for Wiltshire that complaints of adultery constituted only a minority of separation suits: see Ingram, *Church Courts*, 182. London society may have been more willing to see adultery as the end of marriage; the two courts may also have been following different conventions.

[8] Figure 3, in Ch. 2, shows the changing levels of separation suits in relation to other sex and marriage litigation. The numbers recorded here, as those that called witnesses, were also affected by the canons of 1604 which re-established that separations could only be granted if witnesses testified.

[9] In cases recorded in deposition books between 1572 and 1640, 47 men sued women for separation and 57 women sued men.

while the parties in separation cases included tailors, chandlers, and alehouse-keepers, they also included three knights and ladies and several gentry couples.

The two main kinds of suit, allegations of adultery and cruelty, each involved a distinct kind of plea, and the testimonies witnesses gave to the court expose an understanding of marriage in which men's and women's misconduct were read and articulated in very different ways. Women's allegations of life-threatening cruelty were difficult to judge, based on subjective proofs, and hard to measure. Most Reformation divorce doctrine ignored the issue of cruelty, except for the *Reformatio Legum Ecclesiasticarum*, drafted in England in 1552 but never officially confirmed, which proposed that divorces should be granted not only on the grounds of adultery but also for a husband's unjustified violence against his wife.[10] This idea of justification—the reformers' 1551 document referred explicitly to the need husbands might have to punish their wives—made measuring violence difficult. Separations on the grounds of cruelty came less frequently to the court as the seventeenth century wore on, and only a quarter of them (compared to 40 per cent of adultery suits) received final sentences. But the complaint of adultery men brought against their wives had a sound biblical precedent as a cause for separation. In the Protestant rhetoric of marriage, adultery could be understood to dissolve the marital bond of itself.[11] Far more lucidly than violence, it could be read as a breakdown of conjugality: 'The disease of Marriage is Adultery', preached Henry Smith, 'and the medicine thereof is Divorcement.'[12] It depended not on the long stories and subjective judgements necessary to prove cruelty, but on the apparently much less ambiguous evidence of suspicious familiarity, compromising encounters, and sometimes, convenient eavesdropping and spying. And although the church courts, requiring evidence of irredeemable sin, could not interpret such acts as inherently destroying the marital bond, plenty of witnesses told stories in which adultery was both the proof and the source of much broader marital wrongs. Women's sin dissolved marriage more easily than men's.

[10] Phillips, *Putting Asunder*, 89; *Reformation Legum Ecclesiasticarum*, ed. John Fox and Matthew Parker (London, 1640).

[11] As it was, e.g., by the commission which considered the question of the Marquis of Northampton's remarriage after a church court separation on the grounds of his wife's adultery in 1547; and, amongst other marital advice, that of Daniel Rogers, *Matrimoniall Honour, Or, The mutuall Crowne and comfort of godly, loyall, and chaste Marriage* (London, 1642), 167.

[12] Henry Smith, *A Preparative to Marriage* (London, 1591), 108. Smith's sermon was, the subtitle noted, first read at a marriage contract ceremony.

IDEALS OF OBEDIENCE

In the testimonies of marital breakdown that came to the court, men and women spoke at length about their understanding of the ground rules of conjugal relations and the disruptions that destroyed marriage. They ordered their stories through the paradigm provided by the law, in which women's misconduct meant the loss of chastity and men's, the abuse of legitimate power; but behind that paradigm we can also glimpse the models through which contemporary culture understood the marital relationship, and the individual concerns on which women and men acted. Men and women adapted the models into their own stories about the organization and the collapse of conjugal relations.

The most neatly elaborated of cultural models for the household was, as we have seen, unwieldy for most people's use. The idealized orderly household, where hierarchical rules regulated every personal relationship, fitted few families' experiences. The detailed prescriptions for women's behaviour that were listed in conduct books were just as hard to enforce. Nevertheless, the ideals of household order and female conduct tapped into an ideology of marriage which had some considerable currency in everyday exchanges as well as in popular culture. The cultural representations of conjugality with which Londoners might come into contact devoted little attention to complete marital breakdown, separation, or remarriage after widowhood. But they did deal in detail with the dangers of adultery and with marital conflict. Marriage sermons, household advice, ballads, and broadsheet literature all focused on women's adultery as both a pointer to, and a result of, the loss of their entire virtue. The strictures with which women were bound to domesticity, to silence, and to obedience were guaranteed to preserve both chastity and its appearance.[13] On the street, the language of defamation made elaborate and creative use of the conflation of disorderly, unvirtuous behaviour with whoredom. In marriage disputes, some men used exactly similar insults against their wives; and many others told stories about adultery that testified not just to illicit sex, but to the whole spectrum of disturbances associated with it.

The cornerstone of prescriptions for wives was a problematic obedience. Women are enjoined to be submissive, to obey with love, and to enable their own subjugation by choosing carefully a husband whom they can obey. Obedience is the core of both femininity and

[13] The literature of female conduct is surveyed in Suzanne W. Hull, *Chaste, Silent and Obedient: English Books for Women, 1475–1640* (San Marino, 1982).

marriage. The correlations drawn by so many contemporary writers between household and state depend upon a basic assumption of the submission of wives to their husbands. Robert Cleaver prescribed 'For as in a Citie, there is nothing more unequall, than that every man should be like equall: so it is not convenient, that in one house every man should be like and equall together.'[14] In the ordered household it is the husband's duty to command obedience as it is the wife's to give it. The husband is the head of the household's body. William Whately's 1619 wedding sermon told the head of the family 'hee must not stand lower than the shoulders; if he doe, doubtlesse it makes a great deformitie in the family. That house is a misshapen house, and . . . a crump-shouldered, or hutch-backt house.'[15] Popular literature presented a similar message about the 'deformed family' through the depiction of household order subverted. Women who are allowed too much power in the house make fools of their husbands, and ballads describe the process of humiliation which results. One 'Married Man's Complaint' explains:

> I wash the dishes, sweep the house, I dress the wholesome dyet;
> I humour her in everything, because I would be quyet:
> Of every several dish of meat, she'll surely be first taster,
> And I am glad to pick the bones, *she is so much my Master* . . .
> And when I am with her in bed, she doth not use me well, Sir;
> She'l wring my nose, and pull my ears, a pitifull tale to tell, Sir.
> And when I am with her in bed, not meaning to molest her,
> She'l kick me out at her bed's-feet, *and so become my Master.*[16]

Bedroom scenes are central points of tension in ballads like this one. In 'a Dreadful Combat between Bonny Anthony, and his wife', the centrepiece of several seventeenth-century ballads, Anthony is forced to lie on a bed 'as soft as an old Oaken shelf'; on the rare occasion his masterful wife allows him into her bed, she urinates, instead of into the pan they usually use, into a colander which happens to stand in its place, and, Anthony laments, 'It run all about both my stomach and face'. She responds to his complaints with devastating logic:

[14] Robert Cleaver, *A Godly Form of Householde Governement: for the ordering of private Families, according to the direction of Gods word* (London, 1598, and with John Dod, 1616), 174.

[15] William Whately, *A Bride-Bush: Or, A Direction for Married Persons* (London, 1619), 98.

[16] 'My Wife Will be my Master; Or, the Married Man's Complaint against his Unruly Wife . . .' (*c.*1640), BL Roxburghe Ballads, ii. 576 (also printed, eds. W. Chappell and J. W. Ebsworth (London and Hertford, 1871–95)).

I told her sweet Wife you do Urine beside,
She called me Coxcomb, and told me I ly'd
How can it run over before it is come
So near to the top as the length of my thum.[17]

The sexual script is thus reversed and violated: when women replace men as the active players in bed, sexual activity is replaced with a beating, semen with urine. The tension over sexual mastery points up one of the central stresses of the ideology of obedience. The language of love articulated fears about women making fools of men or driving them mad; the sexual role reversals of ballads, exploring female assertiveness in the bedroom, carry the barely disguised message that men are meant to be, always, on top. In the plots of adultery that preoccupy so many husbands, women are consistently, alarmingly, sexually assertive. Their assertiveness has implications for the order of the whole household. Women's adultery violates the conjugal bond, imperils men's honour, and disrupts the domestic economy. The most well-rehearsed scenario of adultery is also the most revealing: the spectre of sex between apprentices and mistresses threatened a revolution in the domestic hierarchy.

While popular culture made it clear that sex was central to marital order and disorder, the advice proffered by clergy was more preoccupied with the 'friendly' love, as central to Renaissance doctrines of marriage advice as to their Puritan successors, that was meant to ease the burden of obedience.[18] Men were advised to regard their wives as helpmeets, 'a friend, and comfort for society, but also a companion for pleasure' (as well as 'in some sort a servant for profite also'). Those who 'usurp such superiority over them, as is commonly used towards slaves' drive their wives to adultery.[19] Marital breakdown, then, is caused not only by the failure of male authority, but by its extremes. But these attempts to settle a balance of conjugal power are betrayed by their own imagery. The metaphors of marriage for which early modern writers ransacked the animal and mechanical kingdoms

[17] 'Couragious Anthony: Or, A Relation of a Dreadful Combat between Bonny Anthony, and his Wife', *The Pepys Ballads*, ed. W. G. Day (Cambridge, 1987), iv. 146; see also, for the same story, 'Poor Anthonys complaint And Lamentation against his miseries of marriage, meeting with a scolding Wife', *Pepys Ballads*, iv. 121, and 'The Scoulding Wife', *Pepys Ballads*, iv. 136.

[18] Kathleen M. Davies, 'The Sacred Condition of Equality: How Original Were Puritan Doctrines of Marriage?', *Social History*, 5 (1977), 563–80.

[19] Alexander Niccholes, *A Discourse, of Marriage and Wiving* (London, 1615), 5; *The Court of Good Counsell. Wherein is set downe the true rules, how a man should choose a good Wife from a bad, and a woman a good Husband from a bad* (London, 1607), sig. C2.

were hopelessly unworkable. Women are described as 'yokefellows'; marriage is the joint efforts of two oxen, or a boat, 'the man and wife as partners like two Owers [oars]'. But the corollary of these images—the picture of the boat ends 'for she is as an under-officer in his Common weale'—proves their impossibility.[20] If one partner is stronger than the other, boats and oxen alike can only go round in circles.

Clearly, these detailed prescriptions for obedience had little relation to the reality of most marriages. The confinement of women to the domestic arena that they advised was, for most women, impracticable. And the total dependence of women upon their husbands that advice literature assumed was prevented by, if nothing else, the positions from which many women married: not from their father's homes, but from widowhood or service, with some experience of financial and social independence. But the broader dialogue about authority and submission and its tensions were more relevant to marital conflict. The marriage service, after all, prescribed a fundamentally unequal relationship, and the balance of power in marriage was at the heart of some of the most violent disputes that came to these courts. In these cases, the moments of violence, adultery, or desertion become the focus of ideas about the financial balance of marriage, the social, verbal, and sexual behaviour of women, and the equilibrium of the household partnership.

ADULTERY IN THE HOUSEHOLD

The plaintiffs and witnesses in adultery suits told stories of illicit sex that depended on some basic assumptions and some familiar storylines. Almost entirely, these stories were about women. While the rules of ecclesiastical justice predicated men's suitability for marriage upon sexual continency as much as they did women's, the practice of the courts shows no evidence that separating couples experienced this in reality. Male adultery was not, in practice, sufficient foundation for a separation suit: women occasionally accused their husbands of adultery, but generally in the much larger context of either cruelty, or desertion and the establishment of a new household with another woman.[21] In contrast, stories of women's adultery focused on single

[20] Smith, *Preparative to Marriage*, 66.

[21] See e.g. Rose Partridge *c.* Robert Partridge (1611), DL/C 220, fo. 651; Jane Croece *c.* Edward Croece (1620), DL/C 226/V, fo. 43^{r-v}.

or repeated incidents, stressing women's betrayal of their husbands, the disruptions of domestic order and the broader vices that followed women's promiscuity; most importantly for the success of the case, they stressed women's refusal to repent and reform. Their testimonies played on themes rehearsed at length in contemporary culture. In plays, ballads, and fiction the story of adultery revolved around some central figures and dramas; sermons and advice literature outlined the larger sins consequent on women's unchastity. The language of insult offered one version of the unchaste woman, in the shape of the whore; many of its associations figured as well in descriptions of adulterous wives. The drama of adultery in the household was a staple plot of Elizabethan theatre, and tales of men being cuckolded by their colleagues, friends, or apprentices came to the courts as well as the stage. Such stories proved suggestive for early modern men and women. At court and on the street, the plots and characters of contemporary culture supplied one means of dramatizing experience.

Adultery cases depended on witnesses. Husbands and neighbours might string together clues from seeing women in suspicious places, at odd times, with dubious company, but in court they needed to give unequivocal evidence of actual acts. The courts heard a whole series of stories from servants, apprentices, or neighbours who, alerted by suspicious behaviour, looked through windows, stood in dark corners, or made holes in walls to watch. A typical observer was George Mathew, a witness in George Marr's adultery suit against his wife Margaret in 1573. Mathew deposed that Edmund Alden had made a partition of painted cloths in the shop he hired from him and set a bedstead behind it, and that 'he was certyfied by divers how that the articulate Margarett Marre did resorte thither unto him divers tymes verye suspiciouslye'. Coming back about ten o'clock one night he saw one of Edmund Alden's boys 'out to buy some wine', and his wife told him 'that she helde a wager, that Margarett Marre was there with the sayde Edmund Alden'. 'That will I knowe', he said, and

> straighte wayes lookinge into the sayde Edmund Aldens bedd roome throughe a hole by his stayers allmost right over his the sayde Aldens bedd, he did then and there espye and see the articulate Margarett Marre lyeing uppon the sayde Edmunde Aldens bedd on her backe with all her clothes upp and him the sayde Edmunde lyinge upon her with his hose all untrussed and downe and so lookynge a while longer to see shortlye whether the sayde Margarett Marre were there or no, he did at lengthe see the sayde Edmunde Alden come of her and sawe her the sayde Margarett lyinge still moste unhonestlye all naked with her clothes still upp.

Mathew's wife supported his testimony with a less explicit story about her trip to see her child at nurse in Essex. She was accompanied by Edmund Alden and when they got to the inn Margaret Marr appeared.

> [T]hey all lay in one great chamber together viz the three women in one bedd . . . and Edmund Alden in another . . . so after a whyll that . . . Margaret Marr had lyen in bedd with the . . . women, she sayd she wold lye no longer there, to be thruste and so rose uppe from her this deponent . . . and went into bedd . . . to Edmund Alden and so lay with hym there in one bedd naked togither all that night . . . and wold not come forthe . . . to this deponents bedd agayn . . . although she . . . did thre or fower tymes call her away, and asked if she wer not ashamed to lye there.[22]

The early modern household was not built for privacy. Most couples had a servant or apprentice who was usually in the house; walls were thin, keyholes large, and partitions of cloth easy to pull aside. Most courts received testimonies like these, and contemporary commentators were apt, as historians have been, to doubt their veracity. Clearly, some holes in walls may have been legal fictions: there were particular conventions for testifying to adultery.

As well as the actual act of adultery, witnesses noticed the circumstances associated with it. Certain kinds of behaviour could be suspicious enough to make the foundation of a whole case. In 1574 witnesses reported the transgressions of an apprentice in a printer's workshop in Paternoster Row. Isacke Bynge was suspected of adultery with the wife of his master, Henry Denham, whose publications included such detailed profiles of household order as *A Briefe and Pleasant Discourse of Duties In Marriage* (by Edmund Tilney, 1568) and *The Monument of Matrons* (Thomas Bentley, 1582). Michael Osborn, another member of the household workshop, watched Isacke Bynge dallying, embracing, and kissing with Elizabeth Denham; noted that as their familiarity increased, he was moved up to his mistress's table, and often went into her garden and the parlour alone with her; and eventually 'according to his dewty and othe' told his master what he had seen, for which he was, he said, 'cruellye beaton and otherwise moch mysused'. Judith Awdry, whose husband also worked with Henry Denham, saw the couple sitting together 'at the table ende in the hall . . . drinckinge of wyne togethers in a glasse . . . the sayde Isacke Bynge was vere famyliar, and she lykewise . . . for she . . . did see the sayde Isack Bynge lay his hande aboute her necke and kysse

[22] George Marr *c.* Margaret Marr (1573), DL/C 211/1, fo. 191^{r-v}, 190^{v}.

her'. When they saw her and noticed she was with child, they called her in to share the wine. Later she reported the incident to her husband, who commented that Isacke Bynge 'seemed to be used more lyke a master then a servante'.[23] Adultery between a woman and her husband's male servant is a familiar situation in separation suits and a constant concern. It presented an obvious and profound threat to the ordered household. Keeping women within the walls was meant to ensure their chastity; if adultery could happen even there, any guarantee was impossible. The prospect of such relations disturbed, too, the balance of hierarchical household order. How could servants, or indeed wives, be properly subjugated to their household masters when they were always capable of cuckolding them?

The domestic drama of adultery encompassed servants not just as potential sexual partners, but as compromised witnesses. Large numbers of the witnesses in marriage cases were bound to the litigants by the ties of service or apprenticeship. To discover an employer in a situation of such vulnerability bestowed upon a servant the power of disclosure and sometimes a conflict of loyalty. Edmund Foster, an apprentice, came to the court in 1609 to testify against his master's wife, Grace Ball. In his master's absence, Edmund had grown suspicious of a friend of his, who had begun making protracted evening visits to the house, and sometimes reappearing for breakfast. Listening on the stairs, he heard Grace and her husband's friend talking in bed; on one occasion, sent on a spurious errand for sausages so that Grace could let her lover out of the house in the morning, he succeeded in trapping the man in the kitchen. Left in charge of the business, Edmund took responsibility too for his master's marriage. His statement expressed anger at her betrayal and her attempts to fool him, and he responded by reporting Grace's behaviour to her brother-in-law.[24] This kind of story-telling reversed the prescribed order of household relations. Good housewives were expected to supervise their servants in all areas of behaviour, including their sexual relationships; servants and apprentices were officially prevented from marrying (although many did), and often faced dismissal if their own contraventions of sexual rules were discovered. The servants in these cases gave evidence against their mistresses, expressing as they did so disapproval, shame, and grief at their behaviour. Others must have

[23] Office *ad prom.* John Osborn *c.* Isacke Byng (1574), DL/C 211/1, fos. 214^{v}–215, 232–3. (John Osborn, the presenter of the case, was Michael Osborn's father.)

[24] Bayly Ball *c.* Grace Ball (1609), DL/C 214, p. 473. The stories in this case are discussed further in the following chapter.

turned a blind eye, for such evidence needed the sponsorship of a suing husband to reach the courts.[25] Witnessing and testifying might have profound implications for a servant's position in the household. In 1612 Walter Brampton bribed his wife's servant, Martha Robinson, to spy on her: he offered her £20 and a gown 'to catche hir mistress in a tricke', and said if she succeeded, she should 'live with him in his house to her owne content and more like a Chylde then a servant'.[26] A servant's knowledge of a mistress's adultery might have effects on household order almost as potent as the act of adultery itself. The dangers of that act for the ordered hierarchy of the house were described in a sermon of 1632 on the biblical story of Joseph propositioned by Potiphar's wife: 'If his Master's wife should have prostituted herself to her servant, her vassall; the censure of her crime would freely have passed; and each common inferiour would have become her Judge.'[27] The moral in this cautionary retelling warns women, as much advice to them did, not so much to be chaste, as to appear so; public knowledge of a woman's unchastity is as dangerous as the sin itself.

The husbands who caught their wives in adultery experienced a familiar and potentially humiliating dilemma. Popular culture made cuckolds the butt of countless jokes, rituals, and songs: most humiliated of all was the 'wittold', the cuckold who condoned his wife's adultery. Perhaps partly to limit the humour contemporaries so easily found in their situation, husbands stressed the enormity of their wives' sins and the profound shock with which they discovered their betrayal. When William Loder discovered his wife Elizabeth's adultery in 1625, he himself told it to their friends, endeavouring to insist on the drama of the situation, and perhaps to forestall the ridicule that might accompany it. Taking them up to her chamber where she was lying in bed, he announced: 'Oh Lord I would I had never lyved to this daye for my wife hath undone me.' This dramatic declaration was received by at least one of his audience with a wilfully innocent response: 'hath she lost you any leases or wrytings?' William answered that 'she had disgraced him and stayned the house playing the whore with his tapster'.[28]

Like defamers, witnesses and litigants in adultery cases often envisaged women's illicit sex as the focus for a general depravity and

[25] On the role of servants in witnessing adultery, see Stone, *Road to Divorce*, 211–30.
[26] Walter Brampton *c.* Agnes Brampton (1612), DL/C 220, fo. 661.
[27] John Featly, *The honor of Chastity. A sermon* (London, 1632), 17.
[28] William Loder *c.* Elizabeth Loder (1615), DL/C 223, fo. 22.

specific threats to the household. Behind much contemporary anxiety about adultery lay, unsurprisingly, the threat of pregnancy. The possibility of a man having to provide for children that he had not fathered was a major source of anxiety with great potential for mockery. Contemporary ballads bring the humiliations of cuckoldry to a peak with the man who 'rockes the Cradle, when the Child's none of his owne'.[29] Where illicit sex was concerned, paternity was conflated with financial responsibility. Margaret Marr told the court the child she had given birth to was her husband's, but another witness reported that she had told him a different story. Thomas Slater, a 50-year-old haberdasher, was walking along in the Royal Exchange, when his friend pointed out 'George Marrs wife' to him, and since Thomas had heard speak of her but not met her, they invited her to a tavern where, over a pint of wine, they had the following conversation:

he . . . seinge the said Margarett Marre bygge with childe did say unto her as followeth what be you with childe, to whome she answered, yea that I am and I am abowt to go into the cuntrey, to my fathers to be browght a bedde, To whome he this deponent and his other frend replyed agayn and sayd in effecte, what have you chosen such a father to your child, that is not able, to kepe you to lye home, or that you be asshamed of . . . to whome she . . . confessed agayn and sayd, that in caryenge home . . . Edmund Aldeyes worcke to hym, to his chamber, he did overcome her so with faire wordes, that at laste she yelded unto his requeste, and so was begott with childe bye hym.[30]

Margaret is culpable, here, not so much for becoming pregnant from adultery, as for doing so improvidently. Had her lover been richer, it is implied, she would have been less 'ashamed'; and in other cases, the words attributed both to adulterous women and to their partners are strikingly unlike shamed confessions. In 1608 William Thackerie deposed that he had found Florence Archdeacon and William Smith committing fornication three weeks after Florence had given birth, and that he heard William Smith confess to fathering the child and say 'that it was a prettie boy and that her . . . husband was never able to gett such a childe'.[31] Agnes Goddard, midwife to Dorothy Kingsland, reported that in answer to her questions as to where her husband was, Dorothy had said that her husband was not the child's father and 'that shee had rather see him hanged then that hee shoulde

[29] 'Rocke the Cradle, John', Roxburghe Ballads, iii. 176.

[30] Marr *c.* Marr, DL/C 211/1, fo. 195^{r-v}.

[31] John Thackerie *c.* Edward Smith & Florence Archdeacon (1608), DL/C 225, fo. 239^{v}.

have byn the father therof'.[32] Both these reports play on the tradition that during or after childbirth was the time for women to talk about the paternity of their children; but the expected guilty confession is replaced with a kind of pride in the result of a sexual competition between men that focuses not on having sex, but on fathering children. Indeed, talking to her brother-in-law, Margaret Marr seems to have spoken of her adultery in terms that elided desire for pregnancy with desire for sexual fulfilment. She acknowledged, he said, having a child by Edmund Alden and 'confessed that the sayd George Marre did not begett that child on her nor did not deserve therfore, and . . . confessed to hym this deponent, that the sayd George Marre was never able to gett a child of her'; she wanted, though, to return to her husband and requested her brother-in-law to mediate between them, and he gave her 'the best councell he could'.[33] Contemporary medical theory held that female orgasm was necessary for conception; one of the concomitants of this belief, contradicted as it must have been by experience, was that sexual pleasure and conception were very closely identified for women. Women's sexual desire and men's sexual facility encompassed and associated conception and pleasure.[34]

Though the possibility of illegitimate pregnancy was the most obvious practical reason for the ideology of sexual double standards, it was not its main focus in practice.[35] Women's adultery was understood to damage a much broader sphere of marital relations, and it was physical, mental, and material disturbances that husbands focused on at the court. Adulterous women engage their husbands in conflict in the house, taking control over communal rooms, locking doors, and breaking into trunks. They are often accused of selling, or removing, the 'household goods': with the end of marital harmony, any notions of joint ownership collapse. As the marriage collapses, so does the character of the wife, and this is made most evident in the care with which husbands and witnesses record the language of adulterous women: rude, loud, seductive, mocking, or threatening, it takes all the forms that characterized 'unfeminine' speech in this period, and with their words, adulterous wives effected one kind of humiliation of their cuckolded husbands. Anne Clemens *als* LePage, from Rouen, brought her husband Gervase to court in 1592, alleging he was physically

[32] Simon Kingsland *c.* Dorothy Kingsland (1617), DL/C 225, fo. 83.

[33] Marr *c.* Marr, DL/C 211/1, fo. 190.

[34] On female sexual pleasure and conception, see Jane Sharp, *The Midwives Book* (London, 1671), 82.

[35] As Keith Thomas points out: 'The Double Standard', *Jl. of the History of Ideas,* 20 (1959), 216.

incapable of consummating their marriage; but her husband's responses drew attention in return to her adultery and her mistreatment of him, alleging that 'untill the time that the producent had lien with the said Peter Lespard he . . . did use and intreat hir with all gentlenes and love, but since that time she hath divers times called him cuckold and said that she wold ly with the said Peter or someother'. He beat her for her 'ill speaches and deedes' and when the French church came to hear of their conflict they were admonished to live together more peaceably; but Anne seems to have managed to achieve some revenge for his beatings, for Gervase also reported that another man, Latore, had 'made an afray upon [him] and beat and misused him in the street' and Anne had told him that 'so oft as he this Respondent beat hir the said Latore should beat him'.[36]

Adultery involved a certain assertion of female autonomy. At the very least, it meant the privileging of female sexual desire over marital stability; it meant, in some cases and for certain periods of time, married women organizing an independent life, sometimes with a child, until they could renegotiate conjugal relations with their husbands. Margaret Marr, visibly pregnant with her lover's child, left her husband to live with her sister, but found they 'could not agree together because . . . her sister did myscall her'. She asked Thomas Fletcher for advice on taking her own house, and he suggested she 'take a house alone, and a litle wench to lerne somethynge'. Thomas Fletcher, married himself and, unlike Margaret, still living with his spouse, told the court that she went on to confide her desires to him, saying:

> Thomas I have no bodye that I may be so bold of to breake my mynde unto as to you nor more that I beare good will unto as to you, so moch that wold to god it had bene your fortune to have bene my husband Then he this deponent answered agayn and sayd, That he never understode so moch of her mynde as nowe, and that she never offered hym so moch frendshipp, And she sayd agayn, that she did not so indede, because she was asshamed to offer it unto hym, and that it is not a womans parte to offer it, but she asked hym this deponent if he wolde or could fynde in his harte to take such parte as Edmunde did (meanynge the articulate Edmunde Alden,) And he this deponent sayd/ Yes, askinge of her where they shuld have a convenyent place therfore, because his house was not fytt and when it shuld be And she sayd agayne, when he . . . wolde, she knewe of a convenyente place therefore, which was (as she sayde) in Ratclyff.

36 Anne Clemens *c.* Gervase LePage (1592), DL/C 214, pp. 258–60. The case resulted in Anne's prosecution for adultery: Office *ad prom.* John Warwell *c.* Anne Clemens *als* LePage (1593), DL/C 214, pp. 442–50.

Thomas 'never obeyed her request', and later she left London to have her child at her father's in the country.[37] If his report of their conversation, over a year later, was an accurate one, it suggested that Margaret found herself outside the conventions both of married life, and of sexual roles; planning to live on her own and preparing for a child that was not her husband's, she makes Thomas an offer that is not normally 'a womans parte'. What she offers is a liaison in which Thomas would take his place alongside her estranged husband and her lover (Thomas makes no reference, in this conversation, to his own wife, except by obliquely pointing out that his house was 'not fytt'.) We need to read this testimony with an eye to its legal utility for Margaret's husband: it suggested, as the practical interpretation of canon law demanded, that she was incorrigibly adulterous. It is none the less revealing of contemporary perceptions of the way adultery changed women and their position, leaving them negotiating their way between sexual availability, independence, new commitments, and reconciliation with their husbands.

In conventional understandings of the effect of women's adultery it was posited as a disturbance of domestic relations that was at once humiliating and threatening. At the Chichester court in 1602 witnesses told how an Arundel woman, Susanna Wilson, staged an elaborate verbal and economic repudiation of her husband James, effectively replacing him in the household with her lover, Thomas Page. James Wilson accused his wife that she allowed Thomas Page 'to eate and drinke and lodge in thyne house contrarie to the good will . . . and expresse commandement of thy sayed husband'; that 'during the tyme of thy overmuch familiaritye with the sayed Thomas Page and of his resort unto thy sayed husbands house . . . thou . . . diddest use or rather abuse thy sayed husband James Wilson unseemely and not becoming an honest wyfe'; and that she shut her husband in his chamber, pinning the door with a knife or stick, while she went to Thomas Page's chamber 'and diddest there continewe and abide with him alone some tyme 2 or 3 howres sometymes untill midnight and sometymes longer'. According to witnesses, Thomas Page was also seen getting money from Susanna, while he was at her house; James Wilson was heard to say 'that he woulde spende 4 pence to dyne or to suppe with his saide wife with a joynte of meat and the saide Susanna Wilson . . . hathe made answeare he should neither dyne nor suppe with her under 6 pence'. Susanna, her maid pointed out, refused to let her husband 'sit

[37] Marr *c.* Marr, DL/C 211/1, fo. 189.

in his owne house either at dynner or supper with her and eate suche meate as she had provided for the said Thomas Page and herself' unless he paid for it, 'as though he were a stranger'; she 'compelled' him to 'sitt by himself and eate such things as he either provided or caused to be provided for himself'. Adultery, here, transforms both the spatial and the economic organization of the household. Susanna withdraws money, provisions, and sexual attention from her husband, and gives them instead to her lover; her husband sits alone instead of with her; he is shut into his room, and out of her bed. The same disorganization of the conventions of consumption was attributed to Alice Arden, accused at her trial of having kept her lover in her own house and feeding him with 'delicate meates' and 'sumptuous apparell', with the full knowledge of her husband.[38] The effects of adultery are seen to strike at the root of the marital household: the shared purse, the preparation of food by women for men, and the space of the bedroom. It is possible, although it is not made explicit, that Susanna was running a victualling business in the house; if so, the economics of commercial provisioning seem to have intersected uncomfortably with those of the conjugal relationship.

Susanna was heard, too, to speak explicitly about her sexual behaviour, saying 'that she woulde never lye with the broken arse knave her husbande any more so longe as she the saide Susanna lived': the phrase circulated locally and was repeated back to her by neighbours trying to effect a reconciliation. It was an image, suggestive of actual impotence, that sealed the humiliation already effected by James's economic subjugation. In many ways, the account of Susanna's reorganization of the household economy is redolent of the conventional tales of cuckoldry that amused and warned early modern husbands.[39] But by the end of the witnesses' testimonies, the story of James's humiliation is overshadowed by another tale: that of the frightening power of his wife. Susanna was said to have threatened 'that excepte the saide Thomas Page . . . did resorte unto the house of the saide James Wilson her husband the saide Susanna woulde make all the vaynes in the harte of her saide husbande to ake'. No one suggested how she meant to do this—by sorcery or love?—but the idea tied in with the reputation Susanna was gathering locally for malevolent

[38] Catherine Belsey, 'Alice Arden's Crime', in *The Subject of Tragedy: Identity and Difference in Renaissance Drama* (London, 1985), 130. The words, from the wardmote book of Faversham, 1551, are quoted in *The Tragedy of Master Arden of Faversham* (1592), ed. M. L. Wine (London, 1973), 160.

[39] See e.g. 'My Wife Will be my Master', Roxburghe Ballads, ii. 576.

power. She was accused of beating a woman servant, who was suing her for her wages; another servant, she was heard to say, had fallen down on her knees and begged her forgiveness after stealing a pot of drink from her; and she was known to have procured an abortion by drinking savin. She was also in court for defaming another woman.[40] In the light of these different invocations, and abuses, of power Susanna's adultery became, in the stories of her neighbours, servants, and husband, not just a cause for his ridicule, but a source of both material loss and actual danger. Husbands telling adultery stories were, at one level, striving to defuse cuckoldry's comic charge.

The range of threats that Susanna Wilson's behaviour posed to her marriage, her household, and her husband were articulated most clearly in the words attributed to her: about her domestic power, her sexual desires, and her antipathy for her husband. In stories like these the speech of adulterous women defines their characters, in line with the cultural association of women's sexuality with their words. It also condemns women out of their own mouths: much stress is laid on Susanna's persistent repudiation of her lawful husband in favour of sexual pleasure with her lover. Her words may work as a model of female sexual assertiveness; their function here, though, is to show how deeply her adultery corrupts her whole character.

Witnesses for another husband paid even more careful attention to his wife's words, questioning her, persuading her to confess, and writing down her replies. In London in 1610, Walter Brampton found his wife Agnes 'at a lewde house with Theophilus Holland'. He brought her home and there, in the presence of Edward Lane and his wife, in whose house they were living, and their servant John Wright, he 'did chardge . . . and accuse her for committing adultery'. The idiom of this occasion is entirely a legal and ecclesiastical one: like a minister or a judge, Agnes' husband charges her, questions her, and hears her confession. At this examination, she responded as she was meant to, according to witnesses: 'in humble and penitent manner as it seemed to this deponent [she did] seriously confesse and acknowledge that shee had comitted adultery or fornication with the said Holland twice, and with the said Sandford, once, and that they had had the carnall use of her bodye'. In this story of formal confrontation Agnes's lan-

[40] Office *c.* Susanna Wilson (1602), WSRO EpI/15/3/15, fo. 103; EpI/11/9, fos. 186^{v}, 188; my attention was drawn to this case by a mention in George Hothersall, 'Matrimonial Problems in West Sussex 1556–1602', *West Sussex History*, 4 (1990), 6–11. For the defamation suit, see Jane Barker *c.* Susanna Wilson (1602), EpI/15/3/15, fo. 50, and EpI/11/9, fo. 130.

guage itself echoes the official idiom: carnal use, adultery, fornication. The scene encouraged the other men present to take a part in this questioning process. The day after Agnes's confession, John Wright, the servant who had witnessed it, took the initiative: 'having a purpose to make freindship between . . . Agnes and her husband and having heard of her incontinent and adulterous life', he wrote out an acknowledgement of her offences for her to read after him; and accordingly she did so, 'voluntarily and submisselie'. However, Agnes's submission seems to have ended there. In other conversations with Edward Lane and John Wright, reported in minute detail to the court, the 'submissive and penitent' tone of her first responses is abandoned. In private, after her first confession, she talked to John Wright about 'her lewdnes and adultery' with Holland and Sandeford and 'confessed . . . that shee had the carnall knowledge of them both . . . of the one with his hose downe and of the other with his points tyed being then nothing ashamed, but rather bragging of her Lewdenes'. Although the legal language of 'carnall knowledge' is still central to this exchange, Agnes's 'confessing' is nothing like a confession. It is, uniquely, she who has the carnal knowledge of them, not the other way around; and the description of their various states of undress only privileges her part more. This kind of boasting was, for contemporaries, the predictable result of women's adultery.

Agnes's sexual assertiveness went, according to John Wright, further than this. When she told him she was going to Bishopsgate Street he suspected she was meeting a lover and questioned her on her return. This time, she gave a different kind of response, and he interpreted it differently.

> [He] did question with her and urge her that shee had bin in their companye, and shee ymagining that this deponent had knowne soe much smiling upon this deponent asked him whether he thought shee had lyen with a married man or a bachelor in that tyme (the sayd Sandeford being a married man and the said Holland a bachelor) and this deponent . . . sayd with a married man, and she then smiling sayd to this deponent that she thought he was a witche, whereby this deponent gathered that shee had lyen with Sandeford . . . and shee then desired this deponent to be secret and not reveale any thing that he knewe or heard or shold knowe by her, saying that he this deponent shold have as much kindenes of her as they had . . . saying that he shold lye with her before any of them, which he might have done, if he had bin soe ill disposed as to yeelde unto her inticements and faire speeches.

His account traces the subtle transformation Agnes has wrought in their conversation: from quasi-legal inquisition to flirtation.

Agnes's adultery made her, in the eyes of her husband and his male associates, a woman beyond redemption. Edward Lane told the court he, and others, had made many attempts to get Agnes Brampton to leave her 'adulterous life', and that she had replied, with the authority of proverbial wisdom, 'that shee could not leave her adulterye or to that effect and that it was rooted in the bone and wold never out of the flesh, and that shee shold answer for her owne sins and that shee must have her pleasure though she were damned for it'. From this he was 'persuaded that shee will never be drawn or persuaded to live honestly with her husband'. In the same vein, Susanna Wilson of Arundel was supposed to have sworn 'she could never lie with her husband again'. To her audience of concerned neighbours, Agnes Brampton 'made lighte of their persuasions . . . and shee hath made a pish of [Edward Lane's] wordes and sette them at nought, and . . . shee hath once or twice sayd . . . that she wold not give over her adulterous life . . . for that shee said noe one man in England could content her'. And finally, Agnes suggested that though she was sinning now, she would not always be tied to her husband. When Edward Lane spoke to her about her husband, he heard her 'boast of the short life of her husband': she told him 'in a kinde of vaunting and joyfull manner that shee had bin with a cunning woman and that her husband shold not live above eighteene weekes'. The cunning woman concerned came to be a bone of contention between the couple, Walter believing that she was a witch, and Agnes claiming that she only saw her for 'merriment sake', to listen to her singing and playing the viol. Agnes's servant had a similar story to report: she heard her 'say to her husband . . . in a kynde of merriment that her first husband lived but nine weeks and if shee had thought that he . . . wold have lived above eighteene weekes shee wold never have married him'. To the same woman, though—and this is the only woman who testifies—Agnes expressed her doubts and fears: 'she sometimes wept and sometimes said a pox on them for roagues they have bin my overthrowe and that she wold not care if it were not for John at Lanes'. If Agnes had really said 'no one man in England could content her', she was also ready to claim her affections *did* lie entirely with one man—John Wright, the servant who questioned her and whom she allegedly propositioned.[41]

Insistence on Agnes's refusal to reform was an important part of Walter's case against her; her own answers to his allegations are not

[41] Brampton *c.* Brampton, DL/C 220, fos. 569^{v}, 570, 573^{v}, 572^{v}–573, 570^{v}, 575, 659^{v}–660.

recorded. Walter's whole case may have been stage-managed; Agnes's servant Martha told the court that Walter had bribed her to watch her mistress and that he had told her he sent Edmund Holland to his house 'of purpose to lye with his wife or to allure her to committe adultery', telling Martha that 'nowe he had gotten securitye for her porcon from her father he wold be divorced from her and wold allowe her noe more then the law wold give her'.[42] But the complex verbal exchanges between Agnes and her various inquisitors suggest, at least, the power of certain stories of adultery. Agnes may have used different languages for her adultery to the men and to her servant: 'confessing', with the penitent attitude expected by the ecclesiastical and legal officialdom her neighbours and husband impersonated; teasing her husband and his allies in a language that was both menacing and subversive; and still breaking down when she was alone with her maid. We might also detect in these different stories two different ways of looking at women's adultery: the self-confident betrayer of monogamous conjugality that the men describe, and the anxious victim of unrequited love that the maid sees. For the men in this case, convincing evidence of Agnes's adultery lay in a portrait of a woman who was rooted in vice, and who used her immoral behaviour to threaten not just her husband's honour, but his life.

The jokes and threats that Agnes Brampton and Susanna Wilson made against their husbands tapped into a specific drama that went much further than the humiliations, economic disturbances, and household disorders that were conventionally associated with women's adultery: the plot of domestic murder. The story that was told of Alice Arden and her lover was only one of the tales of domestic homicide that were so popular in Elizabethan theatre and popular literature, in which handsome young men, often apprentices, cheated elderly husbands of their younger wives, and, in league with the wives, killed the husbands and replaced them in both business and marriage.[43] In law, this scenario involved a double treachery: the murder of husbands by wives, like the murder of masters by servants, was not a felony, but petty treason. Pamphlets, plays, and ballads stressed the household arrangements that domestic homicide violated: husbands were murdered in their kitchens, in their beds, in their sleep, with their

[42] Ibid. 661^{r-v}. Edmund and Theophilus Holland, both accused of adultery with Agnes, may be brothers.

[43] The pamphlet literature, and *Arden of Faversham*, are discussed in Frances E. Dolan, *Dangerous Familiars: Representations of Domestic Crime in England 1550–1700* (Ithaca, NY, 1994), ch. 1.

own kerchiefs, in the sight of their children.[44] This vision cast a powerful shadow. Its conventional features, the threat of attractive apprentices and the absolute amorality of adulterous women, figured, as we have seen, in scenes of potential adultery; as well, some husbands and wives feared, or threatened, murder. Murder was the culmination of the economic, material, and physical consequences of adultery: it was the last danger that adulterous women posed to their husbands.

In another case, the fantasy of husband-murder was conjured up in a lighter way. In 1619 the servants of Sir Francis Ashbey, owner of a large estate in Harefield, Middlesex, gave the court long and detailed testimonies about the suspicious behaviour of his wife Joan with their servant Roger Die. Joan Harmeward, one of the servants, spoke about the way Roger Die had overstepped the limits in his relations with Joan Ashbey as they moved around the house and grounds of Breakspears, the estate Francis had inherited from his father the year before.

> [She] did observe the bould carriage and behaviour of . . . Roger Die, and her [Joan Ashbey's] affection and love to him, in soe much as this deponent hath seene them cast water one at thother, and they have been in the milke house . . . togeither, where they have caused this deponent to skyme the milke bowles for them and have eaten togeither out of one and the same dishe, and where they have toyed and played togeither in verie unseemely manner divers tymes and for the space of an hower or twooe togeither that this deponent hath been ashamed to behold them, the milke house being locked or boulted to them.

Another servant said that Roger 'did with his hand in very familiar manner not fitteing for him to doe strooke her upon the backe side of her gowne and went forth out of the house to walk alone into some walk belonging to Sir Francis his house'. Behaviour like this echoed the innocent conventions of courtship: Roger also asked Joan Harmeward to send her mistress 'a bent silver sixpence', and another woman to buy her some cherries 'as a pledge' from him. At the same time, it was profoundly disruptive. The terms the servants used to describe the situation masked anxiety about privilege and favour in

[44] See e.g. 'The Murder of Page of Plymouth', in *Sundry Strange and Inhumaine Murthers, Lately Committed* (London, 1591), repr. in Joseph H. Marshburn and Alan R. Velie (eds.), *Blood and Knavery: A Collection of English Renaissance Pamphlets and Ballads of Crime and Sin* (Rutherford, NJ, 1973); *A True Relation of the Most Inhumane and bloody Murther, of Master Iames Minister and Preacher . . . Committed by One Lowe his Curate, and Consented unto by His Wife* (London, 1609); *Murther, Murther. Or, A Bloody Relation How Anne Hamton . . . by Poyson Murthered Her Deare Husband* (London, 1641).

the household with the language of shame. John Burbury advised Joan Ashbey 'not to companie with him, for it did breed great distaste to the servants in the house'; Joan Harmeward told the court she was 'ashamed to behold them'; Joan Croste told Joan 'it did not stand with her credit to use such dalliance with one that was but her servant' and told the court of her 'great grief' at witnessing their suspicious behaviour.

But Joan Ashbey and Roger Die's disruptions of their household went one step further than this. They wanted not just to break the bonds of one marriage, but to replace it with another in a simple exchange. A guest of Francis Ashbey, waking at two in the morning to hear 'the rusling of a satten gowne glidinge downe the staires', saw Joan and Roger go out to walk on the heath, where they stayed for an hour and a half; when he asked Joan later how they had passed the time, she told him Roger had been saying to her 'yt was pitty that suche a ladie as she was . . . should want children and that the only meanes to have children was to change the man'. Such words cast Roger in a familiar role, the young, virile lover of a woman wasted on an impotent man; Joan also 'averred' that Roger had 'had the carnal knowledge of her' in, symbolically, the entry of her husband's house. On another occasion, this time in front of witnesses, Roger played on the same kind of vision. John Burbury, domestic servant with the Ashbeys, told the court that one day while he was working in his room and Roger Die was lying on his bed talking to him, Joan came in. Roger lay

> as if he had been asleep . . . [she] nipped him by one of his fingers and thereuppon he started, and . . . said yf I . . . might be soe bould I would nipp you againe, and proceeding in talke togeither he the said Roger Die tould her of a tale, which happned betweene a younge ladie that did not care for her husband so well as she respected another young man, whoe afterwards contrived her husbandes deathe and after whose deathe the younge man and she lyved contently and pleasantly togeither.

They had so much fun with this story that John Burbury asked them if they were not ashamed to make so much noise—'Sir Frances being in the parlour hard by'—and they went away together laughing. The suggestions of these two occasions gave a serious note to the flirtations and courtship rituals other witnesses reported. For Roger, the idea of 'changing the man' in Joan's marriage gave him a chivalrous role quite out of step with his actual situation; far from being the aged, impotent husband of such tales, Francis was in his late twenties, only a year older than Joan; and for all Roger's romantic talk, he ended up cast out of the Ashbeys' service. In court, there was no suggestion that he had, in fact, managed to father a child, or planned a real murder; but the employment in this flirtation of fantasies of exchange, replacement, and 'contriving death' reveals the place literary stories about women's adultery might have in the discourses of real marriage. The tale of the young lady whose lover managed her husband's death could have come from any of the accounts of domestic murder in circulation at the period, but here its moral is turned around. If contemporary literature stressed the overwhelming guilt, and subsequent punishment, of adulterous and murderous wives, the same story could also have a lighter, romantic meaning in which guilt and discovery were replaced with a heroic narrative of rescue and living pleasantly ever after. In this case, the stories Francis Ashbey caused to be repeated in court might well have acquired a longer currency; for the case did not end in a separation, and within a year Joan had given birth to a girl, the couple's only child. Within another four years, Francis had died, aged only 32, and his houses and lands had gone to his younger brother. It would not be surprising if at least some people in Harefield remembered and retold the stories of 1619.[45]

Other testimonies, in contrast, dwelt precisely on the female guilt that was central to narratives of domestic homicide. Jane Burre from Essex confessed to the court in 1611 that her unhappiness with her husband, whom she had been persuaded to marry by others and 'could never of her selfe love and fancie', drove her to plan to poison him:

> ever since theyr sayd marriage she this respondent hath extremely hated the sayd Robert Burre and by reason thereof they have lyved togither very unquietly and with much sorrowe and griefe by reason of the brawles that have bin betwene them . . . she this respondent being weary of the unquiett lyfe that she and her sayd husband led togither did thinke and intend to rid and free herselfe from her sayd husband by poysening of him and hath confessed as muche that she hath had an intent and purpose to poysen him.[46]

[45] Sir Francis Ashbey *c.* Lady Joan Ashbey (1619), DL/C 226/III, fos. 4^v, 6^v, 4, 9^v, 5; DL/C 226/VI, fos. 37^v–38; DL/C 226/III, fo. 9^v; *Collectanea Topographica et Genealogica*, V. 130, 135; *International Genealogical Index* (for Joan Barnett's birth, in Harefield). Francis was knighted by James I in 1617, inherited Breakspears, the largest non-manorial estate in Harefield, in 1618, sued his wife in October 1619, had his daughter Alice baptized in November 1620, and died early in 1624. Joan died in 1635.

[46] Robert Burre *c.* Jane Burre (1611), DL/C 220, fos. 480^v–481.

In 1578 the witnesses against Mary Luff of Fernhurst in Sussex augmented the evidence of her adultery with her own measure of her indifference to her husband: 'she . . . said that yf her husbande was fighting with one whome she never sawe before and were lyke to be kylled of hym she would rather helpe the other then her husbande'. Mary's plans to go away with her lover, Henry Stempe, were alleged to include the wholesale murder of her family. Another witness reported that Mary had told him 'further that the determination of the said Stempe and Mary as she said was to have slayne her father and mother and brother in lawe and her owne syster and that she would have held the candell to the execution'.[47] Barbara Bedell told the London court in 1566 that her adultery had led to her lover planning murder. Three years ago, she said, a married man her husband knew had fallen into great familiarity with her; he had 'had carnalie to do with her divers tymes until at last he wente aboute to make awaye both his wief and her husbande by unlawfull meanes'. Alarmed, she told her husband, who 'took the matter verie angerlyye' and sent her away. She added, to further questioning, that although 'certen of her husbands frends and kinfolkes perceaving the suspicious and unlawfull behaviour of Randulph Watlington and [herself] rebuked her for it and warned her of it; and yet through the temptations of the devil she did not leave the companie of Randulph until her husband put her away'. In her confession, it is the adultery which is the 'temptations of the devil', not murder: murder is the logical consequence.

Figured as the ultimate result of adultery, murder acted as a symbol of the dangers of disordered households, and specifically, the results of women's unchastity. At one level, husband murder is a pragmatic crime: death was the only sure way of exchanging one husband for another, and it is worth remembering in this context that over half the marriages in London were made between couples of whom at least one had already been widowed. At another level, visions of women's murder fitted into the basic vision of whoredom as simultaneously the cause and the corollary of every female vice that underpinned much popular literature, the language of insult, and the stories the men in these cases told of their wives' adultery.[48] Most of all, stories of real or imaginary domestic murder stressed its violation of

[47] Luff *c.* Mary Luff (1578), WSRO Ep/I/11/3, vol. III, fo. 3^{r-v}.

[48] In the popular literature of crime, for example, every kind of women's crime was linked with promiscuity: highwaywomen, thieves, and infanticides as well as murderers were all described as whores.

the spatial and affectional order of marriage and household.[49] In the light of the heavy weight of obedience the ideal household demanded from wives, the prospect of petty treason could seem almost predictable: 'The man, that is not lyked, and loved of his mate, holdeth his life in continuall perill'.[50] Without love, the burden of marriage could not be secure. The cumulative effect of these layers of meaning constructed the sinister side of the drama of adultery that, in insults, ballads, jokes, and rituals, humiliated husbands and made them cuckolds. While, as the stories and taunts of Roger Die and Agnes Brampton show, murder could be an appealing or a teasing fantasy, the threat of murder also compounded the various material, economic, and mental damages attributed to women's adultery, to make the stories of cuckolded husbands not funny, but potentially dangerous. The vision of women's adultery and its dangerous effects outlined in popular, religious, and élite culture gave husbands the key with which to prove their wives irredeemable.

HISTORIES OF VIOLENCE

The proofs of cruelty that women alleged against men required a different kind of evidence of marital breakdown. The threat of mortal danger was incidental in stories of adultery: to pleas of cruelty it was central. While evidence of sexual promiscuity was enough to demonstrate women's unfitness as marital partners, only the proof of life-threatening violence made men unfit husbands. The time-scale of such violence was much longer than that of adultery; single or occasional acts of adultery made the basis for men's cases against their wives, but women's cases against their husbands told whole histories of conjugal violence, some lasting for years. These histories had few cultural models with which to work. The drama of adultery and its consequences was played out at every level of early modern culture; the drama of marital violence was almost invisible. Some advice writers discussed the question, some ballads advocated beating to improve household discipline, and a few murder pamphlets mentioned violence as the context of husband-murder.[51] But the only conventional

[49] For a fuller exploration of these connections in relation to the literature of domestic murder, see Dolan, *Dangerous Familiars*, ch. 1.

[50] Edmund Tilney, *A briefe and pleasant discourse of duties in Mariage* (London, 1568), sig. Bvi.

[51] E.g. Henry Goodcole, *The Adulteresses Funerall Day . . . Or the Burning Downe to Ashes of Alice Clarke . . . for the Unnaturall Poisoning of Fortune Clarke Her Husband* (London, 1635).

stories of violent husbands and battered wives, of the details of men's assertion of authority and the means of women's resistance, seem to have been those that circulated orally, based on rumour and experience, whose traces are visible in these testimonies. Like the testimonies of adultery, their touchstone is the organization of the conjugal household.

Cruelty was a women's complaint as adultery was a men's: the few men who alleged their wives' violence did so as counter-allegations to their wives' stories. The legal basis for separation on these grounds gave no definition that could balance the strict terms defining adultery. Cruelty was a more complex and subjectively determined affair, harder both to measure and to sentence. Contemporary opinion was ambivalent about the acceptability of marital violence. In common law men were entitled to beat their wives, but to do them no 'bodily damage, otherwise than appertaines to the office of a husband for lawfull and reasonable correction'.[52] Many contemporary writers expressed themselves strongly against any measure of violence. The authors of marital advice condemned such means of household rule as cruel, unnecessary, and more likely to produce hatred than submission, and they explained that, since a woman's flesh was her husband's, he was in effect beating himself.[53] 'What is it', asked William Heale, 'that violats the holy rites of matrimony? . . . What is it that breeds horride and domestical massakers?'[54]

For household writers, it was a basic tenet that women were naturally subject to men, and that the household merely needed to be ordered to bring out this natural relationship. Ballads presented violence, rather, as a positive solution to disordered households, finding an answer to female disobedience in the greater exercise of man's natural authority; at the same time, some made it clear that violence signified not reasonable authority, but unacceptable tyranny.[55] Without the need to argue the ethics of beating in words, the satirical print, 'A New yeares guift for shrews', represented a week of male mastery, from the husband's marriage to an unruly wife on Monday, to his cutting a cudgel and beating her, and his final peace (after sending her to the devil) on Sunday (Fig. 9). In all these popular images of marriage, men's

[52] T. E., *The Lawes Resolutions of Womens Rights: or, the Lawes Provision for Woemen* (London, 1632), 128.

[53] See e.g. Smith, *Preparative to Marriage*, 68–74. On contemporary theories about marital violence, see Phillips, *Putting Asunder*, 323–30.

[54] William Heale, *An Apologie for Women* (Oxford, 1609), 29.

[55] See for example 'Couragious Anthony', *Pepys Ballads*, iv. 146; and, in contrast, 'The Maryed Mans lesson', Roxburghe Ballads, i. 510, 511.

FIG. 9. A New yeares guift for Shrews, *c.*1620

violence was figured as a reponse to a very specific female offence: scolding. The cardinal offence of the wives in 'A New yeares guift for Shrews' and in countless ballads is not letting their husbands live 'in quiet'. Men's blows were figured as, most justifiably, a response to women's words, and this equation featured not only in the popular literature of marriage, but in the relations of real marriages. More broadly, the issue of obedience which was key to so much contemporary discussion of femininity and marriage had far-reaching echoes in marital practice. It was in terms of the issue of obedience, and its concomitant strictures on women to keep at home, look chaste, and speak modestly, that violent husbands explained their deeds to their wives, to their neighbours, and to the court.

The measurement of violence, one of the most problematic points of marital separation litigation, was inevitably the crux of litigants' and witnesses' depositions. At the court, women and men fought over the level of violence alleged, men redefining what their wives claimed to be life-threatening violence as 'light chastisement'. In a typical testimony in 1586, Margery Alyver told how she had witnessed the violence of John Farmer to his wife Margaret, neighbours of hers in St Clements. Within a year of their marriage four years earlier, Margery told the court,

> Margarett . . . hathe manie and sondry tymes . . . come unto this deponent . . . and make great mone and complayne unto her, weping and crieinge, and tell this deponent howe cruelly her husband . . . used her and beaten her, showinge this deponent somtymes her eies which was blewe with her husbandes blowes, and tell this deponent that she was throughe her husband crueltye and madenes soe sore and brused in her body that she knewe not what to doe, and that her husband would and had gryped her by the throte, and used her very cruellye wepinge bitterlye: showinge this deponent she was in greate feare of her lyff with hym: And further . . . the said John Farmer had beaten . . . [her] soe greveouslye att one tyme, that she the said Margarett kepte her bed, for the space of 8 or nyne weeks, being sore brused and grypped in her body.

Another neighbour, 'hearing hym a fighting and chyding', went in to part them: 'when she came she founde hym with a cogell in his hand beatinge on his wyff cruellye more like a madd man then anie other'. The court found in Margaret's favour.[56] In another case, when Margaret Bonefant went to see Anne Younge she found her

> bruised and swollen about her head face and body that she was not able to speake nor go nor stir any of her lymes to helpe her selfe, and her jawes were displaced or otherwise so hurt with beating that she was not able to stirre them, and the gristle of her nose was so bruised that untill by the helpe of a surgion it was raysed and the fleshe soupled she could not well fetche or take any breathe at the nose, but seemed as though she were more lyke to die of that beating then to recover and lyve.[57]

The precise description of wounds was crucial to the power of testimonies like these.

Like adultery, the violence which ended marriages was staged in the house, and litigants stress the physical violation of the domestic structure: wives and husbands shut each other in or out of bedchambers and kitchens, men push women down the stairs or threaten to throw them out of windows. In 1614 John Perry explained his violent treatment of his wife Anne on the grounds that she had locked him out

[56] Margaret Bradforth *als* Farmer *c.* John Farmer (1586), DL/C 213, pp. 56, 54; DL/C 611, p. 339.

[57] Anne Younge *als* Lingham *c.* James Younge (1608), DL/C 218, pp. 50–1.

of part of their house:

> when he sent one of his servants into the buttery to fetch him some beer, she got hold of the latch of the buttery dore and would not suffer his . . . servant to goe in . . . this deponent pulling his wife by her cote, she fell downe backwarde and endeavouring to rest herselfe uppon one of her hands, putt one of her fingers oute of joynte.[58]

The violence to which his wife had testified is reinterpreted, here, as her fault: he is defending his rights over the house, she injures herself attempting to exert her authority against his over one room.

Although canon law restricted the definition of cruelty to physical violence, plaintiffs and their witnesses, especially women, attended with as much care to the economic, mental, and verbal cruelty that gave violence its context, revealing the broader popular conception of marital breakdown. Mary Farmer, the servant of a separating couple, deposed that

> she had divers times seen John Kendricke beat Anne Kendricke . . . with his fists, cudgells, and a fireshovell . . . calling her whore and that the child she was great withall was not his and so misuseing her that hee hath not suffered her to lye in the bed with him but hath driven her out of the bed and forced her to come to this deponents bed in another chamber.

She also reported that he had 'cooked victuals away from her refusing to allow her any food or sustenance'; and that Anne had lived apart from him for three years, getting her living by teaching with no help from him.[59] Together, these economic repudiations and verbal insults constituted a wholesale denial of the conjugal bond. Many other marital struggles were fought out over similar areas of contention, with violence closely linked to economic misconduct. In 1614, after living together as man and wife in a gentry household, Charles and Mary Jones moved apart and Charles put Mary to lodge with a widow, Alice Tursen, in Greenwich. There, according to witnesses, Charles often visited her, and 'did very often most cruelly beat the said Mary with his fistes, and punch her . . . as that many tymes she was in danger to be strangled by him'. He called her whore and said 'she had byn all the day at London plaieing the whore', swore 'by many fearfull and greivous oathes that hee would be the death of her', and 'somtymes he did take her by the leggs and drawe her out of the bed and about the house'; refusing to allow her any maintenance, he 'did many tymes take from her her keyes and haveing ransacked her

[58] Anne Perry *c.* John Perry (1614), DL/C 222, fo. 239.

[59] Anne Kendricke *c.* John Kendricke (1613), DL/C 221, fo. 1502^{v}.

chests and coffers carry away with him whatsoever he found there and liked of which she had provided by her owne industrie'. He was also, his wife argued, a danger to her by his adultery, coming home 'diseased' from keeping 'company with dishonest and very dangerous woemen', and 'the surgeons warned her not to accompany with him as her husband and told her that his company was very dangerous unto her'.[60] For once, men's adultery was figured as potent a danger as women's.

At its most extreme, men's cruelty meant not just physical, but mental torment. It made women distracted and desperate; it might be linked, too, with mental possession and bewitching. Elizabeth Williams of Stoke Newington, who sued her husband in 1619, was described by witnesses as driven to mental distraction by him; one said she was 'soe senceles in her understandinge that she knoweth not what she doth', others talked about the strange fits she had. Alice Kadwallader reported that when Elizabeth lay in childbirth she called for a knife to 'make awaie with her selfe', saying 'yt were better for me to end my life presentely then to lyve and be tormented continually by my husband who hath . . . protested with an oathe that he would torment me all the daies of my life'. Her husband's words to the justices who attempted to make peace between them seemed to confirm her account; he apparently 'affirmed . . . that he wold not lyve from his mother and sisters to lyve with her . . . affirming further that he never married her . . . for love but for meanes and sayeing he would use her ten tymes worse then he had before'. But Elizabeth's husband and his family attributed her distraction to possession or witchcraft. Her husband's mother told her father that Elizabeth was bewitched and named the woman he thought had bewitched her. His own version has Elizabeth saying that the devil is calling her, and she 'must goe and breake her necke out of a garrett window'. Confused though the story was, it seems to have been a successful one, for the court declared in Elizabeth's favour.[61]

As much as they describe the breakdown of an intimate personal relationship, and perhaps more easily, marital separation suits tell the tale of a disintegrating household. Like testimonies about adultery, the stories men told to justify their violence focused on the effects of women's misconduct in the household, dwelling in particular on the balance of power in the shared domestic space. Christopher Evans

[60] Mary Jones *c.* Charles Jones (1614), DL/C 222, fos. 70^{v}–71.

[61] Elizabeth Williams *c.* John Williams (1619), DL/C 226/I, fos. 6^{v}, 9–13; DL/C 192, fo. 72^{v}; DL/C 19, fo. 149.

of St Martin's, Ludgate, sued by his wife for cruelty in 1613 after a marriage that had lasted eighteen years and produced six children, told a story which returned again and again to his place in the marital household—also, as it happened, an alehouse, an occupational domestic space especially prone to economic and social tensions. Christopher's wife Anne had already put the house at the centre of her complaint, bringing witnesses to testify that 'shee durst not goe into the house for feare her husband should beat or mischeif her'. In response Christopher's tale stressed the behaviour by which his wife had disrupted 'his house'. He had, he said, often forbidden Humfrey Pritchard his house, but came home to find him there with Anne 'very familiar in unseemely manner'. He beat her 'at his house'. Later Anne spent the night away: 'she was all night abroade . . . at her comeing home the next morning this respondent askeing her where shee had byn all that night shee bad this respondent go looke where upon hee did beat the same Anne with his girdle'. Anne's return home is followed by a series of Christopher's homecomings and his reactions:

> comeing home unto his house and finding the said Anne his wife in companye with one whose companye hee had forbidden her hee did take his skayne or sword and with the same cutt a chaire in peeces and laied it on the fire and burnt it
>
> comeing home and hearing by one of his children that Humphrey Pritchard . . . had been dallieing and plaieing with the foresaide Anne Evans his wife as she lay in her bed . . . hee went unto her and . . . shee took up a chamber pott of earth which stood by the bedside and stroke this respondent with the same upon the head . . . whereuppon he pulled her . . . out of bed and kicked her with his feet.

His story continues, as did so many others, with a battle over the material goods of the shared household: 'plaieing at tables in his owne house for two potts of beare did loose the same And calleing to the foresaid Anne Evans his wife to fill the same beare shee . . . did fall out with this respondent and stroke him on the face with her fist whereuppon this respondent did kicke her downe the staires'.[62] Incidents of violence like these involve both the material objects of the house and its symbolic order: wives infringe the household order, husbands claim to reinforce it.

The simple formulas of the marriage service concerning the bestowal of worldly goods held no guarantee to easy financial relations after the wedding. It might be significant, here, that the wedding

[62] Anne Evans *c.* Christopher Evans (1613), DL/C 221, fos. 1482, 1496v, 1210v–1211v.

promise to endow never became incorporated into the words of marriage contracts as did the promises 'to have and to hold', 'for better, for worse', or 'till death us depart'. Amy Erickson has shown how different familial practice was from marital property doctrine: in the less propertied classes as well as the aristocracy, settlements of property on brides ensured women a separate interest in particular property during marriage.[63] For these couples, the focus of conflict was the bride's portion: its size, its payment, and who spent it. John Williams's threats to his wife followed a conflict with her family over her portion. James Younge's cruelty to his wife arose from a similar dispute, in which he believed he had been cheated of her full estate. He beat her because of it, and when a friend came and said 'she was sory to see his wife in this miserable case', he replied that 'he did thinck her estate had byn better when he married her than he did then fynde it'. She told him 'that was not the waye to knowe or understand of her estate but if he would knowe that it must be his kynde usage of her and not that severitie for that was a waye to make an end of them bothe'. Clearly his violence had already led others to fear he would kill his wife, for he responded 'I am tould I shall be hanged if she die within a yeare and a daye but if I be ther is but one out of the waye'.[64]

In the house, violent disputes often centred on material goods, and particularly the goods which women kept locked away, in their own chests. When William Phillips called for a clean shirt which his wife Margaret had locked in her chest she refused to take it out and 'fell to railing and miscalling him'. He broke up the chest with a hatchet and, he said,

> in the same cheste found bras and pewter which she had stolen from him and previously sworne that she had . . . soulde and given . . . away . . . she with her accustomed terms rascall, roge etc rann to him and scratched the skin of his face . . . and struck his shinnes with her foote that it was not whole of longe tyme and . . . threatened to kill him with a knife.

He denied striking her with the hatchet, and said also that 'he hath bin like to be soddenly slaine with sworde and dagger by one of the producents children, and by her procurement'. A further response revealed the various economic issues at the heart of their conflict. One of Margaret's allegations seems to have been that he did not

[63] Amy Louise Erickson, 'Common Law versus Common Practice: The Use of Marriage Settlements in Early Modern England', *Economic History Review*, 2nd ser., 43/1 (1990), 21–39.

[64] Williams *c.* Williams, DL/C 192, fo. 72; Younge *als* Lingham *c.* Younge, DL/C 218, p. 51. (The 'year and a day' refers to the legal definition of manslaughter.)

allow her sufficient money, but he responded that he had delivered all of her dowry to her as he received it quarterly, that she had kept it under lock and key, and that he had 'allowed unto her sufficient maintenance for a woman of her callinge'. In addition, he suspected that some other economic intrigue was going on. He told the court he had come home one night to hear someone whispering the words 'make away' and 'pay debts', and found Edith Phillips leaving his wife's room. He discovered nothing else because his wife refused to give him the tinder box to light a candle, but he must have guessed Margaret was planning to make away with more of her—or his—belongings.[65] Both husbands and wives regularly accused each other of taking and selling the household goods: it was the final expression of a collapsed economic union. At issue was the central question of shared marital property, an ideal whose full implications many of these women apparently refused. Women witnesses, asked by the court how they lived, referred to their earnings as their own, something with which they supplemented their husband's trade; they perceived the goods they brought to marriage, too, as a personal resource, and many kept them separate, often against the wishes of their husbands; some, like Margaret Phillips, augmented those goods with a 'stolen' portion of the joint household belongings.

While men in cases like these were arguing for their own vision of conjugality, buttressing it by financial deprivation or violence, women were fighting for a different balance. Women with a significant estate were particularly careful of their financial position. Cicely Grimes, according to her husband, refused to live with him unless he left her estate alone: summoned to the court in 1625 to answer her accusations that he had married her bigamously, he explained that 'when this respondent began to looke into her estate she refused to cohabit with him anie longer but tould this respondent that if he would laie with her and not meddle with her estate she would rather live with him then with anie other man'.[66]

Widows were particularly likely to run into conflict over the conjugal economy. With some inherited income, or their own means of support, and children from a previous union, they were the least likely women to find a place in contemporary dialogue about the need for economic and mental subordination to husbands; as well, at least some men saw widows as a profitable marital investment. Margaret

[65] Margaret Phillips *c.* William Phillips (1589), DL/C 213, pp. 544–6, 570–2. Edith was apparently no relation of William's.

[66] Grimes *c.* Grimes, DL/C 193, fo. 147^{v}.

Bradforth, reportedly worth £100 at the time of her remarriage, brought witnesses to testify that her new husband had sold her house lease, two gowns, a 'chomlett kirtle', two silver-plated stone pots, sheets, and gridirons left her by her last husband; instead of her material inheritance, she was left with only the three children from her first marriage and one from her second.[67] In the early 1600s Edward Cleter turned on his new wife, Alice Cleter, the day after their marriage, saying—according to witnesses—'Thinkst thou that I can love such a mustie rustie widdow as thou art thou hast a face that loketh like the back of a tode I married the[e] but to be mayntayned like a man and so I will be.' They had fallen into dispute about his debts, which turned out to be considerably more than he had told her. In the ensuing conflict, he pressured her to pawn the household goods and give him the lease of her house, and became violent, shutting her out of the bedroom, refusing to let her sleep with him, stabbing their pewter full of holes, slashing feather pillows with his daggers, and attempting to smother her. That Christmas she appeared on a neighbour's doorstep 'with her face newly cutt and the blud running downe making her mone . . . and saying that her husband . . . had so cutt her face and misused her', although it was not until four or five years later that she sued him for a series of acts of cruelty.[68]

It may be that remarrying widows were particularly likely targets for marital violence, especially when they married men determined to exert their authority over them, or who married them, as Edward Cleter said he had, 'but to be maintained like a man'; but equally important was that the measure of independence experienced by widows probably gave them more confidence in dealing with the administrative structures of justice, making it easier for them to conceive of suing for separation and return to a single life of which they had already had some experience.[69]

While plaintiffs and their witnesses described a drama whose theatre was the collapsing household, domestic violence was also set on a

[67] Bradforth *als* Farmer *c.* Farmer, DL/C 213, p. 55. ('Chomlett': luxury textile, at this period, angora wool.)

[68] Alice Cleter *als* Millington *c.* Edward Cleter (1609), DL/C 218, pp. 324–7.

[69] For an analysis of the position and independence of widows, see Vivien Brodsky Elliott, 'Widows in Late Elizabethan London: Remarriage, Economic Opportunity, and Family Orientations', in Lloyd Bonfield, Richard M. Smith, and Keith Wrightson (eds.), *The World We Have Gained: Histories of Population and Social Structure* (Oxford, 1986), and, for some of the reasons why widows might avoid remarriage, Barbara Todd, 'The Remarrying Widow: A Stereotype Reconsidered', in Mary Prior (ed.), *Women in English Society 1500–1800* (London, 1985).

larger stage. If 'friends', family, and kin were significant players in the making of marriage, in the breakdown of conjugality their role was equally important and often more problematic. In the stories of violence as in those of adultery, the contours of privacy and publicity in the marital household are contestable. Houses and marriages were at once public and private space, the scene of both social and intimate relationships. But while friends and neighbours witnessed adultery furtively, and spread the word through rumour and common fame, marital violence could be a far more public drama. Margaret Hunt has shown how marital violence in the eighteenth-century city could be 'a dramatic spectacle, played out in the presence of everyone in the immediate vicinity'.[70] In these cases, violent confrontations took place in private, but they often provoked the intervention of servants, friends, and neighbours. Thomas Etheridge caused his wife Margaret to cry out so loud that a youth went running to a neighbour, Robert Walsingham, who came to the house and heard Margaret 'cry out murder murder in a very distracted manner' and found 'her hand stabb by a knife'. Robert asked Thomas 'why he used his wife in soo inhumane a fashion', and in response Thomas 'made answere that he would draw it againe and mediately did so'. On another occasion Margaret's daughter by an earlier marriage went to a neighbour, Katherine Woodcocke, 'crying they were undone for her father in lawe'.[71] To a certain extent, men could be made publicly answerable for their violence to their wives, in the same way that mistreatment of servants led to interventions and confrontations between neighbours. Margery Alyver told the court how she and her neighbours had gone to visit Margaret Farmer sick in bed, 'in danger of death' from her husband's beating: 'this deponent and the reste did playnly perceive that her sicknes came only through her husbands cruell and harde delinge with her in beating and brusing of bodye. And saieth that all the neighbours there and abouts hath made great complaint and spoke againste Farmer for his . . . ill dealing with his wife.' Such interventions were not necessarily effective. In this case, although the neighbours decided to present John Farmer for loose living and for 'never getting anie thing but spending that which his wyff had', the violence went on until Margaret sued her husband at court.[72]

[70] Margaret Hunt, 'Wife Beating, Domesticity and Women's Independence in Eighteenth-Century London', *Gender and History*, 4/1 (1992), 23.

[71] Margaret Etheridge *als* Perkins *c.* Thomas Etheridge (1629), DL/C 231, fo. 104, 104^{v}.

[72] Bradforth *als* Farmer *c.* Farmer, DL/C 213, p. 56.

Not everyone agreed on the point at which domestic violence became a neighbourhood concern. Susan Amussen has argued that the public nature of the family in both ideological and practical terms had implications for the limitation of male violence: men's violence to their wives, like other kinds of violence in the contexts of society and state, was subject to community control.[73] Yet the evidence of communal intervention in men's violence towards their wives suggests that not all members of the community felt the same about the necessity to complain and intervene. It was women, more often than men, who protested to violent husbands, sometimes physically interposing themselves between husband and wife, and coming to court, later, to testify to their female neighbour's precise injuries, and it was women to whom battered wives turned first.

In 1620 Jane Collett, a 63-year-old widow, was called by a servant to come and rescue her mistress, Winifred Vulcombe, from her husband's violence. From the start she found herself embroiled in the physical conflict. The servant girl told her 'that her said master Richard Vulcombe had killed her mistris'; rushing to his house, she found him at the door, 'and this deponent pressing to goe in was repelled by him yett at length this deponent gott into the house'. Finding Winifred lying 'by a fyer side bleeding verie freshly and that exceedingly', with a blow on her head 'so grossley cutt that on might then have turned their twoe fingers in ytt', she called a surgeon and stayed with her until late that night. While Winifred was recovering, her husband came to her room, and although Jane and she had bolted the door against him, he 'with great violence pulled the dore open and in furious manner run unto his wife and taking her with both his handes by the neck said Ah thow whore I have not done with the yett'. It turned into a struggle between Jane and Richard Vulcombe: she 'used all the meanes and strength she could to pull him awaie from her and having in some sorte aswaged his malice and hatred unto his wife gott him forth out of her chamber and shutt him owte'.[74] Violent men were profoundly, angrily resistant to the neighbourhood intervention women mobilized. William Phillips of St Martin's Lane came to the attention of his neighbours for beating his wife Margaret until her face was 'black and blewe and sorly swolne' and she was 'lyke one halfe scaerd outt of her wits'. Neighbours intervened and tried to make peace between them, led by Edith Phillips; William complained

[73] Susan Dwyer Amussen, '"Being Stirred to Much Unquietness": Violence and Domestic Violence in Early Modern England', *Jl. of Women's History*, 6/2 (1994), 70–89.
[74] Winifred Vulcombe *c.* Richard Vulcombe (1620), DL/C 227, fo. 180.

in response 'that he was bewitched by a coople of hagerdlie whores' (meaning Edith and Margaret).[75]

Among couples of a higher social status a very similar drama could be played out. In 1608 a young gentlewoman, Ann Dighton, staying with her husband Thomas at the Earl of Lincoln's house in Chelsea, went to the rooms where another couple were in the same house, 'her face all awashed with tears' saying 'she culd not endure that life meaning . . . her husbandes crueltie towards her'. Mary Morrante took her into her own bed, sending her servant back to get her night clothes, but Thomas 'nipt her . . . very cruelly by the arme', and threatened to break her neck, saying 'your mistris weare better kis my wives tayle then kepe her from me'. Ann Dighton returned with the servant, but Thomas managed to lock them both into his room, beating Ann brutally when she got into bed and refusing to free them even when one of the Earl of Lincoln's men came to intervene; the Earl himself ended up fighting with Thomas.[76] Mary Morrante's husband was in the room with her, but he seems to have taken no part in the battle between Thomas and his wife's allies; only later, after repeated trips to and fro by Ann, Mary, and the servant, each of them brutalized by Thomas, did any men intervene. The drama of violence was understood, it seems, as one fought out—at least at first—by women against men; it is also a drama whose protagonists seem to will to a climax. Why, after all, did Ann have to have her night clothes? Why did Mary Morrante's husband watch the women make repeated forays to Thomas's room, returning with stories of his increasingly dangerous violence to them? In some way, all the participants seem to be waiting for the enclosed drama of marital violence and brutality to a servant to explode into a situation that is clearly unacceptable and that demands, to end it, a fight between men.

Of course, not all women sided with the wife when couples fell into dispute. When Elizabeth Williams's family and friends complained about her mistreatment by her husband, his family gave their own opinions: his sister-in-law told Elizabeth that her brother had 'used her too well'; Elizabeth's plaintive response was 'can a man use his wife too well?'[77] But it was women who engaged with the question of the legitimacy of men's household violence, not, for the most part, other men.

[75] Phillips *c.* Phillips, DL/C 213, pp. 591, 581.

[76] Ann Dighton *als* Hardy *c.* Thomas Dighton (1608), DL/C 218, pp. 15–16, 109–12.

[77] Williams *c.* Williams, DL/C 226/1, fo. 11^{v}.

At the same time that violence and its corollaries destroyed the marital bond, they could also be read as affirming the rules of conjugality. In their own defence, men explained some of the reasons behind marital conflict. They did not deny violence, or argue that it was the result of extraordinary rage or distress: rather, they told stories in which their wives' misconduct provoked a reasonable degree of chastisement. There are few signs here of the drunkenness or broader 'signs of mental disturbance or instability' that Martin Ingram suggests characterized men's violence.[78] What marks the stories of men about their own violence is their emphasis on rationality, on 'moderate correction' as a legitimate part of marriage.[79] Witnesses sometimes spoke of men falling into rages in which they were dangerous and irrational; but in neither the stories of violent husbands, nor those of their wives, does madness, mental distraction, or drunkenness explain violence. Rather, in the histories of marital breakdown violence is represented as a functional characteristic of marital relations. Men's violence in this period was not necessarily conceived as dysfunctional. It was shocking to many advice writers, and it was frequently publicly condemned; but it was not yet the mark of shame that it would become, as Margaret Hunt has argued, in the eighteenth century.[80]

At the court, men measured their own violence with care, emphasizing its rationality in response to women's 'provocation', 'misbehaviour', or 'misuse'. Simon White, answering allegations of cruelty from his wife Elizabeth, replied

> that he hath sondrie tymes . . . being therto muche provoked by the said Elizabeth given her a blow upon the cheeke with his hand . . . And about 4 yeeres now last past . . . he did uppon juste occasion chastise and correcte the said Elizabeth with a small beechen wand for her misusage and intollerable misbehaviour towards him which he did in honest reasonable and moderate sorte.[81]

His words underscore just how differently the signs of marital breakdown, men's violence and women's adultery, could be read: while women's adultery was the epitome of dishonesty, men's violence could be argued to be 'honest'. The phrase 'upon just cause' was another powerful justification. Felix Chambers defended himself that he 'uppon just cause offered by the said Anne . . . did . . . beate or

[78] Ingram, *Church Courts*, 183–4.

[79] Susan Amussen's study illuminates the acceptability of certain levels of violence in Norfolk: Amussen, *Ordered Society*, 128–9.

[80] Hunt, 'Wife Beating', 25.

[81] Elizabeth White *c.* Simon White (1588), DL/C 213, p. 466.

strike the said Anne and curse her and wished the devill to take her and wished that he had never seene her'. He said that Anne had left him—'without anie just cause'—to live with her mother and step-father, and that they were not paying him the 20 marks a year they had promised; it is unclear whether this was the cause of his violence or a response to it.[82] Like the witnesses who testified against them, husbands worked out their own measures of violence and its admissibility. But while women brought witnesses to testify to the exact marks violence left on its recipients, describing black and blue eyes, broken heads, and injured legs, husbands concentrated on their end of it, explaining the precise instruments they used: a hand, 'a beechen wand', 'a small stick of a fagott', or 'a lyttell wyllowe sticke with 3 sprayes'. Their exact memory of the incident was a testimony to the rationality of their behaviour. Women accused of adultery had little option of self-defence: they either denied it, or admitted it and expressed penitence and shame. But men accused of cruelty had considerable room for manœuvre, which they used to defend themselves on the grounds that their violence was a logical extension of the power accorded them in the conjugal economy. Their stories are actuated by a profound resistance to the idea that violence destroyed a marriage. Instead, they turned the blame around, so that the breakdown of conjugality was due to the familiar problems of women's actual, suspected, or potential adultery.

The conventional rhetoric of women's adultery was central to the complaints violent men made against their wives. But as much as, and often more than, women's actual adultery, husbands were concerned with the behaviour conventionally associated with it: their movements outside the house, their speech, and above all, their subjugation. 'An honest wife', prescribed Bullinger's *Christen state of Matrimonye*, 'ought not . . . to go eny where without her husbandes knowledge and leave.'[83] Attempts to enforce such control were one source of marital conflict and men's violence. Thomas Rogers explained that his wife

> havinge made a showe that she would goe to a sermon made at the funerall of one of her neighbours did goe to and spend her time in some other unfitting place with suche company as this respondent did not like of whereupon at her returne being late in the night this respondent being displeased with her did take her by the arme and turne her towarde the staires at this respon-

[82] Anne Chambers *c.* Felix Chambers (1611), DL/C 220, fo. 740v.

[83] Heinrich Bullinger, *The Christen state of Matrimonye*, trans. Miles Coverdale (Antwerp, 1541), fo. 61v.

dents worke howse and withall gave her a spurne with his foote and followeing her downe the same staires gave her three or fower blowes on her head or face.[84]

Thomas Thompkyns told the court his wife had both behaved suspiciously, and—as adulterous wives in these stories often do—spoken to him in unseemly language; his violence was a response to both disorders.

[On] Barthelmew daye last as he and the same Allyce his wyfe were walking togither alonge the Thamysyde to Lambeth Marshe he tolde of her suspicious usinge her selfe with one Edwardes And that not with standinge that he had sondry tymes afore given her warninge and charge not to lett hym resorte to her yett she nothinge regardinge his admonicon did still keape the saide Edwardes companye and lett hym resorte very suspiciously to her bed chamber and into a dark rome behynde his shoppe and there commytted fornicatyon as he is able to prove he tooke up a lyttell wyllowe sticke with 3 sprayes and therewith and for her unhonest and unsemeley language that she spake unto hym at that tyme gave her 4 or 5 blowes on her sholders.

In return Alice had charged her husband with adultery with several women; but her accusation did not stick, and he cleared himself by compurgation and she admitted that she had been persuaded to the charge by others.[85] John Perry made a much more public assault on his wife Anne: like a child, a servant, or a horse, he sent her home:

fynding his wife drinckinge in a private chamber . . . with a couple of vagrant persons taking upp a little small sticke of a brushe fagott gave her twoe or three blowes therewith and wished her to goe home and abstaine from the companie of suche ydle persons.[86]

Complaining of women's misconduct, violent husbands paid particular attention to the emotive issue of their language. Their accounts of what their wives said to them invoke the conventional association of women's sexual unchastity with disorderly words. Abusive, 'immodest' language is both destructive in itself, and the evidence of general marital misconduct. William Phillips, who had abandoned his wife because of what he described as her 'ungodly dealings and unnaturall actes', explained the words which he countered by violence:

(he) hath given her . . . one or two blowes with the backe of his hande upon her cheeke by the provocacion of the same Margarett who uppon some falte

[84] Susan Rogers *c.* Thomas Rogers (1613), DL/C 221, fo. 1193.
[85] Alice Thompkyns *c.* Thomas Thompkyns (1574), DL/C 211/2, fo. 260v.
[86] Perry *c.* Perry, DL/C 222, fo. 239r–v.

that this respondente hath fownde with her hath most uncharitablie and beiondes the bowndes of modestie called this respondente roge rascall whorehunter theefe.[87]

The correlation William drew between women's verbal violence and men's physical violence was one rehearsed and justified in one of the few public defences of wife-beating, *The Husband's Authority Unvail'd*, published in 1650 under the name Moses à Vauts. A tract that invokes personal experience as much as didactic prescription, it describes a precise, justifiable connection between women's words and men's blows. The author proclaims that he had never beat his wife, 'unless this may be called Beating or striking, That, at one time onely (of innumerable Provocations) when, after mild Admonition, shee would not forbear Swearing; but let fly 2 or 3 bloudy, horrid Oaths in my Face, I bestowed so many Flaps with my bare hand alone on her Mouth, the Part Offending'. Like husbands in court, the writer is careful to describe the exact extent of his physical blows; like them, he denies them to be violence at all. Indeed, it is the woman, here, who appears injudicious and violent: she 'lets fly' oaths in his face, he merely 'bestows' reasonable chastisement on 'the Part Offending'. The root of violent husbands' objection to women's over-liberal speech might be seen in à Vauts's explanation of the offensiveness of such words. 'Customary *Scoulding*', he writes, 'and *Clamour* . . . is no Argument of weakness, but of a stubborn and sinfull strength . . . Shall any dare to think, that ever the holy spirit intended a woman to be Tongue-free? to rail, rage, swear, blaspheme, and defy Heaven and her husband?' Words like these not only proclaim unwomanly, unwifely behaviour, but they define that 'stubborn strength' which many violent husbands seem to be seeking to frustrate. The conflation of speech against the husband with speech against God here is no accident. A central plank of the argument is that divine power is vested in the husband, who is therefore entitled to exercise against his wife 'that Knowledge and coactive Power which God hath imparted to him'.[88] Rhetorical in the mould of seventeenth-century gender debates, this text is still revealing of early modern models of men's violence and women's speech.

Few husbands expressed their authority in anything like these rhetorical terms. But equally, none of them displayed any interest in

[87] Phillips *c.* Phillips, DL/C 213, pp. 544–5.

[88] Moses à Vauts, *The Husband's Authority Unvail'd: Wherein It is moderately discussed whether it be fit or lawfull for a good Man, to beat his bad Wife* . . . (London, 1650), 84, 80, 95.

the image that so many preachers used to warn against marital violence, that of husband and wife as one indivisible flesh, in which a husband's violence damaged his own body. To these husbands their wives were all too separate: obedience, not unity, was the keynote of their understanding of marriage, and violence of varying degrees, threatened and real, was the tool with which obedience was to be enforced. In 1613 Thomas Rogers told the court his remedy for his wife's 'liberall' talk.

> This respondent (the said Suzan being more liberall of her speeche than this respondent thought fittinge for her) did . . . once saie that he had heard of a man that had a wife given mutche to talkinge and he perswaded her to be lett bloode in the tongue and thereby made her to talke more mildlie And that he thought he should be faine to use the said Suzan soe . . . And that at another time . . . the said Suzan railing on and abusing this respondent in speeches willed her to hould her peace and said that if she would nott he would pull out her tongue or to the like effecte.[89]

Thomas's 'man that had a wife given much to talking' and threatened to let blood from her tongue was well known: he featured, with his remedy, in a number of contemporary ballads and jokes. Scoggin, the hero of a series of jokes in Andrew Boord's *The First and best Part of Scoggins Iests* (1626), gets a surgeon to help him draw blood, telling his wife 'Dame you have a little hot and proud blood about your heart, and in your stomacke, and if it be not let out it will infect you and many more', although she protests so much that they only manage to bleed her arm and foot; the protagonist of the ballad *A Caution for Scolds* threatens the same cure. Thomas Rogers's words tapped into a body of misogynist discourse, an important source in jokes and proverbs, that offered remedies and responses to enforce men's marital authority, and that recognized at the same time the problematic dynamics of marital power.[90]

In many ways, the conflicts that ended in violence and that were also fought out through battles over words, money, and goods were conflicts over the balance of domestic power. As marriages ran into trouble, men used their financial power to enforce their household authority; women used what economic means they had to establish independent lives. Margery Percy, a remarried widow suing her

[89] Rogers *c.* Rogers, DL/C 221, fo. 1193^{v}.

[90] Andrew Boord, *The First and best Part of Scoggins Iests* (London, 1626: written before 1549), p. 33; 'A Caution for Scolds: Or, A True Way of Taming a Shrew', Roxburghe Ballads, ii. 51. The threat is also obviously related to the bleeding of witches.

husband Christopher in 1590, presented the court with testimonies of the economic and mental hardship he had inflicted on her. Christopher had gone away, leaving her 'in very bare estate for provision' and forbidding the butcher to let her have any food; he

> used very hardd cruell and unkynde words to the producent, threatening her that he would have her into the country not for any love that he bore her . . . but only to hamper her and lock her into a chamber . . . and he hath oftentymes before . . . in scornfull manner said when [she] hath been going abroad with other gentlewomen . . . wayte on my lady, I will pull downe her peacocke feathers.

Witnesses reported his threats to separate her from her friends and her children from a previous marriage, and to 'tame' her. Christopher was aiming specifically to limit his wife's economic and social autonomy. Margery was a widow with seven dependent children and an inheritance of 100 marks, dependent on her not remarrying; Christopher, who styled himself a squire, had assured her his own income was around £500 a year and promised to give £100 to each of her daughters and £100 a year to Margery, 'to maintain Margaret Percy as she was in her old husbands time'. According to Margery's witnesses, Christopher not only broke these promises, but deliberately eroded the financial independence Margery had secured from her previous marriage, and attempted to force her into obeying a vision of an ideally submissive wife, forbidding her social intercourse with other women, threatening to prevent her friends gaining any access to her, and humiliating her in public. His own responses are revealing of his idea of marriage. He explained his behaviour towards Margery's children as a defence of his household authority: 'Walter Gore one of her sonnes, outragiously behavinge hymself towardes this respondent, he . . . rebuked hym as he might lawfully doe in his owne house, and being his father in lawe', and presented his treatment of Margery in the same terms: 'being on a time grievously abused by some that favoured her at Clerkenwell saidd that he . . . did mean to have . . . Margery being his wyff . . . to his owne houses in the contrye where he might be master of his owne house'.[91] The ideal into which Christopher Percy was apparently trying to mould his wife could have come straight from any of the advice manuals, sermons, or homilies of the later sixteenth century; it was particularly unlikely to fit a

[91] Christopher Percy *c.* Margery Percy (1590), DL/C 213, pp. 712–16, 687. (Christopher was originally suing for restitution, but Margery produced witnesses to support her counter-allegations of cruelty and, later, adultery.)

woman with her own inherited income and experience of independent life in between marriages. The literature of marriage advised men not to marry widows for this very reason.

If men's violence was profoundly identified with masculine household authority, the specific context in which early modern culture placed that authority was also important. Images of marriage and the household bound women's sexual chastity up with domestic order: the connection was an important one both in insults about 'whores', and in the concerns of husbands in marital dispute. But while the insults of which women were the main authors paid little attention to the ideology of subjugation and obedience that ruled the ideal household, for husbands in trouble that ideology was very often central. Preachers and prescriptive writers explained the obedience owed by women to their husbands by its similarity to other hierarchical relationships: rulers and subjects, parents and children, and masters and servants; and for some husbands, those connections made sense. Thomas Dighton and his wife Ann, the couple who came to the court in 1608 after a violent battle in the Earl of Lincoln's house, were reported to be ill-suited, and Mary Morrante, who admitted to making the match between them, described them respectively as a man of 'froward crabbed', 'uncivill and rude disposicon' to his wife, 'a younge and timerous', 'very myld gentle and softly natured young gentlewoman'. Thomas's vision of the potential models for the marital relationship was illuminated by the words Mary's maid heard him say to Ann, when she was trying to leave him because of his violence:

> he . . . would gryn most grevously att her . . . and knock one fist uppon an other saying he would chayne her to his bed post and use her as he used Bartholomewe (whom he pretended to be his bondman) and whom he kept chayned at a post with bread and water only to eat and drinck and a pad of straw to lye on like a dogg.[92]

His words push the common connections drawn between relationships of dominance and submission in the household and in society to their extremes. The most violent expression of such threats appears in the mid-sixteenth-century text *A merry Ieste of a shrewde and curste Wyfe, lapped in Morrelles Skin, for her good behavyour* (possibly Shakespeare's source for *The Taming of the Shrew*), in which a scolding wife is subdued by her husband's judicious brutality. The wife complains of her husband's conjugal demands and refuses to follow his commands, swearing 'Thou wouldst fayne the mayster play | But

[92] Dighton *als* Hardy *c.* Dighton, DL/C 218, pp. 17–19.

thou shalt not, by God I make thee sure.' In response, he vows to force her into submission by beating her with birch rods:

> For this I trow I will make her shrinke,
> And low at my pleasure, when I her bed,
> And obey my commaundementes both lowde and still,
> Or else I will make her body bleede,
> And with sharp rods beate her my fill.

His early attempts at this fail, and his wife turns on him, treating him like the fawning animal he wants her to be:

> And lyke a dog she rated him then,
> Saying thus, I set no store
> By thee, thou arte no man:

His final victory over her is brutal: he skins his horse (Morel) and salts the skin, beats his wife until she bleeds, and wraps her in the salted skin until she begs for grace. By the end of the story, the victorious husband is showing off his wife as a model of submission to her family, and threatening her shrewish mother with the skin in her turn.[93] It is worth, apparently, sacrificing a valuable horse to attain domestic order.

While advice writers hotly denied that the relationship they prescribed between husband and wife was akin either to abasement or servitude, slavery was a favourite threat of violent husbands. Stories like this one must have entered the imaginations of husbands preoccupied with the problems of dominance and submission in their own marriages. Such men might also be concerned with their masculine power outside the household. John Williams threatened his wife: 'if thou . . . wilte lyve with me I will . . . make the[e] my slave and my sister Louthers scullion and yf by that means I cannot wearie the[e], I will have the[e] caried to Bedlam . . . from thence to Bridewell and soe to Newgate and from thence thou shalt goe to the gallowes and be hanged.'[94] The idea that women could be their husbands' slaves was a logical consequence of the analogies made with such frequency by contemporary theorists; for this husband, it led on to a much broader scenario of male power over women. John Williams lists a neat progression of institutional punishments, insisting on his authority to enforce not only those with which women were regularly threat-

[93] *A merry Ieste of a shrewde and curst Wyfe, lapped in Morrelles Skin, for her good behavyour* (*c.*1550–60), in J. P. Collier (ed.), Shakespeare's Library, 4 (London, 1875), 440, 444, 445, 446–7.

[94] Williams *c.* Williams (1619), DL/C 226/II, fo. 34v.

ened, imprisonment in Bedlam, for lunacy, and Bridewell, for disorderly behaviour, but also the severest penalties of Newgate and the gallows. Power in the household proves the basis for an imaginary command of the whole process of justice, a threat whose force is weighted by the very real possibility of men's manipulation of at least the lesser of these punishments against women. It was not, either, an entirely notional threat: in another case Thomas Charles, a constable in Holborn, used his authority against his own wife, arresting her when he had 'taken some displeasure against her' and dragging her along the street, proclaiming 'that he had a warrant and that he wold carry her to Newgate'; and the Bridewell court minutes for February 1627, for example, record 'Elizabeth Mitchell, an unruly woman' sent to be kept at Bridewell 'at the request of her husband and at his expense'.[95] In more than one sense, household patriarchy could truly work, as it did in contemporary rhetoric, as the microcosm of the outside world.

The violence of men might be intimately related to issues of gender and power not only inside the household, but outside it. Reproached by a woman who asked him if he had killed his wife with his violence, Thomas Charles replied simply 'What had I cared then I had had my will'.[96] The exercise of men's 'will', and the frustration of that of their wives, was one of the central disputes in these marriages. At a practical level there were considerable barriers to the exercise of absolute male authority over women, one of which was women's power over their own bodies. We have seen how the language of insult, and the stories of adultery, played on women's special insight into the rituals of pregnancy and childbirth: one story here gives us a man's angle on the cultural opacity, to men, of women's bodies. Elizabeth Shawe, suing her husband John for cruelty in 1626, brought witnesses to support a story that linked his violence to her with his broader social behaviour. In the tale that emerged, John's battle with his wife turns into an assault on the authority of all women that was also linked to suggestions of witchcraft. When a neighbour asked them 'why they soe much disagreed', Elizabeth answered that John was 'soe long abroade' and, particularly, 'at the house of one widowe Mason spending her meanes'. John answered 'he did scorne to be subject to any woman'. He bragged to the same neighbour that 'he could make a woman dance naked and that he knew better how

[95] Frances Charles *c.* Thomas Charles (1611), DL/C 220, fo. 512; GL Bridewell Court Book VII (1627), fo. 23.

[96] Charles *c.* Charles, DL/C 220, fo. 512v.

to deliver a woman with childe then any midwife of them all, for he could teach a woman how to be a midwife'; here, his words suggest a familiar male anxiety about women's control over pregnancy. His wife also alleged that he practised witchcraft, showing a friend 'a certaine box wherein a paper was litle bones (which this deponent conceiveth) might be toades bones a peece of a pisell, french flyes, papers of seedes, papers of hornes spells for the toothache and agues and the like trumperies'; she was 'soe much affrighted' at his use of them that 'shee dares no meanes live or cohabite with him'.[97] While John Shawe's box of spells might threaten both men and women, his vocal assertions of power were apparently aimed not just against his wife, but against women generally.

The violence that disrupted marriage was not entirely one-way. While men never sued whole suits on the grounds of women's cruelty, they did use evidence of women's violence as counter-allegations against their wives. Their stories stand in stark contrast to the narratives of rational correction or brutal assaults that formed the centre of cases about men's violence. When men complained of women's violence, they presented it as secretive, unpredictable, and frequently murderous in intent. It had nothing to do with the establishment, or abuse, of hierarchical household power; the tales of women's violence related here bore more relationship to stories of female adultery and its dangerous consequences, than to the narratives of men's violence. Single incidents, not patterns of behaviour, were the focus of dramatic accounts. James Berd told the court he could not take his wife back to him, because 'she did in the night drawe his . . . dagger upon hym when he was in bedd and did come to stycke hym . . . therunto which she had done indede, if he . . . had not avoyded the bedd, and the next day in the morninge she reported to dyvers that she was sorye she had not dispatched hym'. William Phillips, whose story was quoted above, claimed that his wife and her child were plotting to murder him; John White refused to live with his wife Bennett because 'he stood in some feare of his life which he was dryven unto by her former evell life and dealing with him'.[98] Like adultery, women's violence was pictured as so extreme that it threatened murder. And as with adultery, cultural images of women's violence had some resonances for real husbands. If cuckoldry made men fools, being beaten

[97] Elizabeth Shawe *c.* John Shawe (1626), DL/C 230, fo. 212.

[98] Christiana Berd *c.* James Berd (1574), DL/C 211/1, fo. 246; John White *c.* Bennett White (1575), DL/C 212, p. 170.

by their wives was even more humiliating: scolded, beaten husbands were the stock targets of popular ballads and censuring rituals. It might be that to be taken seriously, women's attacks on their husbands had to be lethal. Yet while culture imagined women's violence as a laughing matter, women did assault one another; husbands did fear being killed in the night; and men's anxiety about poisoning loomed high when marriages ran into trouble.[99] Behind the jokes about violent wives lay some very substantial fears.

GENDER AND MARITAL RELATIONS

While suits for marital separation involved a tiny proportion of all marriages, the patterns of testimonies are surprisingly similar. Across different cases and over a period of seventy years, the same themes, conventions, and concerns cropped up again and again. The numbers of cases that ended up in court are not sufficient to allow generalizations about the incidence of adultery or the level of violence in most marriages. But they are exceptionally revealing about the conventions and ideals with which marriage was understood and judged. The perceptions of women's adultery that dominated men's cases against their wives and the justifications men gave for their violence drew their strength from a shared culture that gave meaning to all marriages.

At court, the litigants and witnesses in marriage suits told stories that illuminate the economic, sexual, and power relations of both conflict and concord in marriage. While the two specific complaints of cruelty and adultery served as the basis for much wider stories, they also marked the central difference gender made to marital relations. It was not legal precept that made men sue for adultery and women for violence: rather, the stories which came to the court are demonstrably related to some of the central concerns of couples in conflict. On other legal occasions, for example suits over property at the Court of Requests, husbands and wives produced very much the same kind of complaints about their spouses' misconduct.[100] The stories that surround these allegations situate the specific complaints of adultery and violence in a broader context of marital relations and conflict, structured always around gender difference. The two physical wrongs, adultery and violence, have quite different implications.

[99] See Tim Stretton, 'Women and Litigation at the Elizabethan Court of Requests', Ph.D. thesis (University of Cambridge, 1993), 236, on the implausible frequency with which men at that court claimed their wives were poisoning them.

[100] Stretton, 'Women at the Elizabethan Court of Requests', 228–36.

Contemporary culture envisaged sexual fidelity as the core of women's honour and virtue, and the practice of marital litigation reflected the details of that vision: from women's adultery followed moral debasement, household disorder, and the humiliations of cuckoldry. Men's violence carried no such implications of dishonour; its dangers were purely physical. It bore no explicit relation to the essence of the marriage bond; it was, to a limited extent, legally sanctioned; and it posed no threat to the patriarchal structure of household relations that was enshrined in church teaching and contemporary culture, and which affected, to various extents, the practice of daily household life.

While both men's and women's faults were understood to damage the marital bond, it was women's fault that had the largest and most well-established ramifications. Women's adultery was predictable, disturbing, and dishonest; men's violence was, arguably, tolerable, rational, and honest. With the elaboration of the fault of adultery into a much larger danger, the conceptualization of disturbed marriages placed the weight of the fault much more squarely on women than on men. Women, for whom marriage was understood to be their whole preferment and destiny, were also pictured as constitutionally more disruptive to marriage than men, prone to adulterous longings, and readily susceptible to the wiles of handsome apprentices. In the same way, while contemporary culture invariably pictured women in households, it was simultaneously preoccupied by the dangers women could constitute to the economic and emotional domestic order. When women were believed to have powerful sexual urges, and apprentices were seen as dangerously attractive, the working household embodied a permanent threat of illicit sexual desire. The familiar plot of a woman and her apprentice killing a husband enlarged the threat of women's sexuality to encompass even the destruction of the whole household.

The division of sexual blame through which marital trouble was understood did not carry identical meanings for women and men. While, in the language of sexual insult that elaborated gendered sexual morals, both women and men described a vision of whoredom in which women's sexual misconduct disordered marriages, households, and neighbourhoods, when marriages ran into real trouble loyalties split at least partly along gender lines. When marriage disputes came to court, women and men often told different kinds of stories. Men suing women for adultery brought mostly men (61 per cent) as witnesses; women suing men for violence brought mostly women (64 per cent) as witnesses—the highest percentage of women witnesses of any kind of litigation at the court.[101] Ideologies of sexual morals in which women were primarily to blame, the culmination of which was the practical understanding that only women's adultery destroyed marriage, had cultural and social functions for women as well as men, and were invoked by women in, for example, the language of insult; but in practice, women were less ready than men (and also, probably, less likely to be asked) to testify that a woman's adultery had violated the whole structure of marital relations, and more ready to condemn and try to limit men's violence.

In early modern society, marriage was fundamental both to social structure and to gender order. The proper functioning of both was structured through conjugal power relations. It was in the relations of marriage that the implications of gender difference were most fully put into practice: in economic relations, in the judgement of sexual conduct, and in the balance of power. The experience of marriage, like that of courtship, meant different things for men and women. For everyone marriage was a life stage; for women, marital choices also settled future patterns of work, social life, status, and identity; and if marriage was an intrinsic part of female identity, high rates and expectations of remarriage must have made women's identity a less constant, more changeable one than men's. From the outside, too, marriage looked different for women and men: in practice, men were readier than women to condemn women's adultery and women were likelier to perceive men's violence as unacceptable. Through the rhetoric and practice of marriage, the conventions of gender difference were inscribed not just upon gender relations, but into social relations, social order, and individual identity.

[101] In defamation between women, for example, only 60% of witnesses were women; in marriage cases overall, sued by a roughly equal balance of men and women, 64% of witnesses were men, 36% women.

7
Narratives of Litigation

In the legal battles over slander, conjugal commitment, and marital breakdown, complaints and conflicts were articulated through the stories told in court. The narratives of dispute were composed of a combination of familiar, meaningful themes and telling individual details. Those narratives functioned as part of the broader endeavour in which women and men used the courts; but as stories, they also had their own meanings and projects. In and outside the court, the stories of sexual and marital dispute were tales with their own shape and order, formed by distinctive and gender-related narrative techniques, and inevitably reflecting the conflicts and adjustments of gender relations in the social and domestic sphere.

Narratives like these evade an easy distinction between what they say and how they say it. Their whole structure is dependent on the inferences they provoke and the responses they hope for from the audience for whom they are told.[1] Legal narratives were told to a judicial audience listening for plausibility: the conventions and formulas they used were ones that made sense in canon law. Outside the court they had their own resonances; and this is particularly true for these stories, whose point lay as much in their very telling, as in the decision they were meant to win, but rarely did.

Both in and out of court stories aimed to be plausible and familiar; and they achieved this through presenting their events in the light of morals and judgements. In the words of Hayden White, 'every fully realized story . . . is a kind of allegory, points to a moral, or endows events, whether real or imaginary, with a significance that they do not possess as a mere sequence . . . narrativity is intimately related to the impulse to moralize reality'.[2] In these narratives of everyday life and fiction, stories are told and retold to make points about disputed sex-

[1] Barbara Herrnstein Smith, 'Narrative Versions, Narrative Theories', in W. J. T. Mitchell (ed.), *On Narrative* (Chicago, 1981), 213–18.

[2] Hayden White, 'The Value of Narrativity in the Representation of Reality', in Mitchell (ed.), *On Narrative*, 13–14.

ual, marital, or social behaviour, using stock complaints, characters, and story-lines. While their moralizing was personal and individual, it also depended on the conventions of gender. More broadly, the whole contest of meanings which characterized litigation at the church courts was one liable to be inflected by gender. In marital disputes, witnesses had to ally themselves either with a man's story or a woman's; and very often, both sides were telling an archetypal version, a man's tale of the betrayals of adultery or a woman's tale of the drama of violence. The plots and conventions which were the stock of legal narrative were based on some established stereotypes of women and men, wives and husbands. Again and again, plaintiffs and witnesses returned to figures who were part of both legal convention and neighbourhood talk: wives who deceived their husbands and husbands who nearly killed their wives before neighbours intervened, or alternatively, innocent women misjudged and husbands chastising their unruly wives justifiably. In court, the stereotypes of men and women that populated familiar stories clashed; at one level narratives of litigation reveal the mechanics of conflict between gender stereotypes and gendered stories.

The familiar plots and conventions that supported testimonies in court came from a popular culture which was still primarily oral. The oral culture of early modern society did not disappear with the transition to literacy: some oral culture found its way into print as print shaped oral culture.[3] But the agents of that transmission were almost entirely men. It was mostly men's words through which a primarily oral culture shifted towards a literate one: in a time when literacy was increasing for men but remaining very low for ordinary women, women's cultural agency left few traces. Of course, women and men lived in very much the same cultural world, hearing and using the same set of stories, jokes, and songs. But that culture included nevertheless some stories that made sense primarily to men, and some, harder to trace, that made more sense to women.

If, as I have argued, women and men understood marriage in different terms, the discourse of men's literate culture on marriage might be skewed. Most noticeably, while the literature of marital advice, satire, and jokes contains many stories that resemble those that men told of their adulterous wives, it includes none that tell of men's violence as witnesses at court did. In marital disputes, as we have seen, it was more often women who intervened to protect wives from

[3] On this process, see Adam Fox, 'Aspects of Oral Culture and its Development in Early Modern England', Ph.D. thesis (University of Cambridge, 1992).

violent husbands; the stories they subsequently told to the court suggest that women discussed marital violence in terms of some established story-lines with their own conventions.[4] Some of these themes—like the lethality of men's violence, for example—fulfilled a legal requirement, but were also meaningful outside the court; others, such as the economic and mental cruelty that invariably accompanied men's physical violence, obviously reflected what was likely to happen but at the same time set a pattern for future stories.

The very process of telling stories in court had a personal meaning that had especial point for women. It was, for one thing, a rarer opportunity for them than for most men: throughout the legal system women were less popular witnesses than men, and in the wider contexts of local government and justice women shared in very few of the means of participation that were increasingly open to men of the middling sort. And, in a cultural world where men were increasingly writing down things that were important to them, very few women outside the gentry were able to do so.

For women, witnessing also involved a shift that put them at the centre of dramas of sex, words, and marriage. Litigants were telling stories explicitly about their own experiences, either shaping their own allegations or defending themselves against an accusation; but witnesses, too, retold the stories of plaintiffs by investing them with meanings of their own and centring them on their involvement. The moment of deposing transformed witnesses from spectators into narrators and players in their own dramas. This shift from bystander to actor was especially crucial for women. The scripts of sexual, romantic, and social relations allotted passive parts to women, active parts to men; in, for example, the ritualized exchanges of marriage contracts women negotiated their role with pragmatic creativity. Telling stories gave women both a formal cultural agency—a time in which their words were written down—and a way of putting themselves, as actors, at centre stage. The act of testifying gave a weight to women's words and an attention to women's points of view that was rarely accorded them in law or in culture

The very scope of the church courts makes their records especially important for the history of women's experience and identity. Contemporary culture defined and judged women through their sexual and marital identities: the events that were disputed in court—the

[4] Equally, women's narratives of their own violence had their own conventions: see Garthine Walker, 'Crime, Gender and Social Order in Early Modern Cheshire', Ph.D. thesis (University of Liverpool, 1994), 46–74.

occasions of illicit sex, the negotiations of marital choice, and the histories of marital dispute—represented key moments in women's lives and key elements in women's identities. Mediated and reshaped as they were by lawyers and clerks, the stories women told in court record dramas of autonomy, dependence, and identity.

NARRATIVE SKILLS

The texts that recorded women's and men's narrative answers to plaintiffs' questions share a common shape. Deposing was both an oral and a written event. Clerks recorded carefully every sentence of the witness with the preamble 'she saith that': ostensibly what is written down is a direct transcription of a verbal moment, yet we know that clerical manipulations must have distorted its transposition from voice to text. At the same time, the written account bears many of the hallmarks of oral narrative.[5] Witnesses' tales are designed to be retold verbally; the line of narrative works along a continuous, repetitive path, allowing space for flashbacks, parenthetical explanations, and chronological and spatial shifts to blend different moments towards one theme; and they employ familiar themes and story-lines to explain particular incidents. This distinct method of story-telling allowed room for certain kinds of skills. Narrators told stories that made sense of certain experiences whose meaning was being questioned by the court; as they did so, whether they were principal actors or marginal observers in the events, they presented a personal account that, by its very nature, shifted the focus on to their own part in the drama. In studies of modern oral story-telling, narrative skills have been distinguished particularly in terms of the means by which narrators manage to foreground their purposes and concerns.[6] The same techniques came into play here: witnesses emphasize certain details, suggest connections, and develop variations on familiar story-lines.

The art of testifying at court, practised by witnesses, proctors, and clerks, consisted in reordering selective details into a coherent tale. From the focus of the cases, depositions go on to stress particular times and spaces, centre on the actions of particular characters, close in on important details, and fix more broadly on certain story-lines,

[5] On the distinct shape of oral narrative, see Walter J. Ong, *Orality and Literacy: The Technologizing of the Word* (London, 1982), ch. 3.

[6] See e.g. James Paul Gee, 'The Narrativization of Experience in the Oral Style', in Candace Mitchell and Kathleen Weiler (eds.), *Rewriting Literacy: Culture and the Discourse of the Other* (New York, 1991) and in the same collection, Sarah Michaels, 'Making Connections in Children's Narratives'.

interpretations, and themes. As they answered questions, witnesses managed to tell stories with a chronological logic (if one that is not always immediately coherent) and a narrative time of their own. To questions stating the main allegations of a case, witnesses gave answers whose very openings make their words into a story: 'On St Bartholomews day was a twelvemonth', they start, using the calendrical signs that made most sense to them. They go on to bring together incidents from days or months apart, replacing real time with the narrative's own temporal scheme, ruled by the plot, its configuration, and its ending.[7]

The creation of narrative time sets the scene for a series of other textual shapings at every level. Strategies of opening and placing made sure that witnesses' stories were arranged around their actions, as they were told through their perspectives. As they explain the context, witnesses recall too how they came to be involved, taking care to forestall suggestions that their own part in events was disruptive. Leonard Huckleton, an apprentice who came to the court to testify to his mistress's adultery, explained in his deposition why he was out of his master's house in the evening:

> he this deponent having then occasions of buisnes to be out of his said masters howse in that tyme did by chance aboute eight or nyne of the clocke in an evening the tyme aforesaid meete with the articulate Margery Clerke . . . and being desierous to drincke togeither she wished this deponent to goe [to] John Coppins howse articulate.[8]

The three women who testified to Thomasine Hayward's insults of Joan Searles in Stepney in 1628 all noted why they had heard the incident: 'happening to goe out of her . . . dwelling house'; 'happening to be in the street'; 'passing along the street'.[9] From the start, witnesses attended to their place in proceedings.

Defending rather than witnessing in a suit opened the field for some special skills. Defendants responded to the same questions as witnesses, but instead of elaborating the plaintiff's story, they aimed to retell the contested events from a different angle to present a new story, sufficiently altered to prove their innocence and plausible

[7] See Paul Ricoeur, 'The Human Experience of Time and Narrative', in Mario J. Valdes (ed.), *A Ricoeur Reader* (Hemel Hempstead, 1991), especially p. 110. On the changing observations of saints' days see David Cressy, *Bonfires and Bells: National Memory and the Protestant Calendar in Elizabethan and Stuart England* (London, 1989), ch. 1.

[8] Office *ad prom.* Birche *c.* John Coppyn (1620), DL/C 227, fo. 95.

[9] Joan Serles *c.* Thomasine Hayward (1628), DL/C 231, fos. 257^{v}, 258, 259.

enough to convince a judge. To do this they used strategies typical of defence stories in a legal context: challenging the plaintiff's version, redefining it by stressing different elements, and reconstructing it by placing the focal events in a new and transforming context.[10] Some stuck to simple denial in the words *non credit* (she does not believe it)—or a plea of ignorance —*nescit* (she does not know). Some, admitting the accusation against them, added excuses and requests for mercy. In 1567 Elizabeth Charlewood admitted committing adultery, saying simply she was 'devilishly moved and forgetting her soul hilthe'. Christiane Smith, accused of marrying within the prohibited degrees the widowed husband of her sister, pleaded that 'she did not then know the said marriage to be unlawfull nor that she offended therein . . . she is hartely sorrie for what is past And humblie beseecheth a favorable construction to be made thereof'.[11]

Other defendants reshaped their stories on a grander scale, to provide a new background that would justify what had happened. Claims of marriage contracts or men's cruelty to their wives, where contests at court centred not so much on the truth of events as on their meaning, were particularly open to this kind of rewriting. Agnes Gregory, sued for engaging herself in marriage contracts with two different men, pleaded that she had been forced into it: 'being then of smale yeres and under the rule and government of her frends and kinsfolkes, and being constrained and forced by them muche againste her mynd and conscience, dyd notwithstanding her first promise . . . to the grete daunger of her soule . . . solemnise matrimony with the seid Lynney': her explanation was that somehow she had been mature and independent enough to consent fully to one contract, but two years later she was so easily manipulated by her friends that she entered into another, unwanted and unlawful, one.[12] Her resort to pleas of youth, dependence, and openness to persuasion was typical of women, as we shall see in other stories. Men accused of marital cruelty answered in a quite different tone, explaining their violence as a rational response to their wives' misconduct. James Younge went even further and deftly turned his wife's accusations around so that it was he that was in mortal danger. His wife's 'solen' behaviour, her 'counterfeit' sickness, and her

[10] W. Lance Bennett and Martha S. Feldman, *Reconstructing Reality in the Courtroom* (London, 1981), ch. 5.

[11] John Charlewood *c.* Elizabeth Charlewood (1567), GL MS 9056, fo. 108; Samuel Bowley *c.* Christiane Smith *als* Bowley (1626), DL/C 193, fo. 212.

[12] John Lynney *c.* Agnes Gregory (1567), GL MS 9056, fo. 100.

threats to strike him drove him, he claimed, to sinful despair and self-inflicted injury:

> such hath byn and was the wickedness of the saide Ann his saide wieff towards him this respondent as that she had divers times when he this respondent hath gone out of doors she hath falne down of her knees and prayd to god that he this respondent might never com in at the doors again whereby he this respondent was in a desperate mind about the time articulate for which he is now hartely sory and desireth almighty god to forgive him as that in the morning when he arose (he lying alone as he had don long before and after his sayd wieff refusing his company) he did stabb him self with a knief which he carried to bed with him in the brest in twoe places.[13]

James's guilt is not for his violence to his wife, but for that to himself, and his wife bears the brunt of that guilt for driving him to suicidal despair.[14] It was a consummate achievement in narrative self-defence: the case's result does not survive, but the story effectively transformed one story, wholesale, into another.

All these kinds of narrative craft are representative not just of the voices of witnesses, but those of the other contributors to the final texts of depositions, the plaintiffs who set out the original articles of a case and the clerks and proctors who put them into words. At one level, the part clerks played in depositions means that sentence structure, the word order, and at least some of the words of the resulting documents are not always what witnesses said. More broadly, the mediation of proctors in both the original plaintiff's story, and in witnesses' depositions, did much to shape complaints and memories into pleas and testimonies. The legal process did more than add recognizable formulas and conventions: it provided the whole context in which witnesses' stories had meaning. If witnesses are telling stories, so are proctors and clerks. And, with pages of practice in similar stories behind them, the stories legal personnel were telling might have even more binding conventions for presenting dispute than witnesses did.

But the legal context which shaped their tellings was by no means an alien one to litigants and witnesses. With a background of increasing levels of litigation in all courts, the development of a popular legalism was part of sixteenth- and early seventeenth-century culture. The language women and men used for insults and in courtship, for example, often also had legal meanings that were well known. The

[13] Anne Younge *als* Lingham *c.* James (1608), DL/C 218, pp. 88–9.

[14] On suicide and despair, see Michael MacDonald and Terence R. Murphy, *Sleepless Souls: Suicide in Early Modern England* (Oxford, 1990), ch. 1, especially pp. 35–40.

shape of disputes preliminary to, during, and at the ending of marriage was part of a pattern both in law and in practice. The two-way flow of influences between law and practice meant that legal personnel and witnesses might, very often, be working with the same plans, patterns, and conventions. None of the stories discussed in this chapter is, then, simply a witnesses' tale; but the multilayered and multivalent shape of depositions, bound as they were with restrictions, left space for some very personal tellings.

GENDER, AUTHORITY, AND LAW

At the heart of the depositions of both witnesses and defendants was the narrative shift with which they transposed the case's story into a tale of their part in it. The boundaries of domestic authority, law, and neighbourhood relations complicated that shift: gender and status made a crucial difference to the terms on which witnesses took part in disputes over sex, words, or violence, and correspondingly, to the way in which they told their part.

Witnesses started their answers to questions about disputed events with careful explanations of their precise involvement in them: where they were, what they were doing, and why they were there. Women's answers on these points are often suggestive. To questions about their financial situation, they often responded 'that she is a wife'—or a 'mere wife'—'and doth not know her husbands worth'. Other women gave answers that suggest some of the gendered boundaries of property. Men who spoke of the household spaces referred to them always as theirs: what the clerk recorded as 'his house', 'his shop', would have been phrased first 'my house'. Women talking about the same places used a variety of pronouns: often their houses are 'her [i.e. my] husbands house', while the shops they worked in might be 'her shop', and kitchens and bedchambers are almost invariably theirs alone. In marriage cases these pronouns achieve a particular resonance as women list the household goods removed or sold by their husbands.

The gendered dimensions of credit meant that women were less likely to be asked to witness than men; once they got to court, women were also likely to be cross-questioned in a particular way. The interrogatories that defendants posed to witnesses in longer and more contested suits focused on witnesses' credit and especially on the vulnerable values of women's credit. Women were questioned particularly closely about their truthfulness and about perjury. And women themselves reminded the court of the limitations and weaknesses ascribed to femininity. Some refused to provide all the details of a defamation on grounds of modesty or shame, achieving through references to 'such words as her modestie doth not permit her to repeat' a suggestiveness more effective than the most detailed accounts of obscene words. Others defended or explained themselves as 'sillie', 'weak', or 'greene' women. Ann Elsdon, sued for restitution by a man who abducted her in 1624, described Toby Awdley's earlier attempts to 'intrap this respondent being a sillie weake woman to gett a contract or promise of marriage from her': yet by her own account she answered him sharply—'yf she had had any meaninge that waie . . . she could have ben married longe before unto those that did farr exceede him bothe in wealthe and otherwise'—and, presenting her case, she was well aware of the rules of contracting and marriage.[15] Such claims are the familiar currency of women's self-presentation in male spheres;[16] for these women, insistence on their ignorance or modesty proved a useful tactic for effective story-telling and careful self-defence.

Testifying at court, witnesses centred their stories on themselves as narrators, but they also felt other pulls. Involvement in incidents of illicit sex, defamatory disputes, or dubious marriage contracts could all be legally compromising; joining in slanderous speech and being a party to adultery or bastardy was particularly so for women. As we have seen, women and men intervened in marital disputes in distinct ways; in other kinds of conflicts, women's and men's different relationships to the law came into play. To a certain extent women seem to have had particular kinds of local and semi-formal authority, which they exercised especially in the area of sexual morality. But without the authority that older men in communities often established, or the legal powers that some men had through participation in local justice, women found their involvement in disputes, especially where the secular law was concerned, potentially problematic and compromising.

Joan Smith, an alehouse keeper involved in a defamation case in 1590, told a story in which she was torn between authoritative witnessing and anxiety not to be involved. She began with an explanation that stressed her unfamiliarity with the women litigants, with whom she had gone to Kingsland, in Hackney, to testify to the con-

[15] Toby Awdley *c.* Ann Elsdon (1624), DL/C 193, fos. 138–9. This case ended up in Star Chamber, and Ann's abduction was dramatized in a lost play by Thomas Dekker: C. J. Sisson, *Lost Plays of Shakespeare's Age* (Cambridge, 1930), 80–124.

[16] See also the deprecatory prefaces in which women writers of this period apologize for entering into print: for example, Dorothy Leigh, *The Mothers Blessing: Or, The godly Counsaile of a Gentle-woman* (London, 1627).

stable there in a dispute over money spent in her alehouse: she describes her companions as 'one or two other wench beinge unknowen to this examinante'. On their way, a fight broke out between two of the women. Despite having walked to Hackney and drunk 'a pott of beere or two' with them, Joan Smith cannot name her companions, but later in the deposition she recounts her intervention in the quarrel, this time naming with some reluctance one of the women: 'Dodds wife and wedow Wyatt yf so she be called revyved an old querell that was betweene them And this examinante when she sawe them fighting togither devyded them aswell as she cold and pulled them one from thother.' The fight continued until a local man came to intervene—'then came Crowther busylye to make an ende of that querell and began an other'. It emerges that Joan Smith had become so involved, calling William Crowther a knave because he had hit one of the women, that he tried to put her in the stocks.

Joan's place in her own story is an ambiguous one: she is both insistent on her own attempts to mediate, and ready to deny any familiarity with the women involved. The problem, at the end of the incident, is that her authority is not accepted. Instead William Crowther takes over, and she points out that he did so improperly: 'Mr Harman of Kingeslande was then the constable of the place but Crowther not knowing what doth belonge unto the offyce of a constable more for revenge sake then for anie juste cause of punishment tooke upon him to be deputye for the tyme unto the constable that was sicke.'

It was William Crowther, as a man, who finally assumed the semi-legal authority Joan Smith could not. The triumph of Joan Smith's story is her vindication. She explains that her intervention with Crowther and the course of local justice was aimed to save him from another kind of revenge: 'she knew that her husband wold have byn revenged upon Crowther if he had doone it [i.e. put her in the stocks] but by cause she gott the vyctorye in that matter she wold never lett her husbande knowe it for feare least Crowthers cote shold have byn well lyned for his foolishe attempte'. She emerges from the process of formal justice, exonerated from blame and suggesting that, after all, she was in the right:

> Mr Crowther did comande this respondente and the rest named in this interrogatory to goe before Mr Justyce Machell and when this respondente had made reporte that she was no partye in the brawle betweene Dods wife and thother and that she did not abuse Crowther anie otherwise then that she called him knave . . . for strickinge of a woman the justice dismissed this

respondente and so she left the woman that strocke Dods wife behinde her at the justyce his howse and departed.[17]

Joan Smith's story, as it moves from one kind of formal or informal justice to another, suggests some of the problems of women's position and authority in social disputes.

Men's stories told of a less problematic and more effective relationship with the interests of law. Some stressed their role as mediators. Isaac Thorpe, a witness in Catherine Edwards's case against Robert Sharpe in 1637, recalled

That he . . . heareing of a difference and falling out betweene the parties litigant in this cause being his neighbours and being desirous to make peace and quietnes betweene them . . . sitting at his contestes door Mr Nicholas Shackely . . called Robert Sharpe the partie defendant then passeing by the said door unto him and then and there this deponent and his contest aforesaid desired him to be at peace with the partie plaintiff Catherine Edwardes at the which time the said Sharpe swore he would not and . . . said she was a whore.[18]

Isaac was 83 and had lived in the parish since his youth, while the two disputants were relative newcomers: this must have given him a special authority. Others used their positions as innkeepers or clergy to undertake similar projects, as older friends did in marriage contracts. Mediating like this, men effectively enlisted themselves on the side of the law; like the judges of the church courts, Isaac Thorpe was 'desirous to make peace and quietnes' between the litigants. Amongst the responses of Walter Brampton and the men who lived in the same house as him to his wife's adultery, as we saw in the previous chapter, were a set of interrogations that followed the model of the law in a more pointed way. Both Walter and John Wright, Walter's landlord's servant, 'examined' Agnes Brampton, asking her to 'confess'; John Wright recorded that she did so 'very penitently', and he gave her confession legal standing (it was later produced in court) by writing it down and signing it himself. A later confession he even read back to Agnes, as, in court, witnesses' depositions were read back to them to check, and she repeated his words, 'acknowledging her offences' after him.

With examinations, confessions, and penitence, the series of confrontations between Agnes Brampton and the men who tried to bring her to account read like an imitation of legal processes. When John

[17] Elizabeth Moorefoot *c.* William Crowther (1590), DL/C 213, p. 664.
[18] Catherine Edwards *c.* Robert Sharpe (1637), DL/C 630, fo. 64.

Wright, his employer, and Walter Brampton came to the church court with this story they were asked questions that underlined the official role they had assumed themselves: had they forced the confession from Agnes? Had any undue pressure been used? Edward Lane responded 'onely that his servant John Wright suspected the incontinent life of the said Agnes and wishing well to the party producent laboured to gette her and persuaded her to make the said confessions, to thintent to have the matter plainlie knowne that it might appeare what manner of woman she was'.[19] It seemed to them that the situation required, more than a marital reconciliation, a clear discovery of 'what manner of woman' Agnes was.[20] Men suspected of mistreating their wives, or indeed of adultery, never ended up being questioned like this. The rhetoric of the law, its function as an instrument of both mediation and conflict, played an important part of social relations, but a part that varied for women and for men. In their different contexts, both Agnes Brampton's examination and Joan Smith's narrative of her experiences in Kingsland show the extent to which, while men's legal narratives might ally themselves with the law, women's relationship to the law, its language, and its projects was a potential minefield.

DECEIT AND DISCOVERY

The stories of illicit sex that were central to much of the church court's litigation focused on the sins of women. Witnesses to adultery and defamers told stories of women's sexual misconduct that relied, very often, on the same set of conventions, in which women's adultery infected their whole moral sense, disordered households, and disorganized domestic economies. In both kinds of story the climax was the moment of discovery, the point when honest women were exposed as whores or adulteresses. A domestic drama, adultery was also a public one. Husbands uncovering their wives' adultery shared their shame with their friends or their wife's family; neighbours who suspected women of illicit sex exposed it in public, insisting that it compromised the honesty of the whole neighbourhood.

Both kinds of narrator were concerned particularly with disguised truths. The language of insult, as we have seen, sought to make whores visible; defamers insisted that adultery had physical analogues—a roving eye, the use of cosmetics, or simply pregnancy—that

[19] Walter Brampton *c.* Agnes Brampton (1612), DL/C 220, fos. 573, 570.

[20] For Agnes Brampton's responses, see Ch. 6.

left visible marks on women. Whores were accused of hiding and disguising themselves, of locking doors, and of deceiving both husbands and neighbours. At court, plaintiffs and witnesses told tales of the deceit of women, an established literary trope; in the 1560s a whole collection of stories, alternately biblical or classical and contemporary romances, was devoted to exposing 'The deceyte of women, to the instruction and ensample of men'.[21] It was a peculiarly feminine trope: the ways men destroyed marriage and morals were never construed as secret, deceitful acts.

If the plot of cuckoldry was a well-known and humiliating one, men also had models for triumphing over womens' deceits; and it was these that were mobilized in the service of legal narratives which condemned adulterous women and simultaneously marked the victory of their discoverers, sometimes husbands, sometimes servants or neighbours, and sometimes women. John Poulter of Eastwood in Essex, whose wife Marie was accused of adultery at the court in 1615, was said to have outwitted her deceit with a guile typical of the victorious husbands of popular literature. Samuel Purchas, a London rector, testified to the court that John had told him Marie's adultery with a man named Bradford Berrie was common knowledge, and 'the place of theire usuall meetinge togeither [in the woods nearby] was worne bare by reason of theire resort thither'. John's story, as told to the rector, continued

> the sayd Marie aboute two yeres sithence desired the said John Poulter her husband to goe for a pounde of butter . . . which [he] . . . semed to bee willinge to doe, and that he allsoe distrustinge his saied wiefes lewd and incontinent lief, retired from her, making shewe that hee would goe for the said butter & hid himself aboutes his house in a wood there and watched his said wief, whoe . . . after his goinge out of his said howse made herself readie, and went into his garden and plucked a rose and put the same into her bosome, and then went into a wood in or nere Eastwood, which he sawe and followinge her into a thickett founde the said Bradford Berrie and the said Marie his wief alone togither in such suspitious sort that hee was much offended therat.

John's story, or the rector's report of it, worked in a genre of tales about catching women out; playing on local rumour and 'common fame', and with individual touches like Marie taking the seductive rose from 'his' garden, it was also a conventional tale in which a husband's victory over his deceitful wife balanced the well-rehearsed threat of

[21] Abraham Vele, *The deceyte of women. to the instruction and ensample of all men, yonge and olde* (London, 1563).

adultery. Marie, in fact, received this testimony very much as a story, and sued John Valentine, who had brought the allegation to court instead of her husband, for defamation. Another witness cast doubt on the tale's ending, saying that in the version he heard John found the two together 'distant thone from the other about two or three roodes of and thereuppon he . . . did not present her'.[22] In this context, the repetition of John Poulter's narrative looks as much like the tales that defame women, as legal evidence. Its focus on household errands, on courtship rituals between women and their lovers, and on the trap set by the husband, are all familiar elements in the stories of women's adultery.

It was not just husbands who were deceived by women. Illicit sex had specific legal implications not only for the participants, but for anyone who abetted or concealed them. Witnesses to adultery might, therefore, find themselves in a potentially compromising position, at risk of prosecution for bawdry or harbouring pregnant women. The women and men who had lodged or sheltered adulterous women made a particular feature of their ignorance of the crime: for them, the deceit of adultery was not just a betrayal of marriage but a violation of hospitality. Katherine and Lawrence Hussey, owners of the Rose and Crown inn in Greenwich where Anne Bickmer had given birth to an illegitimate child, told the court a story that traced their mounting suspicions of the deceits practised on them. Anne Bickmer's very name was a deceit: she first appeared to Katherine Hussey as 'a woman who then termed her selfe by the name of Alice Bridges by her fathers name and Alice Smith by the name of an husband whome as shee saied shee had married not long before: whose name as this jurate hath sithens perfectly learned (as she saieth) is Anne Bickmer'. Only a woman could have had so many plausible names; in this story, the shifting identity by which women were defined was part of a larger feminine deceit. William Higham, Anne's partner in adultery, also used a pseudonym, but his was a palindrome of his own, 'Mahgih'; men's identities, it seems, were not as deceptively mutable as women's.

Katherine Hussey's story went on to describe more of Anne's deceptions. Brought by 'a harbinger of . . . the Erle of Leicester', who said she had just married a man called Smith, Anne 'praied this jurate to receyve her as a guest into her howse: and to appoynt her some secret chambre or lodging bicause it might not safely be knowen to

[22] John Valentine *c.* Marie Poulter (1615), DL/C 223, fos. 46ᵛ–47; Poulter *c.* Valentine, (1615), ibid. 212, 214ᵛ. (A roode is about 6–8 yards.)

the parents of the aforenamed Smith for feare least he should be disinherited by them for marrieing that woman withowt their consent'. It was a familiar story, and one that Katherine said she believed, until the behaviour of William Higham, posing as a friend of Anne's, aroused her suspicions: he 'praied this jurate to be chary and carefull of the said Anne he him sellfe then seemeing to be very carefull for her'. As time went on she discovered both of their true names, and after Anne gave birth both Katherine and her husband came to the conclusion that William was the child's father. The economic necessities and emotional context of childbirth were what ultimately exposed Anne's deceit: William gave the game away by paying for her lodging and the child's nursing, asking on his visits 'how his gyrle did', meaning the child, and kissing and 'cherishing' Anne after the birth. Both Katherine and her husband told tales that were concerned centrally with the deceit perpetrated on their hospitality, and their detection of that deceit.[23] More circumstantial than most kinds of evidence offered to the court, stories of illicit sex depended on the witnesses interposing their judgement, establishing guilt through conventional clues: affection, familiarity, secrecy.

Servants were especially well placed to detect the familiar signs of adultery and the deceit of women. In court, the moment of witnessing could transform them into temporary masters of their household, aware, as their real masters were not, of the sexual undercurrents of the domestic order. Most masterly was the story told by Edmund Foster, the 20-year old apprentice to Bayly Ball, who came to witness to the adultery of his mistress, Grace Ball, in 1609. It begins at eight o'clock at night on Christmas Eve. His master was out of town and he was alone in the house with his mistress:

> she sayd to this deponent thus, if I wist no body would come to the dore yow should go to the barbers to have yor haire cutt of which yow might have don all this week and so even as she was thus talking John Whalley . . . knocked at the dore and came in and went upp and stood talking secretly with her . . . and stryght ways she called him this deponent to fetche some beere.

He fetched the beer, and soon Whalley left and his mistress sent him to the barbers, telling him to lock the door 'For quoth she I will go to bed'. When he returned, his suspicions were aroused:

> as he was about to goe to bed he lying in his maisters shopp he saithe he heard his mistris laughe above in her chamber and theruppon he this

[23] Elizabeth Higham *c.* William Higham (1580), DL/C 629, fos. 262^{v}–4^{v}.

deponents shoes being of, went on to the stayers softle harkning did here Whallies voyce talking with her the articulate Grace and heard them kis each other and many words he sayethe he did understand and he sayethe he standing there almost an hour close by the chamber dore did here the bed shake and joggle and crack a great while together and when the bed had don cracking and stirring he did well here and understand John Whallie . . . saye unto her the said Grace I hope I have skoured yow now, I hope so quoth she . . . and laughed at it and then he this deponent being both wearie and cold went downe the stayers into the shopp.

Backtracking again, he remembered hearing some other conversation before the bed started creaking:

he heard them talk together of sundry things namely how many tradesmen wer broken therabouts and likwise he asked whether one Thurston that dwelt therby had had to doe with her or not whearunto she answered no neither Mr Thurston nor any man living had don that to her which he the same Whallie had don . . . Then he . . . asked her what if your husband should knowe that I weare in bed with yow nowe whearunto she answerd saying that is impossible.

'No man living had don that to her which he had don': this fragment of lovers' conversation might be a reference to specific sexual acts, an assertion that John Whalley was more sexually satisfying than Bayly Ball, or an attempt to sustain a fiction of fidelity even in adultery. Edmund Foster's report of the words also brings out some areas of particular concern to him: his mistress is discussing local trade not with her lawful work partners—her husband or their apprentice—but with her husband's friend, now her lover; she believes it is 'impossible' that they should ever be found out, but there she underestimates her apprentice's skills at spying, and his word for word account of what he heard implicitly asserts his victory over her.

This occasion is just the first of a series of further events, in each of which Grace Ball makes a secret assignation with John Whalley, sends her apprentice off on various concocted errands, and is suspected or caught out when he returns home. On Christmas morning, to get John out of the house without Edmund suspecting, she sends her apprentice to fetch a pound of sausages; but Edmund tells a boy to watch the house and hears that John Whalley has come out of it, and when he gets back, John reappears and eats breakfast with his mistress 'with sasages which in his this deponents understanding was for nothing ells but because he this deponent should not think that he the same Whallie had byn ther before'. On 27 December, John Whalley makes another flying visit to the house and leaves with many 'god night god night's and 'god be with yow's, after which Grace sends Edmund for 'one pennyworthe of good sugar', letting in her lover while he is gone; in the morning she sends him to see a house on fire, but this time he manages to lock John Whalley in. Grace then sends him for another pound of sausages, telling him to go to Southwark to get better ones than usual. The days of the festival continue to mark Grace's acts of adultery: on New Year's Day they go through the same routine, Grace sending Edmund out for 'a penny worthe of pyns' and the next morning, 'to looke if Mrs Woodbridge and her husband . . . dined at home'; and on Twelfth Night, she sends him for sugar candy, and the next morning, again, for sausages—whose phallic significance infuses them, by this stage in the narrative, with a symbolic weight of their own.[24]

This catalogue of assignations turns, in Edmund's story, into a battle between Grace's deceptions and his cunning: he locks John Whalley out or in to catch him, sets boys to watch the house, and stands spying outside Grace's room. It is a tale that also maps a shift in Edmund's position, from the dependent servant of his mistress to his master's indignant ally. Responsible in his master's absence for both his shop and his wife, he finds Grace disrupting the household business with adultery and trying to fool him with what he realizes to be 'idle or shewles arrands'. Exasperated by the physical discomfort—it was a long way to the sausage shop, and he gets cold and tired standing listening outside her bedroom—Edmund is also righteously angry at his mistress's attempts at secrecy. Nominally still at her command to run imaginary errands, by the end of this story Edmund has information which puts him in a much more powerful position. Catching his mistress out in crime, he continues to obey her but produces a story against her which he tells, first to her brother-in-law, and later to the court. As he tells it, the story becomes an account of his own victory of perception and proof against her deceits.

The claims pressed by Bayly Ball against his wife were also reconfigured into different stories. Richard Ball, Bayly's brother and the parish priest of St Helens Bishopsgate, told a version that incorporated the tale that Edmund Foster had told him—presumably an earlier form of the one he told to the court—into a narrative about his own action: not as the witness and exposer of adultery, but the mediator. He went to see Grace, who had by now left Bayly and gone to her mother's house, and told her he knew of 'some particular

[24] Bayly Ball *c.* Grace Ball (1609), DL/C 218, pp. 474–80.

speeches' between her and John Whalley. Like other wives, she responded, apparently, with a confession:

at last . . . she the same Grace began with teares to acknowledge her fault sayeing unto him this deponent thus or to this effect, I have byn sundry times tempted to dishonestie bothe when I was a mayd and synce I was maried but I never yelded to dishonestie before now that my husband was out of towne when John Whallie taking opportunitie at my husbands absence urged me to dishonestie and so she confessed unto him this deponent that she had lyne with the same John Whallie fower severall nights and had committed adulterie with him for which she was hartely sorry and desyred him this deponent not to reveale it to her mother but to intreat her husband to forgive her making great lamentacon for her sayed offence.[25]

Richard Ball's focus was on Grace's confession and repentance: both through his kinship to her and his ministry, he is empowered to confront her with her offence. As a minister, he was more entitled to use the language of spiritual discipline—offending, examining, confessing, and forgiving—than the other men who turned to it so readily when they talked to women under suspicion of adultery. His aim is reconciliation, and here he assumes for himself the kind of role the court took on, mediating between husbands and wives; and Grace's greatest fear is apparently not of the discipline of the church, or even the reaction of her husband, but of her mother. Grace's mother's reaction seems to have borne out her fears, for Bayly alleged that when she did hear of her daughter's confession to Richard Ball, she 'wished that she the said Grace Ball wear as deepe under ground as she was above grounde for confesing soe much'.[26]

Finally the story comes to Grace Ball, for her to retell in her defence. By the time the case went to court she had already left Bayly on grounds of cruelty, and it is possible the whole adultery story was set up by her husband. But against his allegations she produced a careful rewriting of her husband's story. Edmund Foster had told a conventional tale of deceit and discovery; Richard Ball had invoked another conventional image, a guilty woman's repentance. In response Grace Ball turned to a storyline that was also familiar, and told a tale about the problems of a woman's part in hospitality. In 1607 Thomas Heywood's *A Woman Kilde with Kindnesse* presented his audiences with a woman whose husband presses his friend on her, instructing her to entertain him, 'use him with all thy loving'st courtesy': she extends the courtesy too far, and dies for it.[27] In 1609 Grace Ball told how her

[25] Ibid. 467–8.

[26] DL/C 15, fo. 74.

[27] Thomas Heywood, *A Woman Kilde with Kindnesse* (London, 1607), II. i. 78.

husband brought friends home, asked her to welcome them, but grew swiftly jealous:

> Bayly Ball her husband being a man that useth much company after such tyme as she was first marryed unto him brought home unto her to his house divers of his companions and acquaintance and commanded her to bid them welcome and there would and did many tymes make them good cheare and many tymes go abroade with them to the tavernes and there make merrie with them, and keepe them companie at the bowling alleys . . . and when he had either lost his money or had byn longe at the taverne with them would then come home unto her and upbraid or hit her in the teethe that she was over familiar with them insomuche that she percieving his jelous humour and disposition and that it bred much disquiet betwixt them oftentimes desired him thatt he would not from thenceforthe bring home to his house any of his companions, but still he brought them thither . . . and when this respondent had at any tymes kept her selfe out of the way and would not be seene of them, as often tymes she did, then her sayd husband would and did fynde fault therewith and quarrell with her because she did not bid them welcome.

When, in September 1608, he introduced John Whalley as 'one of his good frends', told her to make him welcome and invited him 'divers times' to breakfast, she feared 'that her sayd husband would in the ende growe jealous of him', and begged him not to bring him home any longer, but Bayly 'falling into greate rage and anger with her for her sayd speaches did tell her that if she would not be content to suffer the said Mr Whallie to frequent his house, that then he himselfe would wholy forsake and leave it if none of his frends might be welcome to it'. The very morning that Bayly left on his Christmas business trip, Grace said, he 'invited home to his house that morning to breakfast the sayd Whalley and two other younge men of his acquaintance without the privitie of this respondent'; John's further visits, in Bayly's absence, followed naturally from this start.[28] In her other, briefer answers Grace admitted sending Edmund Foster on errands, said that the stories of other witnesses who claimed John Whalley had confessed to Richard Ball were untrue, and contended that she had left Bayly because he mistreated her.

Grace's responses counter the case against her with a complete reshaping of the events, telling a story which begins much earlier with a history of marital conflict over hospitality, introducing precedents of breakfast invitations to explain John's visits and citing moments of violence and verbal abuse to suggest the marital cruelty that is her response to Edmund Foster's narrative of betrayal. It is a tale that

[28] Ball *c.* Ball, DL/C 218, pp. 503–4 ff.

strives at one level to deny her adultery; at the same time, with her stress on Bayly's insistent hospitality and his jealousy, Grace's words read like a plea that, if she *had* committed adultery, it was her husband's fault. For her, as for Edmund Foster, the domestic sphere is fraught with dangers and traps. Marriage, in her story, is a dilemma in which her business role as Bayly's hospitable partner is undermined by his sexual jealousy of her. It is a narrative, with its familiar references and conventions, that she felt would convince the court; it may well also have been part of a discourse other women used to deny or explain adultery in the context of the dilemmas of women's hospitality. Agnes Brampton, the story of whose 'confessions' we heard earlier, accused her husband of setting a trap purposely to catch her in adultery, encouraging another man to visit the house, telling her to treat him kindly, and—according to her maid—planning his wife's adultery in the hope that he would then be able to divorce her.

NARRATIVE AND WOMEN'S IDENTITY

Litigation at the church courts was very often concerned with disputes that had a special centrality to women's lives and female identity: battles for sexual honour, negotations for marriage, and allegations of adultery. Socially, culturally, and legally, the events of sex and marriage were central to women's identity and status as they were not for men. Sexual chastity was a measure of female virtue that could outdo every other way of defining a woman; marriage decided women's names, their legal identity, and their economic, working, and social future. For all witnesses, deposing in court involved representing themselves; for women describing their sexual or marital encounters, it could also mean telling the story of their identity, using languages of dependency, victimization, autonomy, and self-assertion.

The legal and social culture of early modern society accorded less credit to women's words than to men's. In the sphere of sexual conduct this was particularly so; women, especially young women and servants, found it hard to make accusations of seduction, asssault, or rape stick against men. Some of their accusations, indeed, ended up being cited as slander. The narrative opportunities of witnessing provided some women with a way of countering that denial of their tales. Women who testified to the court often described their powerlessness in the face of husbands or suitors, masters or mistresses; but in the very telling of these stories they asserted their control over the events of daily oppression by reconstructing them and shifting the blame.[29] Susan More, a 25-year-old servant made pregnant by her master's friend—well known for his sexual harassment of other women in the neighbourhood[30]—failed to get any maintenance or help from him and was turned away by his wife; but several months later, she found herself giving evidence in a disciplinary case against him for bastardy, on which occasion she was able to place his sexual misconduct and her mistreatment at the centre of a story which in another context could very easily have been told around her guilt.

Thomas Creede started off by buying Susan a pint of wine because, she said, his first wife had been called Susan and they looked so alike. After a few months of meetings he gave her 'so much wine as she . . . was drunck and sicke', took her to a house he knew, and 'had the carnall knowledge of her body'. Drink proves the means by which Susan becomes a passive victim of seduction. In her story, Thomas continues to pursue her: he 'enticed' her to other taverns, sending 'tavern boys' over to her master's house to fetch her when she refused. When she thought she was pregnant he refused to do anything for her, saying 'goe fetch another father for your child if you wil for I mean not to father it, I will shift it of well enoughe and my wief will help to cleere me of this matter and to shift it as she hath shifted me of such matters as this is before now'.

This 'shifting' does not so much clear Thomas, as pass his guilt on to his wife: for Susan, it is increasingly the 'other woman' in the case who is to blame. Susan told her master and mistress of her pregnancy, and they arranged a meeting at which Thomas's wife 'did so terrifie her this deponent with words as she this deponent could not tell what to do she saying that if she this deponent layed her child to her husband she would make her this deponent repent it all the dayes of her lief'; finally Mrs Creede was persuaded to give Susan ten shillings to go away, and escorted her on to a wagon to Cambridge. Susan, 'being not able to endure the uneasie going of the wagon it being in the great frost time last', returned to London, where she failed to find anywhere to stay and ended up sleeping in the street and later in 'a pore womans house' with, in stark contrast to the abundance of food and drink Thomas showered on her during the seduction, nothing to eat for two days. Eventually she was persuaded to have Thomas called to the

[29] Ann Syme's story is quoted in full in Ch. 3.

[30] Anna Berke, Susan's mistress, reported Creede's 'wanton speeches' to her—'she . . . had a sweet paire of lipps and if she wear a good wench she would lett him have some part with her husband'—and his 'earnest' attempts on her chastity: DL/C 218, p. 163.

sessions, at which occasion Mrs Creede promised to send her money and to come and help at the birth, but in the end did neither. Throughout the events of pregnancy, poverty, and homelessness, it seems the only agency Susan has left is verbal: she tells the story to her employers, to Thomas and his wife, and to the sessions. Finally she tells it to the consistory court, not as a prosecutor but as a witness, and her narrative of her experiences takes up eleven pages.[31] Integral to the cultural agency Susan exercised in telling her story was a reorganization of blame, so that the guilt for her pregnancy is not hers. But it was a retelling that eventually shifted the blame away from Thomas too: at the end of Susan's story, it is his wife who is to blame for not saving her from homelessness, hunger, and the ignominy of illegitimate childbirth. Susan remains bound, in some skewed way, by the conventions of moral blame: it is always a woman who bears the responsibility for adultery.

The kind of powerlessness that Susan More recorded in the events of her seduction and pregnancy was used by another, younger woman in a more sophisticated way. Joan Smith, a orphan of around 15, daughter of a freeman and in the wardship of the Lord Mayor, was sued in 1575 by her putative husband, Henry Eaton, for the restitution of conjugal rights he had never enjoyed. Her answers to his allegations told a long story of abduction and clandestine marriage. Her version reads at first very like a petition, couched in the kind of language familiar to those dependent upon the maintenance and favours of the City: 'she ys verie younge and of verye simple sence and capacitie fatherles and motherles, a freemans childe of this Cittie of London and by that means an orphaunte of the same cittie and under the protection and tuition of the Lorde maior and alderman of the said cittie'. As much at issue as her person, it appears, is her money, the inheritance from her father for which Henry Eaton—whose brother Thomas had married her sister—sought to marry her. Joan alleged that she had been intimidated by Thomas Eaton, his wife, 'and other lewde and wycked persons', who threatened that her 'friends' would put her out to service 'to very sharpe mysteris that would everie daye beate and whippe her, and make her wearie of her lyffe'. Already the stress is on the vulnerability of a young girl protected only by 'friends' with dubious loyalties. 'Throughe this feare and other theire craftye perswacions and intisements' Joan was persuaded to go with them, and was dressed in new clothes and taken to a church. There they

[31] John Scales *c.* Thomas Creede (1608), DL/C 218, pp. 138–49.

called for 'an unskilfull minister', and through 'the saide feare and other perswacions and craftye dealinges they procured this respondent having neyther skill judgemente or discretion to judge of matrimonie or whatt belongeth thereto, to saye she knoweth nott nowe whatt'. They took her back to the house of Thomas Eaton, Henry's brother, where 'they kepte her lyke a prisoner the doores faste shutt'. Eventually she was 'rescued' by her friends and her sister, with the help of the Lord Mayor's officers. Taken to the safety of the Mayor's house, her independent judgement and most importantly her power to dissent to marriage returns: she told the court she was 'carried . . . to the house of the saide Lorde maior whereof this respondente was verie gladd and did utterlie mislyke of all that had passed betweene her and the saide Eaton and dissented to the same'. She went on to deny with great care all the customary proofs of the marital bond, returning finally to her rights and position as a freeman's child:

> shee sayeth also that she never had anie acquaintance before with the sayde Henrie Eaton neyther did shee ever love hym or ever had anie occasion by giftes or tokens or other familiar continuance of talke so to do but onelye throughe the feare and treacherie aforesaide neyther had shee ever or hathe anie likinge of hym but hathe and dothe utterlie dissente from hym and all his companions craftye and moste ungodlie devises and practises in this behalfe . . . and moste humblie requirethe that she maye by reason of the premisses be by order of lawe clerelie rydd and sett free from the saide Eaton, whoe ys no free man nor hathe anye thinge in the worlde eyther howse or oughte ells to lyve bye and therfore seekethe to spoile this respondente of that that her father hath lefte her to her utter undooinge and to the moste wycked example of other suche evell disposed persons to practize and doo the lyke.[32]

Throughout the narrative Joan makes unusually explicit moral references to the behaviour of Henry Eaton and his associates, comparing them with her own state: they are 'lewd and wycked', 'craftye', 'ungodlie'; she, in sharp and stirring contrast, is 'very simple', 'in verie greate feare', 'kept lyke a prisoner', and finally, when rescued, is simply 'very gladd'. The Eatons and their friends appear as a mass of strange, crafty abductors; her stress is on her unprotected orphanhood. She chooses to ignore the closeness of her relationship to her captors: in fact Thomas Eaton was her brother-in-law, and the woman she refers to as 'the wyffe of the said Thomas', who takes a principal part in

[32] Henry Eaton *c.* Joan Smith (1575), DL/C 212, pp. 125–7.

frightening and abducting her, is her sister. Orphanhood, here, is a more productive identity than that of bullied sister: the sister she *does* recognize is the one who helps to rescue her. Thomas Eaton's quite different version of events claimed that this sister had threatened to 'putt her to a shrewd mistres, and otherwise did abuse her in many thinges', and that Joan came to him and his wife to beg that she could be 'at their puttinge'.[33] What emerges, in fact, is another story, one where Joan has not too little kin, but too much, and where she is being torn between the persuasions and threats of two sisters. And, while Joan's story suggests that her orphanhood is her central identity, and that she has long been a ward of the City, her father had in fact died only a month before the disputed marriage.

The extraordinary shaping and eloquent pleading of Joan's story, and her youth, make it tempting to assume it was planned by someone else, a proctor or one of the friends to whom she refers. It was still she who told it in court; its rhetoric of vulnerability in the marriage market, pointed up by the final reminder that Henry Eaton's acts are a 'moste wycked example' to 'other suche evell disposed persons to doo the lyke', might be one that made particular sense to girls and women in her position; certainly very similar language and fears structured the stories of other women embroiled in the plots of clandestine marriage. Joan's eloquent self-presentation might incline us to agree, ironically in contradiction of her carefully argued pleas, that she was—as Thomas Eaton claimed—'of wytt sufficient enough to make a resonable answer of her self to any thinge'.[34] Her narrative persona was very different to that of Susan More, yet it was representative in its own way of perceptions of women in relation to sex and marriage. In Susan's story, her poverty and position make her the passive victim of men's wiles; Joan, confident of her privileges and inheritance in the civic community, knows herself to be a marketable prize that men will try to steal, and she deploys what she—or somebody—judges to be an appealing version of her identity and kinship to win her case.

Elizabeth Rogers, at court over another alleged abduction in 1574, also told a tale of her battle against unscrupulous men. Involved in a complicated marriage case with Matthew Goodman who had allegedly married her and contracted himself to another woman, she managed in her statement to rearrange its focus so that the crime of clandestine marriage committed against her became its central question. Like

[33] Ibid. 117, 116. [34] Ibid. 120.

Joan Smith's, the story that Elizabeth presented stressed her lack of understanding. Elizabeth, aged 13, really was under marriageable age,[35] and her witnesses testified that she was 'of her age more childishe witted than commonlie others be of like age'. Agnes Stockdale, an older female neighbour, said 'her demeanour is very childish playing and fighting with young children commonlie', and reported that Elizabeth, being at her house with her two children (aged 4 and 7), had begged her husband 'I pray yowe goffar Stockdale geve me this (meaning some shredes which her husband had being a taylor) to make me a babe of'. She also 'like a young child hath . . . mutch trobled the house of this examinante with her plaie fellowes young children of the streete'. When

> it was first reported that she was carried awaie to be married everie man and woman wondred in the street affirming that she was not yet past making of babes, and too much a jigg and childishe And undoubtedlie she is and is comonly accompted so simple, as it is not possible she shuld knowe what mariadge meaneth neither wilbe able to knowe these dosen yeares except she be otherwise broken, then she is yet, And is more meate to have a will then a husband And both this examinante and all her neighbors . . . doe beleve that with a babe or some sutch trifell a man might easelie enduce her to have twenty husbands almost in one daie.

Her words draw a series of connections to present Elizabeth's immaturity: she plays with 'children' and 'makes babes'; she knows how to make 'babes' out of shreds of cloth, but she does not know about the making of real babies, 'what mariadge meaneth'. Her stress, too, is on the 'breaking' necessary to make wives of girls: Elizabeth plays, begs, bothers, and fights; she has a 'will' instead of a husband, as if the two are incompatible.

Yet the length and care of Elizabeth's own reponses suggests she was considerably more mature and aware than this. Like Joan Smith, she told the court a story that stressed her vulnerability and betrayal by older men and women, but also presented herself as not foolish enough to be entirely taken in by their words. As she was carrying water for her father, Mr Dale told her she was to go with Matthew Goodman over the river 'not uttering the cause of her going thither but bearing her in hand that she sholde at the waters side mete with her father'. She refused, for 'her father had not made her privey to anie such busines but was willed by him to returne quicklie againe and

[35] Elizabeth's age was one of the points at issue in the case; while Matthew Goodman admitted he thought she was 13, his witnesses claimed he had told them she was 15 or 16, and the registration of her birth eventually proved her to be 13.

beside that she should goe with one with whome she was never before acquaynted or had any talk with all'. Only Dale's threats to force her to go made her accompany him, and when they arrived at the wharf and her father was not there 'she chardged Dale that he had deceived her . . . he threatened her that if she spake he wolde make her repent . . . and that no-one purposed her anie hurte and he said Besse be of good cheere thy father hath willed me to carrie the[e] awaie from thy mother to marrie the[e] . . . wheareat she cried owte upon him that he had brought her to that pointe'. It is a drama characterized by men's conspiracies against women: Elizabeth's father, not her mother, is supposed to have intrigued with Dale and Matthew Goodman to carry her away.

As they landed at Limehouse 'divers words' were still passing between Elizabeth and Dale, 'she chardging him that he had delte judaslie with her'. At three or four o'clock the next morning she was 'carried by them to the church and by the waie taught by Dale what she shoulde saie when she cam there who threatened her to throwe her into the water excepte she wolde yelde to saie as he had instructed her'. At the church, 'she sayd certaine woords after the priest which she neither then marked nor nowe remembreth'. She concludes 'because she was not married as other folkes be, she thinketh that she was not married at all'. Other witnesses' reports suggest that she knew at least 'what mariadge meaneth', and managed to avoid its implications: she refused to go to bed in the bride bed that had been provided 'by the goodwief of the house after the countre fashion', and when Matthew went to bed to her, he came back reporting that she 'was not able to lie with a man', and the next day she held up the whole party by complaining that she was sick.[36] Agnes Stockdale's tale of Elizabeth's youthful mentality may, however, have had some basis in fact: unlike Joan Smith, Elizabeth pays little attention to the purposes for which her abductors presumably wanted her; she is more concerned that they persuaded her to disobey her father's orders to go straight home, and the fact they lied to her. Her vision of herself is not yet that of Joan Smith, two years her senior, a vulnerable, marriageable asset.

The keynote of these last stories has been the sexual and marital identities of women, constructed in relation to men. It has been men, in these tales, who pressure or threaten women; these women's stories are about how they responded or coped or suffered at the hands

[36] Marie Bedell *c.* Elizabeth Rogers & Matthew Goodman (1574), DL/C 212, pp. 66–7; Matthew Goodman *c.* Elizabeth Rogers (1574), DL/C 212, pp. 43–4, 61.

of male imperatives. I want to finish with a story that is concerned, instead, about the dynamics of power between women. Nominally a presentation of evidence to support an allegation of adultery, it tells, rather, a domestic drama of displacement, disempowerment, emotional distress, and moral victory. Its narrator is at threat not, as in these last cases, from the dangers of the marriage market and the betrayals of men, but from the configurations of status and power in the sphere of a Catholic gentry household. Displaced in that household, she tells a story whose content and eloquence mean that it constitutes in itself a realignment of domestic authority.

Madelen Plonkett, the 22-year-old daughter of a landed gentleman, from Dethick in Derbyshire, came to the London consistory court in 1591 to testify in a marriage separation suit brought by her brother, Francis Babbington, against his wife, a London alderman's daughter called Julian Roo. Madelen and Francis were the younger siblings of Anthony Babington, attainted in 1586 for plotting with Mary Queen of Scots against Elizabeth I. By the time of this case, Madelen had married the heir to an Irish barony; but before 1588, Madelen told the court, she was keeping house for her brother in his two houses in Nottinghamshire, inherited despite the confiscation from their brother Anthony, and he had charge of her marital portion. When Madelen was 20 this neatly balanced arrangement was upset by the marriage of her brother Francis. She continued to live with the couple, but 'delivered the whole charge of both hir brothers . . . houses' over to his wife Julian.

With this description of her domestic life, Madelen opened a household drama that begins one night when her brother was away. Long before then, she noted, she had

> conceaved soome suspicon of hir said sister in lawe dwelling in house togither of bad delinge and more than modestie required betweene her said sister in lawe and the articulate James Skelton hir brother Francis his man by their often and privett conferences and his overbold familiaritie unmannerlie and fellowlike acquaintance and usage towards hir with continuall continance thearof.

That night,

> she the articulate Julian hir sister in lawe going to bedd (who laye the very next chamber to this deponent having butt a dore betweene them) sent hir maid called Helvetham Brown through this deponents chamber into another chamber beyonde shee this deponent being in hir owne chamber with hir book and accompanied with hir maid whearuppon the maids passing through this deponent began to growe into further imaginacyon of hir former con-

ceipt of hir sister in law, and (after the maid was going) this deponent walked up and down hir chamber and standing by her chimney which is so mayde that one may easilie see all the other chamber whear hir sister lay she this deponent espied hir sister in law in hir smock newly risen out of hir bedd and sawe hir unlock the said Julians door which was by hir bedd side and ledd down a paire of staires into the court, at which sight this deponent marvelled and grewe in further suspicion then beefore.

The architectural details so carefully noted are important: not only are we told how easily Madelen can see into her sister's room, but we are also reminded of Madelen's displaced status in the house. Once in control of all the rooms of the house, she has handed her dominion over to a woman who is now, it appears, misusing their spaces and their connections. Madelen's story continues,

and within a while after the maid aforesaid returned back this deponent then beeing again at her book and so continued untill about 12 of the clock at midnight [at which time] she this deponent hard a kind of softe kn[ock] in her sister in laws chamber and presentlie after this deponent heard plainlie soom rustling in the chamber whearuppon this deponent growing more and more suspitious of some badd dealing and beeing very discontent and impatient with hirselfe and nott able to abide sutch matter as her verie minde did give her and she grew in a manner fullie persuaded of, shee this deponent called hir maid . . . thatt satt by hir who looked steadfastdlie upon hir, and perceiving this deponent oute of her woonted order by hir face and countenance asked hir what shee ayled, and this deponent told hir whatt she suspected in the next chamber whear hir sister in law lay.

By now we know what the story's crisis point is going to be, but Madelen diverts its course to talk about her own mental state, to ensure the story focuses on her own reactions—her 'discontent' and impatience with herself, her maid's concern for her health. Finally, the moment arrives.

thearuppon this deponent took the candle she read by shadowing the light thereof so much as shee could and went to hir said sister in lawes chamber and came to hir sisters beddside and this deponent did easilie and plainlie decearn one to lie in bedd with her, whearuppon this deponent with her hand pulled down the sheet saieing to hir said sister shee could not cover her villainie in that sorte or sutch like woords And the sheet beeing so pulled down this deponent to her great greif and amazement sawe the articulate James Skelton hir said brothers man lie in naked bedd with her said sister in law Julian Babbington whose villainous and beastlie company this deponent began greatlie to abhorr and detest and using such woords as shee thought good then to hir said sister.

Despite all her suspicions, Madelen proclaims herself astonished to find James Skelton. Grieved and amazed at Julian's 'villainy', she decides then and there that she 'abhorrs and detests' the 'villainous and beastlie company' of Julian, 'her sister' nevertheless. Because they are still sisters, Julian and her lover beg Madelen for her mercy, and the story proceeds from this central crisis point into a tale of repentance and resolution:

> the articulate Skelton rose out of hir said sisters bedd in his shirt on the further side and came over a pallat whear the said Julians foresaid mayde lay and took his cloke which lay upon a truncke standing by the said chamber dore and threw the same over his shirt and kneeled down beefore this deponent as she stood by the said bedd side with a candle in hir hand and acknowledged very submissivelie his villainous attempt confessing that in respect thearof hee had not deserved life with divers such like woords to that effect and so departed downe the staires leaving this deponent still talking with hir sister in law Julian And this deponent saith that after mutche talk beetweene hir and hir sister Julian who intreated this deponent to reagarde hir estate and creditt and consider of hir hard fortune and deale with hir frendlie and having persuaded this deponent shee the said Julian called her mayd Brown who lay upon the said pallat at the bedds feet and told hir what was happned and howe this deponent had found hir and thearfore willed and charged hir for hir the said Julians creditt sake to be secret in the same mather So that this deponent saith it was very near three or fower of the clock in the morninge beefore shee departed hir sisters chamber.[37]

Madelen Plonkett, who read books in her bedchamber by candlelight, would have had narrative structures for such a story from all sorts of sources in her head; her social status and her familiarity with the written word must have made her an unusually self-assured witness; and the high status of both litigants may have impelled the clerk to record, or even embellish, the story in the fullest possible detail. Madelen tells a story in—unusually—careful chronological order, in which every event is linked to the next with none of the discontinuities of time and place that characterize so many depositions, and into which she introduces delays that shift the focus on to her own emotional reactions and her reflections on the discovery. From the often unpromising form of questions and answers she tells a story that has a clear beginning, hinting at the potential problems of her financial dependence on her brother and the shifting of household responsibilities between herself and her sister-in-law. It moves on into an opening

[37] Francis Babbington *c.* Julian Babbington *als* Roo (1591), DL/C 214, pp. 53–6; for the family details, *Collectanea Topographica et Genealogica*, viii. 355–8.

sequence of suspicion and mistrust, building on the familiar script of absent husband, adulterous wife, and treacherous servant, and proceeding through the build-up of suspense to its climactic moment of discovery, in which the narrator, displaced in the household by her brother's marriage, takes full control again, leaving her new sister-in-law begging her for clemency and forgiveness, and restoring by her authority the servant to his proper role, subject to her and confessing 'he had not deserved life'. Finally, in a process of apparent resolution, the guilty Julian manages to negotiate her way back to the position she has forfeited by adultery. It is a text that, written, needs no explaining, its shape and its details manipulated to make a tale structured within the modes of contemporary moral tales and dramatic according to textual convention.[38]

The dramatic tension of Madelen's story was achieved precisely through its reference to herself. In court, she was telling a tale whose circumstances no longer shaped her identity and life: by the time the drama of her sister-in-law's adultery reached its conclusion in court, Madelen had left the house for a marriage of her own. Her narrative was a look back into an enclosed household, with all its hidden tensions and dangerous familiarities; as she retold the story of Julian's adultery, she also returned to her own place in that household, attending—as, at the time, only her maid had—to her emotional state, her careful observation, and her masterful handling of the final climax. And the resolution Julian achieves at the end of her tale did not last—for later, Madelen wrote to her brother and told him the whole story. Perhaps she used these same words and forms.[39]

Not all stories in court work as well as this. For the most part the narrative projects of witnesses and defendants find an expression only around the obstacles of clerical interpretation, unchronological memory, and the question–answer form of depositions; written down, the narratives of predominantly illiterate witnesses lost many of their interpretative clues. These stories are, to some extent, exceptional; many more women and men came to court with tales that are much less eloquent and in which they were less deeply involved. But the narrative impulse, and its special meaning for women, was one they

[38] Such moral structures can be found, for example, in murder stories, such as *A Pitilesse Mother, That most unnaturally at one time, murthered two of her owne children at Acton* . . . (London, 1616) and H[enry] G[oodcole], *Heavens Speedie Hue and Cry sent after Lust and Murther* (London, 1635).

[39] Francis and Julian were not, apparently, ever separated. Madelen was murdered, allegedly by a female servant, in Ireland in 1609 (G.E.C., *The Complete Peerage* (London, 1916), iv. 553).

shared. This specific moment of story-telling had resonances outside its legal context, because the stories people told there were also stories they would need or choose to tell to family, friends, or neighbours. The telling of tales about sexual blame, marital misconduct, and household order was one of the ways in which the relations of gender, family, and neighbourhood were worked out. Stories of conflict passed into the oral culture of history and reputation that came to play as women and men related to neighbours, chose marriage partners, or made business decisions.

Using the skills of everyday, oral story-telling, witnesses and defendants told stories that dwelt on particular themes, constructed familiar and individual patterns, and developed plots for personal dramas. Their stories can display a mastery of narrative technique that constitutes in itself a triumph over events that have got out of control. For women, in the context of an institutional, social, and cultural practice that regularly discredited women's words, testifying at court could offer one way of asserting a verbal agency over domestic, sexual, and marital events that had, one way or another, disempowered them. They told stories that vindicated their names and characters; that countered legal, social, and cultural disempowerment; and that could cut right to the heart of their identity.

8

Conclusion

In the civic world of late sixteenth- and early seventeenth-century London, moral discipline made the sexual and marital lives of women and men a public concern. But the moral vision behind the exercise of regulation was not uncontested. The invocation of moral rules in language and litigation reveals a culture in which ideas of honesty, virtue, and honour were the weapons of both gender relations and social relations.

The business of the church courts, ruled as it was by the prescriptions of canon law, was also shaped by popular participation. The exercise of moral discipline involved more than the absorption of the ideals of church and state into popular morality. Transparently, litigation involved complex motives and functions outside the court process: its instigators came to court looking for a legal revenge, for a formal arena in which to tell their story, for the translation of dispute into other directions, and sometimes, for resolution. Historians have tended to treat going to law as essentially a conciliatory process, and to speak of 'malicious' litigation as one, rare, misuse of the court.[1] The realities of the court's business belie any simple division between malicious and non-malicious invocations of the law. Rather, litigation always involved a complex set of motivations and purposes, relating to the material, financial, and verbal weight attached to court proceedings.[2] The court provided men and women with the ammunition to voice, resolve, and perpetuate local and domestic disputes. This perception of litigation has consequences, too, for our understanding of the apparently more straightforward business of disciplinary justice: presenting women and men to the court for sexual, marital, and other

[1] E.g. Martin Ingram, *Church Courts, Sex and Marriage in England, 1570–1640* (Cambridge, 1987), 33, 314, on 'vexatious suits'. See also J. A. Sharpe, 'The People and the Law', in Barry Reay (ed.), *Popular Culture in Seventeenth-Century England* (London, 1985), 253.

[2] Some of these potential purposes are explored in Richard L. Kagan, 'A Golden Age of Litigation: Castile, 1500–1700', in John Bossy (ed.), *Disputes and Settlements: Law and Human Relations in the West* (Cambridge, 1983).

misconduct could, as litigation did, further social disputes quite outside the court's remit.

In early modern London the law held a confirmed place in the fabric of social relations. In the seventeenth century small city parishes of about 200 households sent around twenty sex and marriage cases each decade to the consistory court alone; larger parishes with 1,000 or more households sent about 100.[3] Five times that number were presented for disciplinary offences, and other business went to the archdeaconry court, the commissary court, and the secular law.[4] The mechanics and meanings of litigation and disciplinary justice were common currency in local dispute. Legal sanctions took their place in the range of informal and formal mechanisms available for the pursuit of conflict. The language of the law—citation and prosecution, presentments and defences, standing bail and giving witness—was a familiar one, and the processes of litigation were recognizably invested with the wider concerns that lay behind neighbourhood dispute. A dispute between Ann Yarrington and Ann Croste in 1621 involved an resourceful combination of public rituals and formal actions. After, apparently, one lawsuit between them, Ann Yarrington 'unhosed' Ann Croste in the street, saying to her 'I am shited [punning rudely on cited] to poules [St Pauls] with a shitacon and that at the sute of Ann Croste whoe is my husbands whore.' She produced an old handkerchief from her pocket and continued 'for this ould handkerchefe my husband hath occupied her seaven tymes'.[5] In November, Ann Croste sued Ann Yarrington for a second time, bringing witnesses to testify to her words. The language of insult, the rituals of community shaming, and the procedure of formal justice were a familiar conjunction in the arena of women's dispute. Litigation for defamation, presentments for scolding, accusations of petty theft were all threatened and used as part of the armoury of interpersonal conflict. The court system had a clear identity for early modern people, and that identity was imagined not so much as an abstract institution of moral enforcement, but as a process at once formal and communal, with functions used by both women and men in the course of personal and local conflict.

[3] Calculated from the act books and deposition books for 1631–40, DL/C 232–5, 630, 27.

[4] On the involvement of people in the secular law, see Cynthia B. Herrup, *The Common Peace: Participation and the Criminal Law in Seventeenth-Century England* (Cambridge, 1987), and Robert B. Shoemaker, *Prosecution and Punishment: Petty Crime and the Law in London and Rural Middlesex, c.1660–1725* (Cambridge, 1991).

[5] Ann Croste *als* Butler *c.* Ann Yarrington (1621), DL/C 228, fos. 95^{v}–96.

The development of slander litigation as the court's principal business testifies to the force one such function carried for women. Its significance might be traced to the particular kinds of conflict to which London society was prone: debates about territory in a constantly changing urban topography, about gender roles in a city economy in which women worked publicly, about the nature of marriage at a time of high mortality and in a city with considerable potential for anonymity, and about verbal or sexual behaviour in a mobile, migrant community. Its increase testifies, too, to women's maximization of a rare opportunity of speech, complaint, and legal agency. The London court was more open than others to the exploration of that opportunity. The nature of urban life seems to have involved more public female activity. Women worked, often without a male partner, in markets, alehouses, and shops; in the dockside parishes, many married women were making their own livelihoods in their husbands' absence. Large numbers of unmarried women in service were living under the supervision of employers and, to a degree, friends, but independent of the kind of domestic control parents could enforce. Widowhood, a situation which at any one time, nearly half of London's married women had already experienced, also forced women, temporarily or permanently, into a more autonomous financial and social position.[6] The relative autonomy of urban women, especially in the riverside neighbourhoods of East London, meant that reputation both on the streets and in court became a women's affair.

The transformation of disputes into litigation involved personal purposes and meanings that were not necessarily in accord with the ostensible aims of the court. The gravity of formal litigation fulfilled in itself a certain function, acting as a register of a dispute's seriousness. The extensive financial investment required both attested to the severity of the issue and gave the law a potential consumer's slant: defamers spoke, for example, of 'paying' to call someone a whore. The publicity of complaint offered by legal proceedings added another dimension. In cases of defamation, the court acted as a forum for the articulation of broader conflicts; through complaints about words, the wider disagreements that had led to them could be

[6] An estimated 42% of women marrying in London between 1598 and 1619 were widows: Vivien Brodsky, 'Widows in Late Elizabethan London: Remarriage, Economic Opportunity, and Family Orientations', in Lloyd Bonfield, Richard M. Smith, and Keith Wrightson (eds.) *The World We Have Gained: Histories of Population and Social Structure* (Oxford, 1986).

expressed.[7] For married women, the church courts were one of the few jurisdictions where such conflict could be fought with a legal agency technically equivalent to that of men. The early seventeenth century saw women in London turning in quantity to that opportunity, as they had at the commissary court in the late fifteenth century. At the secular courts, it was not until the early eighteenth century that women's participation in the law through the use of indictments and, more often, recognizances, reached an equal or higher level to that of men.[8]

The court also served a purpose outside that of its practical results. It enabled women and men to rewrite the stories of contested events, and to see their versions recorded, framed by their own life-stories. In the proofs which men and women used to argue for the beginnings and endings of marriage, they rewrote some of the restrictive categories of evidence technically admissible in court. Litigation about marriage contracts came to focus on the broader proofs of affection, words, and tokens that told a much fuller story of pre-conjugal relations. Plaintiffs for marital separation followed popular morals in suing cases distinguished rigidly by gender, enlarging on the basic allegations of adultery or cruelty with stories that covered a whole range of perceived violations of conjugal relations. Litigants and witnesses engaged in a mutual process in which popular practice both influenced and was shaped by law.[9] For witnesses as for litigants, going to court also involved a project of self-representation in an unusually formal context. The moment of deposing required witnesses and defendants to dictate one version of events in their experience, one segment of an autobiography: for some witnesses, and particularly for women, it was a narrative that bore closely on the terms of their identity, autonomy, and authority.

The transformation of the church courts between 1570 and 1640 was related to both legal and social changes. London's society, by nature of its changing population, was in almost constant flux; the 'custom' and 'tradition' which were taken as behaviourial guides in early modern culture lasted less time than ever here. The practice of law was one form of tradition that drew its strength from both innovation and conservatism. The relationship between the people, the law, and the courts constituted a custom of its own, with its own

[7] This process is explained in Simon Roberts, *Order and Dispute: An Introduction to Legal Anthropology* (Oxford, 1971), 52.

[8] Shoemaker, *Prosecution and Punishment,* 211.

[9] On this process, see Sharpe, 'The People and the Law'.

place in popular culture. Most obviously this was true in the case of customary law: at the court of requests, what was presented as long custom might be little more than a generation old.[10] But the same culture of law and custom shaped the character of the church courts. Ecclesiastical jurisdiction depended on canon law that was written down, not customary law based on memory; but the practice of the church courts and the way people used them depended on established and changing popular custom. Business like marriage contract litigation was affected, more than by legal changes, by shifts in popular practice and in men's and women's understanding of what promises of love meant; the court's business changed accordingly. More broadly, the period of this study saw a considerable change in the relationship of women to the church courts.

The early seventeenth century saw women using the consistory court in a new way, in vast numbers, over a mass of very similar disputes. At one level, this reflects a change in women's conceptions of the law, or at least, of this particular branch of it. Reputation became, more surely than it was before, an issue worth going to court over; women, in greater quantities than before, and in greater quantities than men, went to law themselves over it. When the court resumed business after 1660, it became even more firmly established as a women's court.[11] The first surviving depositions after the court's restoration, from 1669, testify that Blanch Wilcox had defamed Anne Browne: 'God forgive mee if I think amisse Anne Browne lay with Anthony Thorpe in the days of her first husband Porringer as often as she did with him.'[12]

In a period when the church courts were losing prestige, and the changing relations between church and state marginalized the ecclesiastical jurisdiction, the church courts were becoming a forum for women. Not all church courts witnessed the shifts towards increased defamation suits and increased female participation; in most places, if

[10] See here Tim Stretton, 'Women, Custom and Equity in the Court of Requests', in Jenny Kermode and Garthine Walker (eds.), *Women, Crime and the Courts in Early Modern England* (London, 1994).

[11] The same was true after 1700: see Tim Meldrum, 'Defamation at the Church Courts: Women and Community Control in London 1700–1745', M.Sc. dissertation (LSE, 1990).

[12] Anne Brown *c.* Blanch Wilcox (1669), DL/C 236, fo. 1. For defamation in the 15th c., see Richard Wunderli, *London Church Courts and Society Before the Reformation* (Cambridge, Mass., 1981), ch. 3; for the 18th and early 19th, Meldrum, 'Defamation at the Church Courts', and Anna Clark, 'Whores and Gossips: Sexual Reputation in London 1770–1825', in Arina Angerman, Geerte Binnema, Annemieke Keunen, Vefie Poels, and Jacqueline Zirkzee (eds.), *Current Issues in Women's History* (London, 1989).

women did come to be the majority of litigants, they did so in the later seventeenth century, rather than the earlier.[13] But in London, the increase of women litigants happened earlier and more conspicuously than anywhere else. Consequently, for the first part of the seventeenth century London women had an established stake in a jurisdiction which—coming under attack as it was—was nevertheless still of considerable importance in the legal and social structure of early modern communities.

The growth of women's litigation for slander was a cumulative movement, inspired in part by the words which spread between women and men about their or their neighbours' use of the court. Whatever the precise contours of that change, it had a very visible effect at the court and in neighbourhood relations. It meant that women emerged as brokers of several kinds of power in neighbourhood, social, and gender relations. The exchanges of words in which women contested reputation in the neighbourhood gained an added power by their legal significance. But women also emerged as legal agents in their own right, a role which early modern institutions were not always willing to grant them. With the significance of law in the social relations of communities, this gave women an important local power; the non-legal, semi-formal rituals in which women claimed a part added to that profile.

The legal and linguistic battles that women and men fought over courtship, marriage, and social relations focused most sharply on gender relations on the domestic stage. The period of this study saw the rhetoric of morals and gender centre on the patriarchal household as the seat of both gender order and social order: the practice of domestic relations, the focal theme of conflicts over sex and marriage, reveals the pivotal place of gender in the patriarchal household order and the society which gave it its meaning. The conventions of popular morals understood sexual sin in the light of domestic transgression: women who made their husbands cuckolds usurped their domestic power, men who were unfaithful to their wives spent the affectional and economic resources of the household outside it. In very similar ways, the women and men in court over marital separation, and those who used the language of insult against each other on the street, used an ideology of sexual sins and their associated transgressions to which the organization, and disorganization, of the con-

[13] See e.g. Susan Dwyer Amussen, *An Ordered Society: Gender and Class in Early Modern England* (Oxford, 1988), 101.

jugal household was central. And while disputes during and after courtship concerned a world with its own gender relations and rules, the transactions that surrounded premarital commitment also presaged the economic and power relations of the conjugal household. The legal dimension of conflicts around sex and marriage revolved around the establishment of domestic relations and their disruption.

The domestic scene loomed large in popular and élite, oral and printed culture. The gulf between prescriptions for the ideal household and everyday life for men, women, children, and servants was manifestly wide, yet ideals of the ordered patriarchal household remained powerful. The precepts of femininity, in particular, which were central to those ideals—obedience, chastity, and keeping at home—made useful rules for husbands trying to control wives and women and men composing insults. Conversely, the visions of gender disorder and unruly femininity that were such a fertile source of humour and sensation in popular literature, functioned both as extreme warnings of, and descriptions of the actual consequences associated with, women's illicit sex.

At a more practical level, disputes over sex and marriage were centrally concerned with the spatial organization of the household. Witnesses to illicit sex paid a particular attention to the domestic geography of adultery, noting the ways adulterous women violated their husbands' space with flirtations in the workplace, drinking in the hall, walks together in the garden, and especially, locked bedroom doors. Defamers paid the same attention to the misconduct they detected behind the walls of respectable houses. Between husbands and wives, marital conflict focused on the shared spaces of conjugal households: wives were accused of locking their husbands out of rooms, husbands of shutting their wives into them; in the kitchen, women might redistribute the food meant for their husbands to other men.

Deeply implicated in the gendered arrangement and conceptualization of household space was the line between publicity and privacy. Despite the precepts of advice literature, in the early modern world masculinity and femininity were not equatable with publicity and privacy; nor was the household a private sphere. The domestic world had a well-established correlation with the public and the political: disordered households had implications for the moral order of society; ecclesiastical and secular discipline, insisting on the accountability of sexual sinners to their neighbourhoods, made that connection real. While the officers of church and state made illicit sex and marriage a public affair with presentation, penance, and fines, ordinary women and men publicized the real or imaginary sexual misdeeds of their neighbours in the language of defamation. The stress on disguise, deceit, locked doors and 'privy' whores that featured in defamers' words insisted that attempts at privacy should be frustrated, and illicit sex made public. The sanctions defamers advocated against whoredom—marking whores, shaming them publicly, and forcing them out of honest neighbourhoods—were a further step in the same direction, elaborating the public implications of private sin.

The project of publicizing the household meant different things for women and for men. While women's adultery, one kind of violation of domestic order, was an established subject for neighbourhood comment and intervention, another kind of disorder—men's violence—was far less so. Implicitly this meant that disruptions of domestic order by women were more concerning, more predictable, and more damaging than those by men; indeed, because men were taken to be the household's masters, the very idea of them infringing domestic order made far less sense than did the idea of women doing so. Women, not men, were domestic dangers: marriage, the sphere in which women's principal identity was defined, was also the sphere in which femininity was perceived as most problematic.

Contemporaries called the church courts 'the bawdy courts': manifestly, their main business dealt, both in terms of discipline and in litigation between people, with sex. The suits that came to dominate the court were nominally entirely about sex. Reading the records of the courts, though, it looks very often as if sex was not what litigation over slander was about: that what was defamatory was *any* words, rumour or gossip, because in theory at least, the goodness of women's name was contingent on not being spoken of at all—a good name meant no name. It is in this light that we might usefully read the testimonies witnesses gave to women's good credit: they record, almost invariably, that they had *heard no evil* of the plaintiff, that she was of good name *for anything they knew*, or that they *never heard otherwise* than that she was of good reputation and calling. And yet sex is manifestly what slander—and women's honour—is about; and the discussion of whoredom, which implicitly and often, in these cases, explicitly, leads on to the act of heterosexual sex, goes right to the heart of gender relations.

Sex was a very good language for other arguments; at one level, the women and men fighting over defamation were engaged in a project to reduce all sorts of other things to sex. At the same time—and this is perhaps precisely why sex could work like this—what people said about sex was central to gender relations and to the subordination of women. In a culture where gender difference made sense primarily in the light of marriage and sex between men and women, it was the act of heterosexual penetrative sex as much as the sex of the body that defined and constructed gender in its patriarchal context.

The most common word early modern women and men used for heterosexual sex was 'occupying'. Men occupied women; the image carries the implication that only one man can occupy, and possess, a woman at once. We might recall, here, the inventories of economic damage with which women and men tried to make sense of the financial ramifications of whoredom for the practices of maintaining, spending, and saving that were meant to characterize the conjugal economy. In this society, sex and money were very closely linked. The word 'whore', which had for the most part lost its original financial meaning, carried far-reaching economic overtones, especially in terms of consumption. The financial transactions associated with whores at once mirrored and disturbed those of marriage.

The ideologies of gendered morality that were so powerful in early modern culture and society involved much more than men's regulation of the sexual, verbal, and physical behaviour of women. At different levels of practice they were subject to different interpretations and they carried changing resonances. In the language of insult it was women more than men who insisted upon the enforcement of sexual standards through a gendered honour, women who used the words that defined a femininity based on sexual honesty. Much of the power of the ideology of sexual honour lay in the fixed, consistent rules it purported to represent. The idea that unchaste women were always whores, and that men had a duty to control the sexuality of their households, featured persistently in contemporary culture; it made the vision of sexual honour a powerful weapon both inside and outside the household. But both the practical rules of morality, and the broader understanding of gender on which they had bearing, were in some degree flexible. Unchastity was by no means always understood to condemn women's whole characters; cuckoldry was not necessarily the source of humour that ballads held it to be. As much as women elaborated the circumstances and implications of whoredom in insults, when real adultery was in question it was men who were the most likely to testify to it. Sexual honour was most powerful as a culture of morality, whose constantly restated rules could shame both men and women, but whose practical implications were hard to pin down.

If the words of dishonour did not necessarily effect material discredit, the ideology of gendered honour remained one of immense power. It was central not just to ideas of morality, but to understandings of masculinity and femininity. It had powerful practical implications—namely, the belief that women's unchastity, but not men's, destroyed marriage. While the years of this study saw a transformation in the shape of business at the church court, the nature of the slander business that came to dominate proceedings remained very much the same. The abusive language of insult that came to dominate the court's proceedings was not specific to the seventeenth century; the same kind of words were being brought to the court two hundred years earlier and kept on coming in the eighteenth century. What was different was the context of sexual insult. The language of abuse and the ideology of sexual honour in which it had meaning carried a constantly changing weight. The word 'whore', constant and persistently offensive as it was, also had variable resonances. The social atmosphere of a neighbourhood, and the power of ideas of reputation in it, determined the precise inflection the word carried. At a much larger level so did the invocation of women's sexuality in the rhetoric of church and state; the organization of sexual culpability could be central to projects of social order. The wider implications of whoredom that were elaborated so fully in the early seventeenth century, its effects on domestic order and male power, made sense in the light of the rhetoric of sermons and literature about the ordered household; the stress defamers laid on purging their streets and parishes of dishonesty reflected some of the tensions of life in a city sustained by immigration and high mobility. In the 1570s women's illicit sex was pursued, along with men's, by the city's governors as part of their campaigns towards order, and the stringent regulation of real whores gave an added power to the use of the word as insult. Shortly after this study ends, in 1650, adultery was made a capital crime for women: at that precise juncture, it was the marital context of women's sexual culpability that carried the most weight.

The fact that few if any women were actually executed following the 1650 act points up a characteristic of the relationship between law, morals, and practice. The language in which the entire blame for illicit sex was laid on women did not mean that accusations of illicit sex invariably destroyed a woman's reputation, or that only women were penalized for sexual sin. But the formal and informal punishment of women for illicit sex both drew strength from, and gave power to, the ideology of different moral standards. The power of calling a woman 'whore' persists to this day: despite the changing inflections of sexual insult of women, it is historically intimately related to the dynamics of patriarchal power. In a changing social and cultural world, the ideology of sexual honour remained central to the definition of femininity, family, and social relations.

If the gendered ideology of morals was pivotal to the operation of patriarchy in family and society, it also provided a set of ideas women might use to negotiate around patriarchal strictures and restrictions. The arrangement of the burden of guilt for illicit sex so that it fell heaviest on women also invested a certain amount of sexual responsibility in women. In law and local government, it was in the area of sexual morals that women had a recognized role: women were assigned responsibility for moral investigation at its most physical level, examining pregnant women and questioning the mothers of illegitimate children. At a more informal level women claimed authority in the same physical and sexual sphere. In the language of insult, the courts, and the popular, informal rituals of censure, women asserted a moral authority to define and sanction sin that in law was confined to men. Words and popular rituals proved, for some women, a route to the local power which men might exercise through more formal avenues.

Women in early modern England negotiated their dependence, autonomy, or authority around the legal and social guarantees of men's primacy. Answering proposals of marriage, they used a language of dependency that might cloak their independent will. Testifying to men's sexual misdeeds, or elaborating sexual insults of other women, they turned their responsibility for sexual honesty around, making it a source of personal and neighbourhood authority. In the practical disputes of marriage, it was often women who intervened most physically against men, and women who came to court asserting the limitations of men's right to chastise their inferiors.

The urban social world left some space for women's initiatives. But at a personal and daily level men's power was consistently enforced at the expense of women's and through the ideologies of gendered morality. Men's insults of women betray a confidence in the mechanisms of justice that assured the culpability of women; whatever the technical penalties for male fornication, they were happy to call women 'my whore' in public. Men's use of the courts testifies to the legal backing such assurance had: women's allegations of sexual assault and rape were countered by men's interpretations of their words as defamation, and men used threats of having women presented as scolds, put in the stocks, or sent to Bridewell, as a way of following personal enmity through a legal custom that offered particular potential for penalizing women for their verbal or sexual behaviour. The church courts were an exception to a legal system that consistently disabled women, but there, too, women's standing was always visibly tenuous.

The church courts' narrowing focus, between 1570 and 1640, on defamation between women does not necesarily testify to a commensurable shift in popular morals; but it does mean that in one formal court a regular and considerable portion of time was devoted to negotiations around an issue that was pivotal to gender relations in patriarchal society. Were the years of this study a time of 'crisis in gender relations', as David Underdown has suggested?[14] It is arguable that if gender relations were becoming especially stressed anywhere in England in this period, it would surely have been in London. There, local communities were characterized by high levels of newcomers, all bringing different histories and expectations. Many would have come from rural areas, where women's work, and probably their social lives, took place in a fairly confined sphere; they ended up in a city where women, both as young servants and as married wives, seemed to have a conspicuous degree of spatial and social freedom. In the city, too, people had the best access to the pamphlets, broadsheets, and plays that dramatized conflict between the sexes, and against whose backdrop Underdown sets the 'crisis'. Contemporary literature certainly gave some credence to the idea of metropolitan gender crisis: polemics about women wearing men's clothes, or acting promiscuously, or 'ramping and roysting' through the streets, all assume an urban, not a rural context. If London itself was in a state of conflict in the late sixteenth century, as some historians have argued, its battles might light particularly on gender order; the search for social and civic order certainly made the regulation of sexual behaviour a prime concern.

[14] David Underdown, 'The Taming of the Scold: the Enforcement of Patriarchal Authority in Early Modern England', in Anthony Fletcher and John Stevenson (eds.), *Order and Disorder in Early Modern England* (Cambridge, 1985). Martin Ingram argues against Underdown's thesis in '"Scolding Women Cucked or Washed": A Crisis in Gender Relations in Early Modern England?', in Kermode and Walker (eds.), *Women, Crime and the Courts*.

At the same time, London's social relations did not necessarily provide the most fertile ground for the kinds of dramas that have been identified as part of a crisis of gender. Prosecutions for scolding, like accusations of witchcraft, involved long histories of neighbourhood dispute. London was a much more mobile society than most villages; relationships between governors and governed were necessarily shaped by its size and relative anonymity; while in many ways its neighbourhoods exhibited patterns of permanence, continuity, and conservatism, it was also often possible for people to disappear, at least temporarily. The kinds of dispute that led, in small towns and isolated communities, to prosecutions for scolding and witchcraft did not take the same shape in London.

The conceptual model of crisis itself is not the best way of analysing gender: we might usefully think, instead, about gender construction and gender relations in early modern England as a perpetual conflict. The definition and implications of gender were always in contest; changes and shifts took place in the shape of conflict, rather than from stability to crisis and back again. If the years of the late sixteenth and early seventeenth century were a time of especially focused anxieties around the mechanics of gender relations, in part because of the power of rhetorics of domestic order, those anxieties also fixed on some perduring tensions in patriarchal relations. The vision of morality that placed sexual blame squarely on women and defined women through their sexual morals retained its power long after the precise inflections of household patriarchy that characterized these years had altered.

The specific configuration of rhetoric and practice that made sixteenth- and seventeenth-century marriage may have been shifting, but the gender relations defined most clearly in conjugal patriarchy endured. The power relations and social meanings of early modern patriarchy were organized around marriage. It was in the disorganization of the sexual, economic, and spatial relations of marriage that the resonances of women's illicit sex were most felt; it was in the daily relations of marriage that gender difference and gender relations were most sharply defined. But what shaped marriage was not so much its context in society and the state, as a gender order based on sexual morals. If marriage and marital order were central to early modern society, that also made gender order central—a gender order that worked from a central definition of the incommensurability of women's and men's sexual morals. The discussion of gender, far from consolidating the complementarity of men and women as husbands

BIBLIOGRAPHY

UNPRINTED SOURCES

Greater London Record Office

Consistory Court Deposition Books, 1572–1640, 1669, 1679–86: DL/C 211/1–2, DL/C 212–14, DL/C 629, DL/C 217–35, DL/C 630, DL/C 236, DL/C 240.

Consistory Court Instance Act Books, 1569–1640: DL/C 8–29, DL/C 611, DL/C 612.

Consistory Court Office Act Books, 1574–5, 1609–11, 1631–3: DL/C 615, DL/C 308–9, DL/C 327.

Consistory Court Personal Answer Books, 1617–38, 1682–8: DL/C 192–4, DL/C 96.

Middlesex Sessions Records MJ/SR 466–479 (1609), MJ/SR 575–581 (1619).

Guildhall Library

Archdeaconry Court Examination Books, 1566, 1632–8: MS 9056, 9057/1.

Commissary Court Act Book, 1587: MS 9064/13.

Commissary Court Assignation Book, 1635–6: MS 9059/1.

Consistory Court Deposition Books, 1622–4, 1627–8: MS 9189/1, MS 9189/2.

Table of Fees: MS 25,188.

Aldersgate Wardmote Minutes, 1467–1801: MS 2050/1.

St Margaret Pattens Churchwardens' Accounts, 1558–1653: MS 4570/2.

Bridewell Court Minute Books, III (1576–9); VIII (1627–34).

Public Record Office, Chancery Lane

Court of Star Chamber Proceedings, 1603–25: STAC 8.

West Sussex Record Office

Chichester Archdeaconry Court Cause Papers, 1572–1631: EpI/15/3/1–2, 5–6, 8–14, 16–17, 19, 21, 23–4, 29, 37, and EpI/15 boxes 118, 122, 125–6, 128, 131–2, 139–40, 142.

Archdeaconry Court Depositions, 1578, 1587, 1596–1608, 1622–38: EpI/11/3, 5, 7–10, 13–16.

Canterbury Cathedral Archives

Canterbury Consistory Court Depositions, 1621–4: X.11.19.

British Library

The Roxburghe Ballads (also printed, eds. W. Chappell and J. W. Ebsworth (London and Hertford, 1871–95)).

PRINTED SOURCES

The Act Book of the Archdeacon of Taunton, ed. C. Jenkins, Somerset Record Soc. 43 (London, 1928).

ANGER, JANE, *Jane Anger her Protection for Women* (London, 1589).

The Araignment and burning of Margaret Ferne-Seede, for the Murther of her late Husband . . . founde deade in Peckham Field neere Lambeth, having once before attempted to poyson him with broth . . . (London, 1608).

The Archdeacon's Court: Liber Actorum, 1584, ed. E. R. C. Brinkworth, Oxfordshire Record Soc. 23–4 (Oxford, 1942–6).

À VAUTS, MOSES, *The Husband's Authority Unvail'd: Wherein It is moderately discussed whether it be fit or lawfull for a good Man, to beat his bad Wife . . .* (London, 1650).

Ballads and Broadsides chiefly of the Elizabethan period, ed. H. L. Collman (London, 1912).

BENTLEY, THOMAS, *The Monument of Matrones: The Fift Lampe of Virginitie* (London, 1582).

BOORD, ANDREW, *The First and best Part of Scoggins Iests* (London, 1626).

BRATHWAIT, RICHARD, *The English Gentleman* (London, 1630).

—— *The English Gentlewoman* (London, 1631).

BRIDGES, JOHN, *A Defence of the Government Established in the Church of England for Ecclesiasticall Matters* (London, 1587).

BULLINGER, HEINRICH, *The Christen state of Matrimonye*, trans. Miles Coverdale (Antwerp, 1541).

BUNNY, EDMUND, *Of Divorce for Adulterie, and Marrying Againe* (Oxford, 1610).

BURY, SAMUEL, *An Account of the Life and Death of Mrs Elizabeth Bury* (Bristol, 1720).

CARTER, THOMAS, *Carters Christian Comon Wealth: Or, Domesticall Dutyes deciphered* (London, 1627).

Child-marriages, Divorces, and Ratifications, etc. in the diocese of Chester, A.D. 1561–6, ed. Frederick J. Furnivall, Early English Text Soc., OS 108 (London, 1897).

CLEAVER, ROBERT, *A Briefe Explanation of the Whole Booke of the Proverbs of Salomon* (London, 1615).

—— *A Godly Form of Householde Governement: for the ordering of private Families, according to the direction of Gods word* (London, 1598, and with John Dod, 1612).

CLERKE, FRANCIS, *Praxis in Curiis Ecclesiasticis* (London, 1596).

C[ONSETT], H[ENRY], *The Practice of the Spiritual or Ecclesiastical Courts* (London, 1685).

COOKE, RICHARD, *A White Sheete, Or A Warning for Whoremongers* (London, 1629).

COSIN, RICHARD, *An Apologie: of, and for Sundrie proceedings by Iurisdiction Ecclesiasticall* (London, 1591).

The Court of Good Counsell. Wherein is set downe the true rules, how a man should choose a good Wife from a bad, and a woman a good Husband from a bad (London, 1607).

CROFTS, ROBERT, *The Lover: or, Nuptiall Love* (London, 1638).

D'URFEY, THOMAS, *Wit and Mirth* (London, 1707).

Depositions and Other Ecclesiastical Proceedings from the Courts of Durham, extending from 1311 to the Reign of Elizabeth, ed. J. Raine, Surtees Society, 21 (London, 1845).

DOVE, JOHN, *Of Divorcement* (London, 1661).

ERASMUS, DESIDERIUS, *A mery dialogue declaring the properties of shrowde shrewes, and honest wyves* (London, 1557).

E., T., *The Lawes Resolutions of Womens Rights: or, The Lawes Provision for Woemen* (London, 1632).

FEATLY, JOHN, *The honor of Chastity. A sermon* (London, 1632).

FIELD, NATHAN, *A Woman is a Weathercock* (1607), ed. J. P. Collier (London, 1829).

G., A., *A briefe discourse of the late murther of master George Saunders* (London, 1573).

GATAKER, THOMAS, *A Good Wife God's Gift: and, A Wife Indeed. Two Mariage Sermons* (London, 1624).

G[IBBON], C[HARLES], *The Praise of a Good Name* (London, 1594).

GODOLPHIN, JOHN, *Reportorium Canonicum; or, An Abridgement of the Ecclesiastical Laws of this Realm* (London, 1678).

G[OODCOLE], H[ENRY], *Heavens Speedie Hue and Cry sent after Lust and Murther* (London, 1635).

Goodcole, Henry, *The wonderfull discoverie of Elizabeth Sawyer a Witch, late of Edmonton, her conviction and condemnation and Death. Together with the relation of the Divels accesse to her, and their conference together* (London, 1621).

—— *The Adulteresses Funerall Day . . . Or the Burning Downe to Ashes of Alice Clarke . . . for the Unnaturall Poisoning of Fortune Clarke Her Husband* (London, 1635).

GOUGE, WILLIAM, *Of Domesticall Duties: Eight Treatises* (London, 1622).

GRIFFITH, MATTHEW, *Bethel: or, A Forme for Families* (London, 1633).

Haec-Vir: Or, the Womanish Man (London, 1620).

HALE, W. H., *A Series of Precedents and Proceedings in Criminal Causes from 1475 to 1640* (London, 1847).

HEALE, WILLIAM, *An Apologie for Women* (Oxford, 1609).

HEYWOOD, JOHN, *A ballad against slander and detraction* (London, 1562).

HEYWOOD, THOMAS, *A Woman Kilde with Kindnesse* (London, 1607).

Hic Mulier; Or, the Man-Woman (London, 1620).

HOWELL, JAMES, *Παροιμιογραφια. Proverbs, or Unsayed Sawes and Adages* (London, 1659).

KYDDE, THOMAS, *The trueth of the most wicked and secret murthering of John Brewen . . . committed by his owne wife, through the provocation of one John Parker whom she loved* (London, 1592), repr. in J. P. Collier (ed.), *Illustrations of Early English Popular Literature* (1863).

LEIGH, DOROTHY, *The Mothers Blessing: Or, The godly Counsaile of a Gentle-woman* (London, 1627).

MACHYN, HENRY, *The Diary of Henry Machyn*, ed. John Gough Nichols, Camden Society (London, 1847).

MARCH, JOHN, *Actions for Slaunder, Or, a Methodicall Collection under certain Grounds and Heads, of what words are Actionable in the Law, and what not?* (London, 1647).

A merry Ieste of a shrewde and curst Wyfe, lapped in Morrelles Skin, for her good behavyour (*c.*1550–60), in J. P. Collier (ed.), Shakespeare's Library, 4 (London, 1875).

Middlesex County Records, ed. John Cordy Jeaffreson (London, 1886–92), 4 vols.

Murther, Murther. Or, A Bloody Relation How Anne Hamton . . . by Poyson Murthered Her Deare Husband (London, 1641).

NICCHOLES, ALEXANDER, *A Discourse, of Marriage and Wiving* (London, 1615).

The Pepys Ballads, ed. W. G. Day (Cambridge, 1987).

A Pepysian Garland: Black-Letter Broadside Ballads of the Years 1595–1639, ed. H. E. Rollins (Cambridge, 1922).

PERKINS, WILLIAM, *A Direction for the Government of the Tongue according to Gods word* (London, 1615).

PHILO-PUTTANUS [FERRANTE PALLAVICINO], *The Whores Rhetorick, Calculated to the Meridian of London* (London, 1683).

PHILOGENES, PANEDONIUS [RICHARD BRATHWAIT], *Ar't asleepe Husband? A Boulster Lecture* (London, 1640).

A Pitilesse Mother, That most unnaturally at one time, murthered two of her owne children at Acton . . . (London, 1616).

PORTER, HENRY, *The Pleasant history of the Two Angry Women of Abington* (London, 1599).

Puritan Manifestoes, ed. W. H. Frere and C. E. Douglas (London, 1907).

REYNER, EDWARD, *Rules for the Government of the Tongue* (London, 1656).

RICH, BARNABE, *My Ladies Looking Glasse. Wherein May be Discerned a Wise Man from a Foole, a Good Woman from a Bad* (London, 1616).

ROGERS, DANIEL, *Matrimoniall Honour, Or, The mutuall Crowne and comfort of godly, loyall, and chaste Marriage* (London, 1642).

ROWLANDS, SAMUEL, *Well met Gossip: or, Tis merrie when Gossips meete* (London, 1619).

—— *A Crew of kind Gossips, all met to be merrie: Complayning of their Husbands, With their Husbands answeres in their own defence* (London, 1613).

SALTER, THOMAS, *A Mirrhor meete for all Mothers, Matrones, and Maidens, intituled the Mirrhor of Modestie* (London, 1579).

Select Cases on Defamation to 1600, ed. R. H. Helmholz, Selden Society 102 (London, 1985).

Sermons and Homilies Appointed to be Read in Churches (London, 1817).

SHARP, JANE, *The Midwives Book* (London, 1671).

SMITH, HENRY, *A Preparative to Marriage* (London, 1591).

S[NAWSEL], R[OBERT], *A Looking Glasse for Maried Folkes* (London, 1619).

SPEGHT, RACHEL, *A Mouzell for Melastomus* (London, 1617).

Sundry Strange and Inhumaine Murthers, Lately Committed (London, 1591), repr. in Joseph H. Marshburn and Alan R. Velie (eds.), *Blood and Knavery: A*

Collection of English Renaissance Pamphlets and Ballads of Crime and Sin (Rutherford, NJ, 1973).

SWETNAM, JOSEPH, *The Araignment of Lewd, Idle, Froward and Unconstant Women* (London, 1615).

SWINBURNE, HENRY, *A Treatise of Spousals, or Matrimonial Contracts* (London, 1686).

TAYLOR, JOHN, *A Common Whore, | With all these Graces Grac'd: | Shee's very honest, | beautifull and chast* (London, 1622).

Three Elizabethan Domestic Tragedies, ed. Keith Sturgess (Harmondsworth, 1969).

TILNEY, EDMUND, *A briefe and pleasant discourse of duties in Mariage* (London, 1568).

The Tragedy of Master Arden of Faversham (1592), ed. M. L. Wine (London, 1973).

A True Relation of the most Inhumane and bloody Murther, of Master Iames Minister and Preacher . . . Committed by one Lowe his Curate, and consented unto by his Wife (London, 1609).

TUKE, THOMAS, *A Treatise against Painting and Tincturing of Men and Women: against Murther and Poysoning: Pride and Ambition: Adulterie and Witchcraft* (London, 1616).

Two most unnaturall and bloodie Murthers: The one by Maister Caverly . . . The other, by Mistris Browne, and her servant Peter, upon her husband (London, 1605).

VAUGHAN, WILLIAM, *The Spirit of Detraction, Coniured and Convicted in Seven Circles* (London, 1611).

VELE, ABRAHAM, *The deceyte of women. to the instruction and ensample of all men, yonge and olde* (London, 1563).

WEB, GEORGE, *The Araignement of an unruly Tongue* (London, 1619).

WHATELEY, WILLIAM, *A Bride-Bush: Or, A Direction for Married Persons* (London, 1619).

WING, JOHN, *The Crowne Conjugall or, The Spouse Royall* (Middelburgh, 1620).

SECONDARY WORKS

ADDY, JOHN, *Sin and Society in Seventeenth-Century England* (London, 1989).

AMUSSEN, SUSAN DWYER, 'Governors and Governed: Class and Gender Relations in English Villages, 1590–1725', Ph.D. thesis (Brown University, 1982).

—— 'Gender, Family and the Social Order 1560–1725' in Fletcher and Stevenson (eds.) *Order and Disorder*.

—— *An Ordered Society: Gender and Class in Early Modern England* (Oxford, 1988).

—— '"Being Stirred to Much Unquietness": Violence and Domestic Violence in Early Modern England', *Jl. of Women's History*, 6/2 (1994), 70–89.

ARCHER, IAN, *The Pursuit of Stability: Social Relations in Elizabethan London* (Cambridge, 1991).

ARCHER, LÉONIE, 'Virgin and Harlot in the Writings of Formative Judaism', *History Workshop Jl.* 24 (1987), 1–16.

ATKINSON, CLARISSA, '"Precious Balsam in a Fragile Glass": The Ideology of Virginity in the Later Middle Ages', *Jl. Family History*, 8 (1983), 131–43.

ATKINSON, J. MAXWELL, and DREW, PAUL, *Order in Court: The Organisation of Verbal Interaction in Judicial Settings* (Basingstoke, 1979).

BAKER, J. H., *An Introduction to English Legal History* (London, 1990).

BALDWIN, F. E., *Sumptuary Legislation and Personal Regulation in England* (Baltimore, 1926).

BARRON, CAROLINE, 'The "Golden Age" of Women in Medieval London', *Reading Medieval Studies*, 15 (1992), 35–58.

BARTHES, ROLAND, 'Introduction to the Structural Analysis of Narratives', in Susan Sontag (ed.), *A Barthes Reader* (London, 1982).

BASHAR, NAZIFE, 'Rape in England between 1550 and 1700', in London Feminist History Group (ed.), *The Sexual Dynamics of History* (London, 1983).

BEIER, A. L., 'Engine of Manufacture: The Trades of London', in Beier and Finlay, *London 1500–1700.*

—— and FINLAY, ROGER (eds.), *London 1500–1700: The Making of the Metropolis* (London, 1986).

BELSEY, CATHERINE, *The Subject of Tragedy: Identity and Difference in Renaissance Drama* (London, 1985).

BEN-AMOS, Ilana Krausman, *Adolescence and Youth in Early Modern England* (New Haven, 1994).

BENNETT, JUDITH M., 'Feminism and History', *Gender and History* 1/3 (1989), 251–72.

BENNETT, W. LANCE, and FELDMAN, MARTHA S., *Reconstructing Reality in the Courtroom* (London, 1981).

BERGER, DAVID G., and WENGER, MORTON G., 'The Ideology of Virginity', *Jl. of Marriage and the Family*, 35 (1973), 666–75.

BOND, RONALD B., '"Dark Deeds Darkly Answered": Thomas Becon's Homily Against Whoredom and Adultery, its Contexts, and its Affiliations with Three Shakespeare Plays', *Sixteenth-Century Jl.* 16 (1985), 191–205.

BOSSY, JOHN (ed.), *Disputes and Settlements: Law and Human Relations in the West* (Cambridge, 1983).

BOULTON, JEREMY, *Neighbourhood and Society: A London Suburb in the Seventeenth Century* (Cambridge, 1987).

BOWLER, CLARA ANN, 'Carted Whores and White Shrouded Apologies: Slander in the County Courts of Seventeenth-Century Virginia', *The Virginia Magazine of History and Biography*, 85/4 (1977), 411–26.

BRANT, CLARE, 'Speaking of Women: Scandal and the Law in the Mid-Eighteenth Century', in Brant and Purkiss (eds.), *Women, Texts and Histories.*

—— and PURKISS, DIANE (eds.), *Women, Texts and Histories, 1575–1760* (London, 1992).

BRAY, ALAN, *Homosexuality in Renaissance England* (London 1982).

BRIGDEN, SUSAN, *London and the Reformation* (Oxford, 1989).

BRINKWORTH, E. R. C., *Shakespeare and the Bawdy Court of Stratford* (London, 1972).

BRODSKY, VIVIEN, 'Mobility and Marriage in Pre-Industrial England: A Demographic and Social Structural Analysis of Geographic and Social Mobility and Aspects of Marriage, 1570–1690, with Particular Reference to London and General Reference to Middlesex, Kent, Essex and Hertfordshire', Ph.D. thesis (University of Cambridge, 1978).

—— 'Widows in Late Elizabethan London: Remarriage, Economic Opportunity, and Family Orientations', in Lloyd Bonfield, Richard M. Smith, and Keith Wrightson (eds.), *The World We Have Gained: Histories of Population and Social Structure* (Oxford, 1986).

BRODSKY ELLIOTT, VIVIEN, 'Single Women in the London Marriage Market: Age, Status and Mobility, 1589–1619', in Outhwaite (ed.), *Marriage and Society*.

BROOKS, C. W., HELMHOLZ, R. H., and STEIN, P. G., *Notaries Public in England since the Reformation* (London, 1991).

BRUNDAGE, JAMES, *Law, Sex and Christian Society in Medieval Europe* (Chicago, 1987).

BURKE, PETER, 'Popular Culture in Seventeenth-Century London', *London Jl.* 3 (1977), 143–62.

—— *Popular Culture in Early Modern Europe* (London, 1978).

—— 'The Art of Insult in Early Modern Italy', *Culture and History*, 2 (1987), 68–79.

BUTLER, JUDITH, *Gender Trouble: Feminism and the Subversion of Identity* (London, 1990).

CAMERON, DEBORAH, *Feminism and Linguistic Theory* (Basingstoke, 1985).

—— 'What is the Nature of Women's Oppression in Language?', *Oxford Literary Review*, 8/1–2 (1986), 79–87.

CAMPBELL, J. K., *Honour, Family and Patronage: A Study of Institutions and Moral Values in a Greek Mountain Community* (Oxford, 1964).

CARLTON, CHARLES, 'The Widow's Tale: Male Myths and Female Reality in Sixteenth and Seventeenth Century England', *Albion*, 10 (1978), 118–29.

CAVALLO, SANDRA, and CERUTTI, SIMONA, 'Female Honor and the Social Control of Reproduction in Piedmont between 1600 and 1800', trans. Mary M. Gallucci, in Edward Muir and Guido Ruggiero (eds.), *Sex and Gender in Historical Perspective* (Baltimore, 1990).

CERTEAU, MICHEL DE, *The Practice of Everyday Life*, trans. Steven Rendall (Berkeley, Calif., 1984).

CHAPMAN, COLIN R., *Ecclesiastical Courts, their Officials, and their Records* (Dursley, 1992).

CHARLES, LINDSEY, and DUFFIN, LORNA (eds.), *Women and Work in Pre-Industrial England* (Beckenham, 1985).

CHAYTOR, MIRANDA, 'Household and Kinship: Ryton in the Late Sixteenth and Early Seventeenth Centuries', *History Workshop Jl.* 10 (1980), 25–60.

CLARK, ALICE, *Working Life of Women in the Seventeenth Century* (1919), ed. Amy Erickson (London, 1992).

CLARK, ANNA, 'Whores and Gossips: Sexual Reputation in London 1770–1825', in Arina Angerman, Geerte Binnema, Annemieke Keunen, Vefie Poels, and Jacqueline Zirkzee (eds.), *Current Issues in Women's History* (London, 1989).

CLARK, SANDRA, *The Elizabethan Pamphleteers: Popular Moralistic Pamphlets 1580–1640* (London, 1983).

COLLIER, JANE FISHBURNE, and YANAGISAKO, SYLVIA JUNKO (eds.), *Gender and Kinship: Essays Toward a Unified Analysis* (Stanford, Calif., 1983).

COX, JANE, *Hatred Pursued Beyond the Grave: Tales of Our Ancestors from the London Church Courts* (HMSO, London, 1993).

CRAWFORD, PATRICIA, 'Katherine and Philip Henry and their Children: A Case Study in Family Ideology', *Trans. of the Historic Society of Lancashire and Cheshire,* 134 (1984), 40–73.

—— 'The Construction and Experience of Maternity in Seventeenth Century England', in Fildes (ed.), *Women as Mothers.*

—— 'Public Duty, Conscience and Women in Early Modern England', in John Morrill, Paul Slack, and Daniel Woolf (eds.), *Public Duty and Private Conscience in Seventeenth-Century England* (Oxford, 1993).

CRESSY, DAVID, *Literacy and the Social Order: Reading and Writing in Tudor and Stuart England* (Cambridge, 1980).

—— *Bonfires and Bells: National Memory and the Protestant Calendar in Elizabethan and Stuart England* (London, 1989).

DAVIES, KATHLEEN M., 'The Sacred Condition of Equality—How Original Were Puritan Doctrines of Marriage?', *Social History*, 5 (1977), 563–80.

DAVIS, NATALIE ZEMON, 'Women on Top: Symbolic Sexual Inversion and Political Disorder in Early Modern Europe', in *Society and Culture in Early Modern Europe* (Stanford, Calif., 1975).

—— 'Boundaries and the Sense of Self in Sixteenth Century France', in Thomas C. Heller, Morton Sosna, and David E. Wellbery (eds.), *Reconstructing Individualism: Autonomy, Individuality and the Self in Western Thought* (Stanford, Calif., 1986).

—— *Fiction in The Archives: Pardon Tales and their Tellers in Sixteenth-Century France* (Cambridge, 1987).

DEKKER, RUDOLF M., and POL, LOTTE C. VAN DE, *The Tradition of Female Transvestism in Early Modern Europe* (Basingstoke, 1989).

DOLAN, FRANCES E., *Dangerous Familiars: Representations of Domestic Crime in England 1550–1700* (Ithaca, NY, 1994).

DOLLIMORE, JONATHAN, *Sexual Dissidence: Augustine to Wilde, Freud to Foucault* (Oxford, 1991).

DONAHUE, CHARLES, JR., 'The Canon Law on the Formation of Marriage and

Social Practice in the Later Middle Ages', *Jl. of Family History,* 8 (1983), 144–58.

DURSTON, CHRIS, '"Unhallowed Wedlocks": The Regulation of Marriage During the English Revolution', *Historical Jl.* 31/1 (1988), 45–59.

ERICKSON, AMY LOUISE, 'Common Law versus Common Practice: The Use of Marriage Settlements in Early Modern England', *Economic History Review,* 2nd ser., 43/1 (1990), 21–39.

—— *Women and Property in Early Modern England* (London, 1993).

FALLER, LINCOLN B., *Turned to Account: The Forms and Functions of Criminal Biography in Late Seventeenth- and Early Eighteenth-Century England* (Cambridge, 1987).

FILDES, VALERIE (ed.), *Women as Mothers in Pre-Industrial England* (London, 1990).

FINCHAM, FRANCIS W. X., 'Notes from the Ecclesiastical Court Records at Somerset House', *Trans. of the Royal Historical Society,* 4th ser., 4 (1921), 103–39.

FINLAY, ROGER, *Population and Metropolis: The Demography of London 1580–1650* (Cambridge, 1981).

—— and SHEARER, BEATRICE, 'Population Growth and Suburban Expansion' in Beier and Finlay (eds.), *London 1500–1700.*

FLEISCHMAN, SUZANNE, 'On the Representation of History and Fiction in the Middle Ages', *History and Theory,* 22 (1972), 278–310.

FLETCHER, ANTHONY, and STEVENSON, JOHN (eds.), *Order and Disorder in Early Modern England* (Cambridge, 1985).

FORD, WYN, 'The Problem of Literacy in Early Modern England', *History,* 78/252 (1993), 22–37.

FOUCAULT, MICHEL, *The History of Sexuality. Volume I: An Introduction,* trans. Robert Hurley (London, 1979).

FOX, ADAM, 'Aspects of Oral Culture and its Development in Early Modern England', Ph.D. thesis (University of Cambridge, 1992).

FOYSTER, ELIZABETH, 'A Laughing Matter? Marital Discord and Gender Control in Seventeenth-Century England', *Rural History,* 4/1 (Apr. 1993), 5–23.

GARBER, MARJORIE, *Vested Interests: Cross-Dressing and Cultural Anxiety* (London, 1992).

GEE, JAMES PAUL, 'The Narrativization of Experience in the Oral Style', in Mitchell and Weiler (eds.), *Rewriting Literacy.*

GILLIS, JOHN, *For Better, For Worse: British Marriages, 1600 to the Present* (Oxford, 1985).

GLUCKMAN, MAX, 'Gossip and Scandal', *Current Anthropology* 4/3 (1963), 307–15.

GODDARD, VICTORIA, 'Honour and Shame: The Control of Women's Sexuality and Group Identity in Naples', in Pat Caplan (ed.), *The Cultural Construction of Sexuality* (London, 1987).

GOTTLIEB, BEATRICE, 'The Meaning of Clandestine Marriage', in Tamara K. Hareven and Robert Wheaton (eds.), *Family and Sexuality in French History* (Philadelphia, 1980).

GOWING, LAURA, 'Women, Sex and Honour: The London Church Courts, 1572–1640', Ph.D. thesis (University of London, 1993).

—— 'Language, Power and the Law: Women's Slander Litigation in Early Modern London', in Kermode and Walker (eds.), *Women, Crime, and the Courts.*

GREENBLATT, STEPHEN, *Learning to Curse: Essays in Early Modern Culture* (London, 1990).

GREGORY, ANNABEL, 'Slander Accusations and Social Control in Late Sixteenth and Early Seventeenth Century England, with Particular Reference to Rye (Sussex), 1590–1615', D.Phil. thesis (University of Sussex, 1984).

GROEBNER, VALENTIN, 'Losing Face, Saving Face: Noses, Honour and Spite in the Late Medieval Town', *History Workshop Jl.* 40 (1995), 1–15.

HAIGH, CHRISTOPHER, 'Slander and the Church Courts in the Sixteenth Century', *Trans. of the Lancashire and Cheshire Antiquarian Society,* 78 (1975), 1–13.

HAIR, PAUL, *Before the Bawdy Court: Selections from Church Court and Other Records Relating to the Correction of Moral Offences in England, Scotland, and New England, 1500–1800* (London, 1972).

HALL, HUBERT, 'Some Elizabethan Penances in the Diocese of Ely', *Trans. of the Royal Historical Society* 3rd. ser., 1 (1907), 263–77.

HANLEY, SARAH, 'Family and State in Early Modern France: The Marriage Pact', in Marilyn J. Boxer and Jean Quataert (eds.), *Connecting Spheres: Women in the Western World, 1500 to the Present* (Oxford, 1987).

HARDING, SUSAN, 'Women and Words in a Spanish Village', in Rayna R. Reiter (ed.), *Toward an Anthropology of Women* (New York, 1975).

HARRIS, OLIVIA, 'Households and Their Boundaries', *History Workshop Jl.* 13 (1982), 143–51.

HELMHOLZ, R. H., *Marriage Litigation in Medieval England* (Cambridge, 1974).

—— *Roman Canon Law in Reformation England* (Cambridge, 1990).

HENDERSON, KATHERINE USHER, and MCMANUS, BARBARA F., *Half-Humankind: Contexts and Texts of the Controversy about Women, 1540–1640* (Urbana, Ill., 1985).

HERRNSTEIN SMITH, BARBARA, 'Narrative Versions, Narrative Theories', in Mitchell (ed.), *On Narrative.*

HERRUP, CYNTHIA B., 'Law and Morality in Seventeenth-Century England', *Past and Present,* 106 (1985), 102–23.

—— *The Common Peace: Participation and the Criminal Law in Seventeenth-Century England* (Cambridge, 1987).

HIGGINS, PATRICIA, 'The Reactions of Women, with Special Reference to Women Petitioners', in Brian Manning (ed.), *Politics, Religion, and the English Civil War* (London, 1973).

HILL, CHRISTOPHER, *Society and Puritanism in Pre-Revolutionary England* (London, 1964).

HOTHERSALL, GEORGE, 'Matrimonial Problems in West Sussex 1556–1602', in *West Sussex History*, 4 (1990), 6–11.

HOULBROOKE, RALPH, 'The Decline of Ecclesiastical Jurisdiction Under the Tudors', in O'Day and Heal (eds.), *Continuity and Change.*

—— *Church Courts and the People During the English Reformation, 1520–1570* (Oxford, 1979).

—— *The English Family 1450–1700* (Harlow, 1984).

—— 'The Making of Marriage in Early Modern England: Evidence from the Records of Matrimonial Contract Litigation', *Jl. of Family History*, 10 (1985), 339–52.

—— 'Women's Social Life and Common Action in England from the Fifteenth Century to the Eve of the Civil War', *Continuity and Change*, 1/2 (1986), 171–89.

HULL, SUZANNE W., *Chaste, Silent and Obedient: English Books for Women, 1475–1640* (San Marino, 1982).

HUNT, MARGARET, 'Wife Beating, Domesticity and Women's Independence in Eighteenth-Century London', *Gender and History*, 4/1 (1992), 10–29.

HUTSON, LORNA, *The Usurer's Daughter: Male Friendship and Fictions of Women in Sixteenth-Century England* (London, 1994).

INGRAM, MARTIN, 'Ecclesiastical Justice in Wiltshire, 1600–1640, With Special Reference to Cases Concerning Sex and Marriage', D.Phil. thesis (University of Oxford, 1976).

—— 'Spousals Litigation in the English Ecclesiastical Courts c.1350–c.1640', in Outhwaite (ed.), *Marriage and Society.*

—— 'Ridings, Rough Music and the "Reform of Popular Culture" in Early Modern England', *Past and Present*, 105 (1984), 79–113.

—— 'Ridings, Rough Music and Mocking Rhymes in Early Modern England', in Reay (ed.), *Popular Culture.*

—— *Church Courts, Sex and Marriage in England, 1570–1640* (Cambridge, 1987).

—— '"Scolding Women Cucked or Washed": A Crisis in Gender Relations in Early Modern England?', in Kermode and Walker (eds.), *Women, Crime and the Courts.*

JACKSON, BERNARD, *Law, Fact and Narrative Coherence* (Merseyside, 1988).

—— 'Narrative Theories and Legal Discourse', in Cristopher Nash (ed.), *Narrative in Culture: The Uses of Storytelling in the Sciences, Philosophy, and Literature* (London, 1990).

JAMES, MERVYN, 'English Politics and the Concept of Honour, 1485–1642' in *Society, Politics and Culture* (Cambridge, 1986).

JARDINE, LISA, '"Why should he call her whore?" Defamation and Desdemona's Case', in Margaret Tudeau-Clayton and Martin Warner (eds.), *Addressing Frank Kermode: Essays in Criticism and Interpretation* (Basingstoke, 1991).

JARDINE, LISA, '"No offence i' th' world": Hamlet and Unlawful Marriage', in Francis Barker, Peter Hulme, and Margaret Iversen (eds.), *Uses of History: Marxism, Postmodernism and the Renaissance* (Manchester, 1991).

JONES, ANN ROSALIND, 'Nets and Bridles: Early Modern Conduct Books and Sixteenth Century Women's Lyrics', in Nancy Armstrong and Leonard Tennenhouse (eds.), *The Ideology of Conduct: Essays on Literature and the History of Sexuality* (London, 1987).

KAGAN, RICHARD L., 'A Golden Age of Litigation: Castile, 1500–1700', in Bossy (ed.), *Disputes and Settlements*.

KARRAS, RUTH MAZO, 'The Regulation of Brothels in Later Medieval England', in Judith M. Bennett, Elizabeth A. Clark, Jean F. O'Barr, B. Anne Viles, and Sarah Westphal-Wihl (eds.), *Sisters and Workers in the Middle Ages* (Chicago, 1989).

KELLY-GADOL, JOAN, 'The Social Relations of the Sexes: Methodological Implications for Women's History', *Signs*, 1 (1976), 809–24.

KERMODE, JENNY, and WALKER, GARTHINE (eds.), *Women, Crime and the Courts in Early Modern England* (London, 1994).

KING, WALTER J., 'Punishment for Bastardy in Early Seventeenth-Century England', *Albion*, 10 (1978), 130–51.

KRAMARE, CHERIS, and TREICHLER, PAULA A. (eds.), *A Feminist Dictionary* (London, 1985).

LANDER, STEPHEN, 'Church Courts and the Reformation in the Diocese of Chichester 1500–1558', in O'Day and Heal (eds.), *Continuity and Change*.

LAQUEUR, THOMAS, 'Crowds, Carnival and the State in English Executions, 1604–1868', in A. L. Beier, David Cannadine, and James M. Rosenheim (eds.), *The First Modern Society: Essays in Honour of Lawrence Stone* (Cambridge, 1989).

—— *Making Sex: Body and Gender from the Greeks to Freud* (Cambridge, Mass., 1990).

LARMINIE, VIVIENNE, 'Marriage and the Family: The Example of the Seventeenth-Century Newdigates', *Midland History*, 9 (1984), 1–22.

LASLETT, PETER, 'Clayworth and Cogenhoe', in Laslett (ed.), *Family Life and Illicit Love in Earlier Generations* (Cambridge, 1977).

LAURETIS, TERESA DE, *Technologies of Gender: Essays on Theory, Film, and Fiction* (Bloomington, Ind., 1988).

LEACH, EDMUND, 'Anthropological Aspects of Language: Animal Categories and Verbal Abuse', in Eric H. Lenneberg (ed.), *New Directions in the Study of Language* (Cambridge, Mass., 1964).

LEITES, EDMUND, 'The Duty to Desire: Love, Friendship and Sexuality in Some Puritan Theories of Marriage', *Jl. of Social History* (1982), 383–408.

MACDONALD, MICHAEL, *Mystical Bedlam: Madness, Anxiety and Healing in Seventeenth-Century England* (Cambridge, 1981).

—— and MURPHY, TERENCE R., *Sleepless Souls: Suicide in Early Modern England* (Oxford, 1990).

McIntosh, Marjorie Keniston, 'Servants and the Household Unit in an Elizabethan English Community', *Jl. of Family History*, 9 (1984), 3–24.

—— *A Community Transformed: The Manor and Liberty of Havering, 1500–1620* (Cambridge, 1991).

Maclean, Ian, *The Renaissance Notion of Woman* (Cambridge, 1980).

McLuskie, Kate, '"'Tis But A Woman's Jar": Family and Kinship in Elizabethan Domestic Drama', *Literature and History*, 9 (1983), 228–39.

Marchant, Ronald A., *The Church Under the Law: Justice, Administration and Discipline in the Diocese of York, 1560–1640* (Cambridge, 1969).

Meldrum, Tim, 'Defamation at the Church Courts: Women and Community Control in London 1700–1745', M.Sc. dissertation (London School of Economics and Political Science, 1990).

Mendelson, Sara Heller, 'Stuart Women's Diaries and Occasional Memoirs', in Prior (ed.) *Women in English Society*.

Michaels, Sarah, 'Making Connections in Children's Narratives', in Mitchell and Weiler (eds.), *Rewriting Literacy*.

Miles, Margaret R., *Carnal Knowing: Female Nakedness and Religious Meaning in the Christian West* (Boston, 1989).

Mitchell, Candace, and Weiler, Kathleen (eds.), *Rewriting Literacy: Culture and the Discourse of the Other* (New York, 1991).

Mitchell, W. J. T. (ed.), *On Narrative* (Chicago, 1981).

Moogk, Peter N., '"Thieving Buggers"' and "Stupid Sluts": Insults and Popular Culture in New France', *William and Mary Quarterly*, 3rd ser., 36/4 (1979), 524–47.

Moore, Henrietta L., *Feminism and Anthropology* (Cambridge, 1988).

Noonan, John T., Jr., 'Power to Choose', *Viator*, 4 (1973), 419–34.

Norton, Mary Beth, 'Gender and Defamation in Seventeenth-Century Maryland', *William and Mary Quarterly*, 3rd ser., 44/1 (1987), 3–39.

O'Day, Rosemary, and Heal, Felicity (eds.), *Continuity and Change: Personnel and Administration of the Church in England* (Leicester, 1976).

O'Hara, Diana, ' "Ruled by my Friends": Aspects of Marriage in the Diocese of Canterbury, c.1540–c.1570', *Continuity and Change*, 6/1 (1991), 9–41.

—— 'The Language of Tokens and the Making of Marriage', *Rural History*, 3/1 (1992), 1–40.

Ong, Walter J., *Orality and Literacy: The Technologizing of the Word* (London, 1982).

Outhwaite, R. B. (ed.), *Marriage and Society: Studies in the Social History of Marriage* (London, 1981).

Owen, Dorothy, *The Records of the Established Church in England Excluding Parochial Records* (London, 1970).

Paine, Robert, 'What is Gossip about? An Alternative Hypothesis', *Man*, NS 2/2 (1967), 278–85.

Pearl, Valerie, 'Change and Stability in Seventeenth-Century London', *London Jl.* 5 (1979), 3–34.

PELLING, MARGARET, 'Appearance and Reality: Barber-Surgeons, the Body and Disease', in Beier and Finlay (eds.), *London 1500–1700.*

PERISTIANY, J. G. (ed.), *Honour and Shame: The Values of Mediterranean Society* (London, 1965).

PERRY, MARY ELIZABETH, *Gender and Disorder in Early Modern Seville* (Princeton, NJ, 1990).

PHILLIPS, RODERICK, *Putting Asunder: A History of Divorce in Western Society* (Cambridge, 1988).

PITT-RIVERS, JULIAN, *The Fate of Shechem or The Politics of Sex* (Cambridge, 1977).

POWER, MICHAEL J., 'The Urban Development of East London, 1550–1700', Ph.D. thesis (University of London, 1971).

—— 'East London Housing in the Seventeenth Century', in Peter Clark and Paul Slack (eds.), *Crisis and Order in English Towns, 1500–1700: Essays in Urban History* (London, 1972).

—— 'A "Crisis" Reconsidered: Social and Demographic Dislocation in London in the 1590s', *London Jl.* 12 (1986), 134–46.

PRIOR, MARY, 'Women and the Urban Economy: Oxford 1500–1800', in Prior (ed.), *Women in English Society.*

—— (ed.), *Women in English Society 1500–1800* (London, 1985).

PURKISS, DIANE, 'Material Girls: The Seventeenth-Century Woman Debate', in Brant and Purkiss (eds.), *Women, Texts and Histories.*

PURVIS, J. S., *An Introduction to Ecclesiastical Records* (London, 1953).

QUAIFE, G. R., *Wanton Wenches and Wayward Wives: Peasants and Illicit Sex in Early Seventeenth-Century England* (London, 1979).

RAPPAPORT, STEVE, *Worlds within Worlds: Structures of Life in Sixteenth-Century London* (Cambridge, 1989).

REAY, BARRY (ed.), *Popular Culture in Seventeenth-Century England* (London, 1985).

RICH, ADRIENNE, 'Compulsory Heterosexuality and Lesbian Existence', *Signs,* 5 (1980), 631–60.

RICOEUR, PAUL, 'The Human Experience of Time and Narrative', in Mario J. Valdes (ed.), *A Ricoeur Reader* (Hemel Hempstead, 1991).

RILEY, DENISE, *Am I That Name? Feminism and the Category of 'Women' in History* (Basingstoke, 1988).

RITCHIE, CARSON I. A., *The Ecclesiastical Courts of York* (Arbroath, 1956).

ROBERTS, MICHAEL, 'Women and Work in Sixteenth-Century English Towns', in Penelope J. Corfield and Derek Keene (eds.), *Work in Towns 850–1850* (Leicester, 1990).

ROBERTS, SIMON, *Order and Dispute: An Introduction to Legal Anthropology* (Oxford, 1971).

ROPER, LYNDAL, *The Holy Household: Women and Morals in Reformation Augsburg* (Oxford, 1989).

—— *Oedipus and the Devil: Witchcraft, Sexuality and Religion in Early Modern Europe* (London, 1994).

ROSSIAUD, JACQUES, *Medieval Prostitution*, trans. Lydia Cochrane (Oxford, 1988).

RUSHTON, PETER, 'Women, Witchcraft and Slander in Early Modern England: Cases from the Durham Church Courts, 1560–1615', *Northern History*, 18 (1982), 116–32.

—— 'The Testament of Gifts: Marriage Tokens and Disputed Contracts in North-East England, 1560–1630', *Folk Life*, 24 (1985/6), 25–31.

—— 'Property, Power and Family Networks: The Problem of Disputed Marriage in Early Modern England', *Jl. of Family History*, 11 (1986), 205–19.

SABEAN, DAVID, *Power in the Blood: Popular Culture and Village Discourse in Early Modern Germany* (Cambridge, 1984).

SAFLEY, THOMAS MAX, *Let No Man Put Asunder: The Control of Marriage in the German South-West* (Kirksville, Miss., 1984).

ST GEORGE, ROBERT, '"Heated" Speech and Literacy', in David D. Hall and David Grayson Allen (eds.), *Seventeenth-Century New England* (Boston, 1985).

SALGĀDO, GĀMINI, *The Elizabethan Underworld* (London, 1977).

SCHOFIELD, JOHN, *The Building of London from the Conquest to the Great Fire* (London, 1984).

SCOTT, JOAN W., 'Gender: A Useful Category for Historical Analysis', in *American Historical Review*, 91 (1986), 1053–76.

SEXTON, JOYCE, *The Slandered Woman in Shakespeare* (Victoria, BC, 1978).

SHANLEY, MARY LYNDON, 'Marriage Contract and Social Contract in Seventeenth-Century English Political Thought', *Western Political Quarterly*, 32/1 (1979), 79–91.

SHARPE, J. A., *Defamation and Sexual Slander in Early Modern England: The Church Courts at York*, Borthwick Papers, 58 (York, 1980).

—— '"Such Disagreement Betwyx Neighbours": Litigation and Human Relations in Early Modern England', in Bossy (ed.), *Disputes and Settlements*.

—— 'The People and the Law', in Reay (ed.), *Popular Culture*.

—— 'Plebeian Marriage in Stuart England: Some Evidence from Popular Literature', *Trans. of the Royal Historical Society*, 5th ser., 36 (1986), 69–90.

SHEEHAN, MICHAEL M., 'The Formation and Stability of Marriage in Fourteenth-Century England: Evidence of an Ely Register', *Mediaeval, Studies*, 43 (1971), 228–63.

SHELFORD, LEONARD, *A Practical Treatise of the Law of Marriage and Divorce* (London, 1841).

SHEPHERD, SIMON, *The Women's Sharp Revenge: Five Women's Pamphlets from the Renaissance* (London, 1985).

SHOEMAKER, ROBERT B., *Prosecution and Punishment: Petty Crime and the Law in London and Rural Middlesex, c.1660–1725* (Cambridge, 1991).

SIIKALA, ANNA-LEENA, *Interpreting Oral Narrative* (Helsinki, 1990).

SISSON, C. J., *Lost Plays of Shakespeare's Age* (Cambridge, 1930), 80–124.

SLATER, MIRIAM, 'The Weightiest Business: Marriage in an Upper-Gentry Family in Seventeenth-Century England', *Past and Present*, 72 (1976), 25–54.

SNEDAKER, KATHRYN HOLMES, 'Story-Telling in Opening Statements: Framing the Argumentation of the Trial', in David Ray Papke (ed.), *Narrative and the Legal Discourse: A Reader in Story-Telling and the Law* (Liverpool, 1991).

SOUDEN, DAVID, 'Pre-Industrial English Local Migration Fields', Ph.D. thesis (University of Cambridge, 1981).

SPUFFORD, MARGARET, *Small Books and Pleasant Histories: Popular Fiction and its Readership in Seventeenth-Century England* (London, 1981).

SØRENSEN, PREBEN MEULENGRACHT, *The Unmanly Man: Concepts of Defamation in Early Northern Society*, trans. Joan Turville-Petre (Odense, 1983).

STALLYBRASS, PETER, 'Patriarchal Territories: The Body Enclosed', in Margaret W. Ferguson, Maureen Quilligan, and Nancy J. Vickers (eds.), *Rewriting the Renaissance* (Chicago, 1986).

—— and WHITE, ALLON, *The Politics and Poetics of Transgression* (London, 1986).

STONE, LAWRENCE, *The Family, Sex and Marriage in England 1500–1800* (London, 1977).

—— *Road to Divorce: England 1530–1987* (Oxford, 1990).

—— *Uncertain Unions: Marriage in England 1660–1753* (Oxford, 1992).

STRETTON, TIM, 'Women and Litigation at the Elizabethan Court of Requests', Ph.D. thesis (University of Cambridge, 1993).

—— 'Women, Custom and Equity in the Court of Requests', in Kermode and Walker (eds.), *Women, Crime and the Courts.*

TENTLER, THOMAS N., *Sin and Confession on the Eve of the Reformation* (Princeton, NJ, 1977).

TILLEY, M. P., *A Dictionary of the Proverbs in England in the Sixteenth and Seventeenth Centuries* (Ann Arbor, 1950).

THOMAS, KEITH, 'The Double Standard', *Jl. of the History of Ideas,* 20 (1959), 195–216.

—— *Religion and the Decline of Magic* (London, 1971).

—— 'The Meaning of Literacy in Early Modern England', in Gerd Baumann (ed.), *The Written Word: Literacy in Transition* (Oxford, 1986).

THOMPSON, JANET A., '"Her Good Name and Credit": The Reputation of Women in Seventeenth-Century Devon', Ph.D. thesis (University of Cincinnati, 1987).

THOMPSON, ROGER, '"Holy Watchfulness" and Communal Conformism: The Functions of Defamation in Early New England Communities', *New England Quarterly,* 56/4 (1983), 504–22.

TODD, BARBARA, 'The Remarrying Widow: A Stereotype Reconsidered', in Prior (ed.), *Women in English Society.*

UNDERDOWN, DAVID, 'The Taming of the Scold: The Enforcement of Patriarchal Authority in Early Modern England', in Fletcher and Stevenson (eds.), *Order and Disorder.*

WACK, MARY FRANCES, *Lovesickness in the Middle Ages: The Viaticum and its Commentaries* (Philadelphia, 1989).

WALKER, GARTHINE, 'Crime, Gender and Social Order in Early Modern Cheshire', Ph.D. thesis (University of Liverpool, 1994).

WHITE, HAYDEN, 'The Value of Narrativity in the Representation of Reality', in Mitchell (ed.), *On Narrative.*

WIESNER, MERRY E., 'Women's Defence of their Public Role', in Mary Beth Rose (ed.), *Women in the Middle Ages and the Renaissance: Literary and Historical Perspectives* (Syracuse, Miss., 1986).

WILLEN, DIANE, 'Women in the Public Sphere in Early Modern England: The Case of the Urban Working Poor', *Sixteenth-Century Jl.* 19 (1988), 559–75.

WITTIG, MONIQUE, 'The Straight Mind', *Feminist Issues,* 1/1 (1980), 103–10.

—— 'On the Social Contract', *Feminist Issues,* 9/1 (1989), 2–12.

WOODBRIDGE, LINDA, *Women in the English Renaissance: Literature and the Nature of Womankind* (Brighton, 1984).

WRIGHT, ADRIAN, 'The Ceremony of Childbirth and its Interpretation', in Fildes (ed.), *Women as Mothers.*

WRIGHTSON, KEITH, 'Household and Kinship in Sixteenth Century England', *History Workshop Jl.* 12 (1981), 151–8.

—— *English Society 1580–1680* (London, 1982).

WRIGLEY, E. A., and SCHOFIELD, R. S., *The Population History of England, 1541–1871: A Reconstruction* (London, 1981).

WUNDERLI, RICHARD, *London Church Courts and Society Before the Reformation* (Cambridge, Mass., 1981).

INDEX

Unless otherwise indicated, all place names, except a few familiar ones, refer to London or Middlesex.